First World War
and Army of Occupation
War Diary
France, Belgium and Germany

3 DIVISION
8 Infantry Brigade
Suffolk Regiment 2nd Battalion,
East Yorkshire Regiment 8th Battalion,
8 Machine Gun Company
and 8 Trench Mortar Battery
4 August 1914 - 31 August 1916

WO95/1424

The Naval & Military Press Ltd
www.nmarchive.com
Published in association with The National Archives

Published by

The Naval & Military Press Ltd

Unit 10 Ridgewood Industrial Park,

Uckfield, East Sussex,

TN22 5QE England

Tel: +44 (0) 1825 749494

www.naval-military-press.com

www.nmarchive.com

This diary has been reprinted in facsimile from the original. Any imperfections are inevitably reproduced and the quality may fall short of modern type and cartographic standards.

Contents

Document type	Place/Title	Date From	Date To
Heading	2 Bn Suffolk Regt. 1914 Aug To 1915 Sept 8 Bn East York Regt. 1915 Sept To 1918 Feb. 8 Machine Gun Company 1916 Jan To 1918 Feb 8 Trench Mortar Bty 1916 May To 1916 Aug		
Heading	3 Division 8 Bde 2nd Bn Suffolk Regt 1914 Aug-1914 Dec		
Heading	14th brigade 5th division 2nd Battalion The Suffolk Regiment August 1914		
War Diary	Curragh Camp	04/08/1914	07/08/1914
War Diary	Curragh	08/08/1914	14/08/1914
War Diary	Havre	15/08/1914	31/08/1914
Miscellaneous	G/2317/suffolk	20/11/1917	20/11/1917
Heading	14th Brigade 5th Division 2nd Battalion The Suffolk Regiment September 1914		
War Diary		01/09/1914	02/09/1914
War Diary	Montge	03/09/1914	03/09/1914
War Diary	Bouleurs	04/09/1914	04/09/1914
War Diary	Favieres	05/09/1914	06/09/1914
War Diary	Plessis St. Avoye	07/09/1914	07/09/1914
War Diary	Coulommiers	08/09/1914	08/09/1914
War Diary	Saacy	09/09/1914	09/09/1914
War Diary	Montreuil	10/09/1914	10/09/1914
War Diary	St. Ouentin	11/09/1914	11/09/1914
War Diary	Billy-Sur-Ourcq	12/09/1914	12/09/1914
War Diary	Chacrise	13/09/1914	13/09/1914
War Diary	N. of M In Missy-Sur-Aisne	14/09/1914	23/09/1914
War Diary	Le Carrier	24/09/1914	30/09/1914
Heading	G.H.Q. Troops 8th Brigade 3rd Division 24.10.14. 2nd Battalion The Suffolk Regiment October 1914		
War Diary	Fere-En-Tardenois	01/10/1914	08/10/1914
War Diary	Abbeville	09/10/1914	13/10/1914
War Diary	St. Omer	14/10/1914	31/10/1914
Miscellaneous	2nd Suffolk Regt 8th Bde.		
Heading	8th Brigade 3rd Division 2nd Battalion The Suffolk Regiment November 1914		
Heading	2nd Suffolk Regt. 8th Brigade Frankferred From 14th Brigade Vol IV 1-30.11.14		
War Diary	Champigny	01/11/1914	06/11/1914
War Diary	Estaires	07/11/1914	08/11/1914
War Diary	Vieille Chapelle	09/11/1914	09/11/1914
War Diary	Givency Le Marrais	10/11/1914	10/11/1914
War Diary	Givency	10/11/1914	11/11/1914
War Diary	Vieille Chapelle	12/11/1914	14/11/1914
War Diary	Lacoutre	15/11/1914	15/11/1914
War Diary	Bailleul	15/11/1914	16/11/1914
War Diary	Wulverghem	17/11/1914	21/11/1914
War Diary	Neuve Eglise	22/11/1914	24/11/1914
War Diary	Douve River	25/11/1914	27/11/1914
War Diary	Westoutre	28/11/1914	30/11/1914

Heading	8th Brigade 3rd Division 2nd Battalion The Suffolk Regiment December 1914		
War Diary	Scherpenburg	01/12/1914	03/12/1914
War Diary	Kemmel	04/12/1914	06/12/1914
War Diary	Westoutre	06/12/1914	14/12/1914
War Diary	Kemmel-Ypres Road	14/12/1914	14/12/1914
War Diary	Petit Bois	14/12/1914	15/12/1914
War Diary	Locre	16/12/1914	18/12/1914
War Diary	Kemmel	18/12/1914	21/12/1914
War Diary	Westoutre	21/12/1914	27/12/1914
War Diary	Kemmel	27/12/1914	31/12/1914
War Diary	Westoutre	31/12/1914	31/12/1914
Heading	3rd Division 8th Infy Bde 2nd Battalion Suffolk Regt. Jan-Sep 1915		
Heading	8th Inf. Bde. 3rd Div 2nd Battn. The Suffolk Regiment January 1915		
War Diary	Westoutre	01/01/1915	03/01/1915
War Diary	Locre	04/01/1915	05/01/1915
War Diary	Vierstraat	05/01/1915	09/01/1915
War Diary	La Clytte	09/01/1915	13/01/1915
War Diary	Vierstraat	13/01/1915	17/01/1915
War Diary	La Clytte	17/01/1915	21/01/1915
War Diary	Vierstraat	21/01/1915	24/01/1915
War Diary	La Clytte	25/01/1915	28/01/1915
War Diary	Vierstraat	29/01/1915	31/01/1915
Heading	8th Inf. Bde. 3rd Div. 2nd Battn. The Suffolk Regiment February 1915		
War Diary	Vierstraat	01/02/1915	02/02/1915
War Diary	La Clytte	03/02/1915	05/02/1915
War Diary	Vierstraat	06/02/1915	09/02/1915
War Diary	La Clytte	10/02/1915	14/02/1915
War Diary	Vierstraat	14/02/1915	17/02/1915
War Diary	La Clytte	18/02/1915	20/02/1915
War Diary	Vierstraat	21/02/1915	24/02/1915
War Diary	La Clytte	25/02/1915	27/02/1915
War Diary	Vierstraat	28/02/1915	28/02/1915
Heading	8th Inf. Bde. 3rd Div. 2nd Battn. The Suffolk Regiment March 1915		
War Diary	Vierstraat	01/03/1915	04/03/1915
War Diary	La Clytte	05/03/1915	08/03/1915
War Diary	Vierstraat	09/03/1915	12/03/1915
War Diary	La Clytte	13/03/1915	16/03/1915
War Diary	J&K. Trenches	16/03/1915	16/03/1915
War Diary	Petit Bois	17/03/1915	17/03/1915
War Diary	Vierstraat	18/03/1915	30/03/1915
War Diary	Westoutre	31/03/1915	31/03/1915
Heading	8th Inf. Bde. 3rd Div. 2nd Battn. The Suffolk Regiment April 1915		
War Diary	Westoutre	01/04/1915	04/04/1915
War Diary	Vierstraat	05/04/1915	11/04/1915
War Diary	Westoutre	12/04/1915	13/04/1915
War Diary	Reninghelst	14/04/1915	23/04/1915
War Diary	Rosen Hill Huts	24/04/1915	30/04/1915
Heading	8th Inf. Bde. 3rd Div. 2nd Battn. The Suffolk Regiment May 1915		
War Diary	Vierstraat	01/05/1915	26/05/1915

War Diary	La Clytte	26/05/1915	28/05/1915
War Diary	C Huts Near Brielen	29/05/1915	31/05/1915
Heading	8th Inf. Bde. 3rd Div. 2nd Battn. The Suffolk Regiment June & July 1915		
War Diary	C.Huts-Brielen Near Ypres	01/06/1915	01/06/1915
War Diary	Ouderdom	02/06/1915	02/06/1915
War Diary	Ypres	03/06/1915	03/06/1915
War Diary	Ouderdom	04/06/1915	05/06/1915
War Diary	Brandhoek	06/06/1915	07/06/1915
War Diary	Hooge	08/06/1915	20/06/1915
War Diary	Brandhoek	21/06/1915	03/07/1915
War Diary	Brandhoek & Hooge	04/07/1915	07/07/1915
War Diary	Brandhoek	08/07/1915	09/07/1915
War Diary	Ypres	10/07/1915	12/07/1915
War Diary	Ramparts-Ypres & Sanctuary Wood	13/07/1915	22/07/1915
War Diary	Brandhoek	23/07/1915	25/07/1915
War Diary	Spoil Bank I.33.B	26/07/1915	31/07/1915
Heading	8th Inf. Bde. 3rd Div. 2nd Battn. The Suffolk Regiment August 1915		
War Diary	Spoil Bank	01/08/1915	31/08/1915
Heading	8th Inf. Bde. 3rd Div. 2nd Battn. The Suffolk Regiment September 1915		
War Diary	Hooge	30/09/1915	30/09/1915
War Diary	Ouder Dom	01/09/1915	02/09/1915
War Diary	Kuisstraat	03/09/1915	23/09/1915
War Diary	Maple Copse	24/09/1915	26/09/1915
War Diary	Hooge	27/09/1915	30/09/1915
Heading	3 Division 8 Bde. 8th Bn East Yorks Regt 1915 Sept.-1915 Dec.		
Heading	Battn. Disembarked Boulogne From England 10.09.15. War Diary 8th Battn. The East Yorkshire Regiment September (9.9.15-28.9.15) 1915		
War Diary	Folkstone	09/09/1915	09/09/1915
War Diary	Moulle	11/09/1915	20/09/1915
War Diary	Ecquedecques	22/09/1915	22/09/1915
War Diary	Noeux Le-Mines	25/09/1915	25/09/1915
War Diary	Loos	25/09/1915	27/09/1915
War Diary	Bethune	28/09/1915	28/09/1915
Heading	21st Division 8th E. Yorks Rgt. Vol.2 Oct 15 To 3rd Div. 15/11/15		
War Diary	Strazeele	03/10/1915	03/10/1915
War Diary	Merris	13/10/1915	13/10/1915
War Diary	Armentieres	14/10/1915	29/10/1915
War Diary	L'Epinette	30/10/1915	30/10/1915
Heading	3rd Division 8th Infy Bde 8th Battalion East Yorks Nov-Dec. 1915		
Heading	8th Inf. Bde. 3rd Div. Battn. Transferred From 62nd Inf. Bde. 21st Div. 15.11.15. War Diary 8th Battn. The East Yorkshire Regiment November 1915		
War Diary	L'Epinette	01/11/1915	06/11/1915
War Diary	Armentieres	06/11/1915	06/11/1915
War Diary	L'Epinette	12/11/1915	12/11/1915
War Diary	Armentieres	12/11/1915	15/11/1915
War Diary	Bailleul	16/11/1915	16/11/1915
War Diary	Steenvorde	17/11/1915	23/11/1915
War Diary	Reninghelst	23/11/1915	29/11/1915

War Diary	Dickebusch	30/11/1915	30/11/1915
Heading	8th Inf Bde 3rd Div. War Diary 8th Battn. The East Yorkshire Regiment December 1915		
War Diary	Dickebusch	01/12/1915	06/12/1915
War Diary	Reninghelst	07/12/1915	13/12/1915
War Diary	Dickebusch	13/12/1915	19/12/1915
War Diary	Renninghelst	21/12/1915	28/12/1915
War Diary	Voormezeele	28/12/1915	31/12/1915
Heading	2 Bn Royal Scots 1914 Aug To 1919 May		
Heading	3rd Division 8th Infy Bde 8th Battalion East Yorkshire Regt Jan-Dec 1916		
Heading	8th Brigade 3rd Division War Diary 8th Battalion East Yorkshire Regiment January 1916		
Heading	8th E. Yorks Vol 5		
War Diary	St Eloi	01/01/1916	04/01/1916
War Diary	Reninghelst	05/01/1916	11/01/1916
War Diary	St Eloi	11/01/1916	18/01/1916
War Diary	Reninghelst	18/01/1916	25/01/1916
War Diary	St Eloi	25/01/1916	31/01/1916
Heading	8th Brigade 3rd Division War Diary 8th Battalion East Yorkshire Regiment February 1916		
Heading	8th E. Yorks Vol 6		
War Diary	St Eloi	01/02/1916	02/02/1916
War Diary	Dickebusch	02/02/1916	03/02/1916
War Diary	Reninghelst	04/02/1916	05/02/1916
War Diary	Norileulinghen	05/02/1916	29/02/1916
War Diary	Ouder Dom	01/03/1916	01/03/1916
Heading	8th Brigade 3rd Division War Diary 8th Battalion East Yorkshire Regiment March 1916		
Heading	3rd Division 8 East Yorks Vol 7		
War Diary	Dickebusch	01/03/1916	01/03/1916
War Diary	Bluff (Trenches)	03/03/1916	06/03/1916
War Diary	Reninghelst	07/03/1916	11/03/1916
War Diary	Scottish Wood	11/03/1916	14/03/1916
War Diary	Reninghelst	15/03/1916	19/03/1916
War Diary	Scottish Wood	20/03/1916	22/03/1916
War Diary	P Sector (Trenches)	22/03/1916	25/03/1916
War Diary	Scottish Wood	25/03/1916	26/03/1916
War Diary	U25 & U26	26/03/1916	27/03/1916
War Diary	U24, 23 23b T3	28/03/1916	01/04/1916
War Diary	Bollaartbeek	31/03/1916	08/04/1916
War Diary	Reninghelst	04/04/1916	05/04/1916
War Diary	R.33.T.3.b.	05/04/1916	14/04/1916
Heading	8th Brigade 3rd Division War Diary 8th Battalion East Yorkshire Regiment April 1916		
War Diary	Bollart Beek	31/03/1916	04/04/1916
War Diary	Berthen	05/04/1916	23/04/1916
War Diary	Ridge Wood	23/04/1916	30/04/1916
Heading	8th Brigade 3rd Division War Diary 8th Battalion East Yorkshire Regiment May 1916		
War Diary	Brasserie (O Sector)	01/05/1916	08/05/1916
War Diary	La Clytte	08/05/1916	15/05/1916
War Diary	La Clytte	13/05/1916	13/05/1916
War Diary	'O' Sector	15/05/1916	22/05/1916
War Diary	'O' Sector	19/05/1916	19/05/1916
War Diary	Ridgewood	22/05/1916	25/05/1916

War Diary	Mt Kokereele	25/05/1916	31/05/1916
Heading	8th Brigade 3rd Division War Diary 8th Battalion East Yorkshire Regiment June 1916		
Miscellaneous	The Officer C A.G. Officer at The Base	11/06/1916	11/06/1916
Miscellaneous	To 3rd Div	10/07/1916	10/07/1916
War Diary	Mt Kokereele (Berthen)	01/06/1916	10/06/1916
War Diary	Mt Kokereele (Berthen)	02/06/1916	12/06/1916
War Diary	P Sector	12/06/1916	20/06/1916
War Diary	P Sector	18/06/1916	21/06/1916
War Diary	St. Martin-Au-Laert	22/06/1916	30/06/1916
Heading	8th Inf Bde 3rd div War Diary 8th Battn. The East Yorkshire Regiment July 1916		
Heading	Diary Of The Attack 13/14th July		
Miscellaneous	8th (S) Bn East Yorkshire Regiment Diary of The Attack, 13th-14th July 1918		
Heading	War Diary		
War Diary	St. Martin-Au-Laert	01/07/1916	01/07/1916
War Diary	Franqueville	02/07/1916	03/07/1916
War Diary	Flesselles	04/07/1916	04/07/1916
War Diary	Cardonnette	05/07/1916	05/07/1916
War Diary	Corbie	06/07/1916	06/07/1916
War Diary	Les Celestins	07/07/1916	07/07/1916
War Diary	Carnoy	08/07/1916	14/07/1916
War Diary	Attack On German Positions	14/07/1916	26/07/1916
War Diary	Happy Valley	26/07/1916	26/07/1916
War Diary	Meaulte	27/07/1916	31/07/1916
Heading	8th Brigade 3rd Division War Diary 8th Battalion East Yorkshire Regiment August 1916		
War Diary	Meaulte	01/08/1916	13/08/1916
War Diary	Happy Valley	13/08/1916	14/08/1916
War Diary	Great Bear	15/08/1916	15/08/1916
War Diary	Carnoy	16/08/1916	17/08/1916
War Diary	Trenches	18/08/1916	18/08/1916
War Diary	Trenches Of Guillemont	18/08/1916	19/08/1916
War Diary	Carnoy	20/08/1916	20/08/1916
War Diary	Meaulte	21/08/1916	23/08/1916
War Diary	Bernaville	23/08/1916	24/08/1916
War Diary	Villiers L'Hopital	25/08/1916	25/08/1916
War Diary	Ecoives	26/08/1916	26/08/1916
War Diary	Bours	27/08/1916	27/08/1916
War Diary	Houchin	28/08/1916	28/08/1916
War Diary	Mazingarbe	29/08/1916	30/08/1916
Miscellaneous	To The Ofc 8th York Bde.	19/08/1916	19/08/1916
Miscellaneous	8th (S) B'n West Yorkshire Regiment Diary of Events On 18th and 19th August 1918.	21/08/1916	21/08/1916
Heading	8th Brigade 3rd Division War Diary 8th Battalion East Yorkshire September 1916		
War Diary	Trenches Hulluch Sector	01/09/1916	08/09/1916
War Diary	Noeux-Les-Mines	09/09/1916	21/09/1916
War Diary	Lozinghem	22/09/1916	22/09/1916
War Diary	Coyecques	23/09/1916	23/09/1916
War Diary	Delettes	24/09/1916	30/09/1916
Heading	8th Brigade 3rd Division War Diary 8th Battalion East Yorkshire Regiment October 1916		
War Diary	Delettes	01/10/1916	05/10/1916
War Diary	Verchin	06/10/1916	07/10/1916

War Diary	Varennes	08/10/1916	08/10/1916
War Diary	Mailly-Maillet Wood	09/10/1916	11/10/1916
War Diary	Bus-Les-Artois	18/10/1916	29/10/1916
War Diary	Courcelles	30/10/1916	31/10/1916
Heading	8th Brigade 3rd Division War Diary 8th Battalion East Yorkshire Regiment November 1916		
War Diary	Courcelles	01/11/1916	01/11/1916
War Diary	Serre Sector	02/11/1916	04/11/1916
War Diary	Louvencourt	05/11/1916	12/11/1916
War Diary	Serre Sector	13/11/1916	14/11/1916
War Diary	Bus Huts	15/11/1916	15/11/1916
War Diary	Serre Sector	16/11/1916	17/11/1916
War Diary	Courcelles	18/11/1916	19/11/1916
War Diary	Bus Huts	20/11/1916	21/11/1916
War Diary	Courcelles	22/11/1916	23/11/1916
War Diary	Serre Sector	24/11/1916	28/11/1916
War Diary	Bus Huts	30/11/1916	30/11/1916
Heading	8th Brigade 3rd Division War Diary 8th Battalion East Yorkshire December 1916		
War Diary	Bus	01/12/1916	04/12/1916
War Diary	Courcelles	04/12/1916	05/12/1916
War Diary	Serre Sector	06/12/1916	08/12/1916
War Diary	Courcelles	09/12/1916	09/12/1916
War Diary	Bus	10/12/1916	15/12/1916
War Diary	Serre Sector	16/12/1916	17/12/1916
War Diary	Bus	17/12/1916	25/12/1916
War Diary	Serre Sector	26/12/1916	29/12/1916
War Diary	Bus	30/12/1916	31/12/1916
Heading	3rd Division War Diaries 8/East Yorks 1917 Jan 1918-1918 Feb		
War Diary	Bus	01/01/1917	11/01/1917
War Diary	Ribeaucourt	12/01/1917	22/01/1917
War Diary	Berneuil	23/01/1917	27/01/1917
War Diary	Auteuile	28/01/1917	28/01/1917
War Diary	Bonniere	29/01/1917	29/01/1917
War Diary	Eroisette & Hericourt	30/01/1917	30/01/1917
War Diary	Ostreville	31/01/1917	07/02/1917
War Diary	Lignereuil	08/02/1917	22/02/1917
War Diary	Hauteville	23/02/1917	27/02/1917
War Diary	Arras	28/02/1917	17/03/1917
War Diary	Hauteville	18/03/1917	20/03/1917
War Diary	Arras	21/03/1917	30/03/1917
War Diary	Hauteville	31/03/1917	04/04/1917
War Diary	Wanquetin	05/04/1917	06/04/1917
War Diary	The Caves Arras	07/04/1917	08/04/1917
War Diary	The Battle	08/04/1917	13/04/1917
War Diary	The Battle & Arras	14/04/1917	14/04/1917
War Diary	Arras	15/04/1917	23/04/1917
War Diary	Brown Line	24/04/1917	30/04/1917
Miscellaneous	8th Inf. Bde. Report On Operations Of April 9th 1917	15/04/1917	15/04/1917
Miscellaneous	Report On Operations Carried Out By The 8th Bn East Yorkshire Regt.	17/05/1917	17/05/1917
War Diary	Monchy	01/05/1917	02/05/1917
War Diary	Monchy The Battle	03/05/1917	05/05/1917
War Diary	Monchy	05/05/1917	06/05/1917
War Diary	Tilloy	07/05/1917	10/05/1917

War Diary	Brownline H34 Central	11/05/1917	11/05/1917
War Diary	Brownline	12/05/1917	14/05/1917
War Diary	Arras	14/05/1917	15/05/1917
War Diary	Berneville	16/05/1917	18/05/1917
War Diary	Gouy-En-Artois	19/05/1917	19/05/1917
War Diary	Izel-Lez-Hameau	20/05/1917	31/05/1917
Miscellaneous	Report On Operation	05/05/1917	05/05/1917
War Diary	Izel-Lez-Hameau	01/06/1917	01/06/1917
War Diary	Arras	02/06/1917	02/06/1917
War Diary	Monchy	03/06/1917	07/06/1917
War Diary	Brown Line	08/06/1917	12/06/1917
War Diary	Arras	13/06/1917	17/06/1917
War Diary	Noyelette	18/06/1917	18/06/1917
War Diary	Etree Wamin	18/06/1917	27/06/1917
War Diary	Lucheux	28/06/1917	29/06/1917
War Diary	Gomiecourt	30/06/1917	30/06/1917
War Diary	Lebucquiere	01/07/1917	02/07/1917
War Diary	In The Field Louverval	03/07/1917	10/07/1917
War Diary	Lebucquiere	11/07/1917	18/07/1917
War Diary	Louverval	19/07/1917	26/07/1917
War Diary	Lebucquiere	27/07/1917	05/08/1917
War Diary	Louverval	06/08/1917	11/08/1917
War Diary	Lebucquiere	12/08/1917	19/08/1917
War Diary	Louverval	20/08/1917	27/08/1917
War Diary	Lebucquiere	28/08/1917	04/09/1917
War Diary	Ytres	05/09/1917	17/09/1917
War Diary	Hiphoek	18/09/1917	20/09/1917
War Diary	Hopoutre	21/09/1917	24/09/1917
War Diary	Brandhoek No.2 Area Details	25/09/1917	30/09/1917
War Diary	Toronto Camp Brandhoek	01/10/1917	02/10/1917
War Diary	Winnezelle Area	03/10/1917	04/10/1917
War Diary	Rennecourt	05/10/1917	05/10/1917
War Diary	Beaulincourt	06/10/1917	12/10/1917
War Diary	Beugnatre	13/10/1917	30/11/1917
War Diary	Noreuil	01/12/1917	16/12/1917
War Diary	Hendecourt	17/12/1917	21/12/1917
War Diary	Mory	22/12/1917	22/12/1917
War Diary	Noreuil	23/12/1917	29/12/1917
War Diary	Hamlincourt	30/12/1917	31/12/1917
Heading	3rd Division 8th Infy Bde 8th Battalion East Yorkshire Regt Jan-Feb 1918		
War Diary	Hamlincourt	01/01/1918	26/01/1918
War Diary	Fontaine Croisilles	27/01/1918	09/02/1918
War Diary	Carlisle Lines	10/02/1918	10/02/1918
War Diary	Berles-Au-Bois	11/02/1918	18/02/1918
Heading	3rd Division 8th Infy Bde Machine Gun Company Jan-Dec 1916		
Heading	8th Brigade 3rd Division War Diary Formed 22nd January 1916 8th Brigade Machine Gun January 1916		
War Diary	Reninghelst	22/01/1916	31/01/1916
Heading	8th Brigade 3rd Division War Diary 8th Brigade Machine Gun Company February 1916		
War Diary		01/02/1916	29/02/1916
Heading	8th Brigade 3rd Division War Diary 8th Brigade Machine Gun Company March 1916		
War Diary		01/03/1916	31/03/1916

Heading	8th Brigade 3rd Division War Diary 8th Brigade Machine Gun April 1916		
War Diary		01/04/1916	30/04/1916
Heading	8th Brigade 3rd Division War Diary 8th Brigade Machine Gun Company May 1916		
Heading	8th Coy. M.G.C. From May 1st to 31st 1916		
War Diary	School Nr Farm La Clytte M.N. & O Trenches	01/05/1916	31/05/1916
Heading	8th Brigade 3rd Division War Diary 8th Brigade Machine Gun Company June 1916		
War Diary		01/06/1916	30/06/1916
Heading	8th Brigade 3rd Div. War Diary 8th Machine Gun Company July 1916		
War Diary		01/07/1916	31/07/1916
Heading	8th Brigade 3rd Division War Diary 8th Brigade Machine Gun Company August 1916		
War Diary	Meaulte	01/08/1916	12/08/1916
War Diary	Happy Valley	13/08/1916	14/08/1916
War Diary	Near Bronfay Farm	15/08/1916	16/08/1916
War Diary	Talus Bois	17/08/1916	20/08/1916
War Diary	Sand Pits	21/08/1916	21/08/1916
War Diary	Meaulte	21/08/1916	23/08/1916
War Diary	Prouville	24/08/1916	25/08/1916
War Diary	Wavans	26/08/1916	26/08/1916
War Diary	Guinecourt	27/08/1916	28/08/1916
War Diary	Haillicourt	29/08/1916	29/08/1916
War Diary	Noeux-Les-Mines	30/08/1916	30/08/1916
War Diary	Philosophe	30/08/1916	31/08/1916
Heading	8th Brigade 3rd Division War Diary 8th Brigade Machine Gun September 1916		
War Diary	Philosophe	01/09/1916	09/09/1916
War Diary	Noeux Les Mines	10/09/1916	19/09/1916
War Diary	Philosophe	19/09/1916	19/09/1916
War Diary	Noeux Les Mines	19/09/1916	21/09/1916
War Diary	Auchel	21/09/1916	22/09/1916
War Diary	Audincthun	22/09/1916	30/09/1916
Heading	8th Brigade 3rd Division War Diary 8th Brigade Machine Gun Company October 1916		
War Diary	Audincthun	01/10/1916	05/10/1916
War Diary	Predefin	06/10/1916	07/10/1916
War Diary	Acheux	08/10/1916	18/10/1916
War Diary	Buswood	19/10/1916	31/10/1916
War Diary	Courcelles	31/10/1916	31/10/1916
Heading	8th Brigade 3rd Division War Diary 8th Brigade Machine Gun Company November 1916		
War Diary	In The Field	01/11/1916	30/11/1916
Heading	8th Brigade 3rd Division War Diary 8th Brigade Machine Gun December 1916		
War Diary		01/12/1916	31/12/1916
Heading	3rd Division War Diaries 8/M.G.C. January To 31st December 1917		
War Diary		01/01/1917	10/01/1917
War Diary	In The Field	11/01/1917	30/04/1917
Miscellaneous	8th Infantry Brigade	17/05/1917	17/05/1917
War Diary	Field	04/05/1917	31/05/1917
Miscellaneous	A Form Messages And Signals	01/05/1917	01/05/1917
Miscellaneous	To 8th Inf. Bde.	03/05/1917	03/05/1917

Miscellaneous	Hostile Artillery List-30/4/17 River Scarpe To Cambrai Road	30/04/1917	30/04/1917
Miscellaneous	These guns had orders to open couering five on		
Miscellaneous	Hostile Artillery List-2/5/17 River Scarpe To Cambrai Road	02/05/1917	02/05/1917
War Diary	In The Field	01/06/1917	04/10/1917
War Diary	Field	04/10/1917	31/12/1917
Heading	3rd Division 8th Infy Bde 8th Machine Gun Company Jan-Feb. 1918		
War Diary	Field	01/01/1918	31/01/1918
War Diary	In The Field	01/02/1918	28/02/1918
Heading	3rd division 8th Infy Bde Trench Mortar Battery May-Aug 1916		
War Diary	M.N.O. Trenches	08/05/1916	31/05/1916
War Diary	St. Martin Au Laert	01/07/1916	01/07/1916
War Diary	Berneuil	02/07/1916	02/07/1916
War Diary	Flesselles	03/07/1916	03/07/1916
War Diary	Alonville	04/07/1916	04/07/1916
War Diary	Corbie	05/07/1916	05/07/1916
War Diary	Bois de Celestines	06/07/1916	06/07/1916
War Diary	Bronfay Farm	07/07/1916	07/07/1916
War Diary	Carnoy	07/07/1916	07/07/1916
War Diary	Montauban	08/07/1916	13/07/1916
War Diary	Trench	14/07/1916	20/07/1916
War Diary	Waterlot Farm	21/07/1916	31/07/1916
War Diary	Meaulte	01/08/1916	12/08/1916
War Diary	Happy Valley	13/08/1916	14/08/1916
War Diary	Bronfay Farm	15/08/1916	15/08/1916
War Diary	Trenches South Of Gaillemont	16/08/1916	20/08/1916
War Diary	Sand Pit	21/08/1916	21/08/1916
War Diary	Meaulte	22/08/1916	23/08/1916
War Diary	Barlette	24/08/1916	25/08/1916
War Diary	Chateau De Beauvoin	25/08/1916	26/08/1916
War Diary	Blangemont	27/08/1916	27/08/1916
War Diary	Tangry	28/08/1916	28/08/1916
War Diary	Ruitz	29/08/1916	29/08/1916
War Diary	Noeux Les Mines	30/08/1916	31/08/1916

2 BN SUFFOLK REGT.

1914 AUG TO 1915 SEPT

8 BN EAST YORK REGT.

1915 SEPT TO 1918 FEB.

8 MACHINE GUN COMPANY.

1916 JAN TO 1918 FEB

8 TRENCH MORTAR BTY

1916 MAY TO 1916 AUG.

1424

~~5TH DIVISION~~
14TH INFY BDE

3 DIVISION
8 BDE

2ND BN SUFFOLK REGT

~~AUG - SEP 1914~~

1914 AUG - 1914 DEC

14th Brigade
5th Division

2nd BATTALION

THE SUFFOLK REGIMENT

AUGUST 1914.

Army Form C. 2418.

2nd Batt. Suffolk Regt 121/512

Instructions regarding War Diaries and Intelligence Summaries are contained in F. S. Regs., Part II. and the Staff Manual respectively. Title pages will be prepared in manuscript.

WAR DIARY
or
INTELLIGENCE SUMMARY
(Erase heading not required.)

Hour, Date, Place	Summary of Events and Information	Remarks and References to Appendices
5.18 pm. 4-8-14 Curragh Camp	Order to Mobilize received.	
	Lieut. Bittleston leaves by 7.5 pm train with Colours + 5 N.C.Os for Depot to assist in conducting Reservists etc.	
5-8-14	Wire O.C. Records stating 584 Reservists required.	
	Total of Unfits etc 172.	
6-8-14	Capt. J.H. Robinson O.C. Details arrives from Depot also Lt Gadd + 2/Lt Pereira from Hythe.	
7-8-14. 7.45 am	400 Reservists arrived under Lt. N.A. Bittleston.	
	Some difficulty about obtain neck collars for Heavy Draught Horses.	

(9 26 6) W 257—976 100,000 1/12 H W V 79/3298

Army Form C. 2118.

Instructions regarding War Diaries and Intelligence Summaries are contained in F. S. Regs., Part II. and the Staff Manual respectively. Title pages will be prepared in manuscript.

WAR DIARY
or
INTELLIGENCE SUMMARY
(Erase heading not required.)

Hour, Date, Place	Summary of Events and Information	Remarks and References to Appendices
6.30 am. 8-8-14 Curragh	2nd Party of Reservists under Capt. Wenn 3rd Suffolk Regt join 176.	
	Mobilization Complete. Battalion Parade at 2.30 pm. 8 Special Reserve officers 3rd Bn. accompany the Battalion to complete War Establishment.	
9th, 10th, 11th, 12th } Curragh	These days spent drilling and route marching. Reservists settle down well. Many of them have left the Colours a long time. Transport working well.	
13th Aug. 9.0 am. Curragh	Part of Headquarters and right half Battalion left the Siding for NORTH WALL. DUBLIN.	
9.30 am	Left Half Bn. do.	
	Trains arrive up to time. The first trainload embarked in S.S. LANFRANC and sailed at 5-45 pm. No ship ready for the 2nd Trainload who spent the night in Barracks in DUBLIN.	

(9 26 6) W 257—976 100,000 4/12 H W V 79/3298

Instructions regarding War Diaries and Intelligence Summaries are contained in F. S. Regs., Part II. and the Staff Manual respectively. Title pages will be prepared in manuscript.

WAR DIARY
or
INTELLIGENCE SUMMARY
(Erase heading not required.)

1st portion extracted and sent to M.

Army Form C. 2118.

Hour, Date, Place	Summary of Events and Information	Remarks and References to Appendices
14-8-14	Right Half Bn. spent a quiet day at sea.	
	Men + horses settled down well, very calm.	
	Left Half Bn. embarked in S.S. POLAND and left at 1-0 pm	Up to this point the Diary was kept by Capt + Adjt A. M. Cuthill
2-0 pm. 15th Aug. HAVRE	Arrived about 2-0 pm - commenced quickly to disembark	From here by Lieut. N.B. Oake
	At 6. p.m. Marched about 5 miles to a rest Camp on a hill. Very wet rained all night.	
Sunday. 16th Aug:	Remained in Camp.	N.B.O.
8. p.m	At. 8. p.m. Marched to railway siding in HAVRE where we met the left half Battalion and entrained together.	
Monday. 17th Aug: 3. a.m.	Train moved off up to time.	N.B.O.
7-30. a.m.	Stopped at ROUEN ½ hr: where coffee was issued to men.	
7. p.m.	Arrived at LE CATEAU and detrained in the dark.	
10. p.m.	Marched off complete.	N.B.O

(9 26 6) W 257—976 100,000 4/12 H W V 79/3298

Army Form C. 2118.

Instructions regarding War Diaries and Intelligence Summaries are contained in F. S. Regs., Part II. and the Staff Manual respectively. Title pages will be prepared in manuscript.

WAR DIARY
or
INTELLIGENCE SUMMARY.

(Erase heading not required.)

Hour, Date, Place	Summary of Events and Information	Remarks and references to Appendices
Tuesday. 18th Aug: 3-30. a.m.	Arrived at LANDRICIES and remained in billets.	N.B.O.
Wednesday. 19th Aug: } Thursday. 20th Aug: }	Remained in billets at LANDRICIES and had exercises in route marching.	N.B.O.
Friday 21st Aug: 6-15. a.m.	Marched off with 14th Infantry Bde.	N.B.O.
4. p.m	Went into billets at St. WAAST.	
Saturday 22nd Aug: 7. a.m.	Marched off at head of Brigade. A + B. Companies forming the Advance Guard.	N.B.O.
2. p.m.	Arrived at HAMIN and went into 'billets'.	

(9 26 6) W 257--976 100,000 4/12 H W V 79/3298

Army Form C. 2118.

Instructions regarding War Diaries and Intelligence Summaries are contained in F. S. Regs., Part II. and the Staff Manual respectively. Title pages will be prepared in manuscript.

WAR DIARY
or
INTELLIGENCE SUMMARY.
(Erase heading not required.)

Hour, Date, Place	Summary of Events and Information	Remarks and references to Appendices
Sunday 23rd Aug:	Guns heard all the morning.	
1. p.m.	C + D Companies sent off to take up an outpost position along the Canal facing N.	
4. p.m. Till dusk.	Outposts engaged in which 3 men where killed and 2/Lt. V. M. G. Phillips wounded.	Cpl: Page. Pt. Flack Pt. Goda[illegible]
	A retirement was ordered.	N.B.O.
Monday. 24th Aug: ~~2 a.m.~~	A + B. Coys. took up outpost position to cover the retirement.	
2. a.m.	C + D Coys. arrive in DOUR	
4. a.m.	Battalion occupies trenches at BOIS de BOUSSU	
11. a.m.	Retirement was ordered.	
6. p.m.	Bivouaced at BAVAY	N.B.O.

(9 26 6) W 257—976 100,000 4/12 H W V 79/3298

Instructions regarding War Diaries and Intelligence Summaries are contained in F. S. Regs., Part II. and the Staff Manual respectively. Title pages will be prepared in manuscript.

WAR DIARY
or
INTELLIGENCE SUMMARY.
(Erase heading not required.)

Army Form C. 2118.

Hour, Date, Place	Summary of Events and Information	Remarks and references to Appendices
Tuesday 25th Aug:	Battalion formed part of Rear Guard in a General retirement.	
9. p.m.	Arrived at MONTAY	
10. p.m.	Bivouaced in a barn near LE CATEAU.	N.B.O.
Wednesday. 26th Aug:		
4-30. a.m.	Battalion took up position in the front line facing LE CATEAU and improved the position with the Entrenching tool as much as time permitted.	Ref: Map. CAMBRAI Sheet NO. 13.
7-30. a.m.	Shrapnel fire commenced on the trenches and proved most effective. The supports to the firing line which were situated just in front of a battery of Field Artillery suffered heavily.	
9. a.m.	Lt. Col. C.A.H. Brett D.S.O. mortally wounded.	1. G.S. Wagon containing Officers Kits was left at REUMONT owing to one of the horses being shot.
12-30 p.m.	Shell fire exceedingly heavy, enfilade fire from the left flank	
4. p.m	A General retirement of the Division.	
10. p.m.	Near BOHAIN a short halt was made when the transport and a few of the Battalion were collected together.	N.B.O.

(9 26 6) W 257—976 100,000 4/12 H W V 79/3298

Instructions regarding War Diaries and Intelligence Summaries are contained in F. S. Regs., Part II. and the Staff Manual respectively. Title pages will be prepared in manuscript.

WAR DIARY
or
INTELLIGENCE SUMMARY.
(Erase heading not required.)

Army Form C. 2118.

Hour, Date, Place	Summary of Events and Information	Remarks and references to Appendices
Thursday, 27th Aug: 5. a.m.	Arrived at St: QUENTIN and halted for 1hr: the Roll Call of the Battalion then told:–	
	2 Officers.	Capt Blackwell. Lieut Oakes.
	1 Medical Officer.	Capt: Phelan RAMC.
	A Coy. 31	
	B " 19	
	C " 38	
	D " 16	
	Attached. 7	
	111	
6. p.m.	Arrived at HAM. More men rejoined from straggling.	
	1st Line Transport except { 1 Water Cart, 1 Cooks Wagon. 1 Cooker. 1 Maltese Cart. } handed over to D. of Cornwall's Light Inf:	
		N.B.?

(9 26 6) W 257—976 100,000 4/12 H W V 79/3298

Army Form C. 2118.

Instructions regarding War Diaries and Intelligence Summaries are contained in F. S. Regs., Part II. and the Staff Manual respectively. Title pages will be prepared in manuscript.

WAR DIARY
or
INTELLIGENCE SUMMARY.

(*Erase heading not required.*)

Hour, Date, Place	Summary of Events and Information	Remarks and references to Appendices
Friday 28th Aug: 4. a. m.	Continued retirement. On the way General French addressed troops by the road side. and congratulated them on their great stand at LE CATEAU. General Smith Dorrien congratulated the Battalion personally mentioning the 1st Bn under his command in S. Africa.	
7. p. m.	Arrived at PONTOISE and bivouaced. Battalion attached to E. Surrey Regt. as a Company Approx: strength 229.	N.B.O
Saturday, 29th Aug:	Remained in bivouac.	
5-30. p. m.	Left Bivouac.	N.B.O.
Sunday. 30th Aug: 3-30. p. m	Arrived at ATTICHY and bivouaced by River AISNE	N.B.O.
Monday. 31st Aug: 9.45. a. m	Left bivouac	
8. p. m.	Arrived at CREPY and bivouaced. The Rear Guard of the Division were still in touch with enemy's Cavalry.	N.B.O

(9 26 6) W 257—976 100,000 4/12 H W V 79/3298

G/2317/SUFFOLK.

Major A.F. Becke,
Committee of Imperial Defence (Military History)
Public Record Office,
Chancery Lane, W. C. 2.

Sir,

In continuation of my letter dated 23/10/17, in reply to your letter dated 23/10/17, relative to the composition of the 2nd. Battn. Suffolk Regt. when it left Ireland for France on the 13/8/1914, I beg to inform you that the composition of the Regiment was:-

Officers,-------------------------------	--27.
Regular Soldiers,------------------------	-563.
Reservists, 9 years Colour Service and 3 years Reserve,-------------	I54.
-do- 8 years Colour Service and 4 years Reserve,--------------	-49.
-do- 7 years Colour Service and 5 years Reserve,--------------	-27.
-do- 3 years Colour Service and 9 years Reserve,-------------	-178.
	998.

I am, Sir,
Your Obedient Servant,

C. Barrow 2/Lieut.

Officer in Charge, Suffolk Section,
No. I. Record Office,
No. 9. District.

Warley,

20/II/17.

14th Brigade.

5th Division.

2nd BATTALION

THE SUFFOLK REGIMENT

SEPTEMBER 1914.

Instructions regarding War Diaries and Intelligence Summaries are contained in F. S. Regs., Part II. and the Staff Manual respectively. Title pages will be prepared in manuscript.

WAR DIARY
or
INTELLIGENCE SUMMARY.
(Erase heading not required.)

Army Form C. 2118.

Hour, Date, Place	Summary of Events and Information	Remarks and references to Appendices
Tuesday 1st Sept. 8. a. m.	Took up an Outpost position, shots heard close to but nothing seen of the enemy.	
10. a. m.	Relieved by a Company of K.O.Y. Light Infantry 13th Bde and retired to ROUVILLE, where with part of 1st Bn E. Surrey Regt formed the Van Guard of a Rear Guard to the Division. No resistance was met with except a few shots from Uhland patrols.	
8-30. p. m.	Bivouaced at NANTEUIL.	N.B.O.
Wednesday 2nd Sept. 3-20. a. m.	Left bivouac and went into billets near MONTGE. The D. of Corn. L. Infantry handed over 1st Line transport of Battalion to 1st Bn E. Surrey Regt.	
7. p. m.	"B" Echelon Transport moved South.	N.B.O.

(9 26 6) W 257—976 100,000 4/12 H W V 79/3298

Army Form C. 2118.

Instructions regarding War Diaries and Intelligence Summaries are contained in F.S. Regs., Part II. and the Staff Manual respectively. Title pages will be prepared in manuscript.

WAR DIARY
or
INTELLIGENCE SUMMARY.
(*Erase heading not required.*)

Hour, Date, Place		Summary of Events and Information	Remarks and references to Appendices
	Thursday 3rd September		
MONTGE	6.a.m.	Left billets.	
	7-8. a.m	Two platoons acted as observation posts at the N.E. end of a wood while Brigade halted on road.	
	6. p.m.	Arrived at BOULEURS and bivouaced	N.B.O.
	Friday 4th September		
BOULEURS	10. a.m	Received information that 1st Reinforcements were expected to arrive between 4 and 5 p.m	
	11. p.m	Left bivouac and retired through CRECY.	N.B.O.
	Saturday 5th September		
FAVIERES.	8-30. a.m	Arrived at FAVIERES and passed 1st Reinforcements on road.	
	10. a.m	Battalion with 1st E. Surrey Regt formed outposts on line F in FAVIERES to V in VILLE facing N.E. Main Body bivouacing near TOURNAN.	N.B.O.

(9 26 6) W 257—976 100,000 4/12 H W V 79/3298

Instructions regarding War Diaries and Intelligence Summaries are contained in F. S. Regs., Part II. and the Staff Manual respectively. Title pages will be prepared in manuscript.

WAR DIARY
or
INTELLIGENCE SUMMARY.
(*Erase heading not required.*)

Army Form C. 2118.

Hour, Date, Place	Summary of Events and Information	Remarks and references to Appendices
FAVIERES. Sunday 6th September 6. a.m.	Outposts withdrawn and advanced through FAVIERES.	
9. a.m.	Halted in a paddock where 1st Reinforcements joined 90 men under Capt Wynn who took over command from Lieut. Oakes.	
	Battalion organized as 2 Companys of 2 Platoons each.	
2-20. p.m.	Advanced N.E. and halted for the night at PLESSIS ST: AVOYE	
10. p.m.	Enemy reported retiring N and E in haste.	N.B.O.
PLESSIS ST: AVOYE Monday Sept 7th	Remained in bivouac during morning.	
11. a.m.	Major Cornish Bowden D. of Corn: L. Infantry took over command of the Battalion.	
2-30. p.m.	Marched off in an Easterly direction in pursuit of the Enemy.	
8. p.m.	Arrived at COULOMMIERS and bivouaced for the night.	
	Sgt Rush and 14 men rejoined.	N.B.O.

Army Form C. 2118.

Instructions regarding War Diaries and Intelligence Summaries are contained in F. S. Regs., Part II. and the Staff Manual respectively. Title pages will be prepared in manuscript.

WAR DIARY
or
INTELLIGENCE SUMMARY.

(Erase heading not required.)

Hour, Date, Place	Summary of Events and Information	Remarks and references to Appendices
COULOMMIERS Tuesday Sept: 8th		
6-5. a.m	Continued the pursuit in a N.N.E direction	
10. a.m	An attack was made by 14th Bde from DOUE on ST: OUEN Battalion and 2/Manchester Regiment in support. Little resistance was met with.	
2. p.m	Battalion formed part of an Advance Guard as far as CHAMPTORTEL	
8. p.m	Bivouaced in a field near ROUGEVILLE. S. of SAACY	NBO
SAACY Wednesday Sept: 9th 5-30. a.m	Continued the pursuit through SAACY the bridge being left intact by the enemy.	
12. noon	An attack was made by 14th Inf: Bde from LE LIMON across the valley on LES MAILLONS D. of Corn. L. Inf on & our left and 1/ Manchester Regt on our right	
1-30. p.m	On arriving at the top of the hill the enemy concealed in the wood on our right opened fire ~~and~~ at close range (150 yds) and shell fire from half left. In the wood fight which continued little advance was made.	
6. p.m	Enemy delivered heavy shell fire on us Very little of enemy could be seen concealed in the thick wood.	NBO

Army Form C. 2118.

Instructions regarding War Diaries and Intelligence Summaries are contained in F. S. Regs., Part II. and the Staff Manual respectively. Title pages will be prepared in manuscript.

WAR DIARY
or
INTELLIGENCE SUMMARY.
(Erase heading not required.)

Hour, Date, Place	Summary of Events and Information	Remarks and references to Appendices
Wednesday (continued) Sept: 9th 6-30 p.m	Withdrew about 200 yards S. of Wood and took up an outpost position facing wood.	
	No event took place during night.	
	In this wood fight the following were casualties.	
	Killed :- Capt. A. Wynn	
	Sgt Clayton.	
	Wounded :- Major Cornish Bowden.	
	C.Q.M.Sgt. F. Williams.	N.B.O.
MONTREUIL Thursday Sept: 10th	Enemy retired during night.	
6. a.m	Outposts withdrawn and Bde formed General Reserve to V Div:	
7- a.m.	Continued the advance through MONTREUIL.	
8. p.m.	Arrived at ST: QUENTIN and bivouaced	
	En route 2nd and 3rd reinforcements joined Battalion 2/Lt. Roe and 93 men. 2/Lt. Wilder and 90 men respectively	
	Strength of Battalion :- Officers { Capt: & Qr Mr W. M. Blackwell, Lieut. N. B. Oakes, 2/Lieut C. C. Roe, 2/Lt. R. C. P. Wilder }	
	Other Ranks 480 (approx:)	N.B.O.

(9 26 6) W 257—976 100,000 4/12 H W V 79/3298

Instructions regarding War Diaries and Intelligence Summaries are contained in F. S. Regs., Part II. and the Staff Manual respectively. Title pages will be prepared in manuscript.

WAR DIARY
or
INTELLIGENCE SUMMARY.
(*Erase heading not required.*)

Army Form C. 2118.

Hour, Date, Place	Summary of Events and Information	Remarks and references to Appendices
ST: QUENTIN Friday Sept. 11th		
5. a.m.	Organized Battalion into 4 equalized Companies (temporarily)	
6-45. a.m.	Left bivouac	
3-45. p.m.	Arrived at BILLY-SUR-OURCQ billeted in R.C. Church	
	Rained hard during afternoon. Wet through.	N.B.O.
BILLY-SUR-OURCQ Saturday Sept 12th		
6-20. a.m.	Left billets and advanced in a N.E. direction via HARTENNES and DROIZY	
	Heavy firing heard all day on our left near SOISSONS	N.B.O.
8. p.m.	Billeted in CHACRISE. Raining hard.	
CHACRISE Sunday Sept 13th		
4-40. a.m.	Left billets	
8. a.m.	Arrived at SERCHES. 14th Inf Bde ordered to make a passage over the R. AISNE at MIN. DES ROCHES. Battalion in Reserve	
6-45. p.m.	Battalion had just crossed river when heavy shelling commenced over it. Crossed river by rafts made by R.E.	
8. p.m.	Formed a line facing N.E. just N. of M in MISSY-SUR-AISNE	
9. p.m.	Surprised by firing to our right and shell fire. One Casualty	Pte Mills
	Slept night in position	N.B.O.

Instructions regarding War Diaries and Intelligence Summaries are contained in F. S. Regs., Part II. and the Staff Manual respectively. Title pages will be prepared in manuscript.

WAR DIARY
or
INTELLIGENCE SUMMARY
(Erase heading not required.)

Army Form C. 2118.

Hour, Date, Place	Summary of Events and Information	Remarks and References to Appendices
N. of M in MISSY-SUR-AISNE		
Monday. Sept: 14th 4.a.m.	Forty men sent back to River bank to bring up rations which supply wagons had left the other side.	
5-30.a.m.	Enemy commenced shelling as ration party returned. This Evidently drawing the fire. One man wounded.	
1.p.m.	100 men with 2/Lt. Roe sent into MISSY village to form posts and guard left flank against snipers.	
	Strength:- Officers. Lieut. Oakes 2/Lt. Roe " Wilder Capt & Qr Mr. Blackwell Other Ranks. 380. (approx:)	N.B.O.
N. of M. in MISSY-SUR-AISNE		
Tuesday. Sept. 15th 1-30.a.m.	Supply wagons brought up rations and waterproof sheets and left again before daylight.	
5.a.m.	Lieut. Reynolds returned from V. Divisional Cyclist Company and took over command of Battalion from Lieut Oakes.	
	Remained in General Reserve all day against the wall in Orchard.	
	Enemy's shells were bursting over us at intervals during the day. Chiefly at dusk.	N.B.O.

Army Form C. 2118.

Instructions regarding War Diaries and Intelligence Summaries are contained in F. S. Regs., Part II. and the Staff Manual respectively. Title pages will be prepared in manuscript.

WAR DIARY
or
INTELLIGENCE SUMMARY
(*Erase heading not required.*)

Hour, Date, Place	Summary of Events and Information	Remarks and References to Appendices
N. of M. in MISSY-SUR-AISNE		
Wednesday Sept: 16th		
1-30. p.m.	Rations brought up by Supply wagons. Several shots were fired at them by Snipers with no result. Remained in same place keeping under cover from view of aeroplanes as much as possible.	
7-30. p.m.	14 Officers with servants joined Battalion. Capt. Temple took over command.	
	The following were the Officers:-	
	Capt: Temple.	
	" Hanbury.	
	" Mowbray.	
	" Cautley.	
	Lieut: Chalmers.	
	" Jackson	
	" Cleave.	
	2/Lt: Dowse.	
	" Wright.	
	" Fraser.	
	" Sparkes.	
	" Trollope.	
	" Taylor.	
	" Thill.	N.B.O.

(9 26 6) W 257—976 100,000 4/12 H W V 79/3298

Army Form C. 2118.

Instructions regarding War Diaries and Intelligence Summaries are contained in F. S. Regs., Part II. and the Staff Manual respectively. Title pages will be prepared in manuscript.

WAR DIARY
or
INTELLIGENCE SUMMARY
(Erase heading not required.)

Hour, Date, Place	Summary of Events and Information	Remarks and References to Appendices
N. of M. in MISSY-SUR-AISNE Thursday Sept: 17th		
1-30. a.m	Rations brought up. All quiet.	
6. a.m.	Battalion Organized into 4 Companys. Each Company 4 platoons Each platoon 2 sections instead of 4 owing to small number of men. The following was the distribution of Officers:- C.O. Capt. Temple. Adjt Lieut. Oakes. Qr Mr Capt. Blackwell. Company Commanders: Capt: Hanbury. A. Coy; " Mowbray. C " ; " Cantley. D " ; Lieut. Reynolds. B "	
	Platoon Commanders:- A. Coy: 2/Lt. Wright. ; " Taylor ; " Thill B. Coy: 2/Lt. Browse. ; " Fraser ; " Sparkes C. Coy: Lieut. Jackson ; 2/Lt. Trollope. ; " Roe. D. Coy: Lieut. Chalmers. ; " Chase. ; 2/Lt. Wilder.	
	Attached: M.O. Capt. Phelan. R.A.M.C.	N.B.O.

(9 26 6) W 257—976 100,000 4/12 H W V 79/3298

Instructions regarding War Diaries and Intelligence Summaries are contained in F. S. Regs., Part II. and the Staff Manual respectively. Title pages will be prepared in manuscript.

WAR DIARY
or
INTELLIGENCE SUMMARY
(Erase heading not required.)

Army Form C. 2118.

Hour, Date, Place	Summary of Events and Information	Remarks and References to Appendices
N. of M. in MISSY-SUR-AISNE. Thursday. Sept. 17th	(Continued).	
	Strength of Battalion:-	
	Officers. 19 and 1. Attached. (M.O.).	
	Other Ranks. 365.	
	A. Coy 95	
	B. Coy 89	
	C. Coy 87	
	D. Coy 94.	
	365	
	Rained hard most of the day.	
11-30. p.m.	"B" Coy. with Lt. Jackson and Cleave sent back to the Ponton Bridge to carry up rations for Battalion and E. Surrey Regt. owing to the bad state of the roads and approaches to Bridge caused by wet weather the supply wagons were unable to cross.	N.B.O.

Army Form C. 2118.

Instructions regarding War Diaries and Intelligence Summaries are contained in F. S. Regs., Part II. and the Staff Manual respectively. Title pages will be prepared in manuscript.

WAR DIARY
or
INTELLIGENCE SUMMARY
(*Erase heading not required.*)

Hour, Date, Place	Summary of Events and Information	Remarks and References to Appendices
N. of M in MISSY-SUR-AISNE		
Friday Sept. 18th		
4-30. a.m.	Stood to arms before dawn.	
	Remained here all day and improved Sanitary arrangements as far as possible.	
	Ground very wet.	
11-p.m	Rations brought up in Limbered Wagon. 1st Line Transport. also an issue of Rhum and Tobacco.	N.B.O.
N. of M in MISSY-SUR-AISNE.		
Saturday. Sept: 19th		
2. a.m.	Bivouac alarmed by firing all round and Searchlight flashes.	
	No event took place.	
	Ground very wet and muddy. Made several pathways with stones from the road-side.	
	Quiet all day.	
11. p.m.	Rations arrived as usual.	N.B.O.

(9 26 6) W 257—976 100,000 4/12 H W V 79/3298

Army Form C. 2118.

Instructions regarding War Diaries and Intelligence Summaries are contained in F. S. Regs., Part II. and the Staff Manual respectively. Title pages will be prepared in manuscript.

WAR DIARY
or
INTELLIGENCE SUMMARY
(Erase heading not required.)

Hour, Date, Place	Summary of Events and Information	Remarks and References to Appendices
N. of M. in MISSY-SUR-AISNE. Sunday. Sept: 20th		
4. a. m.	Stood to arms. One platoon detailed to be ready to fire at hostile aircraft in case of necessity.	
10. p. m	Ration arrived.	N.B.O
N. of M in MISSY-SUR-AISNE. Monday. Sept: 21st		
4. a. m.	Stood to arms. Company parades in morning and afternoon for Musketry Exercises and lecture. (½ hr: each.)	
5.30. p. m	Stood to arms. Firing was heard on our Extreme right but only a few shots at our immediate front.	
10. p. m.	Rations arrived. Capt. Hansbury took over command of Battalion from Capt: Temple by Divisional order.	N.B.O.

(9 26 6) W 257—976 100,000 4/12 H W V 79/3298

Instructions regarding War Diaries and Intelligence Summaries are contained in F. S. Regs., Part II. and the Staff Manual respectively. Title pages will be prepared in manuscript.

WAR DIARY
or
INTELLIGENCE SUMMARY
(Erase heading not required.)

Army Form C. 2118.

Hour, Date, Place	Summary of Events and Information	Remarks and References to Appendices
N. of M. in MISSY-SUR-AISNE. Tuesday. Sept: 22nd.		
4.a.m.	Stood to arms.	
8.30.a.m.	Enemy's artillery opened fire on trenches N. of ST MARGUERITE and searched for our guns close by. One man wounded in thigh.	
2.30.p.m.	Enemy's artillery opened again for about 1. hour. Two men slightly wounded	
8.30 p.m.	Commenced to dig trenches in dark near the Railway facing MISSY. Rations arrived.	
	Capt. Cantly went sick and sent to Base.	N.B.O.
N. of M. in MISSY-SUR-AISNE. Wednesday. Sept: 23rd.		
4.a.m.	Stood to arms.	
8.30.a.m.	Enemy commenced shelling. Cover was taken against the wall.	
9.a.m.	Two machine guns arrived for the Battalion.	
	25 men went sick including 10 for Field Ambulance. Slight Dysentery.	
2.p.m.	Enemy's guns had evidently found our position in the Orchard and opened fire with Shrapnel. Shells bursting high but accurate. The wall was of little protection as direction of fire was from due N. A hostile aeroplane had evidently located our bivouac by the presence of straw and waterproof sheets. Dispersed men by Companies. Some behind farm at Bde. H.Q. and others behind wall running E. and W.	
	Casualties. { 1 Killed { 8 Wounded.	N.B.O.

Army Form C. 2118.

Instructions regarding War Diaries and Intelligence Summaries are contained in F. S. Regs., Part II. and the Staff Manual respectively. Title pages will be prepared in manuscript.

WAR DIARY
or
INTELLIGENCE SUMMARY
(Erase heading not required.)

Hour, Date, Place	Summary of Events and Information	Remarks and References to Appendices
N. of M. in MISSY-SUR-AISNE	(Continued)	
Wednesday. Sept: 23rd 6.p.m.	When dusk waterproof sheets were taken down and rolled up.	
7-30.p.m.	C. Coy. and ½ B. Coy. as 1st Relief dug trenches near Railway facing MISSY.	
11.p.m.	No: 2. Relief, A Coy and ½ B Coy went out to finish digging. D. Coy. blocaded windows in farm house against Shrapnel splinters and commenced bomb-proof Shelters in Orchard.	H.B.O.
LE. CARRIER. Thursday. Sept: 24th 3-30.a.m.	Battalion paraded and marched S. to cross river	
4-30.a.m.	Crossed R. AISNE by the pontoon bridge at MIN DES ROCHES	
5. a. m.	Arrived at LE CARRIER and billeted. Met with a reinforcement of 168 men with Lieut. Squirl-Dawson and 2/Lt. Ainsley. Strength Officers: 19 and 1 attached (M.O.) Other Ranks. 600 (approx:)	H.B.O

(9 26 6) W 257—976 100,000 4/12 H W V 79/3298

Instructions regarding War Diaries and Intelligence Summaries are contained in F. S. Regs., Part II. and the Staff Manual respectively. Title pages will be prepared in manuscript.

WAR DIARY
or
INTELLIGENCE SUMMARY
(Erase heading not required.)

Army Form C. 2118.

Hour, Date, Place	Summary of Events and Information	Remarks and References to Appendices
LE CARRIER. Friday Sept: 25th		
5-30. a.m.	"A" Coy sent to LA GRÈVE N of. V in CROUVELLES to assist R.E. in clearing undergrowth.	
6. a.m.	1st Line Transport sent to a place under cover from view S. of Y in JORY.	
10-30. a.m.	"B" Coy. sent out to relieve "A" Coy	
1. p.m	"C" and "D" Coys sent to outpost position near the road S. of MÉZIERES.	N.B.O.
LE CARRIER. Saturday. Sept: 26th.		
3-30. a.m	"A" and "B" Coys paraded to go and relieve "C" and "D" Coys on Outposts.	
4. p.m.	50 men paraded for digging party to assist R.E. at SERCHES.	
6. p.m.	Order came from Bde. H.Q. to warn units to be in readiness to move at any time.	N.B.O.

(9 26 6) W 257—976 100,000 4/12 H W V 79/3298

Instructions regarding War Diaries and Intelligence Summaries are contained in F. S. Regs., Part II. and the Staff Manual respectively. Title pages will be prepared in manuscript.

WAR DIARY
or
INTELLIGENCE SUMMARY
(Erase heading not required.)

Army Form C. 2118.

Hour, Date, Place	Summary of Events and Information	Remarks and References to Appendices
LE CARRIER.		
Sunday Sept: 27th 3.a.m	Order received that 14/ Bde. will move at once.	
3-30.a.m	Battalion fell in opposite billets ready to move.	
4-30.a.m	Marched through SERCHES to COUVRELLE after receiving order and information that the Germans were crossing the bridge over the R. AISNE at CONDÉ in large numbers.	
6-30.a.m.	No enemy seen and order received to march back to billets leaving one working party of 50 men in COUVRELLE to assist R.E.	
4.p.m	Working party of 50 men paraded and marched to SERCHES.	N.B.O
LE CARRIER. Monday Sept: 28th.	The following working parties to assist R.E. in digging trenches and clearing foreground were furnished at times stated in JURY. 150 men. 7-15.a.m. 150 men 10-30 a.m. 150 men. 6-30. p.m.	
8-30.p.m.	Order received from Bde H.Q. that all units were to hold themselves in readiness to move at short notice.	N.B.O.

(9 26 6) W 257—976 100,000 4/12 H W V 79/3298

Instructions regarding War Diaries and Intelligence Summaries are contained in F. S. Regs., Part II. and the Staff Manual respectively. Title pages will be prepared in manuscript.

WAR DIARY
or
INTELLIGENCE SUMMARY
(Erase heading not required.)

Army Form C. 2118.

Hour, Date, Place	Summary of Events and Information	Remarks and References to Appendices
LE CARRIER.		
Tuesday. Sept: 29th.	Working parties as for previous day were furnished.	
11-30/a.m.	C.O. went round to see trenches which had been dug in the event of a retirement becoming necessary.	
6. p.m.	Received an order from 14/ Bde H.Q. that the Battalion would march at 5.a.m. to FERE-EN-TARDENOIS and relieve the Gordon Highlanders. 1st Line Transport to be handed over to 8th Division and proceed to BRAINE.	N.B.O.
LE CARRIER. Wednesday Sept: 30th. 5.a.m.	Battalion marched off en route to FERE-EN-TARDENOIS viâ SERCHES - ST: MAAST and ACY.	
10-30.a.m.	Arrived at FERE-EN-TARDENOIS. and took over duties and billets from Gordon Highlanders.	
	The following guards were furnished by the Battalion	
	1. Commander-in-Chief's Guard. 1 Sgt: 1 Cpl: + 6 men. 2 posts.	
	2. H^d Q^rs Guard. 1 Cpl: + 3 men 1 post	
	3. Examining Guard. 3 Cpls. + 18. men. by day. 1 Sgt: 3 Cpls + 27 men. by night }	
	4. Stragglers Guard. 1 Sgt. 1 Cpl + 12. men	
	5. Billeting Guard. 1 Sgt. 1 Cpl + 12 men.	N.B.O.

G. H. Q. TROOPS

8th Brigade 3rd Division 24.10.14.

2nd BATTALION

THE SUFFOLK REGIMENT

OCTOBER 1 9 1 4

Army Form C. 2118.

WAR DIARY
or
INTELLIGENCE SUMMARY
(Erase heading not required.)

Instructions regarding War Diaries and Intelligence Summaries are contained in F. S. Regs., Part II. and the Staff Manual respectively. Title pages will be prepared in manuscript.

Hour, Date, Place	Summary of Events and Information	Remarks and References to Appendices
FERE-EN-TARDENOIS. Thursday. Oct: 1st.		
11- a.m. 2. p.m.	} Sgt: Major's parade. as strong as possible.	
	100 men in command of Capt: Temple detailed to practice Guard of Honour daily in the Event of the arrival of the French President.	N.B.O.
FERE-EN-TARDENOIS. Friday Oct: 2nd 7-a.m. 11. a.m.	} Sgt. Major's parade.	
2-30 p.m.	C.O's parade.	
	Order from A.H.Q. that all ranks were to polish their buttons and numerals and complete their kit as far as possible.	N.B.O.

(9 26 6) W 257—976 100,000 4/12 H W V 79/3298

Instructions regarding War Diaries and Intelligence Summaries are contained in F. S. Regs., Part II. and the Staff Manual respectively. Title pages will be prepared in manuscript.

WAR DIARY
or
INTELLIGENCE SUMMARY
(Erase heading not required.)

Army Form C. 2118.

Hour, Date, Place	Summary of Events and Information	Remarks and References to Appendices
FERE-EN-TARDENOIS		
Saturday. 3rd Oct: 3-a.m.	14 men under Lieut Chalmers sent out by motor-cars to a wood about 4 miles away to try and capture about 10 Uhlans which had been reported seen the day before: their bivouac was located but no enemy encountered.	
	Parades as usual.	N.B.O
Sunday 4th October. 10-30 a.m.	Battalion paraded as strong as possible for Church Parade in the field S.E. of the billets	
2-30. p.m.	Companies placed at the disposal of Company Commanders.	N.B.O
Monday 5th October.	Parades as usual.	
3. p.m.	Capt Temple, 2/Lt: Trollope and 50 men acted as Guard of Honour to the French President on his visit to the Commander-in-Chief.	
4-30. p.m.	On receipt of order from G.H.Q. "C & D" Companies marched to BRAINE to report to H.Q. 1st Army Corps for further Orders.	
	Corporal F. S. Wynn. Royal Flying Corps on appointment to the rank of 2nd Lieutenant joined the Battalion and posted to "A" Coy.	N.B.O
Tuesday 6th October. 8. a.m.	Lieut: Col: H. F. Clifford arrived and took over command of the Battalion.	
9. a.m.	Remainder of "C & D" Companies and 1 Machine Gun with Limbered Wagon marched to join their respective Companies at BELLEME CHATEAU, 1 mile N.E. of BRAINE.	N.B.O.

Instructions regarding War Diaries and Intelligence Summaries are contained in F. S. Regs., Part II. and the Staff Manual respectively. Title pages will be prepared in manuscript.

WAR DIARY
or
INTELLIGENCE SUMMARY
(Erase heading not required.)

Army Form C. 2118.

Hour, Date, Place	Summary of Events and Information	Remarks and References to Appendices
FERE-EN-TARDENOIS.		
Wednesday. 7th October. 8.a.m.	Lieut. Chalmers with remainder of Machine Gun Section, marched to join C. & D Companies at BELLEME CHATEAU.	
	Parades as usual.	
12. m.n.	Received wire to say Capt. Mowbray wounded in the foot.	
	Capt. Hansbury took over command of C. Company.	
	Received order to Entrain by two trains the following day.	N.B.O.
Thursday. 8th October. 7-45.a.m	176 men under Capt Temple and 4 other Officers left for Station. The train left at 12. noon.	
9-30.a.m	All transport with Grooms, Cooks etc: marched to Station to load.	
10-45.a.m.	Battalion H.Q. with remainder under C.O. & 7 other officers left for Station. Train left 3. p.m. Times of trains were altered at the last minute to 3 hours later. Route – ORMOY – PLAINE ST: DENIS – CREIL – AMIENS – ABBEVILLE.	N.B.O.
ABBEVILLE. Friday 9th October 10. a.m	1st Train arrived at ABBEVILLE, detrained, marched to Infantry Barracks. and furnished the following Guards:- 1 Sgt: 1 Cpl: and 15 men under an Officer. C-in-C's House. 2. posts. G.H.Q. Office 1 " A.G. " 1 " Palais de Justice. 1 "	
6.30 p.m.	2nd Train arrived and detrained.	
	Men & N.C.O's were quartered in the Barracks CASERNE DE BOIS Officers billeted close by.	N.B.O.

(9 26 6) W 257—976 100,000 4/12 H W V 79/3298

Instructions regarding War Diaries and Intelligence Summaries are contained in F. S. Regs., Part II. and the Staff Manual respectively. Title pages will be prepared in manuscript.

WAR DIARY
or
INTELLIGENCE SUMMARY
(Erase heading not required.)

Army Form C. 2118.

Hour, Date, Place	Summary of Events and Information	Remarks and References to Appendices
ABBEVILLE.		
Saturday. 10th October.	Parades as usual.	
4-30 p.m.	A Guard of Honour consisting of 50 men under Capt: Temple, + 2/Lt Taylor paraded for the arrival of a French General visiting the C-in-C.	N.B.O.
Sunday. 11th October.		
10.a.m.	Battalion paraded for Church parade on Barrack Square as strong as possible.	
	Parades as usual.	N.B.O.
Monday. 12th October.		
11-30.a.m.	The 5th Reinforcement arrived and was posted to A + B Companies temporarily consisting of the following:- 2 Officers. Lieut. E.C.T.B. Williams, and 2/Lt. W.L. Llewellyn. 3 Sgts: 6. Corpls: and 6 L/c.s: and 77. men.	
4.p.m.	Reinforcements paraded for inspection.	
8-30.p.m.	Received Order from G.H.Q. to entrain the following day in two trains.	N.B.O.
Tuesday. 13th October.		
5-15. a.m.	1st Train consisting of 190 men and 7. Officers paraded.	
5-45. a.m.	2nd Train " " 218. " " 9 " Transport, Prisoners + Stragglers.	
	Route – ETAPLES – BOULOGNE – ST: OMER. On arrival at ST: OMER men were quartered at CASERNE DE LA BARRE. The following guards were found:- C-in C, G.H.Q. and Examining Guard. Officers were billeted in the town close to Barracks.	N.B.O

(9 26 6) W 257—976 100,000 4/12 H W V 79/3298

Army Form C. 2118.

WAR DIARY
or
INTELLIGENCE SUMMARY
(Erase heading not required.)

Instructions regarding War Diaries and Intelligence Summaries are contained in F. S. Regs., Part II. and the Staff Manual respectively. Title pages will be prepared in manuscript.

Hour, Date, Place	Summary of Events and Information	Remarks and References to Appendices
ST: OMER.		
Wednesday. 14th October Thursday. 15th " Friday. 16th " Saturday. 17th "	These days spent in doing parades on Square, and Exercises in the preliminary for the Attack.	
Sunday 18th October	9-30. a.m. C.O's. parades. 11 a.m. Church parade. 2-30. p.m. Company Commanders lectured to platoon and section leaders.	N.B.O.
Monday. 19th October Tuesday. 20th "	Parades as usual.	N.B.O.
Wednesday. 21st " ~~Thursday~~	Furnished a Guard of Honour to General Joffre on his visit to C-in-C	N.B.O.
2-30. p.m	"D" Coy and 3 Officers arrived and rejoined Battalion H.Q	
8-30 p.m.	"C" Coy, Machine Gun, and 6 Officers " "	N.B.O.
Thursday. 22nd October 12 noon.	"A" Coy made up to 200 all ranks sent to H.Q 4th Army Corps.	N.B.O.

Army Form C. 2118.

WAR DIARY
or
INTELLIGENCE SUMMARY
(Erase heading not required.)

Instructions regarding War Diaries and Intelligence Summaries are contained in F. S. Regs., Part II. and the Staff Manual respectively. Title pages will be prepared in manuscript.

Hour, Date, Place		Summary of Events and Information	Remarks and References to Appendices
ST. OMER Oct 23rd		"A" coy was ordered back to GHQ. The Battn was put under orders to be ready to move. Lieut DOWSE was sent to PARIS with 2 prisoners.	R
Oct 24th	2.30 P.M.	Parade. Artillery formations practiced. Battn got orders to move by motor bus to VIII Bde at 7.0 A.M. on the following day.	R
Oct 25th	5.0 A.M.	Lieut McDONAGH 3rd Battn ROYAL WEST KENT Regt and 100 men arrived; This brought strength up to 24 officers 745 men.	
	7.0 A.M.	Battn was put on to 34 motor busses; and proceeded via CASSEL to VIEILLE CHAPELLE. [Meeting General FOCH at CASSEL]	R
	11.30 A.M.	On arrival Battn was at once ordered to support IXth Bde: whom we learnt had been attacked in NEUVE CHAPELLE: and been forced to give ground. Bn therefore marched to ROUGE CROIX (1½ miles). On arrival found all was over, & went into billets in support of VIII Bde at a farm. During the day had to remain in trenches: at night sleeping in barns. Got orders to relieve ROYAL SCOTS on the following day in firing line at 3.0 A.M.	R
Oct 26th	4.0 A.M.	C.O. Adjt & O.C. Coys reconnoitred ROYAL SCOTS position.	
	7.0 P.M.	Got orders to stand to arms; as attack had been renewed on NEUVE CHAPELLE	
	1.30 A.M.	Orders to turn in.	
Oct 27th	2.30 A.M.	Paraded to relieve ROYAL SCOTS; and marched to their position EAST & parallel to RUE TOLLOGE. A & B coys were put into the firing line; which was about 400x from the enemy. C & D coys were in the reserve about 600x further back. In the middle of reserve coys behind two haystacks was Battn HQ. Rations etc were issued in [illegible]. All quiet during the day. At 7.0 P.M. Heavy burst of firing from both sides. At 11.30 P.M. the same thing occurred again.	R
Oct 28th		Lieut FRASER shot through the lungs by a rifle bullet. Pte Gray was killed by a rifle bullet. Pte	R

R. Chalmers Lt
for Adjt 2/Suffolk Regt.

Instructions regarding War Diaries and Intelligence Summaries are contained in F. S. Regs., Part II. and the Staff Manual respectively. Title pages will be prepared in manuscript.

WAR DIARY
or
INTELLIGENCE SUMMARY
(Erase heading not required.)

Army Form C. 2118.

Hour, Date, Place	Summary of Events and Information	Remarks and References to Appendices
Oct 29th	since arrival: the firing line in our position suffered great annoyance from snipers in the White House. A battery under command of Major [illegible] fired shell, putting two through it, at our instructions.	R.
	During these days the GERMANS set fire daily to a cottage or haystack to the right or left rear of our position; opening rifle fire at night from their trenches before dawn every day. Reserve trenches & firing line trenches were interchanged every day. Bursts of fire at [illegible] Neither enemy nor ourselves left trenches.	R.
	All this night improved trenches; put up wire; [illegible] out in front of the wire. Put every available employed man into firing line.	R
Oct 30th	Improved entrenchments. Two ½ hour bursts of fire during the night. Heard enemy digging. Ptes Smith & Pryke were killed by rifle bullets.	R
Oct. 31st	Completed communications between Right section firing line & communication trenches and also between Left lines. Got up blankets for the men in the reserve trenches.	R.

R. Chalmers Lt
[illegible] Adjt
[illegible] 2/SUFFOLK Rgt

2nd Suffolk Regt 8th Bde

Date	Officers				Other Ranks		
	Killed	Wounded	Missing		Killed	Wounded	Missing
27.10.14						1	
29.10.14					1	2	-
30.10.14					1	[illegible]	-
30.10.14					1	[illegible]	-
30.10.14					1	4	-

8th Brigade.

3rd Division.

2nd BATTALION

THE SUFFOLK REGIMENT

NOVEMBER 1 9 1 4:

Nil for M.T.?

121/2502.

2nd Suffolk Regt. 8th Brigade.

Transferred from 14th Brigade

Vol IV. 1–30.11.14

nothing for M.T.?

M07

3/8

(9 26 6) W 257—976 100,000 4/12 H W V 79/3298 arrived in billets.

Army Form C. 2118.

WAR DIARY
or
INTELLIGENCE SUMMARY.
(Erase heading not required.)

Instructions regarding War Diaries and Intelligence Summaries are contained in F. S. Regs., Part II. and the Staff Manual respectively. Title pages will be prepared in manuscript.

Hour, Date, Place		Summary of Events and Information	Remarks and references to Appendices
1st Nov. CHAMPIGNY.			
2nd " "		2nd Gurkas on our right beyond the Connt Rangers were shelled	
	2.30 pm	all the morning and left their trenches – 2nd Lt N. LLEWELLYN 3rd Suff wounded.	2/12
3rd " "		In the trenches.	
4th " "		No 9257 Pte Smith, No 8648 Pte Chapman No 5494 Pte Harvey were [3 men] killed in trenches.	
5th " "	12 to 1 pm	Germans shelled trenches & Reserve trenches for an hour.	
	3 pm	Machine gun trench shelled – [No 6315 L/Cpl Beaumont] killed in trenches	
6th		Relieved by 1st Bn Devon Regt. marched to ESTAIRES and billeted.	
7th ESTAIRES.	2.30 am	arrived & billetted.	
"	12 mn	'C' Coy ordered to support LAHORE DIVN	
8 " "	1. am	D " " " " "	
" " "	9. am	Battn marched to VIEILLE. CHAPELLE. & billeted in Farms	
9 VIEILLE CHAPELLE.	5pm	Battn marched to GORRE to support 21st Indian Infy Brigade and Gen JOUBERTS, French Brigade. Bad guiding by GENL JOUBERT'S guide caused a SAA Cart to fall into a Canal — horses were drowned.	
1. GIVENCY.	10. pm	HQ + A + B coys arrived in support Genl JOUBERTS Brigade	
LE MARRAIS		C + D Coys " " " 21st Indn Infy "	
10 GIVENCY.	10 am	Battn ordered to relieve French Regt in trenches	
	7 pm	order cancelled + C+D Coys returned to LEMARRAIS	
11. GIVENCY.	11 am	Battn concentrated at GORRE and marched to old Billets at VIEILLE CHAPELLE	
	2 pm	arrived in billets.	

(9 26 6) W257—976 100,000 4/12 W.V. 79 3298

Army Form C. 2118.

WAR DIARY
or
INTELLIGENCE SUMMARY.
(*Erase heading not required.*)

Instructions regarding War Diaries and Intelligence Summaries are contained in F. S. Regs., Part II. and the Staff Manual respectively. Title pages will be prepared in manuscript.

Hour, Date, Place		Summary of Events and Information	Remarks and references to Appendices
12 VIEILLE CHAPELLE	5 pm	Battn marched to relieve 9th GURKHAS at NEUVE CHAPELLE.	
13 " "		In trenches, shelling all day. 3 men wounded.	
14 " "	9 pm	Relieved by Northampton Regt [from Egypt] marched to LACOUTRE.	
15 LACOUTRE	3 am	arrived & billetted.	
	6 am	Battn in Brigade [following order 2/Roy Scots 2/Suff 4/Midd] marched to BAILLEUL	
BAILLEUL.	4 pm	arrived & billetted.	
16. " "	1.30	Marched & relieved 15th Inf Bde in trenches E of WULVERGHEM	
17 WULVERGHEM.		2/Lt. WILDER. 3rd Bn Suffk Regt was shot in trenches.	
18 " "		2 Lt. McDONAGH. 3rd Bn RW Kent Regt shot in trenches.	
19 " "		Farm where cooking was done for 2 coys in firing line trenches was shelled. no more cooking.	
20 " "		Reserve trenches were shelled - [No 6457 Pte ASHBY 2/Suff Regt] [1 man] killed 4 men wounded -	2/12
21 " "		Relieved by 2/Roy Scots. marched to NEUVE EGLISE billetted	
22 NEUVE EGLISE.		In billets.	
23 " "			
24	6 pm	Relieved 4/Middx Regt	
25 DOUVE. RIVER		In trenches 5 men wounded by Shell fire. Machine gun turned & dug out undamaged. [No 8209 L Sgt HOMBWELL] 1 man shot in trenches	
26 " "		In trenches - dull day Reinforcement Capt. CAUTLEY. + 89 NCOs & men.	
27 " "		clear day much shelling - Relieved by KOYLI. at 8 pm. marched to WESTOUTRE.	
28 WESTOUTRE		In Billets	

(9 26 6) W 257—976 100,000 4/12 H W V 79/3298

Instructions regarding War Diaries and Intelligence Summaries are contained in F. S. Regs., Part II. and the Staff Manual respectively. Title pages will be prepared in manuscript.

WAR DIARY
or
~~INTELLIGENCE SUMMARY~~

(Erase heading not required.)

Army Form C. 2118.

Hour, Date, Place		Summary of Events and Information	Remarks and references to Appendices
November. 29th	WESTOUTRE.	In billets. (washing and issue of fresh clothing etc:)	
30th	"	In billets.	
	4.0 P.M.	Marched with the brigade (WORCESTERS – SUFFOLKS – ROYAL SCOTS – MIDDLESEX. – H.A.C. –) to billets in SHERPENBERG & LOCRE) arrived 5.0 P.M.	

S.C.T.B. Williams Lt.
A/Adjt.
2nd Battn: The Suffolk Regt.

2/12

8th Brigade

3rd Division.

2nd BATTALION

THE SUFFOLK REGIMENT

DECEMBER 1 9 1 4

Instructions regarding War Diaries and Intelligence Summaries are contained in F. S. Regs., Part II. and the Staff Manual respectively. Title pages will be prepared in manuscript.

WAR DIARY
or
INTELLIGENCE SUMMARY.
(Erase heading not required.)

Army Form C. 2118.

Hour, Date, Place		Summary of Events and Information	Remarks and references to Appendices
Dec: 1st	SCHERPENBURG.	Gen: Smith Dorrien inspected the battalion which was drawn up in mass. Lt Col H.F.H Clifford (commdg)	
	3.15 P.M.	A Coy. Capt. Temple. B Coy. Capt de Crespigny. C. Coy Capt Hansburg. D. Coy. Capt Cautley. Adjt. Lt. Williams. [Gen: Smith Dorrien addressed the Battalion]	[initials]
2nd	"	2nd Lt. in billets. Lt Dalling & 65 other ranks arrived.	[initials]
3rd	" 1.0 P.M.	At 1.0 P.M. the battalion lined the LOCRE – SCHERPENBURG Road, facing West. A detachment under Capt Squirl-Dawson and 50 picked men, were paraded at the place where "H. M. The King" presented medals. Afterwards "H M The King" passed slowly along the line in his motor accompanied by Gen. Smith Dorrien & Brig Gen Bowes Comdg our (The 8th) Brigade. Asking a few questions of the Commanding Officer. H.M. proceeded to SCHERPENBURG HILL & viewed our & the German Trenches. On arrival there the artillery fired at the trenches.	2/12
	4.0 P.M.	Batt^n paraded & marched to KEMMEL & took over the trenches from the Royal Scots. [1 Pte Rawlins wounded during the relief.]	[initials]
4th	KEMMEL. 6.0 A.M.	Ptes [Markham & Beckett] killed by the trenches collapsing owing to weather conditions.	
	8.0 A.M.	[Sgt Dunn] killed [CQMS Sawyer. Sgt Place Pte Chimney H] badly wounded owing to hand grenade exploding on being examined. All quiet during the day. [L/C Cross wounded 10.P.M. when digging communication trench. Pte Wyatt killed 11.0 A.M. by German rifle grenade.]	[initials]
5th		All quiet.	[initials]
6th	6.15 P.M.	Relieved by Royal Scots Fusiliers. [L/C Cross died of wounds.] marched independently by Coys from KEMMEL to billets in WESTOUTRE. A draft of 52 men arrived under C.S.M. McGough who rejoined from hospital	[initials]
	WESTOUTRE.		
7th 8th 9th 10th		In billets in WESTOUTRE	[initials]
11th		" " " A draft of 65 men under 2/Lt Roberts arrived about noon.	[initials]
12th 13th		" " " "	[initials]

(9 26 6) W257—976 100,000 4/12 H W V 79/3298

Instructions regarding War Diaries and Intelligence Summaries are contained in F. S. Regs., Part II. and the Staff Manual respectively. Title pages will be prepared in manuscript.

WAR DIARY
or
~~INTELLIGENCE SUMMARY.~~

(Erase heading not required.)

Army Form C. 2118.

Hour, Date, Place		Summary of Events and Information	Remarks and references to Appendices
December.			
WESTOUTRE 14th		Royal Scots & Gordon Highlanders were in close billets in KEMMEL. — Suffolks & Middlesex	
KEMMEL – YPRES ROAD.	2.45 AM.	marched at 2.45 A.M. to a position on main KEMMEL – YPRES road, Suffolks in reserve to Royal Scots. [At 7.0 A.M. a big bombardement of massed French & English artillery took place. At 8.0 A.M. The 8th Bde: Gordon Highlanders on the right, Royal Scots on the left attacked the high ground south of PETIT BOIS and PETIT BOIS respectively. Royal Scots captured a German trench on West edge of PETIT BOIS taking two machine guns and 30 to 40 prisoners and an officer. The Gordon Highlanders could not reach the trench & lost 7 officers & 253 other ranks. The Royal Scots 5 officers and 100 other ranks. The French did not advance on the left. The WYTCHAETE — MESSINES position on the right was not attacked as part of the scheme but fired onto by our trenches.]	2/12
PETIT BOIS	4.30 P.M.	At 4.30 The Battalion moved up to take over the ground secured by the Royal Scots. A. Coy under the command of Capt Temple relieved the Royal Scots in the captured German Trench 20 minutes later he was shot through the head [& fell into the arms of Pte Gibbons. who was shot dead the next day in the same place.] Capt Squirl Dawson then took over command of "A" Coy. That night Pte Martin S.8914. was killed and five others wounded.	[initials]
15th	3.0 P.M.	About 3.0 P.M. some 80 germans appeared about 50 yards in front of "A" Coy dressed in khaki. digging. They were thought to be R.E when recognised as enemy fire was opened. They then signalled "surrender" but on our men going out in two small parties on each flank, to take them over, they were fired on. At this we opened rapid fire on the exposed Germans. [Pte Francis No 7992 who volunteered to take a message across a meadow from PETIT BOIS to the M.G. officer. ran the gauntlet for 80x yards when he was shot dead.]	[initials]

(9 26 6) W257—976 100,000 4/12 H W V 79/3298

Army Form C. 2118.

Instructions regarding War Diaries and Intelligence Summaries are contained in F. S. Regs., Part II. and the Staff Manual respectively. Title pages will be prepared in manuscript.

WAR DIARY
or
INTELLIGENCE SUMMARY.
(Erase heading not required.)

Hour, Date, Place		Summary of Events and Information	Remarks and references to Appendices
December.			
PETIT BOIS 15th	6.0 P.M.	Relieved by the Wiltshire Regt. — Royal Irish Rifles took over the French captured by the Royal Scots. During the relief. The Germans opened fire and we sustained the following casualties. [Ptes 9319 Anderson W. 9475 Dann S. ~~9914 Amstis F~~ 8863 West B. 8270 Watson T.] and three wounded. We then marched to LOCRE.	
LOCRE 16th – 17th		In Billets.	
" 18th		"	
KEMMEL	5.30 P.M.	Took over trenches from the Worcestershire Regt. H.Q. at PIGSTYE FARM	
" 19th		In the trenches. — five men wounded. —	
" 20th		" " " [Pte Chaplin 9039] killed and one wounded.	
21st		" " " — Relieved by Royal Fusiliers about 5.30 P.M. two men wounded during the relief. Battn: marched to WESTOUTRE.	
WESTOUTRE. " 22nd – 26th		In billets in WESTOUTRE. Xmas Day a draft of 82 men under 2Lt Schroader arrived.	
" 27		" " " "	
KEMMEL	5.30 P.M.	Took over the trenches from the H.A.C. H.Q at VROILANDHOEK farm. (1 man wounded Pte Cobbold 9038)	
" 28th		In the trenches.	
" 29th		" " " One man wounded	
" 30th		" " " Pte [Wilson 8790] killed. [Lt Col Bridgford K. Shropshire L.I. Major Wilkinson 7th Terrors. came to learn trench life. Major Cory of the 3rd Div. Staff. visited our trenches]	
" 31st		" " " Relieved about 6.0 P.M. by R.S.F's and 4/R.F.'s. Marched to WESTOUTRE.	
WESTOUTRE.			

G. C. T. B. Williams
Lt & Adjt.
2nd Battn: The Suffolk Regt.

(9 26 6) W 257—976 100,000 4/12 H W V 79/3298

3RD DIVISION
8TH INFY BDE

2ND BATTALION
SUFFOLK REGT.
JAN-SEP 1915

To 76 BDE 3 DIV

8th Inf.Bde.
3rd Div.

2nd BATTN. THE SUFFOLK REGIMENT.

J A N U A R Y

1 9 1 5

Army Form C. 2118.

WAR DIARY

or

INTELLIGENCE SUMMARY

(Erase heading not required.)

Instructions regarding War Diaries and Intelligence Summaries are contained in F. S. Regs., Part II. and the Staff Manual respectively. Title pages will be prepared in manuscript.

Place	Date	Hour	Summary of Events and Information	Remarks and References to Appendices
Jan: 1915				
WESTOUTRE.	1st		In billets	
"	2nd			
	3rd			
LOCRE	4th	5.0 PM.	Marched to fresh billets	
"	5th	2.30 AM.	C.O. Capt Squirl Dawes. Ld Daulty. Lt Sparks rode to VIERSTRAAT Cross Roads to reconnoitre trench area occupied by 80th French Infantry commanded by Col: Michel	
VIERSTRAAT		4.0 PM.	Marched to VIERSTRAAT and took over from the French:	
"	6th		Pioneers workshop for the trenches started. 3 men wounded.	
"	7th		Brig Gen Bowes. Comdg 8th Inf Bde. Major Butler. Brig Major. O.C. R.E. Ryl(?) visited the trenches.	
"	8th		In the trenches. 8 men wounded. No 9429 Pte E Man killed. 1 man wounded	
"	9th		Capt Courtley reported "2 German guns had come into action in Sq: N.18.B. 300x E of the M.G." ?? Hat(?) Gen: Sir Horace Smith-Dorrien Comdg 2nd Army visited Battn: H.Q.	
LA CLYTTE		6.30 PM.	1/ Gordon Highlanders relieved us. Battn: marched into billets in LA CLYTTE.	
"	10th		Capt. C.C. Cobbold joined the Battn: 2/Lt J.R.T. Roberts went sick. In billets	
"	11th		In billets	
"	12th		In billets	
"	13th		In billets	
VIERSTRAAT.		7.0 PM.	Relieved the Gordons	
	14th	11.0 AM.	Major Gen Haldane. G.O.C. 3rd Div: visited the Regt: Carpenters Shop. About noon enemy shelled our trenches landing one shell in it. No 6209 Sgt A Leeks, No 9217 Pte G Bevan No 9124 Pte J. Jordan were killed during the day & 3 men were wounded.	

(9 26 6) W 257—976 100,000 4/12 H W V 79/3298

WAR DIARY
or
INTELLIGENCE SUMMARY
(Erase heading not required.)

Instructions regarding War Diaries and Intelligence Summaries are contained in F. S. Regs., Part II. and the Staff Manual respectively. Title pages will be prepared in manuscript.

Place	Date (Jan: 1915)	Hour	Summary of Events and Information	Remarks and References to Appendices
VIERSTRAAT.	15th	10 A.M.	Major Gen: Wing C.R.A. visited Battn: H.Q. Shelling much as usual. No 8547 Pte Willis A Killed	[illegible]
"	16th		In the trenches. No 6634 Pte H. Giddens – No 8953 Pte Paskell – killed + 3 men wounded.	[illegible]
"	17th	10.30 A.M.	Gen: Wing. C.R.A. visited Battn: H.Q. Relieved by Gordon Highlanders after dark. 1 man wounded. Marched to billets in LA CLYTTE.	[illegible]
LA CLYTTE.	18th		In Billets	
"	19th		In Billets	
"	20th		2Lt. W. G. Crothers and draft of 50 other ranks arrived.	
"	21st		Took over from Gordons about 8.0 P.M.	[illegible]
VIERSTRAAT.	22nd		In the trenches. Life as usual. No 9080 Pte Stanford C & No 6626 Pte Odgen H. Killed.	[illegible]
"	23rd		" " "	[illegible]
	24th		A great deal of rifle fire to the North all day. Very pistol with long barrell issued to the firing line. First installment of pumps for the trenches received.	[illegible]
	25th		Relieved by Gordons from the trenches. 3 men wounded. Marched to billets in LA CLYTTE 8.0 P.M.	[illegible]
LA. CLYTTE.	26th		In billets. Lt Col H.E.H. Clifford + Lt + A/Adjt. S.C.T.B. Williams rode via BAILLEUL to MERRIS to visit the 1st Battn: who had recently landed from England and who were billeted there. Lt Col Wallace Lt Col Clifford Capt + Adjt. Baldon Lt + A/Adjt Williams. Lt + 2nd Godbolt + Lt & M.G. Officer Leach lunched together in the 1st Battn: H.Q. billet. — 1st Battn: were decorated with little yellow castles below the collar on their backs. Major White, visited the 2nd Battn: meeting the C.O. + Adjt. 2nd Battn: each way on the road. Capt W. Blackwell went sick. 2Lt. C. B. Bevan. + 111 Other ranks arrived.	[illegible]

Instructions regarding War Diaries and Intelligence Summaries are contained in F. S. Regs., Part II. and the Staff Manual respectively. Title pages will be prepared in manuscript.

or

INTELLIGENCE SUMMARY

(Erase heading not required.)

Hour, Date, Place		Summary of Events and Information	Remarks and References to Appendices
	January 1915		
LA CLYTTE.	27th. 11.0AM	In billets. A parade was held in a field on the left of the SCHERPENBURG - LA CLYTTE road for the purpose of presenting D.C.M's to the 2nd Suffolk & 4th Middlesex Regts: Major Gen: Haldane Comdg: 3rd Div: attended by Brig Gen Bowes Comdg 8th Bde presented the medals and delivered an address. The following N.C.Os & Men of the 2nd Suffolk Regt were awarded D.C.M's. C.S.M. McGough. Ptes Francis, Fuller & Chinnery. The former only was present, the remainder being killed wounded and sick respectively.	[illegible]
	28th	In billets. Some N.C.Os 2nd Battn: The Suffolk Regt. visited the 1st Battn: at MERRIS.	[illegible]
VIERSTRAAT	29th	Relieved the Gordon Highlanders in the trenches. 2Lt J.J.H. Smith was granted a commission in the 2nd Suffolk Rgt. to which he already belonged. 2Lt N.B Mossop and 80 other ranks joined the Battn:	[illegible]
	30th	In the trenches. Reliable information was received that 3 German Corps had arrived on the front MENIN - COURTRAI. Garrisons in the trenches were increased 25% about midnight a tremendous fusilade was heard somewhere north, in the direction of St ELOI. There was much gunning & numerous lights were thrown up. 36 of our oldest men were sent away to do duty on the L of C. 1 man was wounded.	[illegible]
	31st	In the trenches - usual life - 2 men were wounded.	[illegible]

P. C. T. B. Williams Lt & A/Adjt:
2nd Battn: The Suffolk Regt.

(9 26 6) W 257—976 100,000 4/12 H W V 79/3298

8th Inf.Bde.
3rd Div.

2nd BATTN. THE SUFFOLK REGIMENT.

F E B R U A R Y

1 9 1 5

Instructions regarding War Diaries and Intelligence Summaries are contained in F. S. Regs., Part II. and the Staff Manual respectively. Title pages will be prepared in manuscript.

WAR DIARY
or
INTELLIGENCE SUMMARY.
(Erase heading not required.)

Army Form C. 2118.

Place	Date	Hour	Summary of Events and Information	Remarks and references to Appendices
	February 1915			
VIERSTRAAT	1st		In the trenches 1 man wounded.	Hw.
	2nd		Relieved by Gordon Highlanders about 8.0 pm	Hw
LA CLYTTE	3rd		In billets.	Hw.
	4th		2nd Lieutenants J.V.R. de Castro, A.J. Lowther and M.O. Griffiths arrived.	Hw
	5th		2nd Lieut G. Goodwin arrived.	Hw
VIERSTRAAT	6th		Relieved Gordon Highlanders in Trench area.	Hw.
	7th		In the trenches. Just the ordinary routine. 1 wounded.	Hw
	8th	12 noon	In Trenches. Our artillery shelled HOLLANDSCHESCHUUR FARM for the benefit of H.M. the King of the Belgians who watched it from SCHERPENBERG. 1 [No 9442] Private [S. Rayton] Killed – 2 wounded.	Hw
	9th		In trenches. 2nd Lieut. A.L. Platts and 70 other ranks arrived.	Hw
LA CLYTTE	10th		Relieved by Gordon Highlanders 9 to pm. Prior to relief two German machine guns opened on L 5 Trench with several bursts of fire. No casualties.	Hw.
	11th		In billets. 2nd Lieut J.R.T. Roberts returned from hospital.	Hw
	12th			Hw
	13th			Hw
VIERSTRAAT	14th		Relieved Gordon Highlanders in Trench area – took over 9.5 pm. Our artillery fired all night.	Hw
	15th		In trenches 1 wounded	Hw
	16th		" " Nothing of any interest. 3 wounded.	Hw.

(9 26 6) W 257—976 100,000 4/12 H W V 79/3298

WAR DIARY

or

INTELLIGENCE SUMMARY.

(*Erase heading not required.*)

Instructions regarding War Diaries and Intelligence Summaries are contained in F. S. Regs., Part II. and the Staff Manual respectively. Title pages will be prepared in manuscript.

Hour, Date, Place February 1915		Summary of Events and Information	Remarks and references to Appendices
VIERSTRAAT	17th	Relieved by the Gordon Highlanders. Relief complete at 8.55 pm. 1 Private [E. Tams No 8936] killed. 1 wounded. 2nd Lt E. F. Heavens, and 2nd Lieut L. G. R. Windsor and 47 other ranks arrived.	JSW. JSW.
LA CLYTTE	18th 19th	In billets.	JSW.
	20th	Relieved the Gordon Highlanders - completed 10.5 pm.	JSW.
VIERSTRAAT	21st	In trenches 1 wounded	JSW.
	22nd	" " 1 [No 6684 Pte W. Porter] Killed. 4 wounded.	JSW.
	23rd	" " 1 [No 15261 Pte A. Hammond] Killed 4 wounded.	JSW.
	24th	" " 1 [No 9415 Pte J. Hayward] Killed 4 wounded. Relieved by Gordon Highlanders about 9.0 pm.	JSW.
LA CLYTTE	25th	In billets. [Lieut. Colonel W. B. H. Clifford and Lieut & Adjt C. C. T. B. Williams rode to BAILLEUL and visited Colonel Wallace commanding the 1st Battalion to hear about their recent fighting and heavy casualties] 91 N.C.Os and men arrived.	JSW.
	26th	In billets.	JSW.
	27th	" " Genl Sir Horace Smith Dorrien, Maj. Gen. Haldane and Brig Gen. Bowes visited Battn H.Q to see Private Death's "Suffolk Death Trap." A new form of wire entanglement, and expressed their very high approval of it.	JSW.
VIERSTRAAT.	28th	Relieved Gordon Highlanders. Took over about 10. pm.	JSW.

J S Wyn.. Lt & Adjt
2nd Battn The Suffolk Regt.

8th Inf.Bde.
3rd Div.

2nd BATTN. THE SUFFOLK REGIMENT.

M A R C H

1 9 1 5

Army Form C. 2118.

WAR DIARY
or
INTELLIGENCE SUMMARY.
(Erase heading not required.)

Instructions regarding War Diaries and Intelligence Summaries are contained in F. S. Regs., Part II. and the Staff Manual respectively. Title pages will be prepared in manuscript.

Hour, Date, Place	Summary of Events and Information	Remarks and references to Appendices
March 1915		
VIERSTRAAT 1st–4th	In the trenches usual routine. 1. Pte W. Craske 5477 killed 2 men wounded	
	2. Pte H. Wilson 15221 – Pte B. Cowling 8940 – Pte W. Brown 8178 killed.	
	3. 2Lt G. R.T Roberts was killed whilst sniping from K2A. He had fired about 6 shots when they got him. Pte W. Fendwick 9883 killed & 5 men wounded.	
	4. Sgt J. Wallage 6312 – Pte L Smith 8219 – Pte S Andrews 9044 and 2 men wounded. Relieved by 1st Gordons.	Cas 1st–4th K 1+8 W 7
LA CLYTTE 5th–8th	In billets. The usual work of cleaning and training was carried on	
	8th Took over same trenches from 1st Gordons – one man wounded.	
VIERSTRAAT 9th–12th	9. Cpl G. Manning 9344 killed – 2 men wounded	
	In the trenches – usual routine. 10. 2Lt Wilkinson & 2Lt Lodward joined	Cas 8th–12th K 4 W 4
	11. Pte J Holmes 9768 – Pte H Addison 13049 killed and one man wounded.	
	12. Sgt. J. Jay 9575 killed. Relieved by 1st Gordons.	
LA CLYTTE. 13th	In the same billets as usual.	

(9 26 6) W257—976 100,000 4/12 H W V 79/3298

Army Form C. 2118.

Instructions regarding War Diaries and Intelligence Summaries are contained in F. S. Regs., Part II. and the Staff Manual respectively. Title pages will be prepared in manuscript.

or

~~INTELLIGENCE SUMMARY~~

(Erase heading not required.)

Hour, Date, Place			Summary of Events and Information	Remarks and References to Appendices
	March 1915			
LA CLYTTE	14th	10.30AM.	The Battalion was drawn up in quarter column just south of the villiage on the right of the SCHERPENBURG – LA CLYTTE road in marching order. Brig. Gen Bowes C.B. addressed a complimentary speech to the battalion alluding to its soldierlike bearing.	
		2.15AM	On the same ground the battalion was inspected by Gen: Sir Horace Smith Dorrien Commanding 2nd Army – There were present Gen Sir Charles Fergussen Comdg 2nd Corps. & Brig Gen: Bowes Comdg 8th Inf Bde and their respective staffs. After the inspection Gen: Sir Horace Smith Dorrien mounted the C.O's charger and made a most complimentary speech to the Battn: saying what excellent reports he had had from our general on the work of the Battn: in & out of the trenches. [Lt Col. H.F.H Clifford Comdg. Capt. G.C.B. Williams Adjt. O.C. A Coy. 2/Lt Lygon. O.C. B Coy. 2Lt Sparks. O.C. C Coy 2Lt Oakes O.C. D Coy. 2/Lt Crotty]	2/12
	15th	11.30AM.	The G.O.C. 8th Inf Bde inspected the transport who can only be described as the "rusty buckles"	
		9.00PM	Officers went off to reconnoitre the J. and K trenches.	
	16th	6.30PM	Marched to the trench area and took over from the 3rd Middlesex & 3rd Royal Fusiliers. Although we marched scheduled time the congestion ~~[illegible]~~ in KEMMEL could only be likened to uncontrolled traffic in Piccadilly Circus if the police were removed. The Battn: took over 13 separate trenches, one of them being J.3. where Capt Temple was killed on Dec 14th 1914	

(9 26 6) W 257—976 100,000 4/12 H W V 79/3298

Instructions regarding War Diaries and Intelligence Summaries are contained in F. S. Regs., Part II. and the Staff Manual respectively. Title pages will be prepared in manuscript.

or

INTELLIGENCE SUMMARY

(Erase heading not required.)

Hour, Date, Place	Summary of Events and Information	Remarks and References to Appendices
MARCH 1915		
J & K. Trenches. 16th	In the afternoon a draft of 103 arrived – one man wounded in relief.	
PETIT BOIS 17th	Having taken over 13 trenches, we relinquished them after 24 hours. We were relieved by the Wilts & the Royal Irish Rifles the latter causing us much delay by only taking over half of J.3. We took over our old trenches from the 1st Gordons. (the last time). The M.G. sec was very late in relieving as before we could relieve the Gordons our guns had to be relieved by the Wilts who had in turn to be relieved by some other Regt. in the F. trenches before they could relieve us. – one man wounded	2/12
VIERSTRAAT 18th	one man wounded.	
19th	Brevt. Lt Col Lord Butler left the Brigade much to our regret – on promotion. Sgt. J. Mulley 5294 killed & one man wounded.	Cas. 17th – 20th: K 3. W 4
20th	Sgt T. Rush 10240 – Pte H Tricker 15236 killed one man wounded	
21st	Brig Gen Bowes left for England on relinquishing the command. On his departure he sent a message to all battalions thanking them for the support they had given him on all occasions. Pte. B. Smith 5923 – killed – a man wounded.	

Instructions regarding War Diaries and Intelligence Summaries are contained in F. S. Regs., Part II. and the Staff Manual respectively. Title pages will be prepared in manuscript.

or

INTELLIGENCE SUMMARY

(Erase heading not required.)

Hour, Date, Place		Summary of Events and Information	Remarks and References to Appendices
	MARCH 1915		
VIERSTRAAT	22nd	Pte Bottwell 16163 killed 5 men wounded.	
	23rd	2Lt F. T. Schroder killed 10 men wounded. A rifle grenade landed in L5 doing most of the damage.	Cas. 21st–24th K 1+3 W 20
	24th	Pte S Jessop. 13160 killed 2 men wounded.	
	25th	In trenches [illegible] Pte P. Seeley 8527 & Cpl H. Sparke 8947 killed 5 men wounded.	
	26th	Pte J. Northfield 5462 killed 3 men wounded.	" 25th–28th K4 W12
	27th	2 men wounded.	
	28th	Pte F Barber 12894 killed 2 men wounded.	
	29th	Pte H. Page 12186 killed 3 men wounded.	" 29th–30th K1 W10
	30th	2 men wounded. Relieved by 4th Middlesex Regt. and marched to our old billets of Xmas time in WESTOUTRE.	
WESTOUTRE	31st	In Billets.	Month K 2+23 W 59

[illegible] Capt & Adjt.
2nd Battn: The Suffolk Regt.

6/4/15.

8th Inf.Bde.
3rd Div.

2nd BATTN. THE SUFFOLK REGIMENT.

A P R I L

1 9 1 5

Army Form C. 2118.

Instructions regarding War Diaries and Intelligence Summaries are contained in F. S. Regs., Part II. and the Staff Manual respectively. Title pages will be prepared in manuscript.

WAR DIARY
or
~~INTELLIGENCE SUMMARY~~
(~~Erase heading not required.~~)

Hour, Date, Place		Summary of Events and Information	Remarks and References to Appendices
	April. 1915.		
WESTOUTRE	1st 2nd 3rd 4th	In billets.	[illegible]
VIERSTRAAT	5th	Took over M1 and L trenches from 4th Middlesex Regt. No 5277 Pte H Bruce killed. one man wounded.	[illegible]
	6th	No 8612 Pte J Balford & 9021 Pte G Lewis killed.	[illegible]
	7th	No 8996 Pte G. Ruff killed	[illegible]
	8th	One man wounded	[illegible]
	9th	Bde ordered us to hand over to next Bde 100 paces on left of M.1. No 15470 Pte B Lee & No 5948 Pte F Wheeler killed.	[illegible]
	10th	Germans fired rifle grenades at M.1. [killing No 5589 Pte H Souther & No 12758 Pte J. Taylor and wounding one other	[illegible]
	11th	[4 men wounded] Relieved by 4th Middlesex Regt. - marched to WESTOUTRE.	[illegible]
WESTOUTRE	12th	1st Battn. The Suffolk Regt under the Command of Lt-Col W. B. Wallace marched through WESTOUTRE where the 2nd Battn. was in billets. A mile from WESTOUTRE - Lt Col Gifford comdg the 2nd Battn. and Capt Williams, Adjt met the 1st Battn. at 11.0 AM. The two C.O's and Adjts [The Adjt of the 1st Battn. being Capt Balders] rode at the head of the column; the 1st Battn. being welcomed by large groups of officers and men of its sister Battn. - Close by the village church the 1st Battn. Halted and the men fell out for a quarter of an hour during which time the officers 1st Battn.	[illegible]

Instructions regarding War Diaries and Intelligence Summaries are contained in F. S. Regs., Part II. and the Staff Manual respectively. Title pages will be prepared in manuscript.

WAR DIARY or INTELLIGENCE SUMMARY

(Erase heading not required.)

Hour, Date, Place	Summary of Events and Information	Remarks and References to Appendices
April 1915		
WESTOUTRE 12th	were entertained by the officers of the 2nd Battn: in their temporary mess, and a group of the officers was photographed between the church and the mess. The 1st Battn: then fell in, and amidst the good wishes of all ranks of its sister Battn: marched off to POPERINGHE, being accompanied for the first mile or two by Lt Col Clifford & Capt Williams who then saluted them and wished them "God's speed". It is probable that this is the first occasion in the history of the Regt: that the two Battn's have met — it is certainly the first occasion on active service, and as such is of momentous interest to all connected with it. Some idea may be conveyed to future generations [who care to consult an army list of August 1914] of the magnitude of the wastage of this war if we record the presence at this meeting of regular officers.	
	1st Battn: Lt Col Wallace. Capt Balders (Adjt) Capt Arnold Lt Wood Lt Bradley Lt & Qr Mr Godbolt.	
	2nd Battn: Lt Col Clifford D.S.O Capt Williams (Adjt) Lt Oakes.	
	Since this meeting; of the 1st Battn: Capt Arnold has been killed & Capt Balders & Lt Wood have been wounded East of YPRES, and Lt Col. Clifford has been wounded & Lt Oakes has gone sick from the 2nd Battn: — .	

~~WAR DIARY~~ or

INTELLIGENCE SUMMARY

(~~Erase heading not required.~~)

Instructions regarding War Diaries and Intelligence Summaries are contained in F. S. Regs., Part II. and the Staff Manual respectively. Title pages will be prepared in manuscript.

Place	Date	Hour	Summary of Events and Information	Remarks and References to Appendices
	April 1915			
WESTOUTRE	13th		In billets	
		10 P.M.	The Battn: marched to the ROSENHILL HUTS between LACLYTTE and RENINGHELST	
RENINGHELST	14th 15th 16th 17th		In billets	
			Relieved 4th Middlesex Regt. 3 men wounded.	
	18th		2 men wounded	
	19th		2 men wounded by rifle grenade in M.1. much shelling by "crumps" about 500ˣ over HOWITZER FARM.	
	20th		C.T. between trenches M1 & 25 constructed by "A" Coy under 2Lts Lynn & Winton. Enemys rifle grenade fell in M.G. emplacement in M.1. wounding 5 men another in M1 killing 2 and wounding 3 men. (No 13124 Pte A Steed & 7352 Pte F Morgan killed) 3 more men wounded by bullets.	
	21st		Rifle grenade fired by Germans at dawn & wounded 5 men. By request Howitzers dropped by H.E. shells about HOLLANDSCHESCHUUR FARM	
	22nd		Brigadier visited Battn: H.Q. stayed to tea, went the grand tour of the trenches with the C.O. Backing up with the DUMOL - C.T. At 9.0 P.M. news came that the Germans were using obnoxious gases (against the North Midland Division) which hurt mens eyes. Fighting at Hill 60 had been heard every night lately. No 8880 Pte C Berry - No 9008 Pte J. Pallant & No 9262 Pte A. Skillings killed - 11 men wounded	
	23rd		Relieved by 4th Middlesex Regt: & marched to ROSENHILL HUTS.	

(9 26 6) W 257—976 100,000 4/12 H W V 79/3298

Instructions regarding War Diaries and Intelligence Summaries are contained in F. S. Regs., Part II. and the Staff Manual respectively. Title pages will be prepared in manuscript.

~~WAR DIARY or~~ INTELLIGENCE SUMMARY

(~~Erase heading not required.~~)

Hour, Date, Place	Summary of Events and Information	Remarks and References to Appendices
April 1915		
ROSEN HILL HUTS		
24th, 25th, 26th, 27th, 28th, 29th	In billets – during these days ~~there was~~ a heavy German attack north of YPRES on French and the Canadian division. Gas was extensively used by the enemy.	[illegible initials]
	Relieved 4th Middlesex Regt. in usual trenches. [Lt. A. J. Lowther (son of "The Speaker") dangerously wounded in the head behind L.2. 4 men wounded. Enemy shelled "Confusion Corner" with H.E. Shrapnel & Fizz Bangs at 20 min intervals during the whole night. M.G. emplacement on road between M. 3 & 5 was hit by a shell. M.G. was then placed in C.T. just behind.	[illegible initials]
30th	In the trenches.	Casualties – month. K 15. W. 9 + 40
	7/5/15. G. C. T. B. Williams Capt & Adjt. 2nd Battn. The Suffolk Regt.	

(9 26 6) W 257—976 100,000 4/12 H W V 79/3298

8th Inf.Bde.
3rd Div.

2nd BATTN. THE SUFFOLK REGIMENT.

M A Y

1 9 1 5

Instructions regarding War Diaries and Intelligence Summaries are contained in F. S. Regs., Part II. and the Staff Manual respectively. Title pages will be prepared in manuscript.

WAR DIARY

~~or~~

~~INTELLIGENCE SUMMARY~~

(*Erase heading not required.*)

Army Form C. 2118.

Hour, Date, Place		Summary of Events and Information	Remarks and References to Appendices
May 1st 1915 VIERSTRAAT	In the trenches.	1 man wounded.	
2nd	" " "		
3rd	" " "		
4th	" " "	No 8448 Pte F. Brookes killed one man wounded	
5th	" " "	2Lt A.G. Winton killed - shot in the head behind L2. Lt Col H.F.M. Clifford DSO wounded right arm - remained with the Battn. Two men wounded. Lt N.B. Oakes to Field Ambulance.	
6th	" " "	No 12804 Pte S. Osborne killed two men wounded.	
7th	" " "	Two men wounded	
8th	" " "	No 6055 ~~Pte~~ L. Gray killed one man wounded	
9th	" " "	3 men wounded 2Lt Barber + 2Lt Higgins joined.	
10th	" " "	8th Bde moved into the YPRES salient. The Battn remained in the trenches & was attached to 7th Bde. 3 men wounded	
11th	" " "	No 6658 C.S.M. Gates + 6363 Sgt. T Oakley killed by H.E. Shrapnel outside Bde dugout. 1 man wounded.	
12th	" " "	1 man wounded. 2Lt G.R. Prentice arrived with reinforcement of 23.	
13th	" " "	No 4091 Pte W. Davey killed - 1 man wounded.	
14th	" " "	——	
15th	" " "	——	
16th	" " "	one man wounded.	
17th	" " "	Capt Oakes rejoined from Field Ambulance.	
18th	" " "	one man wounded	
19th	" " "	——	

Army Form C. 2118.

Instructions regarding War Diaries and Intelligence Summaries are contained in F. S. Regs., Part II. and the Staff Manual respectively. Title pages will be prepared in manuscript.

~~WAR DIARY~~ ~~or~~ INTELLIGENCE SUMMARY

(~~Erase heading not required.~~)

~~Hour~~, Date, Place	Summary of Events and Information	Remarks and References to Appendices
May 20th 1915 VIERSTRAAT.	In the trenches. one man wounded	
21st "	" " "	
22nd "	" " " No 1686, Pte Pettit killed one man wounded.	
23rd "	" " " one man wounded.	
24th "	" " "	
25th "	" " " Three men wounded. Lt. Col. HFH Clifford D.S.O. proceeded on 14 days leave to England.	
	Capt C. C. Cobbold assumed command of the Battn:	
26th "	" " " 1 man wounded.	
LA CLYTTE.	Battn: was relieved by the Worcesters 7th Bde. and marched to Billets in the LA CLYTTE HUTS.	
27th "	C & D Coys carried knife rests from DICKEBUSH to near HOOGE going round "SHRAPNEL CORNER" without a casualty, and billeted in "C" Huts near BRIELEN.	
28th "	Remainder of Battn: moved up to the same billets & also carried knife rests without a casualty.	
29th "C" HUTS near BRIELEN.	Half battalion was on digging fatigue near HOOGE nightly.	Cas. month K 1+7. W 1+23
30th		
31st	1 man wounded. Pte Garrod was shot by accident. how it happened is unknown or whether the wound was self inflicted.	

June 1915.

P. C. T. B. Williams Capt & Adjt.
2nd Battn. The Suffolk Regt.

(9 26 6) W 257—976 100,000 4/12 H W V 79/3298

8th Inf.Bde.
3rd Div.

2nd BATTN. THE SUFFOLK REGIMENT.

JUNE & JULY

1 9 1 5

Instructions regarding War Diaries and Intelligence Summaries are contained in F. S. Regs., Part II. and the Staff Manual respectively. Title pages will be prepared in manuscript.

~~INTELLIGENCE~~ SUMMARY

(~~Erase heading not required.~~)

Hour, Date, Place JUNE 1915			Summary of Events and Information	Remarks and References to Appendices
C. HUTS – BRIELEN near YPRES.	1st		digging at night on C.T. from RAILWAY WOOD to SHRAPNEL CORNER one man wounded.	Map Ref. Sheet 28 B Series 1/40000 squared.
OUDERDOM.	2nd	4.0 AM.	after digging ... moved to ~~billets~~ bivouac at G.M.24.A. dug again at night one man wounded	
YPRES.	3rd	7.30 P.M.	Moved to field at H.11.D near YPRES to be in close reserve to Bde who were in trenches stretching from the railway southwards as far as HOOGE. two men wounded digging at night.	
OUDERDOM.	4th	8.0 PM.	Moved back to ~~billets~~ bivouac at G M 24 A. one man wounded digging at night.	
"	5th		Digging at night. Major Sinclair Thompson joined.	
BRANDHOEK	6th		Arrived at fresh bivouac ground about 3.0 P.M. – Major Sinclair Thompson received orders to take over command of the 1st Battn.	
	7th		In bivouac near Brandhoek G.11.B	
	8th		Two Coys sent to dugouts in 1.15.D	
HOOGE	8th		Took over trenches from 1st Gordons. Trenches stretching from I.17.B.38. to western house in HOOGE. – line along MENIN ROAD only held by posts & no one north of the road.	
	9th		Cpl F. Goodwin 6015 Ptes L. Graham 16742 + H Last 12913 killed & 2 men wounded	

(9 26 6) W 257—976 100,000 4/12 H W V 79/3298

Instructions regarding War Diaries and Intelligence Summaries are contained in F. S. Regs., Part II. and the Staff Manual respectively. Title pages will be prepared in manuscript.

~~WAR DIARY or INTELLIGENCE SUMMARY~~

(~~Erase heading not required.~~)

Hour, Date, Place		Summary of Events and Information	Remarks and References to Appendices
JUNE 1915 HOOGE			
10th		2Lt L. Std. Windsor killed by stray shot at night in the head when out by a new trench we were digging in front of the Menin Road eight men wounded.	
11th		Ptes R. Davis 6058 & C Parker 7422 killed seven men wounded.	
12th		Ptes J. Bristowe 15264 & G Salter 15257 killed two men wounded.	
13th		Seven men wounded	
14th		Two men wounded.	
15th		Four men wounded	
16th	4.15AM	3rd Div attacked at 4.15 AM. Railway Wood & the trenches south of it & Y Wood. 1. 11 - B.T.D. got into the Y Wood without any casualties & through it – consequently our own artillery shelled our men heavily as it had been calculated that it would take some time to get through. Worcesters were stopped by bombing about midway between Y Wood & HOOGE.	
	10.00AM	About 10.0 A.M. portions of the KSLI & KRRs of the 14th Div began to arrive about Battn. H.Q. they were supposed to do a fresh attack through our line – they none of them knew where they were & were scattered in odd half coys all the way back to YPRES this was in no way their fault – as practically no guides had been provided & out of 4 officers per battn had done a very short reconnaissance	

Instructions regarding War Diaries and Intelligence Summaries are contained in F. S. Regs., Part II. and the Staff Manual respectively. Title pages will be prepared in manuscript.

or

~~INTELLIGENCE SUMMARY~~

(~~Erase heading not required.~~)

Hour, Date, Place		Summary of Events and Information	Remarks and References to Appendices
	June 1915		
HOOGE	16th	a few days previously - Consequently the battns did not get up to the firing line till about 2.0 P.M. with the help of all our orderlies servants etc: to show them the way. & suffered immense & unnecessary casualties through exposing themselves to artillery in known bad spots Sgt. W. Mills 9041 Pte W. Symonds 12059 Pte H Seeley 6620 Pte A Plumb 12815 Pte L Martin 15369 killed 16 men wounded.	
	17th	2Lt H C N Trollope wounded by shrapnel in arm & foot C.S M. Barker W. killed. twenty men wounded.	
	18th	2Lt G. F Llanena killed by splinter from shell in Y. Wood also 6893 Cpl F Pryke 12836 Pte L Anderson and at night 2Lt J. K. Prentice killed by a bullet in the head while putting out barbed wire near HOOGE & C. S. M. Mc Gough A. 7738. nine men wounded — 2Lt J.J. Thell & 2Lt Hartopp joined.	
	19th	Two men wounded.	
	20th	Nine men wounded. relieved by the Shropshires. 14th Div:	
BRANDHOEK	21st 22nd	} In bivouac — (billets??)	

Instructions regarding War Diaries and Intelligence Summaries are contained in F. S. Regs., Part II. and the Staff Manual respectively. Title pages will be prepared in manuscript.

~~WAR DIARY~~ or INTELLIGENCE SUMMARY

(~~Erase heading not required.~~)

Hour, Date, Place	Summary of Events and Information	Remarks and References to Appendices
June 1915		
BRANDHOEK		
23rd	Bde Sports	[illegible]
24th	2/Lts Boycott-Stanford - Petre - joined Battn:	[illegible]
25th, 26th, 27th	In bivouac	[illegible]
28th	Lt Col Clifford DSO. relinquished command of the Battn. to take over command of the 149th Bde	[illegible]
29th, 30th, July 1, 2nd, 3rd	In bivouac.	[illegible]
BRANDHOEK & HOOGE 4th	2 coys moved into dugouts in SANCTUARY WOOD (A & B Coys)	
5th	one man wounded.	[illegible]
6th	3 men wounded	[illegible]
7th	3 men wounded.	[illegible]
BRANDHOEK 8th	Major C.H. Turner assumed command of the Battn. A & B Coys returned	[illegible]
9th		
YPRES 10th	~~[illegible]~~ Battn: moved into dugouts in H.Q.D.	[illegible]
11th	~~Remainder of~~ one man wounded.	[illegible]
12th	Battn moved. A.B Coys & H.Q. going into the RAMPARTS - YPRES - C & D Coys going into dugouts in SANCTUARY WOOD one man wounded.	[illegible]

Instructions regarding War Diaries and Intelligence Summaries are contained in F. S. Regs., Part II. and the Staff Manual respectively. Title pages will be prepared in manuscript.

~~WAR DIARY~~
~~or~~
INTELLIGENCE SUMMARY
(~~Erase heading not required.~~)

Place	Date	Hour	Summary of Events and Information	Remarks and References to Appendices
	JULY 1915			
RAMPARTS - YPRES & SANCTUARY WOOD	13th			
	14th		3 men wounded	
	15th		3/8202 Pte H Mowld 15241 Pte F Harrington 3/9430 Pte W. Lucas Killed & 4 men wounded.	
	16th		3 men wounded	
	17th		one man wounded	
	18th		3 men wounded.	
	19th	7.0 P.M.	Mine exploded under the German trenches just north of the [illegible] house & HOOGE. & attack by Bde: 4th Mx leading - C.&D. carried bombs etc: to firing line & dug C.T.s etc: at night. Good work done by Lt de Castro & 2Lt Greig. Our bombers were well to the fore & did good work in holding the crater in the evening & the next day - 2Lt Pickard Cambridge who was i/c was specially mentioned by the O.C. 1st G.H. 19180 Pte P. Sagar 3/8311 Pte C. Holmes killed - 4 men wounded. The 2. Coys & H.Q. in ~~the~~ RAMPARTS moved up to the G.H.Q. line 1.16. C.&D.	
	20th	10. P.M.	H.Q. & A & B Coys moved into SANCTUARY WOOD 8415 4/c G. Sansom 3/8727 Pte P Matroni killed & 17 men wounded	
	21st		Two men wounded.	
	22nd	10. P.M.	12931 Pte W. Smith killed 8 men wounded. - Relieved by the 9th K.R.R. & 14th Div. in billets.	
BRANDHOEK	23rd			
	24th	6.0 P.M.	Took over trenches on South side of the canal at SPOILBANK 1.33.A. from the Cheshires. 14th Bde. 2 men wounded.	
	25th			

(9 26 6) W 257—976 100,000 4/12 H W V 79/3298

Instructions regarding War Diaries and Intelligence Summaries are contained in F. S. Regs., Part II. and the Staff Manual respectively. Title pages will be prepared in manuscript.

or

INTELLIGENCE SUMMARY

(*Erase heading not required.*)

Hour, Date, Place		Summary of Events and Information	Remarks and References to Appendices
JULY 1915.			
SPOIL BANK I.33.B	26th	15245 Pte R Miller killed 6 men wounded	[illegible]
	27th	———	
	28th	———	
	29th	Two men wounded.	[illegible]
	30th	Two men wounded. draft of 40 NCOs & men joined Battn.	[illegible]
	31	16782 Pte W. Harvey killed. one man wounded.	[illegible]

G. C. T. B. Williams Capt & Adjt.
2nd Battn The Suffolk Regt.
4th August 1915.

8th Inf.Bde.
3rd Div.

2nd BATTN. THE SUFFOLK REGIMENT.

A U G U S T

1 9 1 5

Army Form C. 2118.

Instructions regarding War Diaries and Intelligence Summaries are contained in F. S. Regs., Part II. and the Staff Manual respectively. Title Pages will be prepared in manuscript.

WAR DIARY
or
INTELLIGENCE SUMMARY
(Erase heading not required.)

Place	Date AUGUST	Hour	Summary of Events and Information	Remarks and references to Appendices
SPOIL BANK	1st		One man wounded — Draft of 13 men joined battn — During the last week eleven mines were heard to go up - all south in the direction of ST ELOI	
	2nd		16457 Pte S. Gooding killed	
	3rd		3/9212 Sgt Howell killed 6 men wounded	
	4th		—	
	5th		13202 Pte J. Ballard killed one man wounded.	
	6th		3 men wounded	
	7th		2Lt J. L. Smith wounded by shell in YPRES. 1 Sgt Master Cook Podley wounded on dump.	
	8th		—	
	9th		19076 Pte J. Nutting killed — During the previous 10 days demonstrations were made most nights & days to try & relieve the pressure at HOOGE after the German Liquid Fire attack on July 30th.	
	10th		3 men wounded — Draft of 50 N.C.Os & men joined the Battn: from the 10th Battn:	
	11th		—	
	12th		—	
	13th		One man wounded	
	14th		—	
	15th		Two men wounded — Two men joined Battn from Base.	
	16th		15230 Pte Randall killed.	
	17th		One man wounded.	
	18th		Two men wounded	
	19th		—	
	20th		7036 Pte Catton killed Capt. N.B. Oakes rejoined from sick leave - Capt. S.C. Phelan R.A.M.C. who had come out with the Battn. in Aug 1914 from the Curragh was posted to 36th F.A. Lt. J.P. Cox R.A.M.C. came in his place	
	21st		19253 Pte F. Goss & 12730 Pte B. King killed one man wounded.	

1875 Wt. W593/826 1,000,000 4/15 J.B.C. & A. A.D.S.S./Forms/C. 2118.

Instructions regarding War Diaries and Intelligence Summaries are contained in F. S. Regs., Part II. and the Staff Manual respectively. Title Pages will be prepared in manuscript.

Army Form C. 2118

~~WAR DIARY or~~ INTELLIGENCE SUMMARY

~~(Erase heading not required.)~~

Place	Date 1915 AUGUST	Hour	Summary of Events and Information	Remarks and references to Appendices
SPOIL BANK	22nd		2Lt. J. K. Stanford & 3 men wounded by shells in dugouts	
	23rd	10.0 P.M.	8955 Pte Lilley killed – Battn. relieved by 6th Sherwoods & returned to bivouac near OUDERDOM. H. 13. c. D.	
	24th		6 M. Gunners joined the Battn:	
	25th–30th		In billets.	
	31st		2Lt D. M. Greig accidentally wounded by a bomb when on a bombing course.	

R. C. T. B. [illegible] Capt & Adjt.
2nd Battn The Suffolk Regt.
4th Sept 1915

1875 Wt. W593/826 1,000,000 4/15 J.B.C. & A. A.D.S.S./Forms/C. 2118.

8th Inf.Bde.
3rd Div.

2nd BATTN. THE SUFFOLK REGIMENT.

S E P T E M B E R

1 9 1 5

Instructions regarding War Diaries and Intelligence Summaries are contained in F. S. Regs., Part II. and the Staff Manual respectively. Title Pages will be prepared in manuscript.

WAR DIARY or ~~INTELLIGENCE SUMMARY~~

(Erase heading not required.)

Army Form C. 2118

Place	Date	Hour	Summary of Events and Information	Remarks and references to Appendices
HOOGE	Sept 30th 1915	3.0 P.M.	Bombers & 1 Coy 4th Mx on the right up B.3 —— The Bombers & 1 Coy 2 R.Sc. centre of the salient – the bombers & 1 Coy 2SK. on the left up B7. The attack was made by "A" Coy under the command of Capt S. C. Smith who was unfortunately killed at the commencement. – The attack succeeded in reaching the western edge of the crater being gallantly led by Capt de Castro in the face of machine gun & rifle fire & also bombs. They were also stopped by barbed wire which Capt de Castro proceeded to cut. – At this period Major Turner in command of the attacking party was killed – also Lt Thill & 2Lt Law. i/c the bombers. & Capt Dealtry was wounded. The attack which had reached this position was forced to retire by enfilade M.G. fire & formed a line out to the right making use of B4. S. & digging a new trench connecting up in the direction of Pollock Street. Where the 2 R.S. were still bombing. This line was strengthened & consolidated during the night by the H.A.C. who were brought up to connect up with the Royal Scots Killed Major C.H. Turner. Capt S.C. Smith. Lt. J.J. Thill. 2Lt C.L.G. Law. 6829 Sgt. S. Seal. 3/9610 Sgt. Hector 5316 Sgt Barber. 15283 Pte Holderness 12862 Pte Oakes 14379 Pte Garrard – 20281 Pte Gosling 16937 Pte Boley 19228 Pte Conway 20361 Pte Frost 19055 Pte Jones 15302 Pte Watts 19283 Pte Benson 15693 Pte Beyanton 8023 Pte Tatum 3/8672 Pte Pick. 19133 Pte Rudd. 8227 L/c Giles 5882 Pte Martin 6828 Cpl Dorling 17424 Pte Crane 13106 Pte Scott. 19067 Pte Harrison. 3/9452 Pte Crane 9510 Pte Maidwell 16944 Pte Hunt. —— Two men missing Capt C.M.E. Dealtry & 84 men wounded G.C.T. Bhollrams 2nd Bn The Suffolk Regt. Capt & Adjt.	

1875 Wt. W593/826 1,000,000 4/15 J.B.C. & A. A.D.S.S./Forms/C. 2118.

Instructions regarding War Diaries and Intelligence Summaries are contained in F. S. Regs., Part II. and the Staff Manual respectively. Title Pages will be prepared in manuscript.

WAR DIARY

~~or~~

~~INTELLIGENCE SUMMARY~~

(~~Erase heading not required.~~)

Army Form C. 2118

2 Suffolk Regt

Place SEPTEMBER	Date 1915	Hour.	Summary of Events and Information	Remarks and references to Appendices
ODDERDOM	1st		} In bivouac	
"	2nd			
KRUISSTRAAT	3rd	6.30P.M.	Batn: less all specialists moved to dugouts in H.23.D. Specialists remained in Camp. – very few dugouts and very wet.	
"	4th		———	
"	5th		3 men wounded	
"	6th		2 men wounded	
"	7th		———	
"	8th		1 man wounded	
"	9th		———	
"	10th		1 man wounded	
"	11th		1 man wounded	
"	12th		———	
"	13th		1 man wounded.	
"	14th		2 men wounded.	
"	15th		6972 Pte Clements – (H.Q. Cook committed suicide – temporality insane)	
"	16th		———	
"	17th		———	
"	18th		one man wounded	
"	19th		———	
"	20th		———	
"	21st		13082 Pte A Sherman killed 6 men wounded.	
"	22nd		———	
			(4th–22nd) Pioneering.	
"	23rd	9.0P.M.	A+B Coys moved from KRUISSTRAAT to MAPLE COPSE	
MAPLE COPSE	24th	9.0AM.	Remainder of Batn: with H.Q. + all details in ODDERDOM except transport moved into MAPLE COPSE – only dugouts for about ½ the number + all very poor ones. Batn dug itself in as well as possible with practically no material preparatory to the next days attack. No19345 Pte Ashley killed two men wounded.	

1875 Wt. W593/826 1,000,000 4/15 J.B.C. & A. A.D.S.S./Forms/C. 2118.

Instructions regarding War Diaries and Intelligence Summaries are contained in F. S. Regs., Part II. and the Staff Manual respectively. Title Pages will be prepared in manuscript.

WAR DIARY

~~or~~

~~INTELLIGENCE SUMMARY~~

~~(Erase heading not required.)~~

Army Form C. 2118

Place	Date	Hour	Summary of Events and Information	Remarks and references to Appendices
MAPLE COPSE	Sept. 25th	3.45 A.M.	Heavy bombardement of the enemy's trenches commenced. At 4.19 two of our mines were exploded under the enemy's trenches and at 4.19½ two more were "sent up". At 4.20 the 8th Bde	
		4.20	attacked. 1st G.H. on left 4th G.H. in Centre 2 R.S. on right and the 4th Mx in reserve in SANCTUARY WOOD & 2SK in reserve in MAPLE COPSE. The 14th Div: cooperated on ~~the~~ the left of the 1st G.H. The 4th G.H. & 2 R.S. gained their objective. The 1st G.H. were however "held up" by $\frac{1}{2}$" wire, which had not previously been located & consequently not cut by the artillery, in front of "The Wall" on the MENIN ROAD. Touch was consequently lost between the 1st & 4th G.H. – The Germans then counterd in a southerly direction from the MENIN ROAD – cut off the 4th G.H. & compelled the 2 R.S. to conform & consequently give up a great portion of the ground they had taken.	
		7.0 P.M.	Took over trenches – appendix C1 - B8 - B7 – with A & B Coys with M.G's & Bombers – B.8.S. & 4.G.H. H.Q. with D Coy & head quarters. from 4th G.H. 4th Mx & R.S No 19437 Pte W. Brewer – 3/8666 Pte W. Jakes – 5854 L/C P Challice 12942 Pte W. Bridges No 12970 Pte A Manning – 15691 Pte W. Pegg – 15663 Pte F Dear killed. 19351 Pte G Berry " Eighteen men wounded	
	26th	11.0 P.M.	General "strafe" on both sides – bombs trench mortars etc: Pte J. Clarke 15229 & Pte C Fryett 15233 killed 4 men wounded.	

1875 Wt. W593/826 1,000,000 4/15 J.B.C. & A. A.D.S.S./Forms/C. 2118.

WAR DIARY
or
~~INTELLIGENCE SUMMARY~~
(Erase heading not required.)

Army Form C. 2118

Instructions regarding War Diaries and Intelligence Summaries are contained in F. S. Regs., Part II. and the Staff Manual respectively. Title Pages will be prepared in manuscript.

Place	Date	Hour	Summary of Events and Information	Remarks and references to Appendices
HOOGE	Sept 1915			
	27th		Two men wounded	
	28th		Two men wounded	
	29th	4.15 PM	Germans exploded a mine under junction of B4 & B7 which was held by 4th Middlesex. Capt Lynn who was in command of A Coy & was holding western half of B7 collected some of the men from B4 who came running back after the mine went up & with some men of his Coy & some Coy Bombers proceeded at once up a portion of B7 which had been vacated by the 4th Mx. He succeeded in getting some way up this trench but was prevented from proceeding further by a party of Germans coming up on his right & rear. He was then wounded but established a line to his right before coming to report progress at Bn H.Q. — It was desired to make a counter attack at once in conjunction with the 4th Mx & 2 R. Scots but owing to their not being a sufficient reserve supply of bombs with the division (all having been sent south) this had to be abandoned for the time being. 2Lt R.F. Deck killed. Capt. T.S. Lynn & 2Lt W.R. Moss [illegible] wounded also 2Lts Hartopp & Spong slightly wounded. No 3/9329 Pte Trenter killed and ten men wounded.	
	30th	2.0 PM	A supply of bombs having been obtained a counter attack was ordered by the G.O.C. 3rd Div. at 2.0 PM which had to be postponed till 3.0 PM owing to the non arrival of the bombs from the Div:	
		3.0 PM	At 3.0 PM the artillery was to bombard the mine crater until 3.15. This did not appear very effective. At 3.15 the attack was to be carried out by the	

1875 Wt. W593/826 1,000,000 4/15 J.B.C. & A. A.D.S.S./Forms/C. 2118.

~~21ST DIVISION~~
~~62ND INFY BDE~~

3 DIVISION

8 WF

8TH BN EAST YORKS REGT

1915 SEP - ~~OCT 1915~~ 1915 DEC

62nd Inf.Bde.
21st Div.

Battn. disembarked
Boulogne from
England 10.9.15.

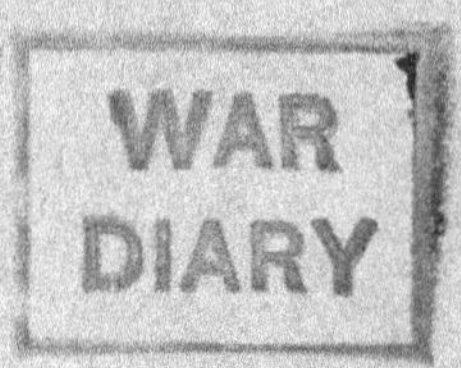

8th BATTN. THE EAST YORKSHIRE REGIMENT.

S E P T E M B E R

(9.9.15 - 28.9.15)

1 9 1 5

Instructions regarding War Diaries and Intelligence Summaries are contained in F. S. Regs., Part II. and the Staff Manual respectively. Title Pages will be prepared in manuscript.

or

~~INTELLIGENCE SUMMARY~~

(Erase heading not required.)

8th East Yorkshire Rgt

Place	Date	Hour	Summary of Events and Information	Remarks and references to Appendices
FOLKSTONE	9/9/15	11 pm	The Battalion Embarked for France — on arriving at BOULOUGNE marched to a rest camp – Entrained at 10.30 pm and Detrained at WATTEN ——	
MOULLE	11/9/15	3 am	Marched into Billets —— from 11/9 to 20/9 carried on with Field Training	
MOULLE	20/9/15	7.10 pm	Marched by road WITTES arriving at 2. a m 21/9/15 went into Bivouac & rested until 7 pm —.	
ECQUEDECQUES	22/9/15	1. a M	arrived and Billeted – approx 8 miles from the Trenches —	
NOEUX-le-MINES	25/9/15	11 aM	Moved from billets – halted for an hour and at 3 pM launched the attack at Enemy from BETHUNE – LENS Road – The direction was for Hill 70 thro' LOOS and over the Slack heaps – We came under heavy artillery fire at 3 pm and so moved in artillery formation — D Coy led the attack with C on the left B & A in support on arriving in the village of LOOS Col B. I. Way was met by the Brig Gen of 145 Bde apparently on account of the obstacles when coming over the enemys trenches the Battalion was straggled out Col Way led on the S E side of the village & formed up about a company & a half – Shells of all classes were falling very thick around and several casualties occurred. D Coy and part of C under Col Way crossed the Slack heap & commenced entrenching C Coy & part of B & about a company of the 10 York organised by the Adjt lined up and moved forward on the right — Major Ingles 2nd in Command formed up the 2 reserve companies in LOOS and went up to the Slack heap and commenced communication trench – at 8. pM the Bn was in line digging in – Companies were re organized – 10 York R on our right — Col Way commanding the left of the Bn & Major Ingles on the Slack heaps	
LOOS	25/9/15			

1875 Wt. W593/826 1,000,000 4/15 J.B.C. & A. A.D.S.S./Forms/C. 2118.

Instructions regarding War Diaries and Intelligence Summaries are contained in F. S. Regs., Part II. and the Staff Manual respectively. Title Pages will be prepared in manuscript.

~~WAR DIARY~~ or INTELLIGENCE ~~SUMMARY~~

(Erase heading not required.)

8th E York Rgt

Place	Date	Hour	Summary of Events and Information	Remarks and references to Appendices
			all the night machine gun fire from the right flank & shells made entrenching difficult — 2 small counter attacks were easily repulsed during the night —	
LOOS	26/9/15	a.m. 10	Lt-Col Way with a party of 120 E York Rgt and a few of the London Rgt & a few Northld Fus made an attack on Hill 70 — the enemy's trenches were however reached, but the flank fire from mach guns on the left & shells made the Bn withdraw. At 11 a m the slack heap was heavily shelled and Col Way was was wounded ordered a slight retirement to the village — heavy casulties from snipers & machine guns occurred and Major Ingles with Capt Moons A Coy kept on the Slack heap and held their position —	
			Part of the Bn retired at 4.30 pm & joined support trenches of 23 Londons W of the Village and remained all night — Shelling by the enemy continued all night — A+B Coys held on the slack heap until relieved by the London &	
LOOS	27/9/15		Gordons at 4 pm. the shelling was incessant at particually during the relief at 6.30pm the Bn was formed up in Bivouac at SAILLY LABOURSE	
			Rain was falling throught the engagement —	
			A roll was called and the Casulty list made for the 3 days action	
			Officers Killed 4. Injured 1 officer ‖ other ranks Killed 21 Gassed 1.	
			" Wounded 11. Gassed 1 " ‖ " " Wounded 132 Gassed & Missing 1.	
BETHUNE	28/9/15		" Missing 1. Wounded & Missing 1 officer ‖ " " Missing 131 Died of wounds 1	
			The Brigade entrained and marched to Rest Camp to be refitted	

[illegible] Major

1875 Wt. W593/826 1,000,000 4/15 J.B.C. & A. A.D.S.S./Forms/C. 2118.

21st ~~3rd~~ Division

121
———
7595

8th E. Yorks: Rgt:

Vol: 2

Oct 15

To 3' Div 15/11/15

Instructions regarding War Diaries and Intelligence Summaries are contained in F. S. Regs., Part II. and the Staff Manual respectively. Title Pages will be prepared in manuscript.

WAR DIARY

~~or~~

~~INTELLIGENCE SUMMARY~~

(*Erase heading not required.*)

8th E York Rgt

Army Form C. 2118

Place	Date	Hour	Summary of Events and Information	Remarks and references to Appendices
STRAZEELE	3/10/15	—	Rested in Billets — until 13/10/15 carried on during that time with Battalion training and Re-equipping troops after action —	
MERRIS	13/10/15	3 pm	Billeted for night	
ARMENTIERES —	14/10/15	5.30 pm	Took up billets	
— do —	15/10/15		Carried out trench digging & construction under command of C.R.E 50th DIV — 2 Coys going by day & 2 by night —	
— do —	24/10/15		Completed work with 50 DIV	
— do —	25/10/15	6.30 pm	A Coy went up to trenches for instruction in trench warfare for 24 hours 2 platoons to 12th Northumberland Fus & 2 platoons to 13th North Fus —	
— do —	26/10/15	6.30 pm	B Coy (less 1 platoon) went up to trenches for instruction for 24 hours attached to 10 York R.	
— do —	27/10/15	6.30 pm	C & D Coys went up to trenches for instruction for 24 hours attached to 10 York R — 12th North'd Fus & 13th North'd Fus —	
— do —	29/10/15	6 pm	The Battalion took over 74 trench to 76 inclusive at L'EPINETTE relieving the 12th & 13th North Fus — the relief was carried out in 3 hours — The night was quiet	
— do —	29/10/15		Major F B Brewis 9th K.O.Y.L.I. ~~billeted~~ took over Temporary Command of Battalion vice Lt-Col Way, wounded —	

1875 Wt. W593/826 1,000,000 4/15 J.B.C. & A. A.D.S.S./Forms/C. 2118.

Sheet 2

Army Form C. 2118

Instructions regarding War Diaries and Intelligence Summaries are contained in F. S. Regs., Part II. and the Staff Manual respectively. Title Pages will be prepared in manuscript.

WAR DIARY
or
~~INTELLIGENCE SUMMARY~~ 8. E. York. R.

(Erase heading not required.)

Place	Date	Hour	Summary of Events and Information	Remarks and references to Appendices
L'EPINETTE	30/10/15	"	Working in Trenches – repairing and building same caused trouble nothing to report situation very quiet –	
"	30/10/15	"	Enemy bombarded firing line about noon seven slight casualties nothing further to report.	

F. S. Brewis
Major. Comdg 8 E York R

1875 Wt. W593/826 1,000,000 4/15 J.B.C. & A. A.D.S.S./Forms/C. 2118.

3RD DIVISION
8TH INFY BDE

8TH BATTALION

EAST YORKS.

NOV-DEC 1915

8th Inf.Bde.
3rd Div.

Battn. transferred
from 62nd Inf.Bde.
21st Div. 15.11.15.

WAR
DIARY

8th BATTN. THE EAST YORKSHIRE REGIMENT.

N O V E M B E R

1 9 1 5

Instructions regarding War Diaries and Intelligence Summaries are contained in F. S. Regs., Part II. and the Staff Manual respectively. Title Pages will be prepared in manuscript.

WAR DIARY
or
~~INTELLIGENCE SUMMARY~~
(Erase heading not required.)

Army Form C. 2118

Place	Date	Hour	Summary of Events and Information	Remarks and references to Appendices
L'EPINETTE	1/11/15		Work in trenches continued – Rain and an odd H.E caused some damage to Bays —— Situation very quiet ——	
—"—	2/11/15 to 6/11/15		Work in trenches continued – Rain caused much damage to Parapets & Paradoes situation very quiet —. Nothing to report situation quiet –	
		5.30 PM	Relief commenced by 10.York R 9.10 pm relief completed. Bn moved into ARMENTIERES in Brigade Reserve –	
ARMENTIERES	6/11/15 to	12/11/15	Found working parties for trench repair &c in L'EPINETTE Trenches. nothing to report during the time in reserve –	
L'EPINETTE	12/11/15	4 pm	Commenced relief of 10.York.R. signallers & Grenadiers taking over 4.15 pM wire from Bde came cancelling the relief	
ARMENTIERES	12/11/15		Received orders the Bn was to be transferred to 8th Inf Bde 3rd DIV	
—"—	13/11/15		Supplied working parties to 10 York R in trenches	
—"—	14/11/15		Supplied working parties to 10 York R & 1st Northumbrian R.E.	
—"—	15/11/15	10 A.M.	Marched to BAILLEUL & billeted for night	
BAILLEUL "	16/11/15	10 A.M.	March to STEENZVORDE reported arrival to 8th Inf Bde – took up Billets near STEENZVORDE – Bde in rest billets ——	

1875 Wt. W593/826 1,000,000 4/15 J.B.C. & A. A.D.S.S./Forms/C. 2118.

Sheet No 2.

Instructions regarding War Diaries and Intelligence Summaries are contained in F. S. Regs., Part II. and the Staff Manual respectively. Title Pages will be prepared in manuscript.

WAR DIARY
or
~~INTELLIGENCE SUMMARY~~
(Erase heading not required.)

Army Form C. 2118

Place	Date	Hour	Summary of Events and Information	Remarks and references to Appendices
STEENVORDE	17/11/15	11.40 A.M.	Brigade marched past Army Commander – Battalion in order of march	
"	19/11/15 to 23/11/15		Carried out Company parades – Brigadier made an informal inspection	
"		9 AM	Battalion in Rest Billets – Carried out Battalion training &c.	
"	23/11/15	9 AM	Bn marched in Brigade to Rest Camp at RENINGHELST entered camp at 4 P.M. Capt J Greene 7th Dragoon Guards arrived as 2nd in Command	
RENINGHELST "	24/11/15	2.30 pm	A Coy went up to trenches for instruction in trench warfare for 2 days attached to 1/R. S. Fus. B Coy attached to 4th R. Fus. for similar period.	
"	25/11/15		Nothing to report	
"	26/11/15	2.30 pm	C Coy relieved A Coy, D Coy relieved B	
"	27/11/15		nothing to report.	
"	28/11/15	5 pm	C & D Coys came from trenches & billeted at DICKEBUSCH	
"	29/11/15	4.30 pm	A & B Coys moved to DICKEBUSCH & joined up with C & D Coys – Bn forming Brigade reserve at DICKEBUSCH.	
DICKEBUSCH	30/11/15		nothing to report	

F A Brewis Major
Cd, 8th East Yorkshire Regt

1875 Wt. W593/826 1,000,000 4/15 J.B.C. & A. A.D.S.S./Forms/C. 2118.

8th Inf.Bde.
3rd Div.

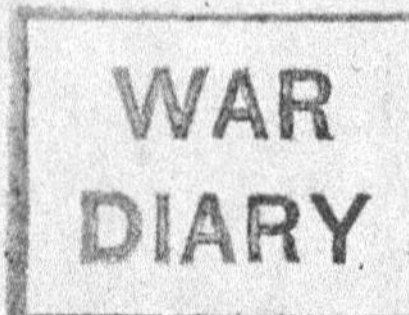

8th BATTN. THE EAST YORKSHIRE REGIMENT.

D E C E M B E R

1 9 1 5

Instructions regarding War Diaries and Intelligence Summaries are contained in F. S. Regs., Part II. and the Staff Manual respectively. Title Pages will be prepared in manuscript.

No. 1.

WAR DIARY
or
INTELLIGENCE SUMMARY
(Erase heading not required.)

8 E York R.

Army Form C. 2118

Place	Date	Hour	Summary of Events and Information	Remarks and references to Appendices
DICKEBUSCH	1/12/15 to		Brigade Reserve, 2 Platoons reinforced 7th K.S.L.I. front line permanently. working parties found each day for R.E. & front line trenches	
do	6/12/15		One Officer & 50 O/Ranks attached 4th Gordons.	
do	6/12/15	4.15	Relieved & marched back to Rest Camp RENINGHELST.	
RENINGHELST	7/12/15 to 13/12/15		Rest ~~billets~~ Camp At RENINGHELST.	
DICKEBUSCH	13/12/15 to	4.30 pm	Brigade Reserve relieved 4th Royal Scots 1 Officer & 2 platoons D Coy in front line trenches 7 KSLI. 2 Machine Guns in Strong Point	
do	21/12/15		Found working parties for trenches & R.E	
do	19/12/15	5.30 AM	Felt slight fumes of Gas attack - ~~then~~ The Bn stood-To and used smoke helmets - no casualties - dispersed at 9. A.M.	
RENINGHELST	21/12/15 to		Rest Camp	
do	28/12/15			

1875 Wt. W593/826 1,000,000 4/15 J.B.C. & A. A.D.S.S./Forms/C. 2118.

Instructions regarding War Diaries and Intelligence Summaries are contained in F. S. Regs., Part II. and the Staff Manual respectively. Title Pages will be prepared in manuscript.

Sheet No.

WAR DIARY
or
~~INTELLIGENCE SUMMARY~~
(Erase heading not required.)

8th York R.

Army Form C. 2118

Place	Date	Hour	Summary of Events and Information	Remarks and references to Appendices
VOORMAZEELE	28/12/15	9. pm	Relief Complete on P Sector of trenches relieved West Yorks – no casualties or hitch in Relief —	
"	29/12/15		Carried on work rebuilding & repairing trenches — patrols report enemy	
"	30/12/15		Quiet = " no activity –	
"	31/12/15		Nothing to report –	

Lt Col
Comg 8th Yorks R

1875 Wt. W593/826 1,000,000 4/15 J.B.C. & A. A.D.S.S./Forms/C. 2118.

2 BN ROYAL SCOTS.

1914 AUG TO 1919 MAY.

1423

2 BN ROYAL SCOTS.

1914 AUG TO 1919 MAY.

1423

3RD DIVISION
8TH INFY BDE

8TH BATTALION.

EAST YORKSHIRE REGT.

JAN - DEC 1916.

8th Brigade.

3rd Division.

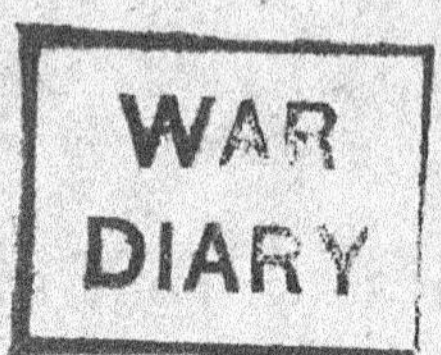

8th BATTALION

EAST YORKSHIRE REGIMENT

JANUARY 1 9 1 6

VII. DIV[N]

8th E. Yorks
Vol: 5

9 Bde

Sheet No1

Instructions regarding War Diaries and Intelligence Summaries are contained in F. S. Regs., Part II. and the Staff Manual respectively. Title Pages will be prepared in manuscript.

WAR DIARY
or
INTELLIGENCE SUMMARY

(Erase heading not required.)

8 E Yorks R

Army Form C. 2118

Place	Date	Hour	Summary of Events and Information	Remarks and references to Appendices
ST ELOI	1/1/16 to	-	Holding P sector of trenches of 8 Bde —	
	4/1/16	8.30 PM	Relieved by 12 W Yorks — on morning of the 4th the G.O.C Div inspected trenches & sent a message of congratulations on work done — weeks work approx 60,000 sand bags filled & placed building parados.	
RENINGHELST	5/1/16 to		Battalion in Rest Camp — carried out usual training — supplied all Bde Fatigues — 10 Offrs & 30 O/Ranks attached to 172 Tunnelling Co —	
	11/1/16	2 pm.	G.O.C. 9 Bde sent letter complimenting the Bn on the good work done during the last tour in Trenches —	
ST ELOI	11/1/16 to	6.30 pm	Relief complete at 6.30 pm. work continued in rebuilding trenches — nothing of any importance occurred beyond minor shelling of P & each day by 7.7 CM shells — Lt Hough was killed while sniping on Jan 18/16 —	
	18/1/16	6.30 pm		
RENINGHELST	18/1/16 to		Relieved by 12 West Yorks — went back to Rest camp training &c — found	
	25/1/16	8.30 pm	a few Fatigues in 1st Line trenches —	
ST ELOI	25/1/16 to	8.30 p.m.	Relieved 12 WEST Yorks in P sector of trenches work continued rebuilding each night efforts were made by ~~—~~ Lt Gould & Lt Samuel to capture one of the enemy for identification — both offrs were out patrolling but could not see anything of an enemy patrol — wind changed E & SE on the 30th for so Bn had to Stand to in case of Gas.	
~~DICKEBUSCH~~	31/1/16 ~~31/~~			

F A Brewis Lieut Col
Cdg 8th East Yorkshire Regt

1875 Wt. W593/826 1,000,000 4/15 J.B.C. & A. A.D.S.S./Forms/C. 2118.

8th Brigade.

3rd Division.

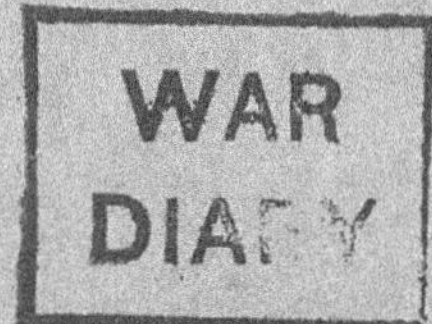

8th BATTALION

EAST YORKSHIRE REGIMENT

FEBRUARY 1 9 1 6

8th E. Yorks
Vol: 6

3d

Instructions regarding War Diaries and Intelligence Summaries are contained in F. S. Regs., Part II. and the Staff Manual respectively. Title Pages will be prepared in manuscript.

WAR DIARY
or
INTELLIGENCE SUMMARY
(Erase heading not required.)

Army Form C. 2118

8, E. York R.

Place	Date	Hour	Summary of Events and Information	Remarks and references to Appendices
ST ELOI	1/2/16		Holding trenches	
	7/2/16	9 pm	Relieved by the 12 West Yorks Rgt.	
DICKEBUSCH	2/2/16	10 pm	Took over billets & attached to 9th Bde as reserve Bn —	
"	3/2/16	12 NOON	Received orders to march to Reninghelst at once & were relieved by L.R.B.	
			Remained in Camp cleaning up etc	
RENINGHELST	5/2/16	1.30 pm	Marched from Reninghelst and entrained at GOEDESVELDT for ARQUES. Marched from here to NORTLEULINGHEM & were relieved by West Riding Regt.	
NORTLEULINGHEM	5/2/16	7. am	Arrived in billets, in relief of the 7th Bn Yorks & Lancs at NORTLEULINGHEM	
	6/2/16 to		Training in rest area at NORTLEULINGHEM. 1st week platoon training. 2nd week Company training 3rd week Battalion manoeuvres etc. Special attention paid to grenade throwing & training of specialists	
	10 – 29 2/16		Training Battalion manoeuvres attack practices	
OUDERDOM	1/3/16		Moved, from rest area to Scottish lines in reserve to 96th Bde	
BLACK				

B. Lewis
Lt Col.
Comm: E. Yorks.

1875 Wt. W593/826 1,000,000 4/15 J.B.C. & A. A.D.S.S./Forms/C. 2118.

8th Brigade.

3rd Division.

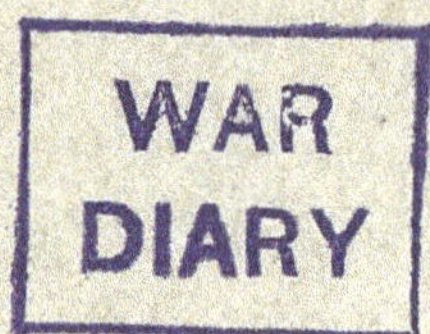

8th BATTALION

EAST YORKSHIRE REGIMENT

MARCH 1 9 1 6

3rd Divn

8 East Yorks

Vol 7

Instructions regarding War Diaries and Intelligence Summaries are contained in F. S. Regs., Part II. and the Staff Manual respectively. Title Pages will be prepared in manuscript.

WAR DIARY or INTELLIGENCE SUMMARY

(Erase heading not required.)

Army Form C. 2118

8th Bn East Yorkshire Regiment.

Place	Date	Hour	Summary of Events and Information	Remarks and references to Appendices
DICKEBUSCH	1/3/16	6 p.m.	Moved into billets. Bn stood to during the night.	
BLUFF (Trenches)	3/3/16		Relieved 1st Gordons. Relief very late in Snowstorm.	
" "	4/3/16		Buried dead, & cleared Trenches of Salvage. Cold weather produced much sickness & bad feet. Evacuated wounded of 76th Brigade & two wounded prisoners.	
" "	5/3/16		Drained C.T's & continued repairing front line & flank communication.	
" "	6/3/16		Relieved by Royal Fusiliers, & conveyed part of way back to "D" Camp Reninghelst by motor buses.	
RENINGHELST	7/3/16 to 11/3/16		Resting in "D" Camp. About cases of "Trench Feet" evacuated.	
SCOTTISH WOOD	11/3/16		Relieved 10th West Yorkshire Regiment. Two Companies in reserve at VOORMEZEELE. Two companies in reserve in SCOTTISH WOOD	
" "	11/3/16 to 14/3/16		Supplied working parties on Q's & R Trenches. Two Companies, "A" & B moved back into DICKEBUSCH on the night of 12/13th.	
RENINGHELST	15/3/16 to 19/3/16		Moved back into "J" Camp as Divisional Reserve. Ordinary Rest Routine. Large Fatigue Parties taken up by buses each evening for work in the Trenches.	
SCOTTISH WOOD	20/3/16 to 22/3/16.		Two Companies "A" & "B" in SCOTTISH WOOD: Two Companies "C" & "D" in DICKEBUSCH. Local Reserves. Quiet time with numerous Trench Fatigues, carrying timber, Trench Mortar ammunition, Grenades, Emergency Rations etc.	
"P" Sector (Trenches)	22/3/16.		Relieved 19th Canadians. H.Q at DEAD DOG FARM.	
" " "	23/3/16		Heavy bombardment of front line with heavy guns, & H.E. Shrapnel, especially on P2A & P4. A number of casualties in "A" & "D" Coys.	
" " "	24/3/16 to 25/3/16		Normal Trench Life. Dumps of ammunition, R.E. Stores, Grenades & Emergency Rations completed in front line.	
SCOTTISH WOOD	25/3/16 to 26/3/16.		One night & day in SCOTTISH WOOD with two Companies in VOORMEZEELE. Relieved 1st GORDONS.	
U25 & U26	26/3/16		Relieved 13th Kings. H.Q in ECLUSE No 7. Two Coys in U25 & 26 & two in Local Support.	
" "	27/3/16.	4.15 a.m.	Explosion of several large mines under the "MOUND" Terrific bombardment of the enemy especially about 2 p.m in afternoon, & during the night. Many Casualties.	

W. Gould Lieut
Adjutant 8 E. Yorks.

1875 Wt. W593/826 1,000,000 4/15 J.B.C. & A. A.D.S.S./Forms/C. 2118.

— 2 —

Army Form C. 2118

Instructions regarding War Diaries and Intelligence Summaries are contained in F. S. Regs., Part II. and the Staff Manual respectively. Title Pages will be prepared in manuscript.

WAR DIARY
or
INTELLIGENCE SUMMARY

(Erase heading not required.)

8th Bn East Yorkshire Regt.

Place	Date	Hour	Summary of Events and Information	Remarks and references to Appendices
U 24, 23, 23b, 13.	28/3/16.		Intermittent shelling by enemy of our front line. H.Q on Canal Bank bombarded by long range naval gun. Three Companies now in front line moved to Right Flank to take over R.S.F. who were badly shaken. H.Q. & "D" Coy moved to BOLLAARTBEEK.	
" " " "	29/3/16.		Shelling continued.	
" " " "	30/3/16		Attack by bombers on our right. Rapid fire by enemy on our trenches. Parapet badly damaged.	
" " " "	31/3/16		Our trenches badly trench mortared. "C" Coy suffered badly, 20 Casualties. All Companies very weak and tired. Shelling again during the night, H.E. & trench mortars.	
" " " "	1/4/16.		Heavy bombardment by our guns, silenced the enemy somewhat. Quiet night. Aeroplanes very active during the day.	
BOLLAARTBEEK	31/3/16. to 1/4/16.		Usual Trench Routine. Bombing attack on the craters. Our men claimed a number of Germans moving towards craters. Heavy shelling on both sides. "C" Coy trench-mortared. Trench breached in several places. Strong working parties at night.	
—do—	2/4/16		SPOIL BANK heavily shelled by guns of all calibres.	
"	3/4/16.		Heavy bombardment by our Artillery at 2a.m. Attack by K.O.R.L on our right which reached objective. Reciprocal shelling during the day. Battalion relieved by 31st Canadians & proceeded to RENINGHELST leaving Lewis Guns & Teams in the line.	
RENINGHELST	4/4/16		Camp Routine. Draft of 1 Officer & 56 Other Ranks.	
"	5/4/16		Moved by Road to BERTHEN Area. H.Q at R.33. b 3.6. (Sheet 27).	
R.33.b 3.6.	5/4/16 to 11/4/16.		Training programme carried out. Specialists training — Lewis Gunners, Signallers, Snipers etc. Lewis Guns returned to Battalion, having suffered many casualties.	
—"—	12/4/16 to 13/4/16.		Moved to LA CLYTTE & supplied night working parties of 270 men on VIERSTRAAT Defences.	
—"—	14/4/16.		Returned to BERTHEN Area.	

W. Gould Lieut
Adjt 8 E. Yorks

1875 Wt. W593/826 1,000,000 4/15 J.B.C. & A. A.D.S.S./Forms/C. 2118.

8th Brigade.

3rd Division

WAR
DIARY

8th BATTALION

EAST YORKSHIRE REGIMENT

APRIL 1 9 1 6

Instructions regarding War Diaries and Intelligence Summaries are contained in F. S. Regs., Part II. and the Staff Manual respectively. Title Pages will be prepared in manuscript.

WAR DIARY
or
~~INTELLIGENCE SUMMARY~~
(Erase heading not required.)

Army Form C. 2118

(9) APRIL. ~~MAY.~~ April 1916.

8 East Yorks

Vol 8

Place	Date	Hour	Summary of Events and Information	Remarks and references to Appendices
BOLLART BEEK	31-3-16 1-4-16		Usual trench routine, bombing attack on the craters; our men claimed a number Germans moving towards craters. Heavy shelling on both sides "6" bay trench - [illegible], trench breached in several places. Strong working parties at night.	
"	2-4-16		SPOIL BANK heavily shelled by guns of all calibres.	
	3-4-16		Heavy bombardment by our artillery at 2 a.m., attack by [illegible] on our right which reached objective; reciprocal shelling during the day. Bn relieved by the 31st Canadians & proceeded to RENINGHELST leaving Lewis guns & teams in the line.	
"	4-4-16		Camp routine. Draft of 1 officer & 56 O.R.	
BERTHEN.	5-4-16		Moved by road to BERTHEN area. Headquarters R 33 b 3 5.	
	5-12		Training programme carried out, [illegible] training, Lewis gunners, Signallers, Snipers etc. Lewis Gunners returned to Bn having suffered many casualties.	
	12-13		Moved to La CLYTTE & supplied night working parties of 240 men on VIERSTRAAT defences.	
	13-4-16		Returned to BERTHEN area.	
	14-23		Training in rest area. Classes for machine gunners, snipers, signallers etc. Coy training.	
RIDGEWOOD	23-24		Marched via SCHERPENBURG & relieved 6th D.L.I. in Bde reserve in RIDGE WOOD	
" "	25-30		Usual reserve routine. Heavy working parties by night on M. [illegible] Poppy Lane etc. Carrying parties etc. for R.E. Day time spent in draining, strengthening dug-outs etc. A little training done in concealed spots in the wood.	

B. Way Lt.Col.
Commanding 8th East Yorks. Regt.

1875 Wt. W593/826 1,000,000 4/15 J.B.C. & A. A.D.S.S./Forms/C. 2118.

8th Brigade.

3rd Division.

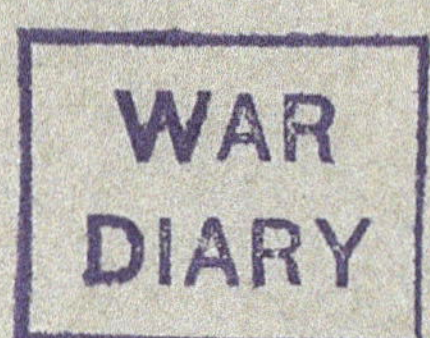

8th BATTALION

EAST YORKSHIRE REGIMENT

MAY 1916

Instructions regarding War Diaries and Intelligence Summaries are contained in F. S. Regs., Part II. and the Staff Manual respectively. Title Pages will be prepared in manuscript.

WAR DIARY or INTELLIGENCE SUMMARY (3)

(Erase heading not required.)

May 1916.

8 East Yorks

Vol 9

Place	Date	Hour	Summary of Events and Information	Remarks and references to Appendices
BRASSERIE (O Sector)	1st		Relieved 7th K.S.L.I in O + N sector of the trenches C + D Coys in the front line. 'A' Coy in redoubts + 'B' Coy mobile reserve.	
" "	2-8		Usual trench routine O2 regularly trench mortared but only a few casualties. Working parties sent up by A + B Coys to work on CHICORY LANE + front line which were frequently damaged by hostile trench mortar bombs	
LA. CLYTTE	8-15		Moved back to Details Camp. 1st day cleaning up. Considerable work done on building new Details Camp. Coy parades during the day.	
" "			working parties in the trenches by night on Poppy Lane. N.11. M supports	
" "	13		Large working party by night 6 officers + 200 men on M supports.	
'O.' SECTOR	15		Relieved 7th K.S.L.I in 'O' + 'N' sector.	
" "	16-22		Usual trench routine, much time spent by night in repairing damage to parapet done by hostile trench mortars on front line. 'A' + 'B' Coys in front line. 'C' in redoubts + D Mobile Reserve.	
" " "	19		Trench mortars very active on O2 + N6. many casualties including one officer wounded.	
RIDGEWOOD	22		Relieved by 7th K.S.L.I + moved into RIDEWOOD as Bde reserve.	
" "	22-25		Usual nightly working parties consisting of most of the Bn, on 'M' supports CHICORY LANE. Poppy Lane etc. Coy training in wood, as far as possible during the day.	
Mt KOKEREELE	(Night) 25-26		Relieved by 9th D.L.I + moved back into Corps Rest area via SCHERPPENBERG + WESTOUTRE	
" "	26-31		2 days complete rest. Programme of Coy training carried out Lewis Gunners & Special Classes. Signallers	

B. I. Way Lt. Col.

Commanding 8th East. Yorks. Regt

1875 Wt. W593/826 1,000,000 4/15 J.B.C. & A. A.D.S.S./Forms/C. 2118.

8th Brigade.

3rd Division.

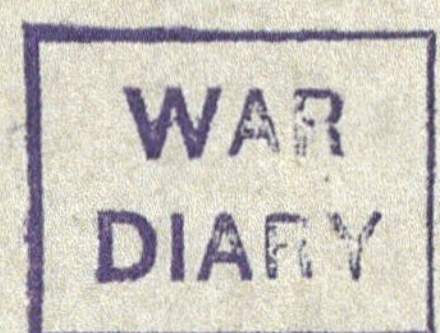

8th BATTALION

EAST YORKSHIRE REGIMENT

JUNE 1916

Confidential

The Officer i/c

A.G.'s Office at the Base

Forwarded.

H. Buxton Maj
for
Major General.
Commanding 3rd Division

11th June 1916.

A.A. & Q.M.G.
A
1815/a/1
3rd DIVISION

To
3 Div

Confidential.

10.7.16.

Reference War Diary for June sent herewith. This has been unavoidably delayed owing to the fact that the Batt has been constantly on the move since the 1st inst.

Frank L Hall 2Lt
Adjt 8 E Yorks

3rd Div. Q.

Forwarded.

Alexander Ryan
Major for G.O.C.
8 Infantry Brigade

10/7/16.

Instructions regarding War Diaries and Intelligence Summaries are contained in F. S. Regs., Part II. and the Staff Manual respectively. Title Pages will be prepared in manuscript.

WAR DIARY ~~or INTELLIGENCE SUMMARY~~

8th (S) Bn East Yorkshire Regiment III

(Erase heading not required.)

June 1916

Army Form C. 2118

8/3

Vol 10

Place	Date	Hour	Summary of Events and Information	Remarks and references to Appendices
Mr KOKEREELE (BERTHEN)	1st - 10th		Training according to programme of work issued to Coys. Special emphasis was paid to training of Lewis Gunners, Signallers, & Snipers.	
" "	2nd		Baths in WESTOUTRE.	
" "	3rd		KING'S Birthday celebrated as a general holiday. Bn sports in 'B' Coy billet - keen interest taken & many competitors.	
" "	5th		Practice move at 2½ hrs notice: successful.	
" "	6th		'Stand to' at 3½ hrs notice finally reduced to 1 hr.	
" "	10th		Moved to DICKEBUSCH HUTS. Long march. Camp shelled during the night.	
" "	11th		Relieved the 12th W. YORKS in the 'P' sectors Trenches 9 - 14 inclusive.	
" "	12th		Canadians attacked further North & regained trenches. All quiet on our part of the line.	
"P" Sector	12th to 20th		Usual Trench Routine. Trench Mortar activity on both sides throughout the tour.	
			Casualties during the week:- Killed 11. Wounded ~~[illegible]~~ 32. No Officer Casualties.	
	18th		Reinforcements arrived from Base:- 1 Officer & 20 Other Ranks.	
	20/21st		Relieved by 27th Bn Canadians, and after relief proceeded to camp at DICKEBUSCH HUTS.	
	~~[illegible]~~ 21st		Left DICKEBUSCH HUTS about 3 p.m. for ZWYNLAND SIDING, POPERINGHE, where the Battalion entrained at 7/45 p.m. after a trying march, under a hot sun. Detrained about 10/45 p.m at ST. OMER. Marched about 2 miles to Billets at ST. MARTIN-AU-LAERT.	
ST. MARTIN-AU-LAERT.	22nd.		Cleaning up equipment &c, - Inspections.	
	23rd		Battalion Field Training - Specialists under their respective Officers. Arrival of draft of 20 Other Ranks	
	24th		Battalion night attack & march. Baths during the day	
	26th		Brigade Route March - 1st Line Transport accompanying Battalions. Ideal Day.	
	27th		Battalion Attack Scheme on Training Area	
	28th		Bde Route March cancelled owing to inclement weather, & Inspections substituted.	

Instructions regarding War Diaries and Intelligence Summaries are contained in F. S. Regs., Part II. and the Staff Manual respectively. Title Pages will be prepared in manuscript.

Army Form C. 2118

WAR DIARY
or
~~INTELLIGENCE SUMMARY~~
(Erase heading not required.)

8th (S) B'n East Yorkshire Regiment.

JUNE 1916.

Place	Date	Hour	Summary of Events and Information	Remarks and references to Appendices
ST. MARTIN-AU-LAERT	29th		Battalion Scheme - Practice Attack in conjunction with 8th Bde M.G. Company on Training Area.	
	30th		Battalion Practice Attack on Training Area. — Arrival of 25 Other Ranks from Base Depot, Reinforcements — Battalion Strength completed to War Establishment.	

B. I. Way [illegible] Lt Col
Comd'g 8th East York Regt

8th Inf.Bde.
3rd Div.

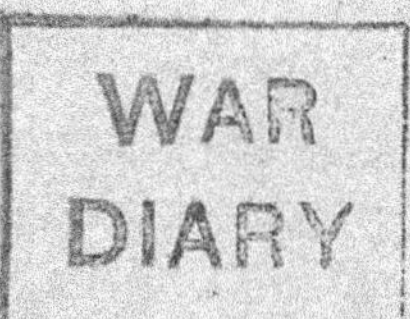

8th BATTN. THE EAST YORKSHIRE REGIMENT.

J U L Y

1 9 1 6

DIARY OF THE ATTACK 13/14th JULY.

8th (S) B'n East Yorkshire Regiment.

DIARY OF THE ATTACK, 13th - 14th July 1916.

9-20p.m.	Left CARNOY and marched along MONTAUBAN Road.
10-15p.m.	Passed MONTAUBAN.
2-0 a.m.	Reached point of Deployment.
3-25a.m.	Artillery lifted and the assault was made. Held up by very strong uncut wire. Enemy opened heavy Rifle and Machine Gun Fire. Estimated number of Machine Guns -- seven. A large number of very lights were sent up, and it was impossible for the men to face the heavy fire, there being a bright light owing to the Flares. Those untouched held their ground, taking cover in shell holes. Colonel B.I. Way, and 2nd Lieut R. Longstaff as Acting Adjutant, retired for the place of assembly, which is under a Bank, and the men proceeded to dig themselves in.
Between 3-30a.m. & 6-45a.m.	The men dug themselves in at the place of assembly.
6-45a.m.	Major Brewis arrived and relieved Colonel B.I. Way who was wounded in the arm and leg. Colonel Way went to the rear.
7-0 a.m.	Machine Guns had been mounted. Stokes Mortars got going and men of the Royal Scots Fusiliers joined the East Yorks. Regt behind the bank.
7-40a.m.	"Whiz-banging" started
7-45a.m.	Lieutenant Hext, Royal Field Artillery, reported that BAZENTIN was in possession of the 9th Brigade, and that a Captain (whose name he did not know) was forming his men up in order to bomb inwards.
7- 5 0a.m.	Major Brewis ordered two guns of the Machine Gun Company to retire back and to take up a position behind covering the right Flank, and placed Lieutenant Newbiggin, 1st Royal Scots Fusiliers, in charge of the extreme right.
7-55a.m.	Intelligence received from 8th Bde that two Companies of the Royal Scots were going to attack the right flank of the objective.
8-0 a.m.	A patrol was sent out by order of the 8th Bde, from the right flank, up to the enemy's wire to see if any of our men were in the enemy's trenches, and holding their own.
8-40a.m.	Colonel Forbes, Commandin g 1st Royal Scots Fusiliers arrived with reinforcements and took over command.
9-8 a.m.	Instructions received from Brigade to send out patrol with the same orders as those for the patrol at 8a.m.
9-30a.m.	Both Patrols reported having been up to the enemy's wire and were certain that the enemy's front line was strongly held. They could hear none of our men in the trench.
9-45a.m.	Stokes Guns fired several rounds.
10-15 a.m.	Another Patrol reported having been up to the enemy's wire and confirmed the previous report as to the enemy front line being strongly held, ~~but~~ they heard ~~no~~ sounds of heavy fightinginside the trenches . This information was passed to Colonel Forbes who was in command
10- 20a.m.	Colonel Forbes sent for Major Brewis (E. York. R.) and it was decided to send all available bombers, supported by two Platoons of the Royal Scots Fusiliers, guided by the Patrol of E. York. Regt., and kept in communication by Signals, 8. E. York. Regt., to try and join ~~heavy fighting~~ [Those fighting in trench →] on the right flank.
10-30a.m.	Message from "SPRING" stating "Bombing is to start from BAZENTIN"
11-10a.m.	Got into communication by Telephone with 8th Bde.
11-15 a.m.	Bde Wire received stating that Indian Cavalry is to go through

Sheet 2.

11-50a.m.	Orders received that the position is to be taken at once at all costs.
12 noon.	Message received from 2nd Lieut. J. C. Hartert, 8th East York. Regt. to say that he has entered both the front and back line ~~fa~~ of the German Trenches , is holding his own and attempting to bomb inwards. He estimated his position to be about S.16 b. 8.2. & 5.
12-15 p.m.	Bombing Party of the Royal Scots appeared on the left. They advanced very quickly and in perfect line, carrying all before them. As they advanced, men lying in shell holes by the wire and in other places along the front, joined in. We all joined in and the fight was over at once.
1-0p.m.	Met the Brigade Major who ordered me to hold from the 9th Division to the 7th K.Shropshire L.I. and to consolidate the position as quickly as possible
2p.m.	Re-organised the Battalion and found the strength to be three Officers, one hundred men, and one Lewis Gun.
5-30p.m.	2nd Lieut. J.C. Hartert and eleven men rejoined.
6 p.m.	2nd Lieut C.M. Pratt arrives from another pat of the Trench where he has been fighting, with six men
	On checking the Battalion we found the following known Casualties:-

Officers.

Killed .... 8.
Wounded.............11.

Other Ranks.

Killed 81
Wounded 218
Missing 141

TOTAL. 19 Officers and 440 Other Ranks.

[signature]

Major,

Commanding 8th (S) B'n East Yorkshire Regiment.

W A R   D I A R Y .

Instructions regarding War Diaries and Intelligence Summaries are contained in F. S. Regs., Part II. and the Staff Manual respectively. Title Pages will be prepared in manuscript.

WAR DIARY

8th (S) Bn East Yorkshire Regiment

~~INTELLIGENCE SUMMARY~~

~~(Erase heading not required.)~~

JULY 1916

Army Form C. 2118. 8/3

Vol XI

Place	Date	Hour	Summary of Events and Information	Remarks and references to Appendices
ST MARTIN-AU-LAERT	1st	8 a.m.	Left Billets at St MARTIN-AU-LAERT, and marched to WIZERNES, where the Battalion entrained for the valley of the Somme. Proceeded by rail via CALAIS-BOULOGNE-ABBEVILLE to CANDAS. Detrained about 8p.m. and marched to FRANQUEVILLE a distance of about five miles. Battalion very weary after a long journey.	
FRANQUEVILLE	2nd		Day spent in resting, & minor inspections. – News received of our offensive on the SOMME Valley.	
— " —	3rd	7 a.m.	Received marching orders. Marched by Brigade, through CANAPLES & HAVERNAS to Billets at FLESSELLES. Very hot day. Distance about 12 miles.	
FLESSELLES	4th	6 p.m.	Brigade marched to CARDONNETTE. Billets for the night. – Weather conditions good.	
CARDONNETTE	5th	— " —	Marched through BUSSY-LES-DAOURS to CORBIE. Distance 14 miles.	
CORBIE	6th	7 p.m.	Left CORBIE & marched via VAUX-SUR-SOMME and SAILLY LAURETTE to LES CELESTINS WOOD, where the Brigade Bivouacked	
LES CELESTINS	7th	10 a.m.	Marched to within three miles of CARNOY, arriving about noon. Rested in field by roadside until about 5 p.m. when the Battalion proceeded to CARNOY, there relieving the 6th BEDFORDS in Brigade Reserve, the remainder of the Bde relieving the remainder of the 53rd Bde.	
CARNOY.	8–12th		Various fatigue parties, carrying ammunition etc., to form Brigade Dump in the QUARRY. Reconnoitring patrols out every night gaining general information re enemy wire, trenches etc., FIGHTING STRENGTH about 20 Officers + 800 Other Ranks	
— " —	night 13th/14th	9-20 pm	Bn Left CARNOY and marched along MONTAUBAN ROAD	
		10-15 pm	Passed MONTAUBAN.	
ATTACK ON GERMAN POSITIONS.	14th	2-0 a.m.	Reached point of deployment. Artillery preparation bombardment.	
		3-25 a.m. to 4/45 am.	Artillery lifted & assault on enemy trenches was made. – Bn held up by uncut wire – Enemy sent up many flare lights – Machine Gun & Rapid Rifle Fire opened on our men by enemy – Men returned to place of assembly under a Bank & dug in – Some remained taking cover in shell holes. Commanding Officer wounded whilst in enemy wire.	

1875 Wt. W593/826 1,000,000 4/15 J.B.C. & A. A.D.S.S./Forms/C. 2118.

— 2 —

Instructions regarding War Diaries and Intelligence Summaries are contained in F. S. Regs., Part II. and the Staff Manual respectively. Title Pages will be prepared in manuscript.

WAR DIARY

8th (S) Bn East Yorkshire Regiment

~~INTELLIGENCE SUMMARY~~

~~(Erase heading not required.)~~

JULY 1916.

Army Form C. 2118

Place	Date	Hour	Summary of Events and Information	Remarks and references to Appendices
ATTACK (CONTD)	14th	6/45am	Second-in-Command (Major F.B. Brewis) arrived & relieved Commanding Officer (Lt-Col. B.I. Way) who was wounded in the leg & arm.	
	"	7-0a.m.	Machine Guns mounted. Stokes Mortars got going. — Men of 1st Royal Scots Fusiliers joined the Battalion behind the Bank.	
	"	7/40a.m.	Enemy shelling commenced. (Small calibre)	
	"	7/45a.m.	Report received that BAZENTIN was in possession of 9th Bde, & our troops were preparing to Bomb inwards.	
	"	7/50a.m.	Two guns of 8. Bde Machine Gun Company retired back and covered the right flank.	
	"	7/55a.m.	Intelligence received that two Companies of 2nd Royal Scots were going to attack right flank of objective	
	"	8/0 a.m.	Patrol sent out from the right flank to enemy's wire, to see if any of our men were in the enemy trenches, & holding their own.	
	"	8/40am	Colonel Forbes, 1st Royal Scots Fus. arrived with reinforcements & took over Command.	
	"	9/6 a.m.	Another Patrol sent out.	
	"	9/30a.m.	Patrols returned — Certain that enemy's front line was strongly held, & could hear none of our men in the trench.	
	"	9/45a.m.	Stokes Guns fired several rounds	
	"	10/15am	Patrol reported heavy fighting in enemy trenches.	
	"	10/20a.m.	Decided to send Bombers & 2 platoons Royal Scots Fus. to try & join heavy fighting in trenches on right flank.	
	"	10/30a.m.	Message received from 2nd Bn The Royal Scots stating "Bombing to start from BAZENTIN"	
	"	11/15a.m.	Wire received from Bde. — "Indian Cavalry is to go through"	
	"	11/30am	Orders received that the position was to be taken at once at all costs.	
	"	12/15p.m.	Bombing party of 2nd Royal Scots appeared on the left, they advanced quickly & carried all before them As they advanced, our men joined in, & the fight was over at once.	

— 3 —

Instructions regarding War Diaries and Intelligence Summaries are contained in F. S. Regs., Part II. and the Staff Manual respectively. Title Pages will be prepared in manuscript.

WAR DIARY

8th (S) Bn East Yorkshire Regiment

~~INTELLIGENCE SUMMARY~~

~~(Erase heading not required.)~~

Army Form C. 2118

JULY 1916

Place	Date	Hour	Summary of Events and Information	Remarks and references to Appendices
ATTACK (CONT.D)	14/7/16	1 p.m.	Received orders to consolidate the position as soon as possible.	
	—.—	2 p.m.	Reorganised the Battalion & found strength to be 3 Officers, 100 Other Ranks and 1 Lewis Gun. On checking the Battalion the following were the known casualties:– Officers: Killed 8, Wounded 11. Other Ranks: Killed 81, Wounded 218, Missing 141. Total 19 Officers & 440 Other Ranks.	
	14/7/16 to 20/7/16		Holding our new position. Heavy bombardments by enemy of our trenches & back area. Gas & lachrymatory Shells. Many casualties. Special attention paid by enemy to QUARRY, roads leading from the QUARRY, & MONTAUBAN.	
	Night 20th/21st.		Relieved from front line by K.O.S.B's, & went back to trenches just NORTH of the QUARRY.	
	22nd.		Moved into BERNAFAY WOOD	
	23rd.		Two Companies were sent to hold the N.E. edge of TRONES WOOD. – Reinforcements:– Draft of 342 O. Ranks from Yorkshire, & York & Lancs Regiments.	
	24th & 25th.		BERNAFAY WOOD. Continual shelling by enemy. The weather throughout the operations was perfect.	
	Night of 25/26th		Relieved by Royal Fusiliers & Bn proceeded to Bivouac at HAPPY VALLEY. – TOTAL CASUALTIES during Operations 29 Officers & 570 Other Ranks.	
HAPPY VALLEY.	26th	4 p.m.	Left HAPPY VALLEY & proceeded to Billets at MEAULTE. – Draft of 27 Other Ranks Northumberland Fusiliers & 2 Officers as reinforcements.	

1875 Wt. W593/826 1,000,000 4/15 J.B.C. & A. A.D.S.S./Forms/C. 2118.

Instructions regarding War Diaries and Intelligence Summaries are contained in F. S. Regs., Part II. and the Staff Manual respectively. Title Pages will be prepared in manuscript.

WAR DIARY
8th (S) Bn East Yorkshire Regiment
~~INTELLIGENCE SUMMARY~~
~~(Erase heading not required.)~~

JULY 1916.

Army Form C. 2118

Place	Date	Hour	Summary of Events and Information	Remarks and references to Appendices
MEAULTE	27th		Cleaning up – Company Inspections – Re-organisation of Companies, Specialists etc., – 5 Officer Reinforcements.	
—"—	28th		Company Route Marches in morning. Afternoon:- Inspection of the Battalion by Brigadier-General. In the course of his speech he expressed the thanks and congratulations of the Divisional & Army Commanders. He said "You are a portion of what is called the New Army. I belong to the old Army, but if this is the new Army, then it is good enough. It is you men in the ranks who have brought about this victory, and it is you whom we thank. In the advance you were held up by the wire, but you hung on. You have been, ~~the~~ in this advance, only a small portion of the troops engaged, but a very important portion, & you performed your task successfully."	
—"—	29th		Morning. Commanding Officers Parade. Afternoon:- Companies at disposal of Coy Commanders.	
—"—	30th.		Sunday:- Church Parade.	
—"—	31st		Morning:- Company Route Marches – Early, to miss the intense heat of the day. Afternoon:- Minor Coy. Inspections.	

[signature]
Major
Commanding 8th (S) Bn East Yorkshire Regiment

1875 Wt. W593/826 1,000,000 4/15 J.B.C. & A. A.D.S.S./Forms/C. 2118.

8th Brigade

3rd Division.

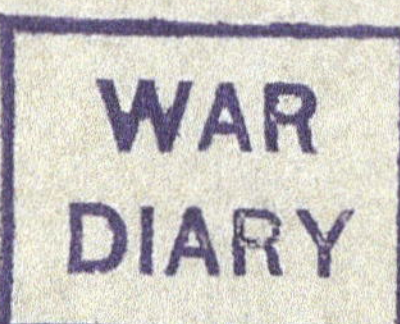

8th BATTALION

EAST YORKSHIRE REGIMENT

AUGUST 1 9 1 6

Attached:- Report on Operations 18th/19th August

Notes on the operation.

Army Form C. 2118

Instructions regarding War Diaries and Intelligence Summaries are contained in F. S. Regs., Part II. and the Staff Manual respectively. Title Pages will be prepared in manuscript.

WAR DIARY
or
INTELLIGENCE SUMMARY
(Erase heading not required.)

8th Bn. East Yorks Regt

Vol 12

Place	Date	Hour	Summary of Events and Information	Remarks and references to Appendices
MEAULTE	1/8/16 to 13/8/16.		Battalion in Billets- Reinforcements arriving. Battalion at Company & B'n Drill. Found minor fatige parties for Brigade.	
Happy Valley.	13/8/16.	4pm	Arrived at Bivouac.	
--do--	14/8/16		Found working parties and carrying parties for Front Line of trenches . A & D Cos moved to the CITADEL (1½miles from B'n H.Q.)	
GREAT BEAR	15/8/16	3.30pm.	Arrived in Bivouac- found working parties etc to the extent of 540men for digging and cable laying.	
CARNOY	16/8/16.	2pm	Bivouaced in old Front Line Trenches near TALUS BOIS wood.	
DO	17/8/16	4pm.	Received orders to stand by to join the 9th Brigade in the line just S.E. of GUILLEMONT.	
DO DO	do	11pm.	B'n proceeded from TALUS BOIS to 9th Bgde and took over Line from the 9th Royal Fusiliers.	
Trenches	18/8/16	4.30am 5.30am ~~x~~	Commanding Officer received attack orders personally from 9th Bgde. Companies arrived at entrance to Communication trench and relief was started. Owing to a single communication trench and numbers of carrying parties and uncleared casualties the relief was not completed until 1.15pm.	
Trenches S.E. of GUILLEMONT.	18/8/16.	11am	Company Commanders and Specialist Officers came to H.Q. for orders etc, which were carefully explained by the C.O.	
		2.45pm.	"B" & "D" Companies under Command of Lieut.W.E.C.Wigfall and Captain H.C. Rollin respectively, each sent two Platoons over the Parapet, forming first wave of attack. Following on about 50 yards interval the remaining Platoons went over, Battalion Grenadiers on either Flank. Each Company took one Lewis Gun. Directly the leading Coys were over the Parapets the Germans opened a heavy Machine Gun Fire from each Flank and shelled heavily with shrapnel and H.E. Our men pushed forward keeping under our Artillery Barage. Capt.Rollin was wounded and Lieut.Wigfall wounded in the leg which was broken. The B'n Bombers entered the German trench on the right	

1875 Wt. W593/826 1,000,000 4/15 J.B.C. & A. A.D.S.S./Forms/C. 2118.

Instructions regarding War Diaries and Intelligence Summaries are contained in F. S. Regs., Part II. and the Staff Manual respectively. Title Pages will be prepared in manuscript.

WAR DIARY
or
INTELLIGENCE SUMMARY
(Erase heading not required.)

Army Form C. 2118

Place	Date	Hour	Summary of Events and Information	Remarks and references to Appendices
Trenches S.E. of GUILLEMONT			(right) and a party of "B" Company under C.S.M. Jackson (killed) obtained a footing on the left part of the German Trench where they held on for more than two hour- the Battalions on either Flank having failed to reach their objective, the remainder of the two Companies then receiving the individual attentions of the XXXXXX Germans, held on in shell holes.	
		4.45pm.	The Leinster Regiment, 24th Division on our left made another attempt to go forward which failed and our men in the German trench after losing heavily withdrew and took up position in our Original Front Line.	
		7.45pm	Flares were sent up to show our positions, orders were received not to attack unless the attacks on our left and right were successful. These attacks never came off.	
	19/8/16		The day was spent getting in the wounded and burying dead and improving the trenches which were very narrow- at night a number of dead were buried about 100 yards from our own trenches in front. Shelling continued heavily all day and several of our own 18pounders(H.E.) and 4.5s dropped into and behind our lines.	
	do	10pm	The relief by the 20th Battalion Lanc.Fusiliers commenced and they were met with the same difficulties as ourselves, narrow and blocked trenches- Relief being completed by 4am on the 20th.	
XXXXXXX CARNOY	20/8/16.	5.15pm	The Battalion took over Dug-outs by old British Front Line and rested. Casualties for two days fighting, 6 Officers wounded, Other Ranks killed 34, wounded 81,missing 46, shell shock 3.	
MEAULTE	21/8/16		Arrived in tents	
DO	22/8/16		Took over Billets. Had 6 N.C.Os and men and two horses badly wounded by bombs dropped by an Aeroplane.	
DO	23/8/16.	6am	Proceeded to Rail head at MERICOURT and entrained, arriving at CANDAS at 4pm.	
BERNAVILLE.	23/8/16		Took over Billets	
DO	24/8/16			

1875 Wt. W593/826 1,000,000 4/15 J.R.C. & A. A.D.S.S./Forms/C. 2118.

Instructions regarding War Diaries and Intelligence Summaries are contained in F. S. Regs., Part II. and the Staff Manual respectively. Title Pages will be prepared in manuscript.

WAR DIARY
or
INTELLIGENCE SUMMARY
(Erase heading not required.)

Army Form C. 2118

Place	Date	Hour	Summary of Events and Information	Remarks and references to Appendices
VILLIERS L'HOPITAL	25/8/16		Arrived by Road and billeted.	
ECOIVES	26/8/16		Arrived by Road and Billeted	
BOURS	27/8/16		Arrived by Road and Billeted	
HOUCHIN	28/8/16		Arrived by Road and Billeted	
Mazingarbe.	29/8/16 30/8/16		Arrived by Road and Billeted 30 Officers inspected the trenches.	
do	31/8/16		Took over trenches from 2nd K.O.Y.L.I.	

1875 Wt. W593/826 1,000,000 4/15 J.B.C. & A. A.D.S.S./Forms/C. 2118.

To the O/C.
8 E York Rt

I

I herewith report on my observation of yesterdays attack. I had a good view from the French trench approx A 6.d. 3.8.

2.45 p.M The Infantry left trenches, the left Battalion, being out about ½ a minute before the Right Battalion – The 8th E Yorkshire being the left – they pushed on steadily and reached Enemy trench ~~S 30 d 2~~. S 30 d 7.1 to T 25. c. 2 8 the Enemy barrage was very intense falling midway between the Jumping off ~~[illegible]~~ trench to the objective trench Shrapnel & machine guns did a lot damage. at 2.50 p.M I noticed several ~~[illegible]~~ Germans retiring towards GUILLEMONT, these may have been orderlies &c as they apparently had no arms –

3.p.M. Impossible to observe owing to ~~[illegible]~~ heavy fire –

3.30 p.M Could see no trace of troops Enemy bombardment still heavy slackening a little at 4 p.M.

4.45 p.M artillery very active outskirts of GUILLMENT reached by Brit troops. Gordons on Right seem to have reached the Sunken Road

A French observer confirmed this a few minutes later –
Enemy artillery barrage again very dense all sight of troops lost in smoke & dust
5.15 p.m. troops on left seemed to have retired – many lying in ~~dugouts~~ shell holes behind the first objective –
During the whole afternoon the enemy were bursting crumps & shrapnel forming a barrage along a line S 6 A. 4. 5 to S 12 d 8 3.

W. B. Richardson Capt
Adjt 8 E York R

Aug 19/16

To 9th Bde
Herewith report as requested of my Adjutant who went off to observe in order to hasten communication

R. B. Brewis Lt Col
Cdg 8th Bn East Yorkshire Regt

19/8/16

8th Bde att 9th Bde

Secret.

8th (S) B'n West Yorkshire Regiment.

DIARY OF EVENTS ON 18th and 19th AUGUST 1916.

18/8/16. 4am. Companies left TALUS BOIS.

--do-- 4.30am Personally received attack orders from Brigade Major of 9th Brigade.

--do-- 5.30am. Companies arrived at the entrance to Communication Trenches, near 9th and 76th Brigade Headquarters, and relief was immediately started. Owing to a single Communication Trench, the number of carrying parties and reliefs going up and down the C.Ts, the narrowness of the trenches and uncleared casualties and the heavy shell fire on the trenches and communication trenches, it took until 1.15 pm before the B'n was settled down in the trenches.

--do-- 11am to 12.15pm. Company Commanders and Specialist Officers went thoroughly into the orders, and plans of positions to be attacked.

1.15pm to 2.45pm. All Officers were busy explaining the objects and points of the Attack to the N.C.Os and men. This was rendered extremely difficult by the narrowness of the trenches and the impossibility of communicating along the whole of the front Line without going round the Support Trenches owing to the heavy shelling and Machine Gun Fire during the time that the men were receiving instructions.

--do-- 2.45pm. "B" and "D" Companies under the Command of Lieut. W.E.O. Wigfall and Captain H.C.Rollin respectively, each sent two Platoons over the Parapet to form the first Wave. Following on, at about 50yards interval appeared the remaining Platoons and Battalion Grenadiers on either Flank. Each Company took one Lewis Gun. Directly the first Line got over the Parapet, the Germans opened with heavy Machine Gun Fire from both Flanks, and Shrapnel Fire. Our men pushed forward, keeping close under the "Barrage". Captain Rollin was wounded by Shrapnel and Lieut.Wigfall had his leg broken. The Battalion Grenadiers got into the enemy's trench on the right and a party of "B" Coy. under C.S.M.Jackson (killed) obtained a footing in the German Trench on the left, where they held on for more than two hours. Meanwhile, the 13th Battalion Middlesex Regiment, of the 24th Division on the left, and the 1st B'n Northumberland Fusiliers of the 9th Brigade on the right, were beaten back, leaving the whole of my attacking Force unsupported, and receiving the undivided attentions of the Germans. As the men could not go forward, they held on in Shell Holes.

--do-- 4.45pm. The Leinster Regiment, 24th Division, on the left, made another attempt to go forward, which failed, and our men in the German Trench, after losing heavily were driven out of the Trench. After Dark, the men managed to crawl back into our Lines.

--do-- 7.45pm. Flares were sent up to see the position of the Front Line. Later, orders were received that we were not to attack again, but if the attacks on our right and left were successful, we were to at once occupy the Trench. These attacks never came off.

19/8/16. The 19th was spent in getting in the wounded, and burying the dead in close vicinity to the front Line and support Lines, and later in the evening a good many dead from over one hundred yards from our trenches

DIARY OF EVENTS ON 18th and 19th AUGUST 1916. Continued.

were buried. Shelling continued very heavily all day, and there was a good deal of shelling of our Trenches by our 18 pdrs (H.E.) and 4.5's.

19/8/16. 10pm. The relief by the 20th Battalion Lancashire Fusiliers which began at about 10pm, was completed after great difficulties about 4am on the 20th. The Battalion moved to CARNOY.

After a check Roll Call, the Casualties of the Battalion wer found to be;

OFFICERS

Wounded........ 6.

Other Ranks

Killed ....35.

Wounded........83.

Missing........46

Hospital....... 3.

167

TOTAL

6 Officers and 167 Other Ranks.

No Lewis Guns, rifles or equipment were lost.
Original sent to 8th Bde

[signature]

Lieut-Colonel,

Commanding 8th (S) B'n East Yorkshire Regiment.

21/8/16.

8th Brigade.

3rd Division.

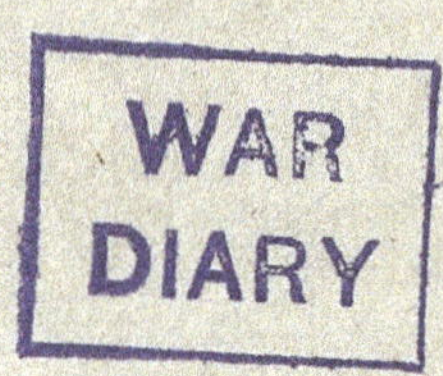

8th BATTALION

EAST YORKSHIRE REGIMENT

SEPTEMBER 1 9 1 6

Instructions regarding War Diaries and Intelligence Summaries are contained in F. S. Regs., Part II. and the Staff Manual respectively. Title pages will be prepared in manuscript.

SEPTEMBER 1916 **WAR DIARY** ~~or~~ ~~INTELLIGENCE SUMMARY.~~

(*Erase heading not required.*)

Army Form C. 2118.

8th (S) Bn East Yorkshire Regiment.

Vol 13

Place	Date	Hour	Summary of Events and Information	Remarks and references to Appendices
TRENCHES HULLUCH SECTOR	1/9/16 to 8/9/16.		Usual Trench Routine. – Wiring parties etc., – Enemy Trench Mortars shewed activity throughout the Tour, resulting in equal retaliation from our Trench Mortar Batteries. – On the night of September 6th, – an organised "strafe" against the enemy was carried out by our Artillery. – Aeroplane brought down by German Aviator, on left portion of our sector, & fell between reserve & front line Trenches. – Casualties slight.	
– " –	– " –	10 a.m.	Relief started. Battalion was relieved by 12th Bn West. Yorks. Regt. Relief completed about 2 p.m. On relief the Battalion proceeded to Hutments at NOEUX-LES-MINES, and remainder of day spent in resting. – Battalion in Divisional Reserve.	
NOEUX-LES-MINES	9/9/16		Cleaning up. Inspections etc.,	
– " –	10/9/16.		Commanding Officer's Inspection by Companies.	
– " –	11/9/16.		Baths allotted to the Battalion from 9-30 am to 5 p.m. – Inspection of Rifles & Arms by Armourer Sergeant.	
– " –	12/9/16.		Parades under Company arrangements. Specialists training. Parties practice rapid wiring.	
– " –	13/9/16.		N.C.O's & men, awarded the Military Medal for bravery etc, during operations on the Somme (14/7/16 to 25/7/16), inspected & presented with the riband by the Brigadier 8th Infantry Brigade. – Company parades under Coy Commanders arrangements.	

2353 Wt. W2544/1454 700,000 5/15 D. D. & L. A.D.S.S./Forms/C. 2118.

SECRET SEPTEMBER 1916. — 2 — WAR DIARY ~~or INTELLIGENCE SUMMARY.~~ 8th (S) Bn East Yorkshire Regiment Army Form C. 2118.

Instructions regarding War Diaries and Intelligence Summaries are contained in F. S. Regs., Part II. and the Staff Manual respectively. Title pages will be prepared in manuscript.

(Erase heading not required.)

Place	Date	Hour	Summary of Events and Information	Remarks and references to Appendices
NOEUX-LES-MINES	13/9/16.	9 p.m.	Carrying party of 480 men, proceeded to Trenches to carry Gas Cylinders to Front Line.	
— " —	14/9/16 to 17/9/16.		Furnished each night carrying parties for Gas Cylinders. Throughout the day Company Commanders Inspections – Kit Inspections etc.	
— " —	18/9/16.		Sunday. – Church Parades & general rest day.	
— " —	19/9/16		C.O's Inspection of newly-formed H.Q. Company, & remaining Companies. Battalion paraded at 2 p.m & marched to practice Trenches near NOEUX-LES-MINES for a Flammenwerfer demonstration. – Draft of 29 Other Ranks arrived from Base, & One Officer. – Small carrying parties at night.	
— " —	20/9/16		Companies at disposal of Company Commanders.	
— " —	21/9/16.	8/30 am.	Battalion received orders to move to Training Area. – Paraded at 8 a.m – Marched off from NOEUX-LES-MINES at 8/30 a.m. & marched via. VERQUIN – LABEUVRIERE – MARLES-LES-MINES to LOZINGHEM, arriving in Billets at 1 p.m. The weather was threatening throughout the march.	
LOZINGHEM	22/9/16.	8 a.m.	Battalion left Billets at LOZINGHEM, & proceeded to march via FERFAY – AMETTES – AUCHY-AU-BOIS ~~to~~ to ESTREE BLANCHE, where the Battalion halted for the mid-day meal. The march was continued about 1/30 p.m via ERNY-ST. JULIEN	

2353 Wt. W2544/1454 700,000 5/15 D. D. & L. A.D.S.S./Forms/C. 2118.

SECRET

Instructions regarding War Diaries and Intelligence Summaries are contained in F. S. Regs., Part II. and the Staff Manual respectively. Title pages will be prepared in manuscript.

SEPTEMBER 1916.

—3—

WAR DIARY ~~or INTELLIGENCE SUMMARY.~~

(Erase heading not required.)

8th (S) B'n East Yorkshire Regiment.

Army Form C. 2118.

Place	Date	Hour	Summary of Events and Information	Remarks and references to Appendices
LOZINGHEM	22/9/16.	1 p.m.	to COYECQUES. Marching conditions were bad owing to the sultry weather, & the fact that only two men fell out on the line of march, speaks highly of the marching qualities of the Battalion. – Took over Billets at COYECQUES about 4/30 p.m. – Length of march about 28 Kilomètres.	
COYECQUES.	23/9/16	2/30 p.m.	Battalion moved into Billets at DELETTES about two Kilomètres march, & about centre of Training Area.	
DELETTES.	24/9/16 to 30/9/16.		First few days spent in building Range, & preparing Training Area, Trenches etc., Signallers, Lewis Gunners, Bombers, & Snipers, training under their respective Officers. Companies at the disposal of Company Commanders. Training consisted of Route marching, Firing on Ranges, Digging practice Trenches etc, On 26/9/16. draft of 80. Other Ranks arrived.	

[illegible]
Lieut.-Colonel,
Commanding 8th (S) B'n East Yorkshire Regiment.

1/10/16.

2353 Wt. W2544/1454 700,000 5/15 D. D. & L. A.D.S.S./Forms/C. 2118.

8th Brigade.

3rd Division.

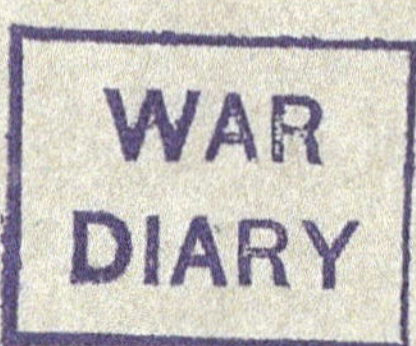

8th BATTALION

EAST YORKSHIRE REGIMENT

OCTOBER 1 9 1 6

SECRET

Instructions regarding War Diaries and Intelligence Summaries are contained in F. S. Regs., Part II. and the Staff Manual respectively. Title pages will be prepared in manuscript.

WAR DIARY or ~~INTELLIGENCE SUMMARY.~~

(Erase heading not required.)

OCTOBER 1916 — 8th (S) Bn East Yorkshire Regt

Army Form C. 2118.

Vol 14

Place	Date	Hour	Summary of Events and Information	Remarks and references to Appendices
DELETTES.	1/10/16 to 4/10/16		Completion of Divisional training. On the 3rd the Attack Practice was carried out by Brigades and finally by Division. Remainder of time occupied in Company + Battalion training, consisting of Attack Practices, Route-marching, etc. — Specialists training under their respective Officers — Weather throughout this period was indifferent —	
— " —	5/10/16.	8/30am.	Battalion left Billets at DELETTES, + marched under instructions from Bde to VERCHIN, arriving in Billets there, about 3 p.m. Showery weather prevailed throughout the march, which was carried out on "heavy" roads. — Distance about 14 miles.	
VERCHIN	6/10/16.		Company parades — Feet Inspections etc.	
— " —	7/10/16.	2/30pm.	Battalion paraded + marched to ST. POL — Intermittent downpours of rain. — entrained at ST. POL at 12-30 p.m + proceeded ~~by~~ via FREVENT + DOULLENS to VARENNES detraining there at 1 p.m. 8/10/16	
VARENNES	8/10/16	2 p.m.	Marched to MAILLY-MAILLET WOOD + encamped there, arriving about ~~[illegible]~~ p.m. — Troops in a weak + tired state having been about 26 hours on road + rail.	
MAILLY-MAILLET WOOD	9/10/16 to 19/10/16		Company training — Supplied working parties for trenches, both during night + day, throughout this period. — Men not on working parties carried out training as usual. — Have specialists trained — On the 19th, a Brigade Scheme was carried out, over marked out trenches. — After this the Battalion proceeded to Billets in the Wood at BUS-LES-ARTOIS	

2353 Wt. W2544/1454 700,000 5/15 D. D. & L. A.D.S.S./Forms/C. 2118.

SECRET

Instructions regarding War Diaries and Intelligence Summaries are contained in F. S. Regs., Part II. and the Staff Manual respectively. Title pages will be prepared in manuscript.

-2-

WAR DIARY

~~INTELLIGENCE SUMMARY.~~

(Erase heading not required.)

8th (S) Bn East Yorkshire Regiment

Army Form C. 2118.

Place	Date	Hour	Summary of Events and Information	Remarks and references to Appendices
BUS-LES-ARTOIS	18/10/16 to 20/10/16		Provided usual working & carrying parties to trenches. – On the 20th a practice attack was again carried out over specially marked area, as a unit of the Brigade. – On the 23rd the practice attack was again carried out by the Division. –	
	27/10/16		On the 27th. "A", "B", & "C" Coys proceeded to the trenches in the SERRE Sector, "B" Coy was attached to the 1st Gordon Highlanders, & "A" & "C" Companies were attached to the 1st Bn Northumberland Fusiliers of the 76th Brigade – During a tour lasting 48 hours, casualties numbering	
	28/10/16		2 Officers & 8 Other Ranks, were sustained. In the 2 Officer Casualties (Captain C. P. Taylor & Lieut J. C. Harter, Killed in Action, 28/10/16) the Battalion lost two of its original Officers.	
	30/10/16		H.Q. & "D" Company, left Billets at BUS-LES-ARTOIS & proceeded to COURCELLES-AU-BOIS to Billets in Barns & Houses. – Here they were joined by "A", "B" & "C" Coys who were relieved from the line.	
COURCELLES	30/10/16		Usual working parties. – A raid which had been organised on the enemy trenches, & which was intended to take place this night, was cancelled owing to inclement weather & the "sticky" state of the ground.	
– . –	31/10/16		Working Parties – Raiding Party again proceeded to trenches, and the raid was carried out. – No prisoners were taken & we suffered Casualties of 1 Officer & 12 O. Ranks (Wounded).	Appendix A

[illegible] Major
Commanding 8th (S) Bn E. Yorkshire Regiment
3/11/16

2353 Wt. W2544/1454 700,000 5/15 D. D. & L. A.D.S.S./Forms/C. 2118.

8th Brigade.

3rd Division.

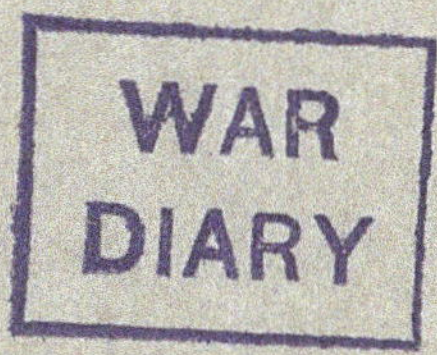

8th BATTALION

EAST YORKSHIRE REGIMENT

NOVEMBER 1 9 1 6

Instructions regarding War Diaries and Intelligence Summaries are contained in F. S. Regs., Part II. and the Staff Manual respectively. Title pages will be prepared in manuscript.

Army Form C. 2118.

8/3

WAR DIARY or ~~INTELLIGENCE SUMMARY~~.

(Erase heading not required.)

NOVEMBER. 1916

8th (S) B'n. East Yorkshire Regt.

Vol 15

(1)

Place	Date	Hour	Summary of Events and Information	Remarks and references to Appendices
COURCELLES	1/11/16		The day was spent in preparing for the trenches, arms, equipment and "Iron Rations" being inspected.	
	-"-	4 pm	The B'n left Billets, Companies at ten minutes interval and marched via COLIN CAMP to the 8th Infty Bgde SERRE SECTOR trenches, relieving the 7th K.S.L.I. Relief was completed about 11.30 p.m.	
SERRE SECTOR	2/11/16 to 4/11/16		Usual trench routine - patrols, working parties etc. Enemy's trench mortars and artillery showed considerable activity throughout the tour, resulting in heavy retaliation from our Batteries.	
	-"-	5 p.m.	Relief commenced by the 1st R.S.F's and completed about 10.30 p.m. On relief the B'n proceeded to Billets at LOUVENCOURT. Casualties during the tour 5 Killed, 10 wounded. The weather was unsettled.	
LOUVENCOURT	5/11/16 to 11/11/16		Company training, special attention was given to the training of Bombers and movements in extended order and Artillery were carried out in preparation for the forthcoming attack. Wiring was practiced and lectures in various subjects given to the N.C.O's.	
	12/11/16		Preparations for the trenches. At 1.30 p.m the B'n marched via BERTRANCOURT to COURCELLES. After a halt of two or three hours, the B'n moved into the trenches, SERRE SECTOR, and took up the positions allotted to them for the attack on the enemy's position.	
SERRE SECTOR	13/11/16	5 a.m.	The B'n was formed up in four waves between FLAG AVENUE and SOUTHERN AV. At 5.45 a.m. the B'n, supporting the 2nd Royal Scots, commenced its advance. The hostile barrage opened quickly and accurately, the rear Company receiving several casualties in the first five minutes. The first two waves of the B'n quickly became merged	

2353 Wt. W2544/1454 700,000 5/15 D. D. & L. A.D.S.S./Forms/C. 2118.

Army Form C. 2118.

WAR DIARY
or
INTELLIGENCE SUMMARY.

(Erase heading not required.)

Instructions regarding War Diaries and Intelligence Summaries are contained in F. S. Regs., Part II. and the Staff Manual respectively. Title pages will be prepared in manuscript.

November 1916 — 8th E.Y.R. — (2)

Place	Date	Hour	Summary of Events and Information	Remarks and references to Appendices
			with the 2nd Royal Scots. A portion of these boys penetrated the German 2nd Line but were checked by rifle and heavy machine gun fire. The third and fourth waves reached the German front line, where large numbers of men of other Units where met retiring and although efforts were made by individual Officers to check the retirement, the retirement was too general to be stopped and the majority of these Companies were carried back to our front line where reorganization was attempted and a defence organized. By 10 a.m. the B'n was practically reformed in the assembly trenches. The remainder of the day was spent in further reorganization and getting in touch with Units on the left and right.	
SERRE SECTOR	14/11/16		Nothing of importance occurred during the day. Heavy shelling on both sides occurred at frequent intervals. About 5 pm relief by the Royal Fusiliers, 9th Brigade, was commenced and completed about 10.30 p.m. On relief the B'n proceeded to Bus Wood Huts. The weather throughout was foggy and unsettled. Casualties during the attack - Officers 2 Killed, 3 wounded. Other ranks - Killed 23, wounded 177, missing 30.	
BUS HUTS	15/11/16		The morning was spent in cleaning arms, equipment etc. Orders to be ready to proceed to the trenches were received and at 8-15 p.m the B'n marched to BUS church and were conveyed to COURCELLES by motor lorries. Relief of the Royal Fusiliers was completed about 2 a.m. on the morning of the 16/11/16.	
SERRE SECTOR	16/11/16 to 17/11/16		Usual trench routine, wiring parties, cleaning of trenches etc. Artillery on both sides showed considerable activity.	

2353 Wt. W2544/1454 700,000 5/15 D. D. & L. A.D.S.S./Forms/C. 2118.

Army Form C. 2118.

WAR DIARY
or
INTELLIGENCE SUMMARY.
(Erase heading not required.)

Instructions regarding War Diaries and Intelligence Summaries are contained in F. S. Regs., Part II. and the Staff Manual respectively. Title pages will be prepared in manuscript.

3

Place	Date	Hour	Summary of Events and Information	Remarks and references to Appendices
SERRE SECTOR	17/11/16	5 p.m.	Relief by the 2nd Royal Scots was commenced but owing to difficulty in reaching the advanced bombing post was not completed until 4 30 a.m 18/11/16. On relief the B'n proceeded to COURCELLES. Casualties during the tour were small. Weather cold and frosty.	
COURCELLES	18/11/16		Cleaning of arms, equipment, clothing etc - inspections.	
— " —	19/11/16		The B'n left billets and marched to BUS WOOD HUTS, arriving there about 3 p.m.	
BUS HUTS	20/11/16		Training was carried out as usual.	
— " —	21/11/16		The B'n moved to COURCELLES and took over billets from the 2nd Royal Scots.	
COURCELLES	22/11/16		Company training, bathing.	
— " —	23/11/16		Preparations for the trenches were made and at 4 p.m the B'n marched to the trenches and relieved the 7th KSLI in the 8th Infty Bgde SERRE SECTOR, relief being completed about 11·30 p.m.	
SERRE SCTR	24/11/16 to		Work on the trenches was carried out. The weather was very wet and considerable difficulty was experienced in keeping the trenches habitable. Relief by the 2nd Royal Scots was completed about midnight and the	
	26/11/16		B'n moved into rear trenches, having received orders to act as a wiring B'n. H.Q at VALLARD.	
	27/11/16 to 28/11/16		Wiring was carried out both day and night in spite of adverse weather. A number of casualties were sustained owing to daylight wiring, three being killed and eight wounded. About noon on the 28th, orders were received to proceed to BUS WOOD HUTS and Companies were dispatched independently	

2353 Wt. W2544/1454 700,000 5/15 D. D. & L. A.D.S.S./Forms/C. 2118.

Army Form C. 2118.

Instructions regarding War Diaries and Intelligence Summaries are contained in F. S. Regs., Part II. and the Staff Manual respectively. Title pages will be prepared in manuscript.

WAR DIARY or ~~INTELLIGENCE SUMMARY~~.

(Erase heading not required.)

(4)

Place	Date	Hour	Summary of Events and Information	Remarks and references to Appendices
			the last party arriving in Billets at BUS about 5 p.m	
BUS HUTS	30/11/16		During the morning the Bn were inspected by the G.O.C. 3rd Division.	
			In the afternoon the Bn moved into Billets in BUS village.	
			B. I. Way. Lieut-Colonel. Commanding 8th (S) Bn East Yorkshire Regiment.	
			1/12/16.	

2353 Wt. W2544/1454 700,000 5/15 D. D. & L. A.D.S.S./Forms/C. 2118.

8th Brigade.

3rd Division.

8th BATTALION

EAST YORKSHIRE REGIMENT

DECEMBER 1 9 1 6

Instructions regarding War Diaries and Intelligence Summaries are contained in F. S. Regs., Part II. and the Staff Manual respectively. Title pages will be prepared in manuscript.

WAR DIARY or ~~INTELLIGENCE SUMMARY.~~

(Erase heading not required.)

Army Form C. 2118.

8th East York. Regt.

December 1916 Secret. Vol 16

Place	Date	Hour	Summary of Events and Information	Remarks and references to Appendices
BUS	1/12/16		Physical training, wiring practice, route marches, Company drill. Special attention was given	
-"-	2/12/16		to the training of new Bombers and machine gunners.	
-"-	3/12/16		Church Parades, Inspection of the Battalion by the Commanding Officer.	
-"-	4/12/16		The usual training was carried out. At 2.30 p.m. the Battalion marched to COURCELLES, arriving	
COURCELLES	"		about 4 p.m. During the night of the 4/5th all available men were employed in the 8th Infty	
-do-	"		Bgde Sector under the direction of the R.E's.	
-do-	5/12/16		Operation orders having been received, preparation for the trench tour was carried out during the	
			morning. At 4-30 p.m. the first Company proceeded to the Serre Sector trenches,	
			followed at intervals by remaining Coys. Relief of the 1st Royal Scots Fus. was completed about 11 p.m.	
SERRE	6/12/16		The usual trench routine was carried out. Efforts were made to improve the condition of the	
SECTOR	7/12/16		trenches, and during the hours of darkness, the wire was strengthened and repaired. A systematic	
			and prearranged bombardment of well known targets in the enemy's rear position was carried at	
			intervals during the two days by our heavy Artillery.	
-do-	8/12/16		Heavy rain necessitated considerable work in keeping the trenches clear of water.	
-"-		5 p.m.	Relief by the 2nd Royal Scots was commenced under favourable conditions, enemy artillery being	
			inactive. By 8-15 p.m. relief was complete and the Bn took over Billets at COURCELLES.	

2353 Wt. W2544/1454 700,000 5/15 D. D. & L. A.D.S.S./Forms/C. 2118.

Army Form C. 2118.

Instructions regarding War Diaries and Intelligence Summaries are contained in F. S. Regs., Part II. and the Staff Manual respectively. Title pages will be prepared in manuscript.

WAR DIARY
or
~~INTELLIGENCE SUMMARY.~~
(Erase heading not required.)

December 1916. Secret

Place	Date	Hour	Summary of Events and Information	Remarks and references to Appendices
COURCELLES	9/12/16		The morning was spent in cleaning of clothes, rifles and equipment.	
		2.30pm.	The B'n marched to BUS and were billeted in the village.	
BUS	10/12/16		Church parade, inspection of Billets, arms and equipment by the C.O.	
-"-	11/12/16. to 14/12/16		With the exception of Specialists, all available men were employed on the roads and 3rd Div. Range. The training of specialists was continued.	
	15/12/16		Two Companies of the B'n marched to the WHITE CITY in reserve to the B'n holding the Line and two Coys were Billeted in Courcelles.	
SERRE SECTOR	16/12/16		The Two Companies from Courcelles and the two from the WHITE CITY relieved the 1st R.S.F in the 8th Infty Bgde Sector, relief being completed about 10-15 p.m.	
-do-	17/18/Dec 16.		The usual trench routine was carried out. Artillery on both sides was very active and our C.T's and dumps were intermittently shelled throughout the tour. On the night of the 18/12/16, relief was commenced about 5-30 p.m by the 2nd Royal Scots, and completed by 9-15 p.m.	
-do-				
BUS			The B'n marched through after relief to the new camp at BUS, with the exception of 126 men who were left at COLIN CAMPS for work on the new railway.	
-"-				
-"- & C.C.	19/12/16.		The B'n rested in the morning. About 2.30 p.m. 160 men moved into Billets at BEAUSSART.	
-"- etc.	20/12/16 to 22/12/16.		Working parties carried out duties at BUS, BEAUSSART and COLIN CAMPS. On the night of the 22nd, the B'n reformed and Billeted in BUS.	

2353 Wt. W2544/1454 700,000 5/15 D. D. & L. A.D.S.S./Forms/C. 2118.

Army Form C. 2118.

Instructions regarding War Diaries and Intelligence Summaries are contained in F. S. Regs., Part II. and the Staff Manual respectively. Title pages will be prepared in manuscript.

WAR DIARY or ~~INTELLIGENCE SUMMARY~~.

(Erase heading not required.)

December 1916 Secret.

Place	Date	Hour	Summary of Events and Information	Remarks and references to Appendices
BUS	23/12/16		Usual Company training was carried out. Specialists under their respective Officers.	
-"-	24/12/16		No work was carried out the day being treated as Christmas Day.	
-"-	25/12/16		Two Coys left BUS during the morning and proceeded to the trenches, relieving the two support companies of the K.S.L.I. in daylight. The two remaining Companies left BUS at 3 p.m. and marched to the trenches. Relief of the two front line Coys was completed about 11.30 p.m.	
SERRE. SECTOR	26/12/16 to 29/12/16		Usual trench routine. The weather was very wet and cold. The enemy's Artillery was more active than usual and our C.T's were heavily shelled throughout the tour. Casualties were light, only three being wounded. Relief was completed about 11.45 pm by the K.S.L.I. and the Bn returned to BUS.	
BUS	30/12/16		The day was spent in the cleaning and inspection of arms, equipment etc.	
-"-	31/12/16		Church parades, inspection of the Bn by the Commanding Officer.	

1/1/17.

Frank E. Dall Major
Cmdg 8th (S) Bn East Yorkshire Regiment

2353 Wt. W2544/1454 700,000 5/15 D. D. & L. A.D.S.S./Forms/C. 2118.

3rd Division

War Diaries

8/East Yorks

~~January to December 31st~~

~~1917~~

1917 JAN – 1918 FEB

DISBANDED

Instructions regarding War Diaries and Intelligence Summaries are contained in F. S. Regs., Part II. and the Staff Manual respectively. Title Pages will be prepared in manuscript.

WAR DIARY
or
INTELLIGENCE SUMMARY
(Erase heading not required.)

Army Form C. 2118

8th Battn East Yorks. Regt.

Vol 17

Place	Date	Hour	Summary of Events and Information	Remarks and references to Appendices
Bus	1.1.17.		New Year's day. By special order of the Corps Commander this day was regarded as a general holiday. The battalion attended the cinematograph show @ Bus.	
	2.1.17		Companies were under their commanders to-day & carried out the following training: Physical drill, Company drill & wiring. Bombers & Lewis Gunners under their respective officers	
	3.1.17.		The morning was spent in preparing for the trenches. At 1pm A & B Companies left Bus for the line, relieving the 7th KSLI in the support trenches. At 3 pm C & D Companies left Bus to relieve the troops in the front line. The relief was complete by 10 pm (no details attend)	
	4.1.17 – 7.1.17		Usual trench routine. Artillery was very active on both sides. Our sector was heavily shelled on several occasions. We had 1 Sergeant & 3 men killed and 12 men wounded.	
	8.1.17		On the afternoon of the 8th the two rear Companies were relieved by the 17th H.L.I. of the 32nd Division @ 7 pm. The relief of the two Companies in the front line was completed by 10.15 pm. The regimental transport left Bus this morning for the new area. At BERTRANCOURT busses were waiting to take our battalion to RIBEAUCOURT. A & B Companies were billeted @ the village & C & D Companies at LANCHES, about a mile away.	
	9.1.17.		The day was spent in resting & scraping mud, washing & shaving.	
	10.1.17		Companies under Company Commanders. To-day Lieut. Col. J.H. de la Perrelle of the 4th Royal Fusiliers took over command of the battalion.	
	11.1.17.		The day was spent in cleaning up, inspections & in arranging of billets. Companies paraded under their commanders for re-organisation into fighting units, as per divisional training scheme. 6 weeks of training lies now before us, as well as sports & competitions.	

1875 Wt. W593/826 1,000,000 4/15 J.B.C. & A. A.D.S.S./Forms/C. 2118.

Instructions regarding War Diaries and Intelligence Summaries are contained in F. S. Regs., Part II. and the Staff Manual respectively. Title pages will be prepared in manuscript.

WAR DIARY

~~or~~

~~INTELLIGENCE SUMMARY.~~

(Erase heading not required.)

Army Form C. 2118.

Place	Date	Hour	Summary of Events and Information	Remarks and references to Appendices
RIBEAU-COURT	12.1.17		(Nothing entered)	
	13.1.17	Saturday [?]	N.C.Os. paraded under R.S.M. for communication drill. Companies under Company Commanders. Drill, & practice of the new sections under their leaders. 2nd Lt R.E.H. Sicke [?] of the 4th Royal Fusiliers joined the battalion to-day & took over the duties of Adjutant in place of Capt Young, who is at present in hospital. 2nd Lt Brock who was A/Adjutant took over duties of Signalling officer.	
	14.1.17	Sun.	Church parade for C of E at 10.30 under R.S.M. All officers of the battalion proceeded to Domart for the interview with the G.O.C. III [?] Division. The General explained his training programme & called upon all units in his division for determination & thoroughness [?]. The first snow of the year fell to-day. Sec Lieut J.M. Blenn [?] rejoined the battalion to-day from leave.	
	15.1.17	Mon.	Now that Companies have been organised into fighting units, the training for the great push commences to-day. For the first three weeks there is to be no work done in the afternoon. Elementary work to start with & a general tightening up of discipline. However we are very hung up for good instructors. G.O.C. 5th Brigade inspected the battalion during training to-day	

2353 Wt. W2544/1454 700,000 5/15 D. D. & L. A.D.S.S./Forms/C. 2118.

Army Form C. 2118.

Instructions regarding War Diaries and Intelligence Summaries are contained in F. S. Regs., Part II. and the Staff Manual respectively. Title pages will be prepared in manuscript.

WAR DIARY
or
INTELLIGENCE SUMMARY.
(Erase heading not required.)

Place	Date	Hour	Summary of Events and Information	Remarks and references to Appendices
RIBEAUCOURT	16.1.17	Tues.	The draft which arrived was posted to Companies. They were inspected by the C.O. They are a better looking lot than the last batch. Most of them have been out before. Some of them however have only had 12 to 15 weeks training. The Regimental Canteen was opened to-day. Companies carried on with training as laid down in programme of work. Lieut Bulwell + 2nd Lts Lamb + Pappa returned from the 3rd Divisional School.	
	17.1.17		Snow fell heavily during the night. Parades therefore took the form of indoor instruction. 2nd Lt Elliott returned this day from 4th Army School. We hear to-day that our battalion will have to move as we are outside our Corps Area. The move is to take place on the 22nd of this month. A concert took place in the canteen which proved to be a great success. The Doctor (Lieut Melrose) proceeded on leave.	
	18.1.17		Companies paraded usual under Company Commanders. The lecture on Physical Training + Bayonet Fighting did not take place. NCOs paraded as usual in the afternoon under the R.S.M. In the evening the Divisional 'Mudlarks' gave us a concert.	

2353 Wt. W2544/1454 700,000 5/15 D. D. & L. A.D.S.S./Forms/C. 2118.

Instructions regarding War Diaries and Intelligence Summaries are contained in F. S. Regs., Part II. and the Staff Manual respectively. Title pages will be prepared in manuscript.

WAR DIARY

or

~~INTELLIGENCE SUMMARY.~~

(Erase heading not required.)

Army Form C. 2118.

Place	Date	Hour	Summary of Events and Information	Remarks and references to Appendices
RIBEAUCOURT	19.1.17		Companies trained as per programme. B & A Companies fired on the range. This morning a draft of 102 men arrived. NCOs & recruits paraded under Adjutant & RSM. The Transport had their Xmas dinner & later a concert was given by a troop from the Mechanical Transport. The G.O.C. visited our area to-day & expressed his satisfaction at what he saw.	
"	20.1.17	Sat.	Lecture @ 9am on Physical Training & Bayonet Fighting. Company training as usual. Football match was postponed owing to a re-draw. 2nd Lt Cole proceeded on leave to-day. 2nd Lts Hayes, Hoyle, Robinson & Micklethwaite joined the battalion to-day from England.	
	21.1.17		Church of England Service in the Recreation Hut @ 10.30. Roman Catholics @ 9.30 in the village Church. Company kit & billet inspection. 2nd Lt Brock & a party proceeded to BERNEUIL to take over billets in our new area. Court of Enquiry was opened to-day on the fire @ the Gum boots Store @ COURCELLES. Major Morris was president of them & 2 Lt Chalmers a member.	

2353 Wt. W2544/1454 700,000 5/15 D. D. & L. A.D.S.S./Forms/C. 2118.

Instructions regarding War Diaries and Intelligence Summaries are contained in F. S. Regs., Part II. and the Staff Manual respectively. Title pages will be prepared in manuscript.

WAR DIARY

or

~~INTELLIGENCE SUMMARY.~~

(*Erase heading not required.*)

Army Form C. 2118.

Place	Date	Hour	Summary of Events and Information	Remarks and references to Appendices
RIBAUCOURT	22.1.17	Mor.	The battalion moved out of RIBEAUCOURT + LANCHES @ 9 am and proceeded to BERNEUIL. There was some trouble with the billeting @ first. The move took till 12 midnight as we had to move all our Canteen + Quartermaster's Stores. A draft of 65 men (Yeomen) arrived to-day. The majority were dirty + ill clad.	
BERNEUIL	23.1.17		Everything was somewhat topsy-turvy to-day. The Gas Officer arrived late. C B + A Companies were lectured to first + A Company last. The G.O.C. 3rd Division visited us to-day, as well as the Brigadier. In the afternoon the usual N.C.O parade took place as well as bayonet fighting for the teams. The weather is fearfully cold + no one seemed quite @ home in them.	
	24.1.17		Company training continues. Attack formations were practiced. To-morrow Companies have to practice the attack on the course which is being taped out. O.C. Companies + Adjutant went to look over the ground. Naturally the course was nothing like ready. The usual parades took place in the afternoon. There was a concert in the evening in the Recreation Hut given by the "Blue Lights". Cpt Smith + 2nd Lt Tyrrell returned from leave to-day.	

2353 Wt. W2544/1454 700,000 5/15 D. D. & L. A.D.S.S./Forms/C. 2118.

Instructions regarding War Diaries and Intelligence Summaries are contained in F. S. Regs., Part II. and the Staff Manual respectively. Title pages will be prepared in manuscript.

WAR DIARY

or

~~INTELLIGENCE SUMMARY.~~

(Erase heading not required.)

Army Form C. 2118.

Place	Date	Hour	Summary of Events and Information	Remarks and references to Appendices
BERNEUIL	25.1.17		Companies proceeded to the training ground. Even to-day the course had not been finished. It was rather a job to find the exact position of things. G.O.C. 3rd Division was on the ground as well. The Companies trained till 12.45 & were then marched home by the drums. The weather still continues to be very cold. The usual parades took place in the afternoon. 2nd/Lt James returned from a bombing Course to-day.	
"	25.1.17		Companies under Company Commanders. Attack formation practiced. In the afternoon were the usual N.C.O. & Bombing parades. The Brigadier was round during the afternoon. There was a concert in the evening in the Recreation Hut. 2nd Lt Le Breton returned from leave to-day.	
"	26.1.17		Company training under Company Commanders. B Coy provided a digging party in the afternoon for extending & improving the existing trenches. 2nd Lt Murray had D Company Bombers on the ground for training purposes. N.C.Os under the RSM &	

2353 Wt. W2544/1454 700,000 5/15 D. D. & L. A.D.S.S./Forms/C. 2118.

Army Form C. 2118.

WAR DIARY
or
INTELLIGENCE SUMMARY.
(Erase heading not required.)

Instructions regarding War Diaries and Intelligence Summaries are contained in F. S. Regs., Part II. and the Staff Manual respectively. Title pages will be prepared in manuscript.

Place	Date	Hour	Summary of Events and Information	Remarks and references to Appendices
BERNEUIL			and Sergeant Instructor for bayonet fighting.	
	27th.1.17.		To-day we received definite news that we would have to move from our present billeting area the division to be ready to move to-morrow. this is very upsetting news as we have just got everything settled + the Canteen going well. Companies carried on their training under Company Commanders. As far as possible everything in the Q.M. Stores was packed + got ready for the move. there was a concert in the Canteen by the "Pop offs" which was a great success. Move orders from the Brigade arrived @ about 9 p.m.	
AUTEUILE	28th.1.17.		the battalion was ready to march off @ 12 noon from Berneuil our destination was Auteuil via Montrelet, Bonneville, Beauval. the weather was very cold. the battalion came along very well and + on arrival at Auteuil at 5 pm only 4 men had fallen out. Billets were quite good. Move orders for the following day came at 6 am on the 29th.	

Instructions regarding War Diaries and Intelligence Summaries are contained in F. S. Regs., Part II. and the Staff Manual respectively. Title pages will be prepared in manuscript.

WAR DIARY
or
INTELLIGENCE SUMMARY.
(Erase heading not required.)

Army Form C. 2118.

Place	Date	Hour	Summary of Events and Information	Remarks and references to Appendices
BONNIERE	29.1.17		The Battalion left Authieule at 9 30 am for Bonniere, via Doullens Bouquemaison and arrived at about 4 p.m. The weather still continues very cold.	
CROISETTE + HÉRICOURT	30.1.17		The Battalion moved off @ 8.15 for Croisette + Hericourt, via Frevent, Nuncq, Ecoivres and arrived in at about 1 p.m. C.O. met all officers @ 4 pm @ H.Q. Mess Hericourt.	
OSTREVILLE	31.1.17		The Battalion marched off @ 9.20 this morning from Croisette for Ostreville, via, St POL for Ostreville and arrived at 12.30 p.m. Snow had fallen during the night which made going rather difficult. Two men fell [illegible]	

2353 Wt. W2544/1454 700,000 5/15 D. D. & L. A.D.S.S./Forms/C. 2118.

Instructions regarding War Diaries and Intelligence Summaries are contained in F. S. Regs., Part II. and the Staff Manual respectively. Title pages will be prepared in manuscript.

WAR DIARY
or
INTELLIGENCE SUMMARY.
(Erase heading not required.)

Army Form C. 2118.

8th East Yorks. Regt. Vol 18

Place	Date	Hour	Summary of Events and Information	Remarks and references to Appendices
OSTREVILLE	1.2.17.		Weather as cold as ever. More snow fell during the night. All Company bombers & some officers were under the Bombing officer for practice. Lewis Gun Instruction in the afternoon for officers. Companies were at the disposal of Company Commanders. Lieut. Block returned to-day from hospital. 2nd Lieut McIntosh rejoined his own battalion to-day.	
"	2.2.17.		Company bombers bombing. Battalion route march, via, MARQUAY, BAILLEUL, MONCHY, ORLENCOURT, OSTREVILLE. Return @ 1 pm. There was a service for Roman Catholics in the afternoon. Inspection by companies by the O.C. Companies.	
"	3.2.17.		Companies under Company Commanders in attack formation. Bombing & rifle grenade practice by Bombing officer. The Commanding Officer inspected the battalion by Companies during the afternoon. Lieut H.S. Williams proceeded on leave this day.	
	4.2.17.		Holy Communion @ 8.30 am & 11.45 am. Parade service @ 9.30-11.30 by Companies, there being no space available large enough for the whole battalion. 2nd Lieut Cole returned from leave to-day & takes over the duties of L.G.O. during the absence of Lieut Williams.	

2353 Wt. W2544/1454 700,000 5/15 D. D. & L. A.D.S.S./Forms/C. 2118.

Instructions regarding War Diaries and Intelligence Summaries are contained in F. S. Regs., Part II. and the Staff Manual respectively. Title pages will be prepared in manuscript.

WAR DIARY
or
INTELLIGENCE SUMMARY.
(*Erase heading not required.*)

Army Form C. 2118.

Place	Date	Hour	Summary of Events and Information	Remarks and references to Appendices
[C]OSTREVILLE	5.2.17.		The battalion practiced the attack during the morning over a system of taped out trenches, Drums representing the "barrage". Company bombers during the afternoon in Rifle Grenade practice.	
"	6.2.17.		Companies at range practice + attack formations. Inspection of transport during the afternoon by Commanding Officer. Major H.L. Wright arrived to-day + assumed duties as second in command. Lieut N.H. Watson joined the battalion to-day + is posted to "D" Company.	
"	7.2.17		Companies under Company Commanders. Range practice + attack formations. Bombing under bombing officer. Preparation for to-morrows move. Billeting parties under Major Morris set out this morning for LIGNEREUIL.	
LIGNEREUIL	8.2.17.		Battalion paraded ready to move off @ 7¹⁵ am. The weather still continues very cold. Arrived at LIGNEREUIL at 12 noon. Billets for men are good + plentiful. Officers are badly off. Battalion soon settled down to its new Quarters. The Division are in the same village. Training ground is good. There are two rifle ranges. 'B' Coy is billeted @ BLAVINCOURT, about a mile from here	

2353 Wt. W2544/1454 700,000 5/15 D. D. & L. A.D.S.S./Forms/C. 2118.

Army Form C. 2118.

Instructions regarding War Diaries and Intelligence Summaries are contained in F. S. Regs., Part II. and the Staff Manual respectively. Title pages will be prepared in manuscript.

WAR DIARY
or
INTELLIGENCE SUMMARY.
(Erase heading not required.)

Place	Date	Hour	Summary of Events and Information	Remarks and references to Appendices
LIGNEREUIL	9.2.17		Physical Training Companies under Company Commanders. Bombing as detailed by the bombing officer. Captain Ward of the General List joined the battalion for duty from the 212 Infantry Brigade Staff, and is posted to 'B' Company.	
"	10.2.17.		Training as usual. The Divisional Gas Officer attended to-day & gave a lecture & demonstrations in Gas. An N.C.O. went round all Companies for the purpose of fitting helmets. The G.O.C. III Division came round the battalion during training. Expressed his satisfaction with what he saw.	
"	11.2.17.		Church Parade @ 11 am. Two Companies attended. During the afternoon Battalion Headquarters were moved from the present place to the Chateau, which had been vacated in the morning.	
"	12.2.17		Companies continue training as per programme. The Regimental Canteen is being fitted up in the Chateau grounds & promises to surpass anything we have had previously. The weather is breaking, it was much milder to-day.	

2353 Wt. W2544/1454 700,000 5/15 D. D. & L. A.D.S.S./Forms/C. 2118.

Instructions regarding War Diaries and Intelligence Summaries are contained in F. S. Regs., Part II. and the Staff Manual respectively. Title pages will be prepared in manuscript.

WAR DIARY
or
INTELLIGENCE SUMMARY.
(Erase heading not required.)

Army Form C. 2118.

Place	Date	Hour	Summary of Events and Information	Remarks and references to Appendices
LIGNEREUIL	13. 2. 17.		Range practices for D Company & Company training under Company Commanders. C Company went on a working party of spitlocking a system of trenches which are eventually to be dug 4'6" x 2'6" for practice purposes. Two Companies went digging in the morning & two in the afternoon. The ground was very hard & progress was comparatively slow. 2Lt Godfrey & Craig were admitted to hospital.	
"	14.2.17.		Digging party as yesterday. Otherwise nothing to report. 2nd Lt Chalmers was admitted to hospital to-day. The Colonel proceeded on leave to-day, by car to Boulogne.	
"	15.2.17.		Usual digging party & training during the morning.	
	16.2.17		Working party during the morning & training in the afternoon. Range practice for A Company. 2nd Lieut C. Murray was admitted to hospital to-day.	
	17.2.17		Working party & training as usual. 2nd Lieut Chalmers returned from hospital to-day. 2nd Lieut Gappa [illegible] struck off the strength of the battalion. Medical board in England.	

2353 Wt. W2544/1454 700,000 5/15 D. D. & L. A.D.S.S./Forms/C. 2118.

Army Form C. 2118.

Instructions regarding War Diaries and Intelligence Summaries are contained in F. S. Regs., Part II. and the Staff Manual respectively. Title pages will be prepared in manuscript.

WAR DIARY
or
INTELLIGENCE SUMMARY.
(Erase heading not required.)

Place	Date	Hour	Summary of Events and Information	Remarks and references to Appendices
LISNEREUIL	18.2.17		Church parade & Holy Communion service in the Recreation Hut. The battalion have at last secured a clean change of underclothes & baths are being carried on. To-day a draft of 8 men joined the battalion from the base.	
"	19.2.17		Working party & training. [illegible] & the ground in a very sloppy state. C.S.M. Mabbott joined the battalion yesterday & takes up duties as Regimental Sgt Major. Capt B L Hard was admitted to hospital on the 17th. There was a concert in the evening by the 4th Army Troupe.	
"	20.2.17		Working party during the morning as usual. Rain most of the afternoon so parades were confined to indoor subjects. In the evening we were entertained by the 3rd Cinema in our Canteen.	
"	21.2.17		Working party as usual during the morning & training during the afternoon. The concert which should have taken place to-day was unable to come owing to the transport difficulties.	
	22.2.17		Training in Company attack. New formations practised according to G.H.Q instructions. Major Wright & officers were proceeding up the line to ARRAS but that was cancelled on the road. Concert was held in the Canteen in the evening by the 6th Corps Concert Party. Huge success.	

2353 Wt. W2544/1454 700,000 5/15 D. D. & L. A.D.S.S./Forms/C. 2118.

Instructions regarding War Diaries and Intelligence Summaries are contained in F. S. Regs., Part II. and the Staff Manual respectively. Title pages will be prepared in manuscript.

WAR DIARY
or
INTELLIGENCE SUMMARY.
(Erase heading not required.)

Army Form C. 2118.

Place	Date	Hour	Summary of Events and Information	Remarks and references to Appendices
HAUTEVILLE	23.2.17		Major Wright + Company Commanders proceeded to Arras to look over the billets which we are to take over in the immediate future. The battalion paraded @ 11^{30} am ready to march off. HAUTEVILLE was reached @ 2 pm. Billets for men are good, officers poor.	
"	24.2.17		Companies under Company Commanders for attack practice + close order drill. Weather improving + much milder.	
"	25.2.17		Holy Communion + Church parade Services. Quiet day + nothing to report. Good news from SERRE.	
"	26.2.17		Inspection of all men's kit by Commanding Officer during the morning. Companies under Company Commanders. Issue + reading of orders to men re. Arras.	
"	27.2.17		Close order drill + arms drill. Bombing + Lewis Gun instruction. Capt Young returns from Course. Lieut Pappa turns up from England. Better news still from Serre. There was a Cinema performance in the evening by Divisional Cinema.	

2353 Wt. W2544/1454 700,000 5/15 D. D. & L. A.D.S.S./Forms/C. 2118.

Instructions regarding War Diaries and Intelligence Summaries are contained in F. S. Regs., Part II. and the Staff Manual respectively. Title pages will be prepared in manuscript.

WAR DIARY
or
INTELLIGENCE SUMMARY.
(Erase heading not required.)

Army Form C. 2118.

Place	Date	Hour	Summary of Events and Information	Remarks and references to Appendices
ARRAS	28.2.17.		During the morning general clean up of billets + preparation for move to ARRAS. Battalion parade @ 4pm ready to march off. Lieut-Col. J.N. de la Perrelle joined the battalion at HARLUS. Battalion arrived in ARRAS at 7.30 pm. B, C, D Company + Batt. HQ billetted in ARRAS. A Company found the garrison for the ST. SAUVEUR Redoubt. Battalion in billets + position by 8.30 pm. Capt Young returns from Course + takes over command of A Company.	

2353 Wt. W2544/1454 700,000 5/15 D. D. & L. A.D.S.S./Forms/C. 2118.

Instructions regarding War Diaries and Intelligence Summaries are contained in F. S. Regs., Part II. and the Staff Manual respectively. Title pages will be prepared in manuscript.

WAR DIARY
or
INTELLIGENCE SUMMARY.
(Erase heading not required.)

Army Form C. 2118.

8th Yorks Regt
Vol 19

Place	Date	Hour	Summary of Events and Information	Remarks and references to Appendices
ARRAS	1.3.17.		A fine day. The Commanding Officer made a tour of inspection of the battalion front with G.O.C. 8th Infantry Brigade. The R.I.F. are holding the line. Trenches were in fairly good condition but are in need of repair. Situation very quiet except for one German gun firing on "Straf Wood". Remainder of battalion were out on a working party outside ARRAS during the afternoon. Major Marris left the battalion to-day for England to be attached to the 7th Training battalion. 2nd Lt Blum also left for England to take up a post in the Chinese Labour Battalions. ~~Sgt~~ Pte Higginson was wounded to-day by rifle or M.G. bullet standing outside bivouac Canteen. M.O. sicks. Lieut Smith has been unwell during the last fortnight. He was unable to perform any duties to-day.	
ARRAS	2.3.17		Fine day. Commanding Officer made a tour of our sector. Company Commanders & Specialists as well. Situation very quiet. Trenches on the left of line are not as good as on the right. ST. SAVEUR Redoubt requires repair. 2Lt Hoyle returned from Divisional Gunnery Course to-day. M.O's relief arrived this evening. There was no working party to-day. Corps Commander visited Battalion Headquarters to-day.	

Army Form C. 2118.

Instructions regarding War Diaries and Intelligence Summaries are contained in F. S. Regs., Part II. and the Staff Manual respectively. Title pages will be prepared in manuscript.

WAR DIARY
or
INTELLIGENCE SUMMARY.

(Erase heading not required.)

Place	Date	Hour	Summary of Events and Information	Remarks and references to Appendices
ARRAS	3.3.17.		Fine day. Tour of the trenches made by Commanding Officer + Corps Commander. Slight shelling in the St Sauveur Redoubt during the afternoon. 2/Lt W R Moore joined the Battalion, + 2/Lt W S Murray returned from hospital. The Mess entertained the Brigadier at dinner. C.Q.M.S Goddard wounded by shrapnel outside the Company Billet.	
ARRAS	4.3.17		Fine day. Tour of the trenches by Commanding Officer preparatory to taking over. Usual working parties in the morning. The Battalion relieved the 1st Royal Scots Fusiliers in this sector. The night was quiet throughout. The trenches were in a good condition. Work was done preparing for the raid, which was to be made the following morning	
ARRAS	5.3.17.		Snow fell during the previous night and this morning. A raid took place at 8.50 a.m by the 1st Gordon Highlanders from our sector on to the opposite German front line. They captured 21 prisoners and 1 machine gun. Five slightly wounded was the number of their casualties. German artillery retaliation was very weak in comparison. An observer, Pte Bragg, was killed by a rifle grenade landing in the trench. Our front trench on the left was given a warm time as the result of the raid	
ARRAS	6.3.17.		Trenches in a muddy condition as a result of melting of the previous days' snow. Slight frost during the night. Severe bombardment on our front both in the afternoon and evening especially about 8.30 p.m. One casualty occurred during this bombardment, as the result of a shell landing on the parapet	

2353 Wt. W2544/1454 700,000 5/15 D. D. & L. A.D.S.S./Forms/C. 2118.

Instructions regarding War Diaries and Intelligence Summaries are contained in F. S. Regs., Part II. and the Staff Manual respectively. Title pages will be prepared in manuscript.

WAR DIARY
or
INTELLIGENCE SUMMARY.
(*Erase heading not required.*)

Army Form C. 2118.

Place	Date	Hour	Summary of Events and Information	Remarks and references to Appendices
ARRAS	7.3.17		Frost during the early morning. Intensely cold and dull throughout the day. Severe bombardment on left front by Trench Mortars during the morning. On the left of our sector severe bombardment of enemy lines at 8 p m and at 11p m by divisional artillery on our left. Casualties five, two killed and three wounded	
ARRAS	8.3.17		Snow in the early morning. Warmer later in the day. Left front company and centre front subject to shelling about 7a m. Barrage placed on front line of our front, then on to support line. No incident occurred. Lieut Watson slightly wounded by shrapnel, but remaining with the battalion. Casualties four. The Battalion was relieved by the 1st R. S. F in the evening. This relief was successfully effected, and the Battalion returned to billets in the town	
ARRAS	9.3.17		Slightly warmer. Usual working parties supplied by the Battalion while in rest billets. The Commanding Officer of the 7th K. S. L I entertained at dinner, Reverend Vokes at lunch. 2/Lieut Woodhouse attached to the Battalion for Intelligence work.	
ARRAS	10.3.17		Dull, foggy day throughout, accentuated towards the evening. Tour made of the cellars & caves, to be later occupied by the Battalion. Working parties again supplied by the Battalion. 1st R S F have during this period suffered no casualties. Remainder of the day uneventful. 2/Lieut Hoyle left for course at Cammeres	

Instructions regarding War Diaries and Intelligence Summaries are contained in F. S. Regs., Part II. and the Staff Manual respectively. Title pages will be prepared in manuscript.

WAR DIARY
or
INTELLIGENCE SUMMARY.
(Erase heading not required.)

Army Form C. 2118.

Place	Date	Hour	Summary of Events and Information	Remarks and references to Appendices
ARRAS	11.3.17		Weather, fine and warm in the morning turning to dull and wet in the evening. Tour of the caves + cellars made by officers of the Battalion. 2/Lt MICKLETHWAITE returned from course. Arras subjected to shelling during which some twenty to thirty shells fell in the town, fortunately causing few casualties	
ARRAS	12.3.17.		Dull, rainy day throughout, making trenches in a filthy condition. A few shells again fell in Arras. The Battalion relieved the 1st R.S.F. in the line, relief complete at 10.30 p.m. Heavy shelling on left sector at 11 p.m. Casualties 4 killed, 4 wounded.	
ARRAS	13.3.17.		Weather, dull and misty. Trenches in very muddy condition. Continued shelling on left sector. Retaliation asked for twice and on each occasion at least one hour late. During afternoon two or three whiz bangs fell behind Battalion H.Q without great damage. Casualties for day 2 killed, 2 wounded, on left sector.	
ARRAS	14.3.17		Clearer day with occasional light shower. Trenches still very muddy owing to weather conditions. Great trench mortar activity on to our left sector. At 4 p.m the afternoon, several shells fell in the neighbourhood of Battalion H.Q., one falling outside the Mess, hitting the opposite house and causing two casualties (wounded).	

Instructions regarding War Diaries and Intelligence Summaries are contained in F. S. Regs., Part II. and the Staff Manual respectively. Title pages will be prepared in manuscript.

WAR DIARY
or
INTELLIGENCE SUMMARY.
(Erase heading not required.)

Army Form C. 2118.

Place	Date	Hour	Summary of Events and Information	Remarks and references to Appendices
ARRAS	15.3.17		Dull misty morning. In the early morning ~~at~~ between 5.20 a.m and 5.40 a.m, the enemy made a raid on the division on our left, and the fringe of this raid touched our extreme left. One machine gun was put out of action, and also a bombing post: the former by a bomb and the latter in the centre company as the result of the barrage. 2/Lt J. M. LAMB is missing, but believed prisoner of war. Two men are also missing, but believed prisoner of war. Total casualties as result of raid, Missing believed prisoner 1 officer, 2 other ranks, killed 3, wounded 19. Shell, undetonated, landed through Mess kitchen.	
ARRAS	16.3.17		Weather clearer, still slightly dull. Frost during the night of the 15/16th. Daylight relief carried out when we were relieved by the 1st R.S.F.; the relief was effected without incident, and great calm had prevailed during the night 15/16th. One company remained in St SAUVEUR Defences till the 18th. The remainder of the Battalion returned to rest billets in ARRAS. 2/Lt SOUTHWELL returned from course.	
ARRAS	17.3.17		Temperature much warmer, with sunshine. Working party by one company. The Battalion moved from Arras at night for Wanquetin where they stayed for the night. A Company still remains in the St SAUVEUR Redoubt and two platoons also remain in ARRAS for work with the R.E's.	

2353 Wt. W2544/1454 700,000 5/15 D. D. & L. A.D.S.S./Forms/C. 2118.

Army Form C. 2118.

WAR DIARY
or
INTELLIGENCE SUMMARY.
(Erase heading not required.)

Instructions regarding War Diaries and Intelligence Summaries are contained in F. S. Regs., Part II. and the Staff Manual respectively. Title pages will be prepared in manuscript.

Place	Date	Hour	Summary of Events and Information	Remarks and references to Appendices
HAUTEVILLE	18.3.17		The temperature is still warm, but becomes cooler towards the evening. The Battalion moved from WANQUETIN to HAUTEVILLE in the afternoon and took over the old billets. A company from ST SAUVEUR rejoined the Battalion at this place late in the evening. The Germans rumoured to have retreated to beyond their fourth line before Arras. A Company suffered two casualties through shell bursting in Redoubt. Casualties two (wounded).	
HAUTEVILLE	19.3.17		Misty dull day, with slight rain. General cleaning up after the previous tour of the trenches. Rumours that the Germans had retreated from their line in front of Arras & confirmed later in the day.	
HAUTEVILLE	20.3.17		Raining most of the day, with snow. Usual parades in the morning while in rest. The Battalion was ordered to move in the evening to ARRAS for the purpose of working parties. Raining on most of the march up.	
ARRAS	21.3.17		Misty dull day. The Battalion still in billets, but Headquarters changed in the evening. ARRAS shelled during the day, particularly near the Station, causing several casualties. One man, Pte Duffy, slightly wounded during this shelling. All companies on working parties on communication trenches at night.	

2353 Wt. W2544/1454 700,000 5/15 D. D. & L. A.D.S.S./Forms/C. 2118.

Army Form C. 2118.

Instructions regarding War Diaries and Intelligence Summaries are contained in F. S. Regs., Part II. and the Staff Manual respectively. Title pages will be prepared in manuscript.

WAR DIARY
or
INTELLIGENCE SUMMARY.
(Erase heading not required.)

Place	Date	Hour	Summary of Events and Information	Remarks and references to Appendices
ARRAS	22.3.17		Dull day, with snow at intervals. ARRAS again shelled causing a few casualties to other troops. All Companies at night on usual working parties on trenches, to be used as assembly positions	
ARRAS	23.3.17		Bright day, with slight frost. ARRAS shelled at intervals during the day. The Battalion is quartered in cellars. All companies on the usual working party. On the whole everything very quiet. Lt H. Cole went to course at Army School.	
ARRAS	24.3.17		Bright day, with large amount of sunshine. Frost during previous night. All officers of the Battalion photographed in a group as a reminiscence of Arras. Usual working party by all companies. Change to summer time on this day at 11 p.m and all clocks advanced by one hour.	
ARRAS	25.3.17		Morning very bright with sunshine tending towards rain in the evening. Usual working parties by all companies at night. The French Commandant of Arras entertained. 2/Lts F.H. PRINCE; A.W. PRINCE; S.B. WILSON; L.G. RUSSELL; joined the Battalion from England and were taken on the strength.	
ARRAS	26.3.17		Raining most of the day and evening. Working parties both morning and at night as usual. Conference of Battalion Commanders at VI Corps Headquarters. Remainder of day passed without incident of note.	

2353 Wt. W2544/1454 700,000 5/15 D. D. & L. A.D.S.S./Forms/C. 2118.

Army Form C. 2118.

Instructions regarding War Diaries and Intelligence Summaries are contained in F. S. Regs., Part II. and the Staff Manual respectively. Title pages will be prepared in manuscript.

WAR DIARY
or
INTELLIGENCE SUMMARY.
(Erase heading not required.)

Place	Date	Hour	Summary of Events and Information	Remarks and references to Appendices
ARRAS	27.3.17.		Weather very dull with many showers. 2/Lt H. FRANKS joined the Battalion from England, and was taken on the strength. Usual working party during the evening. One casualty, slightly wounded.	
ARRAS	28.3.17.		Very fine day, but rather cold. Usual working party on assembly trenches. Shelling of ARRAS, especially near the Station. No other incident of note.	
ARRAS	29.3.17.		Heavy rain throughout the day, without cessation. Usual working party on trenches which finished the work required during the night. Slight shelling of ARRAS during the day.	
ARRAS	30.3.17.		Weather fine with occasional showers. The Battalion still in billets but left in the evening for HAUTEVILLE, the training area. Shelling of ARRAS, one shell bursting near a party of men of this Battalion, causing two casualties, one killed (Pte Hymans), one seriously wounded (Pte Gattergood).	
HAUTEVILLE	31.3.17.		Weather fine, warm sunshine. Battalion on parade addressed by the G.O.C. 8th Brigade in the morning. In the afternoon the whole Battalion practised methods of attack, diamond formation etc.	

[illegible] Lieut
Adjutant

2353 Wt. W2544/1454 700,000 5/15 D. D. & L. A.D.S.S./Forms/C. 2118.

Instructions regarding War Diaries and Intelligence Summaries are contained in F. S. Regs., Part II. and the Staff Manual respectively. Title pages will be prepared in manuscript.

WAR DIARY
or
INTELLIGENCE SUMMARY.
(Erase heading not required.)

8th Bn E Yorks

8/3

Vol 20

Army Form C. 2118.

Place	Date	Hour	Summary of Events and Information	Remarks and references to Appendices
HAUTEVILLE	1.Apr 17.		Dull rainy day throughout. Usual parades by all Companies, attack formations, bombing and machine gun instruction.	
HAUTEVILLE	2.4.17.		Dull day, cold north wind, intermittent snow. Usual parades by Companies when in rest. Final preparations for forthcoming offensive.	
HAUTEVILLE	3.4.17.		Cold, but fine in the morning tending to rain in the evening. Parades by all Companies to practise attack formations. Final preparations for forthcoming offensive.	
"	4.4.17		Weather still very unsettled which hinders our training considerably. All Commanding Officers were interviewed by the G.O.C. III Division at 8th Inf Bde H.Q. The morning was spent in cleaning up billets & in general preparations for the move to WANQUETIN. The Commanding Officer inspected the battalion at 12 noon. He asked all men "to put their backs into their work during forthcoming operations." – The battalion moved off @ 3.15 pm & was billetted in NISSEN huts @ WANQUETIN.	
WANQUETIN	5.4.17		The morning was spent in dumping our blanket, greatcoats, packs & jerkins. Battle stores were issued. At 2.30 pm there was a celebration of the Holy Communion. Orders were received for us to march off to ARRAS at 7.35 pm but the move was cancelled for 24 hours.	

2353 Wt. W2544/1454 700,000 5/15 D. D. & L. A.D.S.S./Forms/C. 2118.

Instructions regarding War Diaries and Intelligence Summaries are contained in F. S. Regs., Part II. and the Staff Manual respectively. Title pages will be prepared in manuscript.

WAR DIARY
or
INTELLIGENCE SUMMARY.
(Erase heading not required.)

Army Form C. 2118.

Place	Date	Hour	Summary of Events and Information	Remarks and references to Appendices
WANQUETIN	6.4.17		Weather appalling. Preparations were made for the move in the evening. The day was a dreary one waiting for the hour of departure. The battalion paraded & marched off @ 7.28 pm. G.O.C. III Divisional saw us off. He expressed his confidence that we should do well. The Divisional band played the battalion out at the starting point to the tune of "Take me back to Blighty". Men were in good spirits. We arrived in ARRAS at the sewer entrance at 11.30 pm. Some congestion. At 2 am the battalion was installed in the AUCKLAND CAVES.	
THE CAVES ARRAS	7.4.17.		Cold dark & smelly was our dwelling place. However we made the best of it. Conference at Brigade HQ at 11 am. Otherwise nothing to report. Companies held concerts in the evening. Everyone full of "buck". Up above our guns were pumping letters into Germany.	
"	8.4.17		Brigade Conference at 11 am. More about the BROWN LINE & final points settled. To-morrow is "DER TAG". The Bombardments continues day & night. Huns scarcely replies. Sleep impossible, too cold. During the evening the 9th Brigade moves into position via our CAVES, 76th Bde follow.	
THE BATTLE.			Brigade & Battalion operation orders attached. At 2 am 8th East Yorks leave their Caves & move into position in the assembly trenches. By 3 am everything is ready. A weary night of waiting. TANKS come puffing along & take up position. At 4 am the guns cease firing.	

2353 Wt. W2544/1454 700,000 5/15 D. D. & L. A.D.S.S./Forms/C. 2118.

Instructions regarding War Diaries and Intelligence Summaries are contained in F. S. Regs., Part II. and the Staff Manual respectively. Title pages will be prepared in manuscript.

WAR DIARY
or
INTELLIGENCE SUMMARY.
(Erase heading not required.)

Army Form C. 2118.

Place	Date	Hour	Summary of Events and Information	Remarks and references to Appendices
THE BATTLE	9.4.17		Everything is quiet once more. Zero hour arrives 5.30 am. Off go all the guns, guns & more guns everywhere. By 7 am the 76th Brigade with the 1st Gordons + 10 Royal Welsh Fusiliers leading, supported by the 8th K.O.R.L. had captured by the entire front line system. It was now time for the 9th Brigade to advance. In the front line were the 4th ROYAL FUSILIERS 12th West Yorks + 13th Kings supported by the 2nd Suffolks + 1st Northumberland Fusiliers. TILLOY was carefully mopped up, Bois de Boeufs cleared & the HARP captured by 9.30 am. At 10.30 am the 8th Brigade went forward with the 1st Royal Scots + 7th KSLI in the front line, followed by the 8th East Yorks + supported by the 2nd Royal Scots Fusiliers. The enemy shelling was not very severe. There were very few dead lying about. Most of the dead were German. Most of the enemy were killed + buried alive or dead in their dug outs, where they had been caught like so many rats. Just before Headquarters got to the HARP 2nd Lieut TYRRELL was killed by a sniper. 2nd Lieut CHALMERS was also wounded earlier on in the Assembly trenches but he returned to his company. On we went. By this time most of the battalion had been absorbed in the front line. Battalion Headquarters were established in some	

2353 Wt. W2544/1454 700,000 5/15 D. D. & L. A.D.S.S./Forms/C. 2118.

Instructions regarding War Diaries and Intelligence Summaries are contained in F. S. Regs., Part II. and the Staff Manual respectively. Title pages will be prepared in manuscript.

WAR DIARY
or
INTELLIGENCE SUMMARY.
(Erase heading not required.)

Army Form C. 2118.

Place	Date	Hour	Summary of Events and Information	Remarks and references to Appendices
			Gun pits of the WANCOURT Road. Many prisoners were now coming back. They all said they were fed up with war. Reports were now coming back from the front line that operations were being hung up on account of cross machine gun fire. Reinforcements were sent up, 1st RSF, 1st Gordons & the K.O.R.L. going forward. 2nd Lt James, Wilson, Kinnear, Corrie had become casualties. It was now getting late in the afternoon & the BROWN LINE had not yet been captured. Battalion HQ went forward. The 1st Gordons were to attack @ 7 pm, supported by the King's Own Royal Lancasters. The 8th Bde were to attack @ the same time. The attack failed, machine gun fire from FEUCHY holding up our infantry & causing many casualties. 2nd Lt HOYLE was killed in this attempt. 2nd Lt PRINCE F.H. was killed during the afternoon. 2nd Lieut WATSON was wounded & C.S.M. APPLEBY was killed in BOIS DE BOEUFS. Night came on & everything was quiet again. The enemy made no attempt to counter attack.	
THE BATTLE	10.4.17		At 2 am orders were received from Division that the 9th Brigade would attack the BROWN LINE at 8.15 am. There was a conference @ Brigade. The attack was eventually postponed till 12 noon. Artillery support was to be had. Battalion Headquarters moved forward to a dug out in the Sunken Road.	

Instructions regarding War Diaries and Intelligence Summaries are contained in F. S. Regs., Part II. and the Staff Manual respectively. Title pages will be prepared in manuscript.

WAR DIARY
or
INTELLIGENCE SUMMARY.

(Erase heading not required.)

Army Form C. 2118.

Place	Date	Hour	Summary of Events and Information	Remarks and references to Appendices
			Preparations were made, Ammunition & bombs were brought up. At 11.45 am the artillery opened fire on the front line & the Infantry advanced to the attack. Left to Right. KSLI, RSF, RS, EY. The enemy fled & the position was captured by 12.30 pm. Fifty prisoners were taken. 2nd Lieut ELLIOTT was killed, 2nd Lt SOUTHWELL was wounded & died later. 2nd Lieut FRANKS was wounded. The BROWN LINE was consolidated. The enemy shelled somewhat otherwise nothing to report. The Cavalry came up [?] & took up position. They were fairly heavily shelled all night.	
THE BATTLE	11.4.17		Battalion Headquarters moved up to the front line. The 12th & 14th Divisions were relieved during the night. The 11th Division was to continue the attack, the final objective being VIS-EN-ARTOIS. 2nd Lieut Moore & 2nd Lieut Bedale [?] were both wounded. We had only 3 officers left with the battalion. Cpt Hayes, 2nd Lt Cox, Robinson & Micklethwaite joined the battalion later on. The weather was terrible, snow & rain. Very cold wind. 2nd Lt Craig took command of A Coy, 2nd Lt Pappa B Coy, Cpt Smith C Coy, Cpt Hayes D Coy. 9th E. Yorks [?] with the other battalions of the Brigade now hold the BROWN LINE & are to hold	

Instructions regarding War Diaries and Intelligence Summaries are contained in F. S. Regs., Part II. and the Staff Manual respectively. Title pages will be prepared in manuscript.

WAR DIARY
or
INTELLIGENCE SUMMARY.

(*Erase heading not required.*)

Army Form C. 2118.

Place	Date	Hour	Summary of Events and Information	Remarks and references to Appendices
			themselves in readiness to support any further attacks to be made by the 9th Brigade on GUEMAPPE	
THE BATTLE	12.4.17		The weather still continues to be very unsettled occasionally the Seventh Royal Scots send a fighting patrol into WANCOURT & find the place to be evacuated. Patrol sent towards GUEMAPPE also report that the village is clear, but no certain. The 9th Brigade came up & took over the advanced positions, 12th West Yorks & 1st Northumberland Fusiliers supported by 4th Royal Fusiliers & 13th Kings respectively. A large mine was exploded in GUEMAPPE during the afternoon. Night came on again cold & quiet. Men are getting very weary.	
THE BATTLE	13.4.17		The day started fine. Hostile shelling from the Right (to south). An attack by the 9th Brigade on GUEMAPPE & Ridge ~~was~~ to be undertaken to-day, in conjunction with the 50th & 29th Divisions N & S. The final objective being VIS-EN-ARTOIS. The 8th Brigade were to support the 9th where necessary. The 29th Division attack was cancelled. The attack was launched @ 7 pm & was a complete failure. The 9th Brigade suffered many casualties. The 8th Brigade was not called upon. It was now getting dark, no further operations were undertaken. The 3rd Division was relieved during the night by the . Division	

Instructions regarding War Diaries and Intelligence Summaries are contained in F. S. Regs., Part II. and the Staff Manual respectively. Title pages will be prepared in manuscript.

WAR DIARY
or
INTELLIGENCE SUMMARY.
(Erase heading not required.)

Army Form C. 2118.

Place	Date	Hour	Summary of Events and Information	Remarks and references to Appendices
THE BATTLE + ARRAS	14.4.17		At 1230 pm we were informed that we were no longer required + so the battalion left the BROWN LINE for billets in ARRAS arriving there between 2 + 3 am. Nothing in particular was done during the day. Billets were rearranged otherwise nothing to report.	
ARRAS	15/4/17		Rain. Quiet day. Casualty reports + many other reports were rendered to Brigade. News from Lieuts Moore + Chalmers who are both in Hospital in France somewhere. The Divisional Commander came round to Bn H.Q. + expressed his great satisfaction with the battalion. The remainder of the day was uneventful.	
ARRAS	16.4.17		Nothing much doing. Companies refitted with clothing + deficiencies made up. Billets of all battalions were changed + after some confusion we settled in our old Headquarters RUE GAUGIERE. Otherwise nothing to report.	
ARRAS	17.4.17		Battalion paraded @ 9.30 am on the Race Course. Owing to wet weather the parade was cancelled. Company Officers' meeting @ H.Q. Draft of 136 O.R. with 2nd Lieut Mathews arrived from the 37th I.B.D. A poor looking lot of men most of them of the C2 + C3 class. Many of them have not been out before. 2nd Lieut Mathews takes over command of B Coy. Capt Young returned as well as 2nd Lt Knee. The remainder of the day was uneventful	

2353 Wt. W2544/1454 700,000 5/15 D. D. & L. A.D.S.S./Forms/C. 2118.

Instructions regarding War Diaries and Intelligence Summaries are contained in F. S. Regs., Part II. and the Staff Manual respectively. Title pages will be prepared in manuscript.

WAR DIARY
or
INTELLIGENCE SUMMARY.
(Erase heading not required.)

Army Form C. 2118.

Place	Date	Hour	Summary of Events and Information	Remarks and references to Appendices
ARRAS	18/4/17		Rain, rain, always more rain. Instructions in bombing & Lewis Gunning carried on in billets. Good news from the French push. The usual parades & training of the battalion. Enemy shell ARRAS with H.E. & Gas shells. Otherwise nothing to report.	
"	19/4/17		Usual training in the morning. N.C.O.s parade in the afternoon.	
"	20/4/17		Training the morning. Draft arrived 2nd Lieut Edwards + 136 O.R. Capt Young & 2nd Lt L Milton rejoin battalion from FREVENT. The physique of the men not too bad. Concert to-night & merry evening by Depot Extracts	
"	21/4/17		Companies in attack practice. Recruits & N.C.Os in the afternoon under the R.S.M. G.O.C. inspected the Draft @ 2 pm. A further reinforcement of 46 O.R. arrived at 6 pm from 37th I.B.D. Otherwise nothing of importance to report. Officers joined 2nd Lt Salton, Outram, Esc, Bibby, Cole, McIntyre & Blittaun.	
"	22/4/17		Battalion parade @ 9.30 am for battalion in attack. Weather fair. Parade finished @ 12 noon. Concert in the afternoon by the Band of the 4th East Yorks.	
"	23/4/17		The attack by the 17, 15, 29 & 50 Divisions was launched @ 4 this morning. 3rd Division in Corps reserve hoping against hope that we shall not be called upon. Weather fine. There was no news of the	

2353 Wt. W2544/1454 700,000 5/15 D. D. & L. A.D.S.S./Forms/C. 2118.

Instructions regarding War Diaries and Intelligence Summaries are contained in F. S. Regs., Part II. and the Staff Manual respectively. Title pages will be prepared in manuscript.

WAR DIARY
or
INTELLIGENCE SUMMARY.
(Erase heading not required.)

Army Form C. 2118.

Place	Date	Hour	Summary of Events and Information	Remarks and references to Appendices
ARRAS	23/4/17		attack until 1 pm when we received orders to proceed to the GLENGARRY TRENCH + await further orders. We left ARRAS at 9.15 pm R S Fus. followed us + took up position on our right. R F + K S L I in support. Position was taken up by 3.30 pm. Weather fine + sunny. No shelling. We were scarcely settled when we received orders to to man the BROWN LINE. At 4.30 pm the battalion moved off there was no shelling until we reached the BROWN LINE. The position was occupied by 6.30 pm. Cpl Cunningham was the only casualty coming up. K.O.S.B Gordons + H L I of the 15 Div were in our line. The night was quiet. CAMBRAI ROAD was shelled during the night causing D Company one killed + 3 wounded.	
BROWN LINE	24/4/17		Glorious weather. Morning quiet. At 4.15 pm 15th Division attacked the BLUE LINE. The position then was, 17th Div no advance, 29th + 50 Divisions in BLUE LINE, 15 Div about to attack. The attack succeeded + some prisoners taken. BROWN LINE shelled at 6 pm. At 8 pm we received orders to take over that part of the B. LINE, N. of the CAMBRAI Road held by the 10th R. H. Fus. 9 pm the move started + was completed by midnight. Rotten trenches + bad accomodation for officers. Bn HQ in a machine Gun emplacement. The night was fairly quiet	

2353 Wt. W2544/1454 700,000 5/15 D. D. & L. A.D.S.S./Forms/C. 2118.

Instructions regarding War Diaries and Intelligence Summaries are contained in F. S. Regs., Part II. and the Staff Manual respectively. Title pages will be prepared in manuscript.

WAR DIARY
or
INTELLIGENCE SUMMARY.
(Erase heading not required.)

Army Form C. 2118.

Place	Date	Hour	Summary of Events and Information	Remarks and references to Appendices
BROWN LINE	25/4/17		At 3.30 am the 17 Division attacked its sector of BLUE LINE. Objectives partially gained. Enemy machine gun & rifle fire v. severe. BROWN LINE shelled & A Company suffer 1 killed & 5 wounded, including Sgt Howard. The remainder of day was uneventful.	
"	26/4/17		Quiet in our part. MONCHY badly shelled as usual. Battalion move from its present position to cheap dug outs off the FEUCHY ROAD. General anxiety that MONCHY might be severely attacked. 8th Bn East Yorks to hold itself in readiness to proceed at a moment's notice to support 76th Infantry Bde. Our guns fire incessantly day & night. Sleep for troops out of the question, yet we are what we are in admirable "Rest billets" (!)	
"	27/4/17		Enemy shelled round Bn HQ for several hours during the night. This was most upsetting. Fortunately we are spared. Quiet again towards morning. We have to stand by all day in our "bund". Two slight casualties in 'C' Coy. Heavy shelling around Bn HQ. Night quiet.	
	28/4/17		Weather fine which is one big blessing. 12th Division attack in order to complete task left undone by 17th Division. RIFLE-BAYONET TRENCH partially captured. Battalion stands by again. Things are fairly OK with us. 8th E.Y. take over Bn Headquarters [struck out] from K.S.L.I. in the BROWN LINE. A good dug out. Night Quiet. BROWN LINE tried, but not the usual British thoroughness [illegible] in places	

Instructions regarding War Diaries and Intelligence Summaries are contained in F. S. Regs., Part II. and the Staff Manual respectively. Title pages will be prepared in manuscript.

WAR DIARY
or
INTELLIGENCE SUMMARY.
(Erase heading not required.)

Army Form C. 2118.

Place	Date	Hour	Summary of Events and Information	Remarks and references to Appendices
BROWN LINE	28/4/17		C.O. goes back to Details for two days. Major Wright takes over Command.	
"	29/4/17		Fine & very warm. Morning quiet. Hostile shelling reported to have slackened considerably. Company Commanders reconnoitre trenches & approaches during the afternoon. Enemy shells batteries near BROWN LINE & all around Bn. H.Q. Captain Hoyer killed & 2nd Lieut Brittain wounded. 3 men killed & 2 wounded. Cox takes over command of D Coy. pro tem. Hostile shelling resumed after a short stop. MONCHY, FOSSE FARM & MONCHY DEFENCES heavily shelled during the afternoon. The night was fairly quiet.	
"	30/4/17		Fine weather continues. Great artillery fight @ 3 am which lasted till about 4.30 am. Situation normal @ 5 am. Major Wright, Cox & Matthews went round the line. There was a conference @ Brigade H Quarters @ 11 am. Brigadier was wounded to-day. Brigade Signalling Officer killed by the same shell. Colonel returned from details this morning. Afternoon quiet & uneventful. All plans & preliminary orders issued for the next attack on the RED LINE. Arrangements made for the relief of the 1st R.S.F. in the line. Battalion moved off @ 8.15 pm. There was little hostile shelling. Relief complete by 10.20 pm the night was fairly quiet.	

R.H. Dillon Lieut & Adj.

2353 Wt. W2544/1454 700,000 5/15 D. D. & L. A.D.S.S./Forms/C. 2118.

8th Inf. Bde.

Report on Operations of April 9th 1917.

The 8th Bn East Yorkshire Regt., less one Company were in support to the two leading Battalions, - 2nd Bn The Royal Scots, and the 7th K.S.L.I.

"C" Company was told off as a Mopping Up Company, two platoons being allotted to each of the attacking Battalions. This Company carried on its work of mopping up and finally became absorbed in the attacking Battalions.

The remaining Companies, moved forward in support and gradually became absorbed in the attacking Battalions.

The leading wave had gone too far forward and filled up gaps which appeared to exist in the attacking Battalions, until such time as the attacking line was held up by heavy machine Gun fire from FEUCHY.

Acting on instructions issued to Company Commanders, they supported the Gordons, who had to withdraw at the same time owing to heavy machine Gun fire. Two Companies then took up a position on the Sunken road, which was consolidated where we were joined up by the Bedfords later on during the night, the right Companies having taken up a position North and South of the NANTES TRENCH which was also consolidated.

Later on during the night, acting on instructions from the G.O.C. 8th Inf. Bde., the Battalion was re-organised preparatory to the attack which was successfully carried out on the 10th inst, and the position consolidated.

[signature]

Lieut.-Colonel,
Commanding 8th Bn East Yorkshire Regt.

15/4/17.

REPORT ON OPERATIOBS CARRIED OUT BY THE

8th BN EAST YORKSHIRE REGT.

during the period April 23rd to May 15th 1917.

****

April 23rd. The attack by the 17th, 15th, 29th and 30th Divisions was launched at 4 am. this morning. We were in Corps Reserve. The attack continued until 1 pm when we received orders to proceed to Glengarry Trench and await further orders. We left ARRAS at 2.15 pm. R.S.F'S followed us and took up position on our right. Royal Scots and K.S.L.I. in support.

Position was taken up by 3.15 pm. weather fine, no shelling. We had scarcely settled when we received orders to move to the BROWN LINE.At 4.30 pm. the Battalion moved off. There was no shelling until the BROWN LINE was reached- this position was occupied by 6.30 pm. We had one Casualty coming up. K.O.S.B., GORDONS, and H.L.I. of the 15th Division were in the line. The night was quiet. CAMBRAI ROAD was shelled during the night. "D" Coy. had one killed and one man wounded.

April 24th. Fine weather-morning quiet.

At 4.15 pm. 15th Division attacked the BLUE LINE . The position there was 17th Division in Advance, 29th and 50th Divisions in the BLUE LINE , 15th Division about to attack. This attack succeeded, and some prisoners were taken. BROWN LINE shelled at 6 pm. At 8 pm. we received orders to take over that part of the BROWN LINE, NORTH of the CAMBRAI ROAD held by the 10th R.D.F'S. At 9 pm, the move started, and was completed by midnight. Poor trenches and bad accomodation for Officers. B.H.Q. in Machine Gun Emplacement. The night was fairly quiet.

April 25th. At 3.30 am. the 17th Division attacked its sector of the BLUE LINE. Objectives partially gained. Enemy machine gun and rifle fire very severe. BROWN LINE shelled and "D" Coy. suffer 1 Killed an d 5 wounded, (including Sgt Howard). The remainder of the day was uneventful.

April 26th. Quiet in our part. MONCHY badly shelled as usual. Battalion moves from its present position to deep dugouts off the FEUCHY ROAD. General anxiety that MONCHY might be severely attacked. 8th East Yorks. to be in readiness to move at a moments notice, to support 76th Infantry Brigade. Our guns fire ceaselessly day and night. Sleep for troops out of the question, yet we are told we are in "excellent rest billets ".

April 27th. Enemy shelled Battalion Headquarters for several hours during the night . Quiet again towards the morning. We have to "stand by" all the day. Two slight casualties in "C" Coy. More shelling round Battalion Headquarters. Night quiet.

April 28th. Weather fine. 12th Division attack in order to complete task left undone by 17th Division. RIFLE and BAYONET TRENCH partially captured. Battalion "stands by" again. 8th Bn East Yorks. take over Battalion Headquarters from the 7th K.S.L.I. in the BROWN LINE. Night quiet. BROWN LINE WIRED.

April 29th. Fine and very warm. Morning quiet. Hostile shelling reported to have slackened considerably. Company Commanders reconnoitre trenches and approaches during the afternoon. Enemy shells batteries near the BROWN LINE, and all around B.H.Q. Captain Hayes killed, 2/Lt. Brittain wounded, 3 men killed and two wounded. 2/Lt. A.J.Cox takes over command of "D" Coy. pro tem. Hostile shelling resumed after a short stop. MONCHY, FOSSE FARM, and MONCHY DEFENCES heavily shelled during the afternoon. The night was fairly quiet.

April 30th. Fine weather continues . Great artillery fight at 3 am. which lasted till about 4.30 am. Situation normal again at 5 am. Major Wright, Cox and Lieut. Matthews went round the line. There was a conference at Brigade Headquarters at 11am. Brigadier was wounded today. Wireless Officer killed by the same shell. Afternoon quiet and uneventful. All plans and preliminary orders issued for the next attack on the RED LINE. Arrangements made for the relief of the R.S.F. in the line. Battalion moved off at 8.15 pm. There was little hostile shelling . Relief complete by 10.30 pm. The night was fairly quiet.

May 1st. The enemy put up a heavy barrage in the morning mostly ~~xxxxxxx~~ behind our front line. MONCHY was shelled intermittently during the day. The R.S.F. returned to take up their Battle Position, also the Royal Scots. Night quiet except for usual shelling of MONCHY.

May 2nd. Morning quiet. MONCHY shelled as usual. German batteries were subjected to a heavy Gas Shell bombardment which caused him to do the same in the evening. while the relief was taking place and other troops were moving into their assembly positions. A number of casualties occurred and a panic ensued. K.S.L.I. joined us in our Headquarters.

May 3rd MONCHY - THE BATTLE. The troops were scarcely in position and many were caught in the open. Zero hour was very dark. The enemy was very quick with his barrage No reports were received until late in the day, when news that the attack was a failure filtered through. A few yards were gained here and there, and many of our people got behind the German Front Line, but the enemy got in behind and from the flanks with his machine guns and our casualties were very heavy. A few posts were put out in front of the 8th Bde sector, but could not be held without very great loss of life. Other Brigades were back in their o front lines by nightfall. The total casualties were 35 killed, 161 wounded, and 39 missing. Officer casualties were also very heavy. At 9.30 pm, there was a terrible "straf" no doubt the Germans thought we would try a night attack. Remainder of night fairly quiet. All night long the wounded came in.

May 4th. As expected, orders were received to reorganise in view of future operations. This could not take place until after dark. Wounded were evacuated in NO MAN'S LAND under the Red Cross Flag. MONCHY and the outskirts were heavily shelled all day and night. Wounded still come walking and crawling in. After dark reorganisation took place. Battalion Headquarters were intermittently crumped all day. All details and last draft rejoin the Battalion in the line. Work on posts and trenches commenced.

May 5th. Comparatively quiet. Relief expected, but instead of rekief we find large working parties, for consolidation purposes.

May 6th. We are to be relieved tonight. Relief commence ed at 10 pm. Complete 5.30 am.

May 7th. Battalion now in old German Front Line North of TILLOY.

May 8th. Nothing to report.

May 9th. Working party in the evening. Digging Communication Trench, WEST of MONCHY.

May 10th. Battalion takes up position in the BROWN LINE, North of CAMBRAI LINE. Working party on C.T. West of MONCHY in the evening.

May 11th. 12th Division attacked TOOL TRENCH, and gained their objective. Working party during the evening deepening trench South of MONCHY.

May 12th. 76th Infantry Brigade attack DEVIL'S TRENCH. Usual working party at night.

May 13th. Working party on VINE STREET. C.T. at night.

May 14th. BROWN LINE quiet during the day. We were relieved by the ESSEX Regiment. Relief commenced 11.45 pm. and was complete by 1 am. Battalion marched to ARRAS, arriving 3 am.15/5/17. Billetted at LEVIS BARRACKS.

May 15th. Left ARRAS 8.45 am. and arrived at BERNEVILLE at 11 am.

Lieut.-Colonel,
Commanding 8th Bn East Yorkshire Regt.

17/5/17.

Instructions regarding War Diaries and Intelligence Summaries are contained in F. S. Regs., Part II. and the Staff Manual respectively. Title pages will be prepared in manuscript.

WAR DIARY
or
INTELLIGENCE SUMMARY.
(Erase heading not required.)

Army Form C. 2118.

8 E York Rgt
Vol 21

8/3

Place	Date	Hour	Summary of Events and Information	Remarks and references to Appendices
MONCHY.	1/5/17.		The month of May has started well with real hot weather. Practice barrage this morning. Enemy put heavy barrage on & mostly behind our front line. Remainder of day quiet. One killed and three wounded. Monchy shelled intermittently all day. R.S.F. return to the line to take up their battle position & also the Royal Scots. Night quiet except for usual shelling of MONCHY and its outskirts.	
	2/5/17		Fine and warm. Morning quiet & uneventful. MONCHY shelled as usual as well as the vicinity of H.Q. German batteries were subjected to heavy gas shell bombardment. During the evening while the relief was taking place and troops were moving into their assembly positions, the enemy retaliated. Quite a number of casualties were caused. It was a horrible night. Quite one of the worst in this period.	
MONCHY the Battle	3/5/17.		At 3-45 am the attack started. Enemy was very quick with his barrage. 2/Lt Knee was killed before the start. The attack was not successful, but posts were established	

A5834 Wt. W4973/M687 750,000 8/16 D. D. & L. Ltd. Forms/C.2118/13.

Instructions regarding War Diaries and Intelligence Summaries are contained in F. S. Regs., Part II. and the Staff Manual respectively. Title pages will be prepared in manuscript.

WAR DIARY
or
INTELLIGENCE SUMMARY.
(Erase heading not required.)

Army Form C. 2118.

Place	Date	Hour	Summary of Events and Information	Remarks and references to Appendices
MONCHY The Battle (cont'd)	3/5/17		in front of the 8th Bde sector. The battalion had many casualties. Our good Padré, Capt C. W. Mitchell was mortally wounded during the afternoon while attending to our wounded under terrible shell fire. Other officers killed were 2nd Lt Dalton Cox, McIntyre. 2nd Lt Price died of wounds. 2nd Lt Le Breton Edwards were wounded. 2nd Lt Bibby is missing. Total casualties. 35 killed 161 wounded 39 missing.	
—	4/5/17		Orders were received, in view of further operations, to re-organise. Wounded were evacuated from no man's land under the Red Cross flag. At dark re-organisation taken place. Capt Smith, 2Lts Pappa & Murray all details and last draft join the battalion in the line. Work on posts & trenches commenced. Work on posts and trenches commenced.	
—	5/5/17		Batt H.Q. intermittently shelled all night. Day comparatively quiet. At night working parties on posts, C.T's out to them. DALE TRENCH made into a fire step. 2Lt Pappa killed on this job.	

A5834 Wt. W4973/M687 750,000 8/16 D. D. & L. Ltd. Forms/C.2118/13.

Instructions regarding War Diaries and Intelligence Summaries are contained in F. S. Regs., Part II. and the Staff Manual respectively. Title pages will be prepared in manuscript.

WAR DIARY
or
INTELLIGENCE SUMMARY.
(Erase heading not required.)

Army Form C. 2118.

Place	Date	Hour	Summary of Events and Information	Remarks and references to Appendices
MONCHY	5/5/17		He was buried where he fell. Works proceeded under heavy sniping and occasional shelling. – Casualties 20.	
	6/5/17		A lovely day. Hostile shelling as usual but situation generally quieter. We are to be relieved to-night by the 9th Bde "Shaking out" to the South & taking over our front and joining up with the 56th Div. Relief commences @ 10pm. At 5.30am message received that relief was complete.	
TILLOY	7/5/17		Battalion now in old German trench system N. of Tilloy. Baths for men in ARRAS. Rest, repairs and refitting commenced. Weather beautifully fine.	
	8/5/17		Weather beautiful and fine. Very quiet life nothing to report. Thunder is in the air. A little rain towards night.	

A5834 Wt. W4973/M687 750,000 8/16 D. D. & L. Ltd. Forms/C.2118/13.

Instructions regarding War Diaries and Intelligence Summaries are contained in F. S. Regs., Part II. and the Staff Manual respectively. Title pages will be prepared in manuscript.

WAR DIARY
or
INTELLIGENCE SUMMARY.
(Erase heading not required.)

Army Form C. 2118.

Place	Date	Hour	Summary of Events and Information	Remarks and references to Appendices
TILLOY	8/5/17		~~Weather beautiful & fine. Very quiet. Nothing to report [illegible] At the [illegible] night~~	
"	9/5/17		Wet morning & miles of mud. Clear during the day. Working parties in the evening. Capt Young wounded & departs	
"	10/5/17		Fine day. Nothing of importance. Battalion takes up position in the BROWN LINE, N. of CAMBRAI ROAD. Heavy artillery fire @ 8pm. Companies out on working party. Night fairly quiet & uneventful.	
BROWN LINE H34 central	11/5/17		Fine day very warm. Quiet morning except for occasional shells on the FEUCHY Road. Nothing much to report. During the afternoon strong points W & N of MONCHY were reconnoitred. BROWN LINE & batteries in rear were shelled all the afternoon. At 8.30pm 12 Division attack TOOL trench. 164 men on working party. The results of the attack were good. Corps on our left gaining all objectives & the 168 Bde. of the 56 Division gaining TOOL TRENCH & CAVALRY FARM.	

2353 Wt. W2544/1454 700,000 5/15 D. D. & L. A.D.S.S./Forms/C. 2118.

Instructions regarding War Diaries and Intelligence Summaries are contained in F. S. Regs., Part II. and the Staff Manual respectively. Title pages will be prepared in manuscript.

WAR DIARY
or
INTELLIGENCE SUMMARY.
(Erase heading not required.)

Army Form C. 2118.

Place	Date	Hour	Summary of Events and Information	Remarks and references to Appendices
BROWN LINE	12/5/17		Weather very fine & warm. Hostile Artillery less active. Attack by 76th Brigade on DEVILS TRENCH. Usual working parties at night, & the last we hope.	
"	13/5/17		Weather still very fine & warm. BROWN LINE has been very quiet to-day. Result of yesterday's attacks not known, believed to be bad. Working party in the evening of 183 men on VINE STREET C.T.	
"	14/5/17		Weather fine. We are to be relieved to-night. The day was spent in cleaning surroundings of trenches & collecting salvage. Transport came up early in the day for the purpose of removing blankets & great coats. At 11.30 pm. some elements of the 1st ESSEX turned up & the relief was complete @ 1 am. Companies marched independently to ARRAS. Enemy did not worry at all with shell fire.	
ARRAS			Arrived in billets just before dawn & got there in broad day light. An early start was necessary and	

2353 Wt. W2544/1454 700,000 5/15 D. D. & L. A.D.S.S./Forms/C. 2118.

Instructions regarding War Diaries and Intelligence Summaries are contained in F. S. Regs., Part II. and the Staff Manual respectively. Title pages will be prepared in manuscript.

WAR DIARY
or
INTELLIGENCE SUMMARY.
(Erase heading not required.)

Army Form C. 2118.

Place	Date	Hour	Summary of Events and Information	Remarks and references to Appendices
	15/5/17		day Battalion was clear of billets by 9.0 am & marched by companies to BERNEVILLE. Everything in the shape of billets had been previously arranged. At DAINVILLE the battalion formed up less D coy who had taken the wrong turning. Battalion arrived in BERNEVILLE about dinner time. All men were accomodated in one large barn and altogether billets were very satisfactory.	
BERNEVILLE	16/5/17		The day was spent quietly namely in cleaning clothes & equipment, haircutting etc. Weather still splendid. Nothing further to report.	
"	17/5/17		Companies paraded under company commanders. G.O.C. Division should have inspected the battalion but on account of the rain was cancelled. Lt. J. A. Stephens & Lt. G. E. R. Lacey joined the battalion for duty.	
"	18/5/17		The Battn. marched to GOUY-EN-ARTOIS where the night was spent. On the route the battalion marched past the major general	

A5834 Wt. W4973/M687 750,000 8/16 D. D. & L. Ltd. Forms/C.2118/13.

Instructions regarding War Diaries and Intelligence Summaries are contained in F. S. Regs., Part II. and the Staff Manual respectively. Title pages will be prepared in manuscript.

WAR DIARY
or
INTELLIGENCE SUMMARY.
(*Erase heading not required.*)

Army Form C. 2118.

Place	Date	Hour	Summary of Events and Information	Remarks and references to Appendices
Gouy-en-Artois	19/5/17		The Battalion left Gouy-en-Artois at 9.0 am and marched to Izel-lez-Hameau, for re-organisation and training.	
Izel-lez-Hameau	20/5/17		The Battalion paraded for Divine Service on the village Green. The service was conducted by the senior Padre of the Division.	
"	21/5/17		Training commenced. The Battn. marched to the training ground at Givenchy-le-Noble and carried out the programme of training Part 1. Major Monro, M. Gordon Hldrs. joined the Battn as 2nd i/c	
	22/5/17		On account of the rain, training had to be carried out in billets. Lt. H.S. Williams returned to duty and took over the command of 'A' coy from Lt Stephens who took over duties as assistant adjutant and L.G.O.	
	23/5/17		Fine day. Hot and sunny. Battn carried out training on the training ground near IZEL-LEZ-HAMEAU	

A5834 Wt. W4973/M687 750,000 8/16 D. D. & L. Ltd. Forms/C.2118/13.

Army Form C. 2118.

Instructions regarding War Diaries and Intelligence Summaries are contained in F. S. Regs., Part II. and the Staff Manual respectively. Title pages will be prepared in manuscript.

WAR DIARY
or
INTELLIGENCE SUMMARY.
(Erase heading not required.)

Place	Date	Hour	Summary of Events and Information	Remarks and references to Appendices
IZEL-LEZ-HAMEAU	23/5/17	(cont)	Lt. Col. de la Perelle, Lt. Fulton, 2/Lt. Murray, proceeded on leave to England.	
	24/5/17		Fine day & very hot. Battn at training. The Major General inspected the Battn. at work.	
	25/5/17		Good weather still holds. Battn paraded according to programme – section training. In the evening the Battn. played the 2nd Royal Scots at football. We lost, the result being 2 – 1.	
	26/5/17		Very hot and sunny. Section training. Football match in the afternoon A coy v B coy. B. won 2 – nil. The "Elegant Extracts" 4th RF's, gave an excellent show on the village green.	

A5834 Wt. W4973/M687 750,000 8/16 D. D. & L. Ltd. Forms/C.2118/13.

Instructions regarding War Diaries and Intelligence Summaries are contained in F. S. Regs., Part II. and the Staff Manual respectively. Title pages will be prepared in manuscript.

WAR DIARY
or
INTELLIGENCE SUMMARY.
(Erase heading not required.)

Army Form C. 2118.

Place	Date	Hour	Summary of Events and Information	Remarks and references to Appendices
IZEL-LEZ-HAMEAU.	27/5/15		Still very hot and sunny. Battn parade for Divine Service on the Village Green at 9-45 am.	
	28/5/17		The glorious weather still continues. A company fired on the range in the morning & B in the afternoon. In the morning Capt. Coulton gave a lecture on P.T. and B.F at which the Battn was well represented. There was a demonstration to Officers and N.C.O's after the lecture.	
	29/5/17		The Battn paraded as usual. Capt J. H. Coles arrived from the 2nd E.Y.R. and took over command of 'B' Coy. Capt. B.C. Ruck-Keene. C.F took over duties as Chaplain. 2nd Lts Ashbridge, Bright & Bolton joined the Battalion to-day.	
	30/5/17		The Battn paraded and C & D Coy did range practice and A & B threw live bombs. The Snipers fired on the long range near BOIS-DU-FAYE.	

A5834 Wt. W4973/M687 750,000 8/16 D. D. & L. Ltd. Forms/C.2118/13.

Army Form C. 2118.

Instructions regarding War Diaries and Intelligence Summaries are contained in F. S. Regs., Part II. and the Staff Manual respectively. Title pages will be prepared in manuscript.

WAR DIARY
or
INTELLIGENCE SUMMARY.

(Erase heading not required.)

Place	Date	Hour	Summary of Events and Information	Remarks and references to Appendices
IZEL-LEZ-HAMEAU	31/3/15.		Battn paraded as usual. The C.O. and Compy. Commanders proceeded by bus to reconnoitre the line in front of ~~[illegible]~~ ARRAS	
			[illegible] Lieut + Adjutant	

A5834 Wt. W4973/M687 750,000 8/16 D. D. & L. Ltd. Forms/C.2118/13.

Report on Operation of 3.5.17

The 8th East Yorks were formed up [illegible] on the following Order.

On the Right B Co supported by D
on the left C Co supported by A.
The leading companies had formed up in SHRAPNEL TRENCH which was vacated by 2nd ROYAL SCOTS FUSILIERS

The Battalion moved forward at ZERO hour but owing to the heavy smoke – combined with the darkness they found it difficult to move on any definite point or points.

A Platoon commander of the Right hand leading company found himself advancing up a small ridge which [illegible] S of the copse in O 8 central where he was up against M.G. fire – he was joined by a K.S.L.I. Officer [illegible] they moved forward together, the K.S.L.I. Officer was killed as well as a number of men & as the place was bristling with M.G.s & the copse occupied by

8th E YORKS MAY 17

occupied by snipers he settled down in shell hole returning at night to HILL TRENCH with eleven men on receipt of orders to do so from Bn H.Q.

The left hand leading company moved forward some men getting forward as far as the enemy front line where they were met with M.G. fire which was also enfilading them.

My right-hand support company moved forward apparently losing direction. The company commander found himself well forward with four men & tried to locate the enemy who were still firing at them with M.G's & snipers. As it was getting light they discovered the enemy had some men behind them & it later became evident that they had crossed the enemy line where the trenches were not connected. He got back with one Sergeant, who had been wounded, his orderly & one other man.

The left hand support company went off & got up to the enemy's line where they were held up. Some of them stayed in HILL TRENCH from where they reported position

8th E YORKS MAY 1917

position - on receipt of this report I immediately ordered them to go forward and support the leading battalion.

On receipt of instructions the Officer commanding this company immediately re-organised all the men he had & prepared to move forward after arranging with the F.O.O. to have a barrage.

We reorganised the battalion later in the day in HULL TRENCH throwing out an outpost line in accordance with verbal instructions received from the Brigade Commander.

The men were in good heart & moved forward readily. I attribute the result to the Heavy Smoke, combined with the darkness which prevented people locating their points of direction. In addition to the the enemy Barrage was very heavy to which must be added the very effective use he made of M.Guns both from the front but also enfilading the attacking troops.

J. [illegible] [illegible] Lt Col
Com'g 8/East York

5 5/7

8th E YORKS

Instructions regarding War Diaries and Intelligence Summaries are contained in F. S. Regs., Part II. and the Staff Manual respectively. Title pages will be prepared in manuscript.

WAR DIARY
or
~~INTELLIGENCE SUMMARY.~~
(Erase heading not required.)

8th Battn East Yorkshire Regt. Vol 22

Army Form C. 2118.

Place	Date	Hour	Summary of Events and Information	Remarks and references to Appendices
IZEL-LEZ-HAMEAU	1917 June 1st		Reveille at 4.30 am. Everything packed and ready by 7.0 am. Battalion paraded at 7.15 am and marched to embussing point. Column started at 8.30 am. Weather beautiful. Arrival in ARRAS at 11 am. Battalion billetted in Baudimont for the night. H.Q. in Rue Louez Dieux. No shelling. Nothing to report.	
ARRAS.	June 2nd		Morning fairly quiet. Few shells near railway. Weather fine but becoming dull. Battalion prepares to move. First Company moved off at 8 pm. Guides at Infantry dry weather track. Relief complete at 1.0 am. Lewis Guns cause some delay. Battalion occupies Hill Trench, Sale & Shrapnel Trench. 2 men wounded going in. Night quiet. Nothing to report. 2Lt G. W. Cubble joins battalion for duty.	
MONCHY.	June 3rd		Glorious weather, morning fairly quiet. SHRAPNEL TRENCH shelled intermittently all day. 3 men of A coy killed in HILL TRENCH. Enemy shelled fairly heavily in the evening. Work on trenches progressing well. C.O. returned from leave.	
do.	June 4th		Nothing much to report. Situation quiet. Cpl Wright sniped a German near TWIN COPSE. At 9-15 pm enemy heavily shelled GRAPE, SHRAPNEL, CANISTER, & the usual targets in the back area. Our ration parties were caught in VINE STREET & we suffered about 10 casualties. The remainder of night fairly quiet. Battalion is making	

Instructions regarding War Diaries and Intelligence Summaries are contained in F. S. Regs., Part II. and the Staff Manual respectively. Title pages will be prepared in manuscript.

WAR DIARY
or
INTELLIGENCE SUMMARY.
(Erase heading not required.)

Army Form C. 2118.

Place	Date	Hour	Summary of Events and Information	Remarks and references to Appendices
			making excellent progress in the trenches, considering the impossible number in each company. The following Officers joined the battalion to-day. Page, Geraghty, Buckle, Hall, Keith & Arment	
MONCHY.	Jun 5		At 2-15 am enemy shelled the usual targets very heavily for ½ an hour. Some more casualties were inflicted. Morning and afternoon quiet. 2nd Lt. Cuttle was killed in SHRAPNEL TRENCH. A most unfortunate occurrence and regretted by all. He was buried in the cemetery near MONCHY by our Padre. The usual noise at about 10.0pm – otherwise quiet. A few gas shells were fired	
do.	Jun. 6th		A slight strafe started at 3 am and lasted for about ½ hour. 2nd Lt. Ritson was wounded & CSM Rosindale badly wounded in the stomach. Several other casualties occurred bringing our total so far up to 1. Offr killed 1. Off wounded 1. W.O. wounded 4. OR killed 27 O.R wounded. Early morning quiet.	
do	Jun. 7th		Day was quiet except for occasional shelling. Shelling rather more severe in the evening. Elements of the K.S.L.I. came along during the day in order to take over. The relief was rather a tricky one as the battalion had to find umpteen working parties. However the relief went on and at 2.30 am the relief was reported complete at 1.15 am. The battalion	

Instructions regarding War Diaries and Intelligence Summaries are contained in F. S. Regs., Part II. and the Staff Manual respectively. Title pages will be prepared in manuscript.

WAR DIARY
or
INTELLIGENCE SUMMARY.
(Erase heading not required.)

Army Form C. 2118.

Place	Date	Hour	Summary of Events and Information	Remarks and references to Appendices
			was accomodated in the famous rest billets of BROWN LINE which during the last two days had been very badly pounded. Although in rest billets and close support the battalion will have to find numerous working parties which should keep every man employed nightly up to a late hour	
BROWN LINE	June 8th		Colonel de la Perelle rejoined the battalion = in Brown line = Day uneventful working parties all over the neighbourhood. No hostile shelling. Entertainment up North began @ 3.0 a.m. going well – so report Day	
do.	June 9th		Orders that Bde is side-stepping to-night consequently to-night we have to take up position in BROWN LINE south of CAMBRAI ROAD, practically move was completed by 7.0 pm. the usual working parties all over the countryside were found by the battalion. Day uneventful, but fine but not quite so sunny. Night quiet though our shelling – not very heavy was persistant.	
do.	June 10th		Fine and Sunny nothing to report. working parties in the evening	

A5834 Wt. W4973/M687 750,000 8/16 D. D. & L. Ltd. Forms/C.2118/13.

Instructions regarding War Diaries and Intelligence Summaries are contained in F. S. Regs., Part II. and the Staff Manual respectively. Title pages will be prepared in manuscript.

WAR DIARY
or
INTELLIGENCE SUMMARY.
(Erase heading not required.)

Army Form C. 2118.

Place	Date	Hour	Summary of Events and Information	Remarks and references to Appendices
BROWN LINE	June 11th		Heavy rain in the early morning which rather flooded out H.Q. dug-out & the trenches. Cleared up at 11.0 am. Nothing to report. Everything quiet. Relief to-morrow night. Usual working parties in the evening.	
do.	June 12th		Fine and bright. Enemy heavily shell ARRAS with aeroplane observation. Aeroplane brought down by a direct hit from Anti-Aircraft Guns. Brown Line was slightly bumped during the night. Day was generally quiet. The battalion was relieved in Brown Line by 10th R.W.F. Relief complete by 11.30 pm. The battalion moved into ARRAS and occupied billets in GRAND PLACE. Battn H.Q. in RUE de GAMBETTA.	
ARRAS.	June 13th		Very hot and sunny and very quiet. Battn rested in the morning. In afternoon it bathed and generally cleaned up.	
do.	June 14th		Sunny with nice breeze blowing. Companies under company commanders are being refitted. — No parades. In the afternoon the Elegant Extracts gave a show for the battalion in the Salle des Concerts. Most enjoyable.	

A5834 Wt. W4973/M687 750,000 8/16 D. D. & L. Ltd. Forms/C.2118/13.

Instructions regarding War Diaries and Intelligence Summaries are contained in F. S. Regs., Part II. and the Staff Manual respectively. Title pages will be prepared in manuscript.

WAR DIARY
or
INTELLIGENCE SUMMARY.
(*Erase heading not required.*)

Army Form C. 2118.

Place	Date	Hour	Summary of Events and Information	Remarks and references to Appendices
ARRAS	June 15/17		The hottest day we have had. The Battn is "standing to" ready to move at ½ hrs notice. Lieut Browse joins the Battn and takes over duties as Quartermaster. 2/Lts Davis & Canswick joined the battalion for duty.	
do.	16/6/17		Very hot day. Battalion had orders to stand to ready to move into the line at a moments notice. Fortunately our services were not required. The parties in the strong points were relieved at night.	
do	17/6/17		The Battn moved from ARRAS to NOVELETTE. March commenced at 4.30 am from road junction just N of A in FAUBERG D'AMIENS. Owing to the terrific heat the ~~[illegible]~~ large number of ~~[illegible]~~ 11 "fell out". Battn arrived at NOVELETTE at 10-45 am. The men from the "strong points" were conveyed by motor lorry.	
NOVELETTE to	18/6/17		The Battn paraded at 6.30 am and marched to ETREE WAMIN. It was a very hot march. 11 men fell out, 8 ~~[illegible]~~ of whom fainted in the ranks, owing to the intense heat. The move for to-morrow is cancelled. The order was	

A5834 Wt. W4973/M687 750,000 8/16 D. D. & L. Ltd. Forms/C.2118/13.

Instructions regarding War Diaries and Intelligence Summaries are contained in F. S. Regs., Part II. and the Staff Manual respectively. Title pages will be prepared in manuscript.

WAR DIARY
or
INTELLIGENCE SUMMARY.
(Erase heading not required.)

Army Form C. 2118.

Place	Date	Hour	Summary of Events and Information	Remarks and references to Appendices
ETREE WAMIN	18/6/17		welcomed as everyone was very tired. Lt Dicke & 2Lt Geraghty proceeded to England on leave.	
do	19/6/17		Not quite so hot to-day. Companies under company Commanders Physical Drill after breakfast and fitting equipment. A draft of Capt Ball and 121 ORs joined the Battn.	
do	20/6/17		Parades under company arrangements. Nothing to report.	
	21/6/17		Training commenced in earnest. Companies were each able to have the use of the Bayonet Fighting Course erected by the Pioneers of the Battn. Thunder was in the air throughout the day & we had several heavy showers. Much cooler. 2/Lt Hutson rejoined from hospital	
	22/6/17		Much cooler & rather dull. A coy. commenced firing on the range. Turned out very wet in the afternoon.	

A5834 Wt. W4973/M687 750,000 8/16 D. D. & L. Ltd. Forms/C.2118/13.

Instructions regarding War Diaries and Intelligence Summaries are contained in F. S. Regs., Part II. and the Staff Manual respectively. Title pages will be prepared in manuscript.

WAR DIARY
or
INTELLIGENCE SUMMARY.
(Erase heading not required.)

Army Form C. 2118.

Place	Date	Hour	Summary of Events and Information	Remarks and references to Appendices
ETRÉE WAMIN	23/6/17		Very sunny not too hot. The battalion bathed at BERLENCOURT, C & D coys on the range. Nothing to report.	
do.	24/6/17		Fine day and sunny. Battn paraded for Divine service at 9.30 am Nothing further to report.	
do	25/6/17		Fairly cool but sunny. The whole battalion fired on the range starting with A Coy at 6.0 am. Turned out very wet at night.	
do	26/6/17		Glorious day. Everything fresh after the rain during the night. The Battn less D coy fired on the range. All Lewis Gun teams fired on the range in the afternoon. D coy was inspected by the Brigadier at 11.30 am. The Divisional Band played for the battalion and was very much appreciated.	
do	27/6/17		The Battalion moved to LUCHEUX starting at 7.0 am. Quite a pleasant march as it was delightfully cool. Quite a change after the hot days.	

A5834 Wt. W4973/M687 750,000 8/16 D. D. & L. Ltd. Forms/C.2118/13.

Instructions regarding War Diaries and Intelligence Summaries are contained in F. S. Regs., Part II. and the Staff Manual respectively. Title pages will be prepared in manuscript.

WAR DIARY
or
INTELLIGENCE SUMMARY.
(Erase heading not required.)

Army Form C. 2118.

Place	Date	Hour	Summary of Events and Information	Remarks and references to Appendices
LUCHEUX	28/6/17		Very wet in early morning. A coy fired on the range in the morning. D coy in the afternoon. B+C coys were inspected by the C O at 10.0 am. The C.O & Adjutant attend a conference concerning the new move, at Bde H.Q.	
do	29/6/17		The Battalion leaves LUCHEUX in two parties to entrain at DOULLENS. 1st party H.Q. A+B coys. 2nd party C+D coys. The battalion proceeded from DOULLENS to ACHIET-LE-GRAND. The journey was remarkably good and lasted only about 2½ hours. The battalion to GOMIECOURT from ACHIET-LE-GRAND and spent the night under canvas just outside the village. Lt. REH Dicke rejoined from leave to the UK	
GOMIECOURT	31/6/17		Very dull, windy & wet. The Battalion marched from GOMIECOURT to LEBUCQUIERE. A miserable march on account of the rain. Not a house in the village is whole. Only 2 men fell out & were admitted to F.A.	
			[illegible] Colonel Com'dg 8/East Yorks 1/7/17	

A5834 Wt. W4973/M687 750,000 8/16 D. D. & L. Ltd. Forms/C.2118/13.

Army Form C. 2118.

Instructions regarding War Diaries and Intelligence Summaries are contained in F. S. Regs., Part II. and the Staff Manual respectively. Title pages will be prepared in manuscript.

WAR DIARY
or
INTELLIGENCE SUMMARY.
(Erase heading not required.)

8th East Yorks. Regt.

Vol 23

Place	Date	Hour	Summary of Events and Information	Remarks and references to Appendices
LEBUCQUIÈRE	1/7/17		The day was spent quietly. The Church Parade was cancelled on account of the rain. The C.O, 2/i/c, O's C Companies, ~~[illegible]~~, and platoon commanders reconnoitred the line.	
do.	2/7/17		To-day is sunny and everything is fresh after the rain. Companies are at the disposal of Company Commanders. Enemy shelled the neighbourhood of our village all the morning, otherwise nothing of importance to report. Battalion moved off at 10 pm to take over the line from 1/8 Worcesters.	
In the Line LOUVERVAL	3/7/17		Relief completed by 2 am. CO + Major [illegible] went round the line. Night quiet except for shelling by our guns. Remainder of day quiet + uneventful. Weather fine. 2nd Lt Buckle was very slightly wounded in the hand, but remained at duty.	
"	4/7/17		Quiet + uneventful. Practically no shelling. Patrols out at night as usual but they did not come in contact with enemy. 2nd Lt [illegible] [illegible] the battalion.	
"	5/7/17		Night + early morning quiet. Weather fair. 14 OR joined battalion yesterday from 37th I.B.D. 2nd Lt [illegible] took a patrol out + discovered a newly dug [illegible] of trench. German [illegible] were left in trench as well as a telephone wire. Nothing unusual on our front.	
"	6/7/17		Our artillery rather more active during the night + early morning. Hostile artillery shelled LOUVERVAL [illegible] times [illegible] near MORCHIES. Capt. Wright M. + 2nd Lt Wright A.E. joined battalion to-day. Day uneventful.	

A5834 Wt. W4973/M687 750,000 8/16 D. D. & L. Ltd. Forms/C.2118/13.

Instructions regarding War Diaries and Intelligence Summaries are contained in F. S. Regs., Part II. and the Staff Manual respectively. Title pages will be prepared in manuscript.

WAR DIARY
or
INTELLIGENCE SUMMARY.
(Erase heading not required.)

Army Form C. 2118.

Place	Date	Hour	Summary of Events and Information	Remarks and references to Appendices
In the line LOUVERVAL	7.7.17		Nothing in particular to report. Successful patrol by Capt [illegible] + 2nd Lt Lamb to enemy crater. Hostile artillery less active during the day. Weather fine & warm.	
"	8.7.17		Fine day again. Artillery quiet during the day. Nothing to report. Patrol again in the evening to the crater. Severe opposition encountered from enemy. No casualties. Remainder of day quiet & uneventful.	
"	9.7.17		Nothing to report. 'A' Coy patrol took possession of an advanced post & held it throughout the following day. Nothing occurred.	
"	10.7.17		Quiet day. Relief took place to-night by the Royal Welsh Fusiliers. Guides at BEETROOT Factory @ 10.45 pm. Relief complete 12.45 am. Battalion returned to billets in LEBUCQUIERE & arrived between 2 & 3 in the morning.	
LEBUCQUIERE	11.7.17		Weather glorious. Day spent in resting & cleaning up.	
	12/7/17		Glorious weather. The morning was spent in training. During the rest of the day the Battn bathed at BEUGNY.	
"	13/7/17		Still hot & sunny. Parades were cancelled as the task of digging a C.T. has been allotted to the battalion.	
	14/7/17		Much cooler & rather dull. The Battn rested after the night work	

A5834 Wt. W4973/M687 750,000 8/16 D. D. & L. Ltd. Forms/C.2118/13.

Instructions regarding War Diaries and Intelligence Summaries are contained in F. S. Regs., Part II. and the Staff Manual respectively. Title pages will be prepared in manuscript.

WAR DIARY
or
INTELLIGENCE SUMMARY.
(Erase heading not required.)

Army Form C. 2118.

Place	Date	Hour	Summary of Events and Information	Remarks and references to Appendices
LEBUCQUIERE	15/7/17		The men on working party got very wet so that the Church Parade was cancelled in order that they might dry their clothes	
"	16/7/17		No parade. men resting after working party. Usual working party to-night.	
	17/7/17		Rather dull. Battalion resting after working party	
~~Louv~~ "	18/7/17		Quiet day nothing to report. Working parties cancelled on account of our going into the line tomorrow night. Divisional Band paid us a visit.	
LOUVERVAL	19/7/17		Quiet day. Preparation for relief. Cpt Armitage & Cole proceed on leave. Relief complete by 1230 pm.	
"	20/7/17		Same Bn HQ. All very quiet. Nothing to report.	
"	21/7/17		Uneventful nothing to report. A Coy's patrol encountered enemy patrol & sustained two casualties (wounded). Night otherwise quiet.	
"	22/7/17		Nothing to report. Weather fine day quiet. No patrols	

A5834 Wt. W4973/M687 750,000 8/16 D. D. & L. Ltd. Forms/C.2118/13.

Instructions regarding War Diaries and Intelligence Summaries are contained in F. S. Regs., Part II. and the Staff Manual respectively. Title pages will be prepared in manuscript.

WAR DIARY
or
INTELLIGENCE SUMMARY.
(Erase heading not required.)

Army Form C. 2118.

Place	Date	Hour	Summary of Events and Information	Remarks and references to Appendices
LOUVERVAL	23/7/17		Weather still continues fine & warm. Nothing to report from the line. Night quiet.	
"	24/7/17		Weather fine & warm. Artillery activity less than usual. Aeroplanes very busy on both sides. Many enemy planes up as well as our own.	
"	25.7.17		Nothing of importance to report. Capt the Rev Rusk. Keene proceeded on leave to England. Capt. Wright joins details from the line. Patrols out all night but no encounters.	
	26.7.17		Day quiet & uneventful, although enemy artillery was rather more active than usual. Relief took place to-night by the 1st Royal Scots Fusiliers. Quiet night. Cambrai Road slightly shelled. Relief complete by 12.30 am.	
LEBUCQUIÈRE	27.7.17		Long rest. Cleaning up. No parades. Doctor goes into hospital. Capt Smith returns from U.K. leave	
"	28.7.17		Early parade cancelled since we have to find a digging party to-night. Baths during the morning & afternoon. 250 men required for digging C.T.	

A5834 Wt. W4973/M687 750,000 8/16 D. D. & L. Ltd. Forms/C.2118/13.

Instructions regarding War Diaries and Intelligence Summaries are contained in F. S. Regs., Part II. and the Staff Manual respectively. Title pages will be prepared in manuscript.

WAR DIARY
or
INTELLIGENCE SUMMARY.
(Erase heading not required.)

Army Form C. 2118.

Place	Date	Hour	Summary of Events and Information	Remarks and references to Appendices
LEBUCQUIÈRE	29.7.17.		No early parade. Quiet morning owing to the work last night. Slight rain. Young Officers bayonet fighting class under C.S.M. Sawyer of the Army School. Otherwise nothing to report.	
"	30.7.17.		Weather breaking. Terrible thunderstorm. Lightning strikes a tree near battalion HQ. Parades washed out, though a certain amount of work was done in the morning. 'C' Company fired on the range.	
"	31.7.17.		Battalion is being inspected to-morrow by Corps Commander General Woollcombe. Parade rehearsed. Apparently everything went off very well. Afternoon spent in cleaning up. 'B' Company fired on the range.	
				[illegible]

A5834 Wt. W4973/M687 750,000 8/16 D. D. & L. Ltd. Forms/C.2118/13.

Instructions regarding War Diaries and Intelligence Summaries are contained in F. S. Regs., Part II. and the Staff Manual respectively. Title pages will be prepared in manuscript.

8th EAST YORKSHIRE Regt.

WAR DIARY or INTELLIGENCE SUMMARY.

(Erase heading not required.)

Army Form C. 2118.

Vol 24

Place	Date	Hour	Summary of Events and Information	Remarks and references to Appendices
LEBUCQUIERE	1.8.17		Morning it rained very hard, but cleared towards the afternoon & the battalion paraded for inspection by General Holcomb, in [illegible], transport in rear. Turn out was good & the march past good. [illegible] Otherwise nothing of importance.	
"	2.8.17		Rain all day. No parades & nothing of importance happened.	
"	3.8.17		More rain. Preparation for the line. We relieve the 1st R.S.F. in the LOUVERVAL sector. Relief complete 12.30 am. Weather bad. Capt H Cole returned from leave to-day	
	4.8.17		More rain. The following is a copy of a letter received from Division & Brigade on the previous day's inspection. "The Divisional Commander was much pleased with the smart appearance & drill of the 8th Battalion East Yorkshire Regiment this afternoon. He remarked the saluting was good & the transport most creditable." From Brigade: "The G.O.C. 8th Infantry Brigade has much pleasure in forwarding this letter & directs me to add that he also was much pleased with the parade & today that it reflects great credit on the Officer Commanding & on all the men on parade. He directs that the remarks of the Major General Commanding be notified to all concerned in the Battalion." Day uneventful except @ 11 pm when the S.O.S. on the left Brigade was fired which provoked a bombardment.	
	5.8.17		Weather gloriously fine. Artillery practically nil. Aerial activity only very little. Evening quiet. At 11 pm a little excitement was caused by left of Brigade on our left firing the S.O.S. This spread until it reached our left & the S.O.S. on our left was fired. Barrage was very prompt. Nothing further happened. Padre returned from leave to-day.	

A5834 Wt. W4973/M687 750,000 8/16 D. D. & L. Ltd. Forms/C.2118/13.

WAR DIARY
or
INTELLIGENCE SUMMARY.
(Erase heading not required.)

Instructions regarding War Diaries and Intelligence Summaries are contained in F. S. Regs., Part II. and the Staff Manual respectively. Title pages will be prepared in manuscript.

Army Form C. 2118.

Place	Date	Hour	Summary of Events and Information	Remarks and references to Appendices
LOUVERVAL	6.8.17		Day fine but one of the quietest. No shelling by enemy. Aerial activity slight between 7 + 8 pm. Night very quiet. 2nd Lieut G. Hall returns from Bombing school. Nothing to report.	
"	7.8.17		Fine day. As quiet as ever. G.O.C. 3rd Division came up to Battalion Headquarters. A Company make a reconnaissance of the position they entered leading to moon Crater reported unoccupied. No enemy seen. Remainder of day uneventful.	
"	8.8.17		Fine Rain later. Very quiet day. INCHY Road slightly shelled during the afternoon. Capt. Ball MC leaves to-day for 2 months training reinforcements at ETAPLES. The raid by A Company fixed for to-night. Zero hour 10 pm. Night fine. Raiding Party set off under 2nd Lt Lamb & 2nd Lt Beadle. After three hours + red rockets (the signal to withdraw was fired) Party returned having found both Crater & Trench empty.	
"	9.8.17		Usual quiet day. Corps Commander accompanied by Divisional Commander visited the line. He expressed his satisfaction with what he saw. Remainder of day quiet & uneventful.	
	10.8.17		Day uneventful. Nothing to report. Padre returned from leave.	
	11.8.17		Quiet day. 1st RSF relieved us in the line in the evening. Relief complete 12 30 am 12/8. 150 men from A+B Coys remain in the line to continue on working parties. 2nd Lt Cranswick in charge of detachment.	

Instructions regarding War Diaries and Intelligence Summaries are contained in F. S. Regs., Part II. and the Staff Manual respectively. Title pages will be prepared in manuscript.

Army Form C. 2118.

WAR DIARY
or
INTELLIGENCE SUMMARY.
(Erase heading not required.)

Place	Date	Hour	Summary of Events and Information	Remarks and references to Appendices
LEBUCQUIERE	12/8/17		Battalion returned to LEBUCQUIERE during the early hours of the morning. Church parade fixed for 12^15 but the inclemency of the weather caused parade to be cancelled. Voluntary parade in the Cinema. Day spent quietly. Capt Armitage returned from leave yesterday. Lt Mathews takes over Command of B Coy. Capt Armitage takes over Command of C Coy. Capt Williams proceeded on leave.	
"	13/8/17		Day spent in cleaning up, baths & refitting. During the afternoon C & D Companies fired on the range & fixed up barbed wire entanglements. There is to be a competition in wiring next Saturday	
"	14/8/17		C & D Companies under Coy Commanders in Platoon training, musketry & wiring – Lewis Guns on range. 'A' Coy & platoon of B Coy returned from LOUVERVAL at 4.30 A.M. & spent day in cleaning up. 5 Offs & 150 O.R. of C & D Coys went to LOUVERVAL to replace A & B. 2nd Lt Godfrey in charge. Returned owing to bad state of the weather. 2nd Lt L Arkwright takes over command of 'A' Coy during absence of Capt H S Williams. 2nd Lt T C Greatly proceeded to L.G. course. Day fine but heavy thunder & lightning & deluge of rain about 8 P.M.	
"	15/8/17		Coys under Coy Commanders in platoon training, wiring & range practice 'A' & 'B' on range. 5 Offs & 150 OR of 'C' & 'D' Coys as mentioned on 14th proceeded to LOUVERVAL N.C.O. at 2.30 P.M under R.S.M. Day fine except for thunder burst & heavy rain about 4.30 P.M. 2nd Lt A. Robinson returned from course at AA Battery.	

Instructions regarding War Diaries and Intelligence Summaries are contained in F. S. Regs., Part II. and the Staff Manual respectively. Title pages will be prepared in manuscript.

WAR DIARY
or
INTELLIGENCE SUMMARY.
(Erase heading not required.)

Army Form C. 2118.

Place	Date	Hour	Summary of Events and Information	Remarks and references to Appendices
LE BUCQUIERE	16/8/17		Very heavy rain in early hours, remainder of day fine. Coys under Coy Commanders. 'A' 'B' Coy at Velu Baths. Major Lennard was found. O.C. Companies & platoon Commanders reconnoitred line held by Right Battalion. Lt R.M. Fulton promoted Temp. Captain; Lt R.S. H. Duke appointed acting Captain & 2nd Lt H. Godfrey promoted Temp. Lieut. 2nd Lt Hall appointed Bn: Bombing Officer. Divisional Band played in Camp at 5.0 P.M.	
"	17/8/17		Day fine & very warm. Two enemy planes over during forenoon – AA opened fire – Result NIL. Coys under O.C. & on Bombing Ground doing line practice. Inter-platoon Competitions being held on Saturday. Brigade Concert Troupe gave entertainment to Battalion – very good.	
"	18/8/17		~~Day fine~~ Coys under Coy Commanders. – 'C' & 'D' Coys returned from Louverval. C.O. Coy Commanders & M.O at one day Gas Course at Divisional Gas School Fremicourt. 'Elegant Extracts' gave entertainment in field near H.Q. Mess. Lt Lacey & 2nd Lt Davies reported from course. Lt Buckton reported after handing Town Majorship of LE BUCQUIERE etc over to Major Sinclair of Canadian Army. Day was fine except for heavy shower of rain about 5-30 P.M.	
"	19/8/17		Day fine & warm. Church Parade 9.30 P.M. Inter Platoon Sports. Results. 100x 1st Sgt Holman (C); 2nd Pte Foster (D) – Tug of War 'B' Coy beat 'D' Coy. – Bombing Bull's Eye. 1st Pte Ager (D); 2nd Pte Hemsley (C); 3rd Pte Kirtley (D) Bombing Long Distance 1st L/C Masterman (C) 2nd Cpl Higgins (D) – Boot Race 1st Cpl Gold (D) 2nd Pte Nickerson (C); 3rd Pte Bevill (C) – Rapid Wiring 20 men, 20 yds in 20 minutes 1st 'C' Coy; 2nd 'D' Coy. Sports not finished as postponed till night relief. Battalion relieved 1st R.S.F. in Left Sector. 2nd Lt Birkett proceeded to Rest Camp. 2nd Lt Dimmer reported from Hospital. Relief was completed by 11.30 P.M.	

A5834 Wt. W4973/M687 750,000 8/16 D. D. & L. Ltd. Forms/C.2118/13.

Instructions regarding War Diaries and Intelligence Summaries are contained in F. S. Regs., Part II. and the Staff Manual respectively. Title pages will be prepared in manuscript.

WAR DIARY
or
INTELLIGENCE SUMMARY.
(*Erase heading not required.*)

Army Form [illegible]118.

Place	Date	Hour	Summary of Events and Information	Remarks and references to Appendices
LOUVERVAL	20/8/17		Day quiet. One of our batteries behind Louverval heavily engaged by hostile artillery observed by aeroplane; this last all afternoon otherwise nothing to report. 2nd Lt Dinnock [illegible] rejoins Battalion. Night quiet. Men worked well on digging new trenches. Army Corps & Divisional Commanders paid a visit to the Intermediate Line.	
"	21/8/17		Day quiet. Hostile Artillery - Nil. Enemy aircraft inactive except for a short time in the evening. Usual working parties in the evening. Nothing to report.	
"	22/8/17		Fine day. Quiet. Little hostile aerial activity & practically no shelling of the back area. Slight shelling on R post caused casualties of one killed & one wounded in "B" Coy.	
"	23/8/17		Quiet generally. Usually working parties at night on joining up posts otherwise nothing to report.	
"	24/8/17		Same as yesterday.	
"	25/8/17		Quiet day. One shell fell in J 5.4, killing one man & wounding another, otherwise nothing to report. Large working party in evening joining up posts. Another N.C.O. wounded.	
"	26/8/17		Quiet day. R.S. attempted a raid on enemy posts in R. [illegible] driven off otherwise nothing to report.	
"	27/8/17		Nothing to report. Bn relieved by 1st R.S.F. "B & D" Coys left detachment behind. Very heavy rain for greater part of day.	

A-[illegible] Wt. W4973/M687 750,000 8/16 D. D. & L. Ltd. Forms/C.2118/13.

Instructions regarding War Diaries and Intelligence Summaries are contained in F. S. Regs., Part II. and the Staff Manual respectively. Title pages will be prepared in manuscript.

WAR DIARY
or
INTELLIGENCE SUMMARY.
(Erase heading not required.)

Army Form C. 2118.

Place	Date	Hour	Summary of Events and Information	Remarks and references to Appendices
LE BUCQUIERE	28/8/17		Spent quietly. Heavy rain in early morning also strong wind. Working party on Assault Course range. Col, Capt Armitage & Lt. Buckston & Matthews at Listening Apparatus Demonstration. Lt Matthews made Acting Captain while in command of a Coy. 2nd Lt Fletcher struck off strength.	
"	29/8/17.		Coys cleaning up & refitting. Baths at Velu. Working parties on ranges at Velu Dump. Rain during day. 2nd Lt Gils went on course. Brigadier round.	
"	30/8/17.		'B' & 'D' Coy detachments return. Spent day quietly. 'A' & 'C' Coys sent detachment to Louverval. Corps Commander round. Usual working parties on ranges at Velu. Padre returned from course. 2nd Lt Hall returned from C.C.S. Major (A/Lt Col) J.M. de la Rue Russell reported in Gazette to be in command of a Batt. & to be Lt Col with seniority from 10/1/17. Lt (A/Major) D.C. Drummond M.C. to be Temp Major from 22/5/17. Rain during day	?
"	31/8/17.		'B' & 'D' Coys at Velu Baths & refitting. Rain off & on during day. Balloonatics gave entertainment in Cinema. Usual working parties on ranges & Velu.	

[illegible] Capt. 1917.

A5834 Wt. W4973/M687 750,000 8/16 D. D. & L. Ltd. Forms/C.2118/13.

3/8

Army Form C. 2118.

Sh. East Yorkshire Regiment

Instructions regarding War Diaries and Intelligence Summaries are contained in F. S. Regs., Part II. and the Staff Manual respectively. Title pages will be prepared in manuscript.

WAR DIARY
or
INTELLIGENCE SUMMARY.

(Erase heading not required.)

Vol 25

Place	Date	Hour	Summary of Events and Information	Remarks and references to Appendices
LE BUCQUIERE	1/9/17.		Coys reorganised into two platoons. Platoons practice attack. Platoons of "C" Coy carry out attack with live grenade practice under Platoon Commanders. Capt. Col[illegible], Capt. Armit[illegible], Capt. Williams & 2nd Lt. [illegible] at Divisional Gas School. Model platoon of "A" Coy carry out same practice as "C" in afternoon.	
	2/9/17		Church parade. Kit inspection by C.O. 2nd Lt [illegible] reconnoitre new Camp at YTRES. Detachment of "A" & "B" return from Longueval. Detachment of "C" (2 Offrs & 76 OR) go to Longueval. Major [illegible] struck off strength owing to being ordered Medical Board.	
	3/9/17		Day fine. Coys under O.C. Coy practicing training. "A" on Bombing Ground from 9/12. "B" from 2/5. All under Platoon Commanders for live [illegible] firing. Box Respirators of all Offrs & men tested in Gas at Div. Gas School. "C" & "D" at 1 PM today. "A" & "B" at 1 PM tomorrow. Brigade Troupe gave show in Cinema.	
	4/9/17.		Detachment of "C" Coy returned to Le Bucquiere. Coys under O.C. Coy. "D" Coy on Bombing Ground practicing grenade barrage. 2nd Lt. Batty transferred from "A" to "D". Battalion moved to YTRES for intensive training. [illegible] Camp handed over to Q.W.R.	
YTRES	5/9/17		Coys in preliminary musketry, platoon in offensive action. Close Order Drill & Musketry. 2Lt A. Robinson appointed as Musketry Officer. Lt Buckton posted to "A" Coy in command of Capt. Williams going to England. Day generally good. Hostile aeroplanes, very high up, were well over our lines. Our A.A. fired heavily but with no result.	

Instructions regarding War Diaries and Intelligence Summaries are contained in F. S. Regs., Part II. and the Staff Manual respectively. Title pages will be prepared in manuscript.

WAR DIARY
or
INTELLIGENCE SUMMARY.
(Erase heading not required.)

Army Form C. 2118.

Place	Date	Hour	Summary of Events and Information	Remarks and references to Appendices
YTRES	6/9/17.		Fine day except for one or two showers. Coy in Close Order Drill, artillery formation on range, bayonet fighting & grenade (rifle) work. 'C' & 'D' Coy at Baths in evening. 2 Lt Birkett returned from Rest Camp.	
"	7/9/17		Miserable morning but later on turned out fine day. Coy in Close Order Drill, platoon in attack, covering fire & rapid extension (practice also on range), bayonet fighting & rifle grenade work 2 Lt Bladon (late C.S.M. 5th Battalion) reported. 2nd Lt R. Webster reported & posted to 'D' Coy.	
"	8/9/17		Day fine tho' very misty in early morning. All morning parades cancelled. Battn paraded at 12 noon & moved to area between Rocquigny, ~~[illegible]~~ Barastre & Bus & practised the attack. Returned to Camp about 6 P.M. Hostile aeroplane well over our way - fired on by A.A. with no result. 'A' Coy at Baths in morning.	
"	9/9/17.		Church parade on Batn. Parade Ground. 'C' Coy on range. All Officers attended C.Os conference after parade. Commanding Officer & all Officers at G.O.Cs lecture in Cinema, Barastre at 5 P.M. Competitions postponed from 19th Augt completed today. Results - 120x flat Race (Transport). 1st Morton; 2nd Barrass; 3rd Maud. Mounted Wrestling 1st Barrass; 2nd Maud. Alarm Race 1st Mosley 'B'; 2nd Robson 'C'; 3rd Bewell 'C'. Lewis Gun Shoot: 1st Sykes 'C'; 2nd Ella 'D'. Cross Country Race, 1st L/C Morton 'A'. 2nd Tomlinson 'A'; 3rd Houghton 'C'. 3 Legged Race, 1st Campbell, 2nd Woodman, 3rd Glossop. Mule Race 1st Cpl Ankers H/Q; 2nd Jackson 'C'. The Commanding Officer ~~[illegible]~~ presented the prizes. 2nd Lt R. Webster went on Recognition of aircraft course at Lealvillers. Football Competition. 8th S.Y.R. v Cheshire R.E. Result Draw 1-1. Replay on 10th inst.	

Instructions regarding War Diaries and Intelligence Summaries are contained in F. S. Regs., Part II. and the Staff Manual respectively. Title pages will be prepared in manuscript.

WAR DIARY
or
INTELLIGENCE SUMMARY.
(Erase heading not required.)

Army Form C. 2118.

Place	Date	Hour	Summary of Events and Information	Remarks and references to Appendices
YTRES	10/9/17.		Coys under O.C. Coys. Morning - Coys in attacks & on range. Afternoon Lewis Gun practice, ~~Rifle~~ Live Grenade practice, Musketry & Close Order Drill. New draft inspected by G.O.C. Yukon Pack demonstration at Bde. H.Q. Lt Buckton takes over 'A' Coy during absence of Capt Williams for dental treatment. Capt Williams proceeds to Etaples for treatment. 2nd Lt Cranswick to G.H.Q. Lewis Gun Course. 2nd Lt R Webster proceeds to Recognition of aircraft course.	?
do	11/9/17.		Battn practice Battn in attack on Divisional Training Area. Lewis Gun instruction in afternoon. Day fine. Football competition 8th EY beat Cheshire RE by 3 to 2 after extra time. Very good game.	
do	12/9/17		Battn proceed to long range at Le Transloy. 2nd Lt S.B. Lush joined Battn & posted to 'D' Coy. 2nd Lt Bladon posted to 'C' Coy. 'A' Coy at baths. Football Competition. 2nd R.S. beat 8th E.Y. by 1-0 after a very give & take game. A draw would have been more equitable result.	?
do	13/9/17.		Day dull. Coys in Close Order Drill & attack practice during forenoon. In afternoon, Coys on range, musketry, bayonet fighting & Bombing practice also Lewis Gun instruction. 2nd Lt E L Kidd reported. New draft under 2nd Lt Kissell went to Rocquigny for purpose of testing Box Respirators in Gas. All Officers attended C.O's conference re Brigade in attack which comes off tomorrow.	

A5834 Wt. W4973/M687 750,000 8/16 D. D. & L. Ltd. Forms/C.2118/13.

Instructions regarding War Diaries and Intelligence Summaries are contained in F. S. Regs., Part II. and the Staff Manual respectively. Title pages will be prepared in manuscript.

WAR DIARY
or
INTELLIGENCE SUMMARY.
(*Erase heading not required.*)

Army Form C. 2118.

Place	Date	Hour	Summary of Events and Information	Remarks and references to Appendices
YTRES.	14/9/17.		Brigade practice attack on Div: Training Area. Battn move off at 8 A.M. Day dull & not very promising, threatening rain. 2nd Lt Webster returns from Aeroplane Spotting course. 2nd Lt Bladon proceeds on leave. Lewis Gun instruction & Bombing in afternoon. 2nd Lt Robinson & party proceed in advance as Billeting Party.	
"	15/9/17		Musketry on long range cancelled. Coys under Coy Commanders. New draft put thro: tests on bombing ground. Yukon Pack demonstration. Showery in morning but fine later on. 2nd Lt Ward & Craig return from Courses. 2nd Lt Ashbridge proceeds to Brigade Depot Coy. Major Smithard reports.	
"	16/9/17.		Church parade. Bishop of Khartoum gave service in open air theatre in Little Wood. Day very warm.	
"	17/9/17.		Day cloudy. Coys under Coy Commanders. New draft do Live Rifle Grenade work. Battalion prepare to move off at 10 P.M. for BAPAUME en route to new Area. 'C' Coy detailed as Detraining Coy for Bde & move to PROVEN in Bde Train. Grand night for marching.	
HIPHOEK.	18/9/17.		Battalion entrained at BAPAUME EAST STN. left at 4 A.M. arrived at PROVEN at 2 P.M. & detrained. Battalion moved off about 3 P.M. & arrived at HIPHOEK about 5.30 P.M. Rain during march.	
"	19/9/17		Coys under O.C. Coys in musketry etc. ~~[illegible]~~ C.O. & all Officers go to V Corps H.Q. for conference at 5.30 P.M. Day bright & warm.	
"	20/9/17		Battalion move off at 9.10 & march to HOPOUTRE (J 15.a.0.1) All under canvas. Battn arrives about 1 PM Day bright & warm.	

Instructions regarding War Diaries and Intelligence Summaries are contained in F. S. Regs., Part II. and the Staff Manual respectively. Title pages will be prepared in manuscript.

WAR DIARY
or
INTELLIGENCE SUMMARY.
(*Erase heading not required.*)

Army Form C. 2118.

Place	Date	Hour	Summary of Events and Information	Remarks and references to Appendices
HOPOUTRE	21/9/17.		Coys under O.C. Coys. Officers proceed to Corps H.Q. to see model of ground over which attack will take place. Hostile Bombing Aeroplanes attempt to come over about 9 P.M. but are picked up by searchlights & driven off by A.A. etc. C.O. at conference. Battalion in good form.	
"	22/9/17.		Coys under O.C. Coys in musketry, platoon in attack etc. Hostile air raid about 12 noon, driven off by A.A. Commanding Officer, Adjutant & other officers reconnoitre line. Companies practice assembling on Assembly ground in afternoon & at night. Brigadier round. Day fine. Men in good spirits.	
"	23/9/17.		Church Parade cancelled owing to late order that Corps Commander would visit & see Battalions on manoeuvres from 11.15 A.M. to 1 P.M. Coys practise attack on ground with points marked on Company frontage only owing to ground without crops being unavailable. Major General came round only. Major & officers reconnoitre line. Another hostile raid but not near our lines. Day very warm. Men very keen [?] fresh as they were before Arras show.	
"	24/9/17.		General preparation & tests for move up the line in evening. Three Coys go by train, remaining Coy by buses. Brigadier spoke to men on coming attack & wished them best of luck. Men cheered Brigadier at the finish. All ranks in fine form & good spirits. Officers left out: Major Smithard, 2nd Lt C.S. Murray (Asst Adjt), Capt Matthews, Lt Buckton, 2 Lts Hall & Gates [?]. Capt Armitage goes to 76th Bde as Liaison Officer. 2 Lts Cranswick & A Robinson also act as Liaison Officers. Battalion moved off at 5 P.M. to Poperinghe. Day fine, warm.	

Instructions regarding War Diaries and Intelligence Summaries are contained in F. S. Regs., Part II. and the Staff Manual respectively. Title pages will be prepared in manuscript.

WAR DIARY
or
INTELLIGENCE SUMMARY.
(Erase heading not required.)

Army Form C. 2118.

Place	Date	Hour	Summary of Events and Information	Remarks and references to Appendices
Brandhoek No 2 Area Details	25/9/17		Details moved up here last night. Battalion have quiet day at Potijze as all unnecessary movement is prohibited. Battalion moves to Assembly Trenches about 9 P.M. It is a glorious day & if tomorrow is the same, the men should be bright cheery & go forward in fine style. 2nd Lt W.L. Robinson reported from IV Corps School. 25 O.R. are detailed according to instructions to report to 8th F.A. Ascertain afterwards that it was the 7th F.A. they go to.	
"	26/9/17		Day of battle. The Battalion was in position of Assembly by 4 A.M. Some slight shelling caused some casualties in the Battalion including 2nd Lt Sharman who though slightly wounded in the head preferred to remain with his Company. At 5.30 AM the attack commenced. The barrage was thick & effective. At 7 AM, 8th East Yorks had taken its objective. 4 machine guns & 15 prisoners being captured. Some resistance was offered from 2 or 3 Pill Boxes. Many casualties were inflicted on the enemy. Special courage was shown by Cpls Lowe, Watson, Bigley & Rathbone, each one of these N.C.Os capturing a machine gun single handed. The attack progressed & finally by 10 AM the Blue Line was captured. The first counterattack was driven off; the second counterattack which was more severe, took place at 6 P.M, caused the leading troops to fall back a little, but a further counter-attack by the Brigade recaptured nearly all of the lost ground. The remainder of the night was uneventful.	

A5834 Wt. W4973/M687 750,000 8/16 D. D. & L. Ltd. Forms/C.2118/13.

Instructions regarding War Diaries and Intelligence Summaries are contained in F. S. Regs., Part II. and the Staff Manual respectively. Title pages will be prepared in manuscript.

WAR DIARY
or
INTELLIGENCE SUMMARY.
(Erase heading not required.)

Army Form C. 2118.

Place	Date	Hour	Summary of Events and Information	Remarks and references to Appendices
Brandhoek Area 2 Detail			Casualties among Officers, so far, were Capt Rev Ruck Keene killed; 2nd Lt Diment killed: the following Officers were wounded, Lt Godfrey, 2nd Lts Buckland, Page, Keith, Wright, Lamb & Lt Johnstone. During the night the troops were reorganised & the position gained, consolidated.	
"	27/9/17		The enemy shelling was severe over the whole area which had been captured. Our artillery was prompt. In the evening the enemy put down a severe barrage behind the front line. Our barrage was prompt & effective, the enemy was unable to leave his trenches, the remainder of the night was uneventful except for the shelling of certain localities. The following casualties among Officers occurred during the day - 2nd Lt Geraghty killed, 2nd Lts Leach, Davies & Robinson wounded.	
"	28/9/17		The usual early morning shelling commenced at an early hour. the morning was fairly quiet. In the evening about 6 P.M. our line was subjected to a bombardment. Casualties however were slight. Capt Matthews proceeds to 19th Corps Lewis Gun Course.	
"	29/9/17		Day was fairly quiet. 2nd Lt Robinson wounded. At 6 P.M. the enemy severely bombarded our trenches & wounded Capts Smith & Cole & 2nd Lt Cole. [In the evening, as soon after dark as possible, the 4th Royal Fusiliers relieved 8th East Yorks, the relief was accomplished	

A5834 Wt. W4973/M687 750,000 8/16 D. D. & L. Ltd. Forms/C.2118/13.

Army Form C. 2118.

Instructions regarding War Diaries and Intelligence Summaries are contained in F. S. Regs., Part II. and the Staff Manual respectively. Title pages will be prepared in manuscript.

WAR DIARY
or
INTELLIGENCE SUMMARY.
(Erase heading not required.)

Place	Date	Hour	Summary of Events and Information	Remarks and references to Appendices
Brandhoek Area 2 Details			without any hitch. The battalion was withdrawn to some reserve trenches near BAVARIA HOUSE on the YPRES - ZONNEBEKE ROAD, the night was quiet except for a few gas shells. 2nd Lts King & Outram return from IV Corps School.	
"	30/9/17		The day was quiet but was area was subjected to some slight shelling with heavy shells. Battalion rested all day. At 8-30 P.M. the Battalion moved off to a Camp south of YPRES for the night.	
			2nd Lt Buckton proceeds to 4th Army Infantry School.	
			2nd Lt Bladon reported back from UK leave.	

[illegible] Capt
Adj. for Lt Col Commanding

A5834 Wt. W4973/M687 750,000 8/16 D. D. & L. Ltd. Forms/C.2118/13.

Instructions regarding War Diaries and Intelligence Summaries are contained in F. S. Regs., Part II. and the Staff Manual respectively. Title pages will be prepared in manuscript.

8th Bn East Yorkshire Regt

WAR DIARY
or
INTELLIGENCE SUMMARY.
(Erase heading not required.)

October 1917

Army Form C. 2118.

8 E York Rgt
Vol 26

Place	Date	Hour	Summary of Events and Information	Remarks and references to Appendices
TORONTO CAMP BRANDHOEK	1/10/17		Battalion arrives from Ypres South Camp about 10 A.M. Day fine. Men spend day quietly. Night disturbed by Bombing Raids. 2nd Lt Craig goes on UK leave.	
"	2/10/17		Battalion moves by Bus to WINNEZEELE AREA. Very [illegible] [illegible].	
WINNEZEELE AREA	3/10/17		Brigade parade in field behind Bde HQ at 9-30 AM. Major General addressed whole on the satisfactory manner in which the recent attack was carried out. Coys under Coy Commanders & at Baths. 2/Lt Russell, Ward, Wessel & Capt Young & draft of 75 join Battalion. 2/Lt Cranswick commands 'A' Coy in absence of Lt Kirkham & 2nd Lt [illegible]. 'D' Coy in absence of Capt Cole.	
"	4/10/17		Battalion moves to RENNESCURE preparatory to entraining tomorrow for BAPAUME. Billets very scattered. Rain off & on during day. Major [illegible] returns to 7th K.S.L.I.	
RENNESCURE	5/10/17		General preparation for movement of area. Battalion entrain at ST OMER about 7 P.M. Day fine but night journey bitterly cold.	
~~BAPAUME~~ BEAULINCOURT	6/10/17		Battalion arrives about 5 A.M. Dark & rain falling. Everyone very miserable after cold night journey. Battalion moves to 'R' Camp BEAULINCOURT. Night was very cold. Nissen Huts in the Camp have been erected in a scattered manner.	
BEAULINCOURT	7/10/17		Church parade at 10 A.M. Very wet most of day & very cold. Concert arranged by Padre postponed till tomorrow night. Capt Armitage takes over Second in Command pending return of Major [illegible]. Capt Young commands 'A' Coy.	
"	8/10/17		Coys under Coy Commanders for reorganisation (4 sections, Rifle, Bomber, Lewis Gun & Rifle Grenadiers) & refitting. Brigadier inspects [illegible]. Day very windy & bitterly cold, heavy rain falls.	

Instructions regarding War Diaries and Intelligence Summaries are contained in F. S. Regs., Part II. and the Staff Manual respectively. Title pages will be prepared in manuscript.

WAR DIARY
or
INTELLIGENCE SUMMARY.
(Erase heading not required.)

Army Form C. 2118.

Place	Date	Hour	Summary of Events and Information	Remarks and references to Appendices
BEAULINCOURT	9/10/17		Very windy & occasional showers of rain. Coys under Coy Commanders at Close Order Drill, P.T. 'A' Coy in morning. N.C.Os under R.S.M. 2/Lt [illegible] made [illegible] [illegible] Officer.	
"	10/10/17		Very heavy rain in forenoon. Coys in Close Order Drill, P.T., Coy [illegible] A & B Coy in morning. One L.G. team per platoon under instruction for [illegible]. Reserve team to be obtained as soon as possible. 2/Lt Buckle, Blood, & J. Holt [illegible] Small Arms School for 14 day course.	
"	11/10/17		Day dull but cold wind blowing. Coys in P.T., Close Order Drill, [illegible] Coy Drill. N.C.Os under R.S.M. Lewis Gun instruction. Capt. & Col [illegible]. 2nd Lt Kidd goes to Hospital.	
"	12/10/17		Battalion moved to Beugnatre Area Camp H.11.b.9.0. Moved off 9.45 A.M. arrived 11.45 A.M. Day dull & rain falls in latter part of day. Capt Armitage & Adjutant reconnoitre 2nd line of Defence.	
BEUGNATRE	13/10/17		Coys on P.T., Musketry, Coy Drill, 'B' Coy training, L.G. instruction, Lecture by platoon Officers & N.C.Os under R.S.M. Day fine	
"	14/10/17		Church Parade in Canteen at Beugnatre. 'D' Coy fire Lewis Gun on short range. O.C. Coys reconnoitre Intermediate line	
	15/10/17.		Coys on P.T., Coy Drill etc. 'A' Coy Lewis Gun on short range in forenoon. B & C Coy in afternoon. Capt. [illegible] Lt. [illegible] returned from Dental Hospital. Lt Hutchinson reported & posted to 'B' Coy. Day fine except for occasional shower. Lt Craig returned from U.K. leave. Commanding Officer, Capt. Armitage & Adjutant reconnoitre line	

A5834 Wt. W4973/M687 750,000 8/16 D. D. & L. Ltd. Forms/C.2118/13.

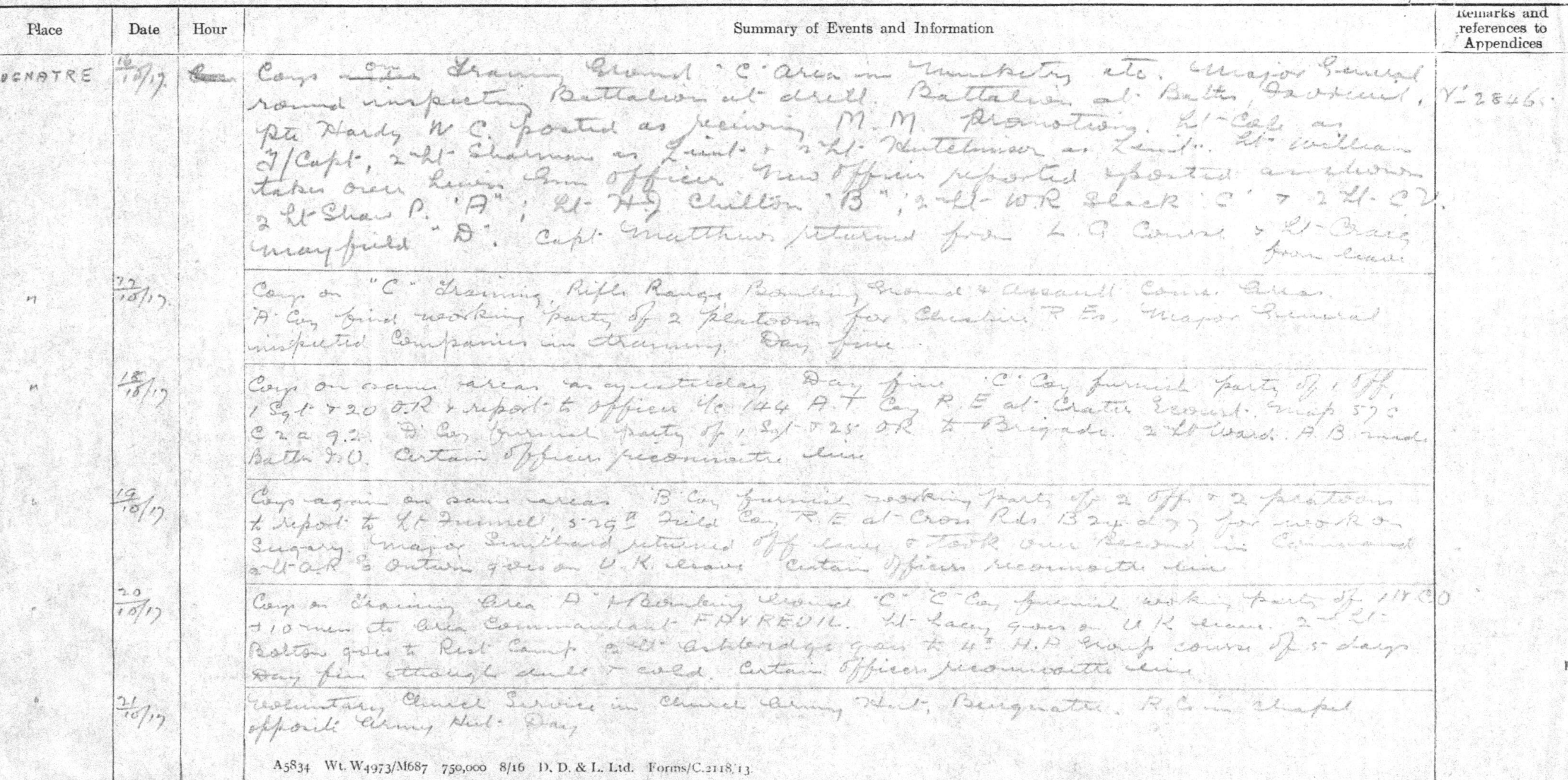

Instructions regarding War Diaries and Intelligence Summaries are contained in F. S. Regs., Part II. and the Staff Manual respectively. Title pages will be prepared in manuscript.

WAR DIARY
or
INTELLIGENCE SUMMARY.
(Erase heading not required.)

Army Form C. 2118.

Place	Date	Hour	Summary of Events and Information	Remarks and references to Appendices
BEUGNATRE	16/10/17		Coys on Training Ground "C" Area in Musketry etc. Major General round inspecting Battalion at drill. Battalion at Baths [illegible]. Pte Hardy W C posted as receiving M.M. Promotions. Lt-Col as T/Capt., 2nd Lt Sharman as Lieut. & 2nd Lt. Huntelmner as Lieut. Lt. William takes over Lewis Gun Officer. New Officers reported & posted as follows 2 Lt Shaw P. "A"; Lt. H.J Chilton "B"; 2nd Lt. W.R Slack "C" & 2 Lt. C.J Mayfield "D". Capt Matthews returned from L.G. Course & Lt Craig from leave	No 2846.
"	17/10/17		Coys on "C" Training Rifle Range, Bombing Ground & Assault Course Areas. "A" Coy find working party of 2 platoons for [illegible] R.Es. Major General inspected Companies in training. Day fine	
"	18/10/17		Coys on same areas as yesterday. Day fine. "C" Coy furnish party of 1 Off. 1 Sgt & 20 O.R & report to Officer i/c 144 A.T Coy R.E at Crater [illegible]. Map 57C C.2.a.9.2. "D" Coy furnish party of 1 Sgt & 25 O.R to Brigade. 2 Lt Ward A.B made Bath O. Certain Officers reconnoitre line	
"	19/10/17		Coys again on same areas. "B" Coy furnish working party of 2 Off & 2 platoons to report to Lt Funnell, 529th Field Coy R.E at Cross Rds B.24.d.7.7. for work on Sugary. Major Smithard returned off leave & took over Second in Command. 2 Lt O.R. & Ontwin goes on U.K. leave. Certain Officers reconnoitre line	
"	20/10/17		Coys on Training Area "A" & Bombing Ground "C". "C" Coy furnish working party of 1 N.C.O. & 10 men to Area Commandant FAVREUIL. Lt Lacy goes on U.K. leave. 2nd Lt Bolton goes to Rest Camp. 2nd Lt Ashbridge goes to 4th H.A Group course of 5 days. Day fine although dull & cold. Certain Officers reconnoitre line	
"	21/10/17		Voluntary Church Service in Church Army Hut, Beugnatre. R.C in Chapel opposite Army Hut. Day	

A5834 Wt. W4973/M687 750,000 8/16 D. D. & L. Ltd. Forms/C.2118/13.

Army Form C. 2118.

WAR DIARY
or
INTELLIGENCE SUMMARY.
(Erase heading not required.)

Instructions regarding War Diaries and Intelligence Summaries are contained in F. S. Regs., Part II. and the Staff Manual respectively. Title pages will be prepared in manuscript.

Place	Date	Hour	Summary of Events and Information	Remarks and references to Appendices
BEUGNATRE	22/10/17		Companies on Training Area "C", Assault Course "C" Range "C" + Bombing Ground "C". Special attention paid to Close Order Drill. "C" Coy practice Patrol work by night. Day fine.	
"	23/10/17		Day wet + cold. Parades cancelled. Men lectured to in Huts by Officers + N.C.Os on various subjects. 2Lt A White "C" Coy + 2Lt H Stakesby "D" Coy joined + posted to Coys as shown.	
"	24/10/17		Coys on P.T., Pre Musketry, Close Order + Arms Drill, Coy Drill, Range + "B" + "D" Coys on night patrol practice. N.C.Os under R.S.M. + working parties under instruction. 2Lt [illegible] goes to Corps Depot. Day fine	
"	25/10/17		Night very stormy – heavy wind + rain. All parades cancelled as whole Battalion out as working party on various works. 2Lt [illegible] rejoined from Hospital.	
"	26/10/17.		Coys on P.T. Preliminary Musketry, Coy Drill, Arms Drill + Artillery attack formation. "D" Coy on range. N.C.Os under R.S.M. Day fine	
"	27/10/17.		Coys on P.T., preliminary Musketry + Close Order Drill. "C" Coy furnishes working parties of 2 Off. + 2 platoons to 529th Field Coy R.E. + 1 Off., 1 N.C.O. + 20 men to 144th A.T. Coy R.E. Day fine though cloudy.	
"	28/10/17		Voluntary Church Parade in Church Army Hut. 2Lt Williams made Battalion L.G. Officer. 2Lt [illegible] goes on U.K. leave.	
"	29/10/17		Coys on usual training. "B" Coy furnish working party of 1 Off. 1 N.C.O. + 20 men to 144th A.T. Coy R.E. 2Lt Buckle returns from L.G. Course.	
"	30/10/17.		Coys on training as yesterday. Capt Armitage takes over second in command. 2Lt Ashbridge commands "D" Coy during absence of Capt. Cole. Battalion relieves 12th W. Yorks Regt in NOREUIL SECTOR. G.O.C. inspected model platoon	(A) [illegible]
"	31/10/17.		Relief was complete at 10 pm [illegible] Slight hostile shelling of Bn H.Q. + NOREUIL Road during the night [illegible] Patrols. Day uneventful. Weather fine. Work continued in the evening on forming up posts. Night quiet.	

A5834 Wt. W4973/M687 750,000 8/16 D. D. & L. Ltd. Forms/C.2118/13.

Instructions regarding War Diaries and Intelligence Summaries are contained in F. S. Regs., Part II. and the Staff Manual respectively. Title pages will be prepared in manuscript.

WAR DIARY or INTELLIGENCE SUMMARY.

(Erase heading not required.)

Army Form C. 2118.

8 X E York Re Vol 27

Place	Date	Hour	Summary of Events and Information	Remarks and references to Appendices
	1-11-17		Day fine. Slight hostile activity against battery positions N. of Noreuil Road during the morning. "C" Coys left was shelled with light shells & minnies. Brigadier visited the line. Night quiet. Inspection of Battalion wire.	
	2-11-17		Day uneventful. G.O.C. Division visited the line. Slight shelling at Tyne Dump. Usual working parties in the evening. A patrol under 2/Lt A.B. Ward encountered a hostile patrol & a fight ensued in which a German N.C.O. is certain to have been killed & others wounded. Great skill & gallantry was shewn by 2/Lt Ward & Cpl. Loft, who, between them, carried Pte. Norman who had been seriously wounded. He unfortunately died of his injuries. A letter of congratulation reached the Battalion in the evening from the Brigadier, which ran as follows:- C.O. 8th Bn. East Yorks Regt - I have read the report of your patrol last night with great interest & congratulate the officer in charge. It is in this way we are able to keep absolute control of what we call "No Man's Land". It is possible some Boche were killed & if so, we should be able to obtain an identification. I hope your wounded men are doing well. (Sgd) W. James B.G. Another patrol under 2/Lt G. Bladen went out to reconnoitre an enemy post. He approached quite close to the wire & although fired on did not return until he had finished his task.	

A7092). Wt. W12839/M1293. 750,000. 1/17. D. D & L., Ltd. Forms/C2118/14.

Instructions regarding War Diaries and Intelligence Summaries are contained in F. S. Regs., Part II. and the Staff Manual respectively. Title pages will be prepared in manuscript.

WAR DIARY
or
INTELLIGENCE SUMMARY.
(*Erase heading not required.*)

Army Form C. 2118.

Place	Date	Hour	Summary of Events and Information	Remarks and references to Appendices
	3-11-17		Day quiet & uneventful. Lt. Oatum returns from leave U.K. also Lt. Laurie. Lt. Batten proceeded on Artillery Course. Hostile shelling & M.G. fire Nil. Heavy mist all day. Usual working parties in the evening. A Company sent out a patrol under Lt. McCammick and R. Wessels to try and reconnoitre gap in enemy wire. They were unable to reach the gap on account of hostile M.G. fire opening on to this point blank range. Patrol returned without any casualties.	
	4-11-17		Quiet day. Uneventful. Publication of honors & awards among officers of the Division. Otherwise, nothing to report. B.G. went round Battalion sector.	
	5-11-17		Nothing to report.	
	6-11-17		Quiet day. Arrangements for relief made with 1st R.S.F. Relief complete by 4 p.m. Battalion withdraws to support at Norevil.	
	7-11-17		Severe rain. Day quiet. Two American officers attached to the Battalion for instruction. Battalion furnish various working parties night & day.	
	8-11-17		Usual routine of working parties.	
	9-11-17		Nothing to report.	

A7092). Wt. W12839/M1293 750,000. 1/17. D. D & L., Ltd. Forms/C2118/14.

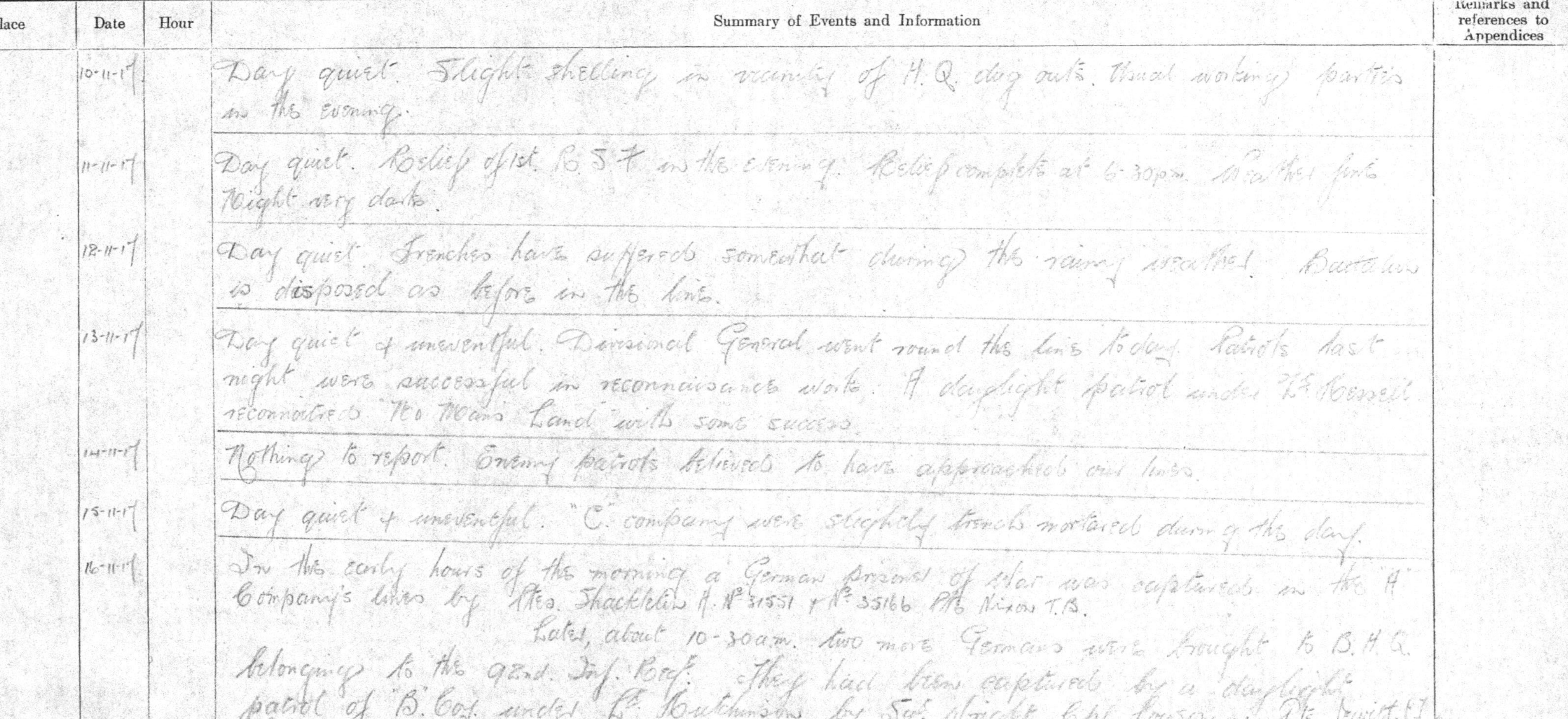

Instructions regarding War Diaries and Intelligence Summaries are contained in F. S. Regs., Part II. and the Staff Manual respectively. Title pages will be prepared in manuscript.

WAR DIARY
or
INTELLIGENCE SUMMARY.
(Erase heading not required.)

Army Form C. 2118.

Place	Date	Hour	Summary of Events and Information	Remarks and references to Appendices
	10-11-17		Day quiet. Slight shelling in vicinity of H.Q. dug outs. Usual working parties in the evening.	
	11-11-17		Day quiet. Relief of 1st R.S.F. in the evening. Relief complete at 6-30pm. Weather fine. Night very dark.	
	12-11-17		Day quiet. Trenches have suffered somewhat during the rainy weather. Battalion is disposed as before in the line.	
	13-11-17		Day quiet & uneventful. Divisional General went round the line today. Patrols last night were successful in reconnaissance work. A daylight patrol under 2Lt Hessell reconnoitred No Mans Land with some success.	
	14-11-17		Nothing to report. Enemy patrols believed to have approached our lines.	
	15-11-17		Day quiet & uneventful. "C" company were slightly trench mortared during the day.	
	16-11-17		In the early hours of the morning a German prisoner of war was captured in the "A" Company's lines by Ptes. Shacklelin A. No 31551 & No 35166 Pte Nixon T.B. Later, about 10-30a.m. two more Germans were brought to B.H.Q. belonging to the 92nd Inf. Regt. They had been captured by a daylight patrol of "B" Coy under Lt Hutchinson by Sgt Wright, Cpl Lowson & Pte Jewitt F.L. The party returned safely to our lines at 10-45a.m. without any casualties.	

A5834 Wt. W4973/M687 750,000 8/16 D. D. & L. Ltd. Forms/C.2118/13.

Instructions regarding War Diaries and Intelligence Summaries are contained in F. S. Regs., Part II. and the Staff Manual respectively. Title pages will be prepared in manuscript.

WAR DIARY
or
INTELLIGENCE SUMMARY.

(Erase heading not required.)

Army Form C. 2118.

Place	Date	Hour	Summary of Events and Information	Remarks and references to Appendices
	16-11-17 (continued)		One prisoner was killed on the way back as he became troublesome. 'C' Company were slightly trench mortared during the afternoon.	
	17-11-17		Nothing unusual to report. Hostile artillery is somewhat more active.	
	18-11-17		C.O's conference at Division. General preparations for an advance. No details to hand.	
	19-11-17		Daylight relief by Royal Scots Fusiliers which was completed by 5-45pm. Battalion withdraws to Brigade Support at Noreuil.	
	20-11-17		At 6.20am the big battle started. VI Corps so far only engaged in minor operations which were very successfully carried out by the 16th (Irish) Division & the 9th Inf Bge, the former capturing 400 prisoners - the latter 70 odd & only sustaining 2 casualties. The evening was fairly quiet. Good news from the South. From Situation Report. Satisfactory progress in the South. Advance to a depth of 5 miles. 3rd Div front situation normal. 9th Bge lost 150 yards on the left of their attack. Weather rainy. Brigade standing-to to advance at any moment. So far, there has been no signs of enemy retiring.	
	21-11-17		Weather poor & drizzling all day. News hopeful. Masnières on our right has been taken. Otherwise news very scarce.	

A5834 Wt. W4973/M687 750,000 8/16 D. D. & L. Ltd. Forms/C.2118/13.

Instructions regarding War Diaries and Intelligence Summaries are contained in F. S. Regs., Part II. and the Staff Manual respectively. Title pages will be prepared in manuscript.

WAR DIARY
or
INTELLIGENCE SUMMARY.

(Erase heading not required.)

Army Form C. 2118.

Place	Date	Hour	Summary of Events and Information	Remarks and references to Appendices
	22/11/17		Day dull but no rain. Enemy has not withdrawn during the night. Vicinity round Bn.H.Q. shelled. Also battery positions in rear. Our aircraft active. News still continues favourable but no signs of us having yet to move forward.	
	23/11/17		Early morning shelling of battery positions in rear of B.H.Q. Our aircraft active. Artillery action against REINCOURT. Intense bombardment during the evening. BOURLON WOOD captured and FONTAINE-NOTRE-DAME captured.	
	24/11/17		Early morning bombardment of REINCOURT and again at 10am. Aircraft active. Hostile artillery shelling valley of NOREUIL. Capt. Armitage to be A/Major. Lieut Buckston to be A/Captain. Otherwise day uneventful.	
	25/11/17		Day uneventful. Hostile artillery active against NOREUIL. Orders to relieve 1st R.S.F. today. Relief complete 8 ... B.H.Q. vicinity shelled intermittently all night. Lieut McAndrews & 2Lt Hand return from leave. 2Lt Hall proceeds on leave.	
	26/11/17		Hostile artillery active against "C" Company. D & B Company as well as B.H.Q. Patrols do good work in reconnaissance. Casualties today - 2 killed 1 wounded.	
	27/11/17		Hostile shelling practically all night. Our artillery & aircraft active. 2 wounded today.	
	28/11/17		Usual hostile activity morning & night & intermittent shelling during the day. Killed. 2Lt Slack & 2 O.R. wounded. Hostile aircraft increased daily.	
	29/11/17		Nothing of importance except for heavy hostile shelling morning & night. 2Lt Blaxon to hospital sick. Many men to hospital sick. Heavy gas shell bombardment of NOREUIL Valley. Battalion was to have been relieved today by 5th Bn. Royal Fusiliers but this was eventually cancelled. Suspected mining on RAILWAY RESERVE being investigated.	
	30-11-17		B.H.Q. heavily shelled at 8.0am today. Some direct hits obtained. Some shelling of front line. Casualties 2 OR wounded.	

A7092). Wt. W12839/M1293. 750,000. 1/17. D. D & L., Ltd. Forms/C2118/14.

9

Instructions regarding War Diaries and Intelligence Summaries are contained in F. S. Regs., Part II. and the Staff Manual respectively. Title pages will be prepared in manuscript.

WAR DIARY
or
INTELLIGENCE SUMMARY.
(Erase heading not required.)

Army Form C. 2118.

8th E. Yorks

Vol 28

Place	Date	Hour	Summary of Events and Information	Remarks and references to Appendices
NOREUIL	1/12/17		Battalion withdrawn to Brigade Support at Noreuil, relieved by 1st R.S.F. One man killed by sniper whilst on patrol with 2nd Lt Hessel who accomplished excellent work in reconnaissance. B.G.C. congratulation received	
"	2/12/17		Nothing eventful to report. Usual working parties found by Battalion. Capt. R.E.H. Locke and Lieut Fulton proceed on leave	
"	3/12/17		2nd Lt Edwards rejoined. Pte J.T. Jewitt awarded the D.C. Medal 1st to the Battalion. Usual working parties were found. Weather cold with sharp frost during the night	
"	4/12/17		Bn. H.Q. and surroundings heavily shelled between 1 am and 4 am. 1 O.R. wounded. Enemy Aircraft fairly active. Every available man on working party during the night. Weather still very cold and frosty	
"	5/12/17		Battalion ordered to take up new disposition immediately in support of 2 Bns at 2.45 am in view of expected hostile operations. 2nd Royal Scots took over our dispositions to develop next of hostile attack and the Bn relieved the 1st R.S.F. in the front line at night. 2nd Lt White proceeds on Lewis Gun Course. Weather still frosty & dry	
"	6/12/17		Capt Wright rejoins from hospital and Lt Marsden joins the Battalion. Front fairly quiet but hostile Artillery very active against battery position. Enemy aircraft over our lines at 6 pm	

A7092). Wt. W12839/M1293. 750,000. 1/17. D. D & L., Ltd. Forms/C2118/14.

Instructions regarding War Diaries and Intelligence Summaries are contained in F. S. Regs., Part II. and the Staff Manual respectively. Title pages will be prepared in manuscript.

WAR DIARY
or
INTELLIGENCE SUMMARY.
(Erase heading not required.)

Army Form C. 2118.

Place	Date	Hour	Summary of Events and Information	Remarks and references to Appendices
NOREUIL	7/12/17		Heavy hostile shelling of batteries. Considerable aerial activity on our part two formations of 14 and 12 respectively flew over the enemy lines. One hostile machine flew very low over our front at 10.30 am but was driven off by Machine and Anti A.C. guns. 2nd Lt R Benson proceeded on leave to UK. Bn H.Q. shelled during the night. Weather still cold with drizzly rain.	
"	8/12/17		Major C E Franklin proceeds to join the 12th S.W.B. 2nd Lt Newman C proceed to Warloy 3rd Army Musketry School. Hostile shelling of batteries in rear heavier than usual. Bn H.Q. again shelled about 6 pm. Night very dark and rainy.	
"	9/12/17		Day uneventful. Enemy exceptionally quiet. Weather dull and wet. Lt Chilton and 2nd Lt Webb, Becket and Butler return from courses.	
"	10/12/17		2nd Lt Webber went down to Field Ambulance. Trench stores were checked prior to relief. Enemy quiet in front but shelled batteries in rear intermittently. Weather cold and showery.	
"	11/12/17		Relieved by 4th R.F. and proceeded to Camp at Moy. Relief completed by 9 p.m. Arrived Moy about 11 pm.	
	12/12/17		Battalion "stood to arms" at 6.30 am. Order received at 7 am to move to 2nd line Corps Reserve at Vaux. Moved off at 7.10 am	

A7092). Wt. W12839/M1293 750,000. 1/17. D. D & L., Ltd. Forms/C2118/14.

Army Form C. 2118.

Instructions regarding War Diaries and Intelligence Summaries are contained in F. S. Regs., Part II. and the Staff Manual respectively. Title pages will be prepared in manuscript.

WAR DIARY
or
INTELLIGENCE SUMMARY.
(Erase heading not required.)

Place	Date	Hour	Summary of Events and Information	Remarks and references to Appendices
	12/12/17		Orders received in Vaux to return to Ivry. Arrived in Camp about 9.40 a.m. At 10.30 a.m. again received orders to move to second line. Battalion in position by noon. Remained until 5 pm when orders were received to move to intermediate line and to be under orders of 9th Brigade. Companies in position about 7 pm. Bn H Qrs at Iggares Corner.	
	13/12/17		Night quiet and very cold. 2 O/R wounded. 2nd Lt Ashbridge proceeded to detail camp in order to proceed to Etaples on L. Gun Course. At 7 pm orders were received to be ready to move to Halifax Support, and at 10 pm 2 companies proceeded to Halifax Support and relieved 2 Companies of the 4th R F. Bn H Qrs moved to Hobart Avenue. Relief complete about 11.20 pm. C Coy on right and D Coy on left were the positions of 2 companies in Halifax support, the left Coy also holding C 5/ and C / . A and B Coys remained in the Intermediate line under Command of Major Armitage who had to provide working parties of 100 strong.	
	14/12/17		No change in disposition. 12 noon Lieut Marsden proceeded to detail camp owing to nervous breakdown. Weather cold and miserable. Day and night passed quietly.	

A7092). Wt. W12839/M1293. 750,000. 1/17. D, D & L., Ltd. Forms/C2118/14.

Instructions regarding War Diaries and Intelligence Summaries are contained in F. S. Regs., Part II. and the Staff Manual respectively. Title pages will be prepared in manuscript.

WAR DIARY
or
INTELLIGENCE SUMMARY.

(Erase heading not required.)

Army Form C. 2118.

Place	Date	Hour	Summary of Events and Information	Remarks and references to Appendices
Noreuil	15/12/17		Stood to at 6.30 am. Heavy bombardment on our left but on S[illegible] 2.30 pm. heavy barrage on our left and Bn stood to until 3.30 pm. Weather cold. Night passed quietly. Provided working parties of 100 for 9th Brigade	
"	16/12/17		All quiet. Orders for relief received. 2 Companies in Hindenburg Support to be relieved by 2 Companies of the 11th Essex and the supporting companies by the K.S.L.I. Casualties 1 O/R killed. Capt Young wounded and 3 O/R wounded. Relief complete at 11.35 pm	
			Battalion marched to Ervillers and embussed for Blairville	
Hendecourt	17/12/17		Nothing to report. Bn cleaning up and resting. Weather hard clear and frosty	
"	18/12/17		Bn still at Hendecourt. Re-fitting and were bathed at Blairville. Weather still continues frosty. [illegible] C.H. Silk returns to Bn. and Lt S. [illegible] and 2nd Lt [illegible] returns from Course.	
"	19/12/17		Nothing to report. Bn carried out Physical training and Coy Inspection	
"	20/12/17		Capt R.E.H. Hicks returns from Leave. Coys under Coy Commanders. Preparation for the line.	

A7092). Wt. W12839/M1293. 750,000. 1/17. D. D & L., Ltd. Forms/C2118/14.

Army Form C. 2118.

Instructions regarding War Diaries and Intelligence Summaries are contained in F. S. Regs., Part II. and the Staff Manual respectively. Title pages will be prepared in manuscript.

WAR DIARY
or
INTELLIGENCE SUMMARY.
(Erase heading not required.)

Place	Date	Hour	Summary of Events and Information	Remarks and references to Appendices
HENDECOURT	21.12.17		Battalion paraded ready to move off at 8.30am. Route HAMELINCOURT to the MORY AREA. Battalion went into Camp here.	
MORY	22.12.17		Coys under Company Commanders. Battalion moved off by Companies for the line at 5pm to relieve 1st Bn the Buffs in NOREUIL support. Relief complete at 8pm. Night quiet.	
NOREUIL	23.12.17		Fine, cold & frosty weather. Day quiet. 3 big shells at Bn HQ. One casualty.	
"	24.12.17		Day quiet. Major General came round also Brigadier. Many others Xmas wishes. Usual working parties at work. 3 casualties to B Coy. CSM Burton left the battalion to-day to take a commission.	
"	25.12.17		Day cloudy. Some rain. Day quiet nothing to report. Hostile Artillery active on the right during the evening. Hostile & our aircraft active during the morning.	
"	26.12		Fresh snow falls. Situation quiet. Hostile shelling slight. Hostile aeroplanes very active. KSLI form up at Bn HQ. 3 casualties today.	
"	27.12.17		Situation quiet. Some hostile shelling near Igarni Corner. 10 casualties. 3 of our men wounded. 2Lt Robinson returns from leave. 2Lt King proceeds to UK Leave. KSLI moved off this evening.	
"	28.12.17		Very cold & fine. Aerial activity considerable. Capt Cole returns from hospital. CO Argyll & Sutherlands comes up & arranged relief for tomorrow night. Usual working parties at night.	
"	29.12.17		Fine day. Very quiet. Relief commenced in good time & was complete at 7.40pm. Battalion marched to Camp at HAMELINCOURT. CLONMEL Camp. Arriving between 11 & 12 midnight.	

A7092). Wt. W12839/M1293 750,000. 1/17. D. D & L., Ltd. Forms/C2118/14.

Instructions regarding War Diaries and Intelligence Summaries are contained in F. S. Regs., Part II. and the Staff Manual respectively. Title pages will be prepared in manuscript.

WAR DIARY
or
INTELLIGENCE SUMMARY.

(Erase heading not required.)

Army Form C. 2118.

Place	Date	Hour	Summary of Events and Information	Remarks and references to Appendices
[illegible]court	30.12.17		Day spent in cleaning & refitting. Lt Col [illegible] [illegible] Paris. Major Armitage takes over Command [illegible] + Lt Col [illegible] takes over Command of 8th Inf Bde	
"	31.12.17		Companies under Company Commanders [illegible] to [illegible] Brigade Commander [illegible] during the morning. Day uneventful.	

[illegible] Armitage Major
Comdg 8th Bn East Yorks

A7092). Wt. W12839/M1293. 750,000. 1/17. D. D & L., Ltd. Forms/C2118/14.

3RD DIVISION
8TH INFY BDE

8TH BATTALION

EAST YORKSHIRE REGT.

JAN-FEB 1918.

DISBAN

Instructions regarding War Diaries and Intelligence Summaries are contained in F. S. Regs., Part II. and the Staff Manual respectively. Title pages will be prepared in manuscript.

WAR DIARY
or
INTELLIGENCE SUMMARY.
(Erase heading not required.)

8th East Yorkshire Regt

Army Form C. 2118. 8/3

Vol 29

Place	Date	Hour	Summary of Events and Information	Remarks and references to Appendices
HAPLINCOURT	1.1	18	New Year's Day. Companies under Coy Commander. 2/Lt Bolton returns from UK Leave.	
"	2.1.	18	Battalion parade at 8.45 am. Company Training.	
"	3.1.	18	Training commences. Commanding Officer awarded D.S.O.	
"	4.1.	18	Training. Day uneventful	
"	5.1.	18	Training. Corps Commander payed us a visit this morning. Also Brigade Comdr. Hun attack at Bullecourt repulsed. R.S.M. Mobbott awarded M.C. Colonel returns from Paris. H.Q. officers entertained at dinner at the Sgts Mess	
"	6.1.	18	Usual Church services. H.Q. Xmas dinner	
"	7.1.	18	Training. Weather better. Transport dinner in the evening. Two Companies proceed to Xmas Pantomime on invitation of Padre. General inspection by Corps Commander to morrow	
"	8.1.	18	Bitterly cold with blizzards. Inspection took place at 2.30 pm. Otherwise day was uneventful. 2 Coys proceed to Pantomime.	
"	9.1.	18	Training. Reinforcements of 38 o.ranks today. H.Q. Coy to Pantomime	
"	10.1.	18	Training. Model Platoon inspection by C.O. B Coy won	

A7092). Wt. W12839/M1293. 750,000. 1/17. D. D & L., Ltd. Forms/C2118/14.

Instructions regarding War Diaries and Intelligence Summaries are contained in F. S. Regs., Part II. and the Staff Manual respectively. Title pages will be prepared in manuscript.

WAR DIARY
or
INTELLIGENCE SUMMARY.
(*Erase heading not required.*)

Army Form C. 2118.

Place	Date	Hour	Summary of Events and Information	Remarks and references to Appendices
HAMLINCOURT	11.1.18		Usual Training. Day uneventful. Padre left us to-day & so did our interpreter Badour	
"	12.1.18		Training during the morning. Games afternoon. Officers play at Rugger. C.O. left the battalion to-day for attachment to French Armies in the Field. Major C de W Armitage takes over Command. 2/Lt Ashbridge rejoins from Course	
"	13.1.18		Church of England Service by Major Fisher. Also Wesleyan Service. Day uneventful. 2/Lt Batty, Bessels, Ward, Shaw rejoin from Course.	
"	14.1.18		Training. Range practices. 2/Lt Batty proceeds on leave. 2/Lt Crang & Hale struck off strength.	
"	15.1.18		Rain all day. Instruction carried on indoors. B.G.C. dined at Bn H.Q.	
	16.1.18		More rain, more instruction in doors.	
	17.1.18		Weather unsettled. First day of working Parties. Parties left camp at 3 pm.	
	18.1.18		Nothing to Report. Working Parties in the evening.	
	19.1.18		Nothing to Report. Usual Working Parties	
	20.1.18		Working Parties in the evening. Major Armitage visited work.	
	21.1.18		Uneventful. Major Armitage & Coy Commanders visit new sector.	
	22.1.18		Nothing to Report	
	23.1.18			

A7092). Wt. W12839/M1293 750,000. 1/17. D. D & L., Ltd. Forms/C2118/14.

Instructions regarding War Diaries and Intelligence Summaries are contained in F. S. Regs., Part II. and the Staff Manual respectively. Title pages will be prepared in manuscript.

WAR DIARY
or
INTELLIGENCE SUMMARY.
(Erase heading not required.)

Army Form C. 2118.

Place	Date	Hour	Summary of Events and Information	Remarks and references to Appendices
HAMLINCOURT	23/1		Day uneventful. Various working parties. Period has now been extended to the 26th.	
"	24/1		Lecturing [illegible] Divisional Commander addressed all officers of the Brigade	
"	25/1		B.G.C. inspected B Coy Model Platoon. Battalion baths & preparation for the line	
"	26/1		Battalion left Camp at 4pm to relieve ~~2nd Lincolns~~ 11th Suffolks, 34th Division in support. Relief complete 10pm	
FONTAINE CROISILLES	27/1		Battalion moved off from support & relieved 10th LINCOLNS in left Battalion Sector. Relief complete by 7.30pm. Situation quiet.	
"	28/1		Day quiet uneventful. B.G.C. visited the line.	
"	29/1		Major General & B.G.C. visited the line	
"	30/1		Quiet day. C.O. returns from French Armies. Sgt [illegible] & Sgt Stevenson awarded Belgian Croix de Guerre	
"	31/1		Quiet day. Relief by 2nd Roy Scots commenced at 11am during night. Relief complete 6pm. Bn withdrawn to support.	

[illegible signature] 3/2/18

A7092). Wt. W12839/M1293 750,000. 1/17. D. D & L., Ltd. Forms/C2118/14.

Army Form C. 2118.

8 E York Regt

Vol 30

Instructions regarding War Diaries and Intelligence Summaries are contained in F. S. Regs., Part II. and the Staff Manual respectively. Title pages will be prepared in manuscript.

WAR DIARY
or
INTELLIGENCE SUMMARY.
(Erase heading not required.)

Place	Date	Hour	Summary of Events and Information	Remarks and references to Appendices
1.2.18 FONTAINE CROISILLES	1.2.18		Day quiet & uneventful. Working Parties for all units day & night	
"	2.2.18		Day uneventful. Usual working Parties.	
"	3.2.18		Day uneventful. Usual working Parties. First intimation that the 8th Battalion East Yorkshire Regt is to be disbanded.	
"	4.2.18		Relief of the 2nd Bn Royal Scots is Cancelled. Day uneventful	
"	5.2.18		Letter from the 2nd Battalion the Royal Scots, ~~copy~~ original of which is attached. Remainder of day uneventful. Lieut H.S. Williams returns from leave.	
"	6.2.18		Day uneventful. G.O.C. came round during the morning. Battalion to leave the line on the 8th inst.	
"	7.2.18		Inter Brigade relief. 5th East Yorks take over Right Support Battalion dispositions. Our move Cancelled. Lord Nunburnholme to inspect the battalion tomorrow	
	8.2.18		Early morning bombardment by the enemy all along the Divisional front. Attempted raid by them on the 7th K.S.L.I. failed. B.G.C. came round the line during the morning. LORD NUNBURNHOLME visited the battalion during the afternoon	

A7092). Wt. W12839/M1293 750,000. 1/17. D. D & L., Ltd. Forms/C2118/14.

Instructions regarding War Diaries and Intelligence Summaries are contained in F. S. Regs., Part II. and the Staff Manual respectively. Title pages will be prepared in manuscript.

WAR DIARY
or
INTELLIGENCE SUMMARY.
(Erase heading not required.)

Army Form C. 2118.

8 E York Regt
Vol

Place	Date	Hour	Summary of Events and Information	Remarks and references to Appendices
FONTAINE CROISILLE	9.2.18.		Orders received that battalion is to be withdrawn on the morning of the 10/2/18. Quiet day. Some slight trench [illegible] shelling round D Coy Area.	
CARLISLE LINES	10.2.18.		At 5 am Companies moved off from their support positions & proceeded to BOYELLES where Breakfast was served. Battalion moved off at 9.30 am for CARLISLE LINES, near BEAURAINS. Afternoon spent in cleaning up & preparing for to-morrow's march to BERLES-AU-BOIS.	
BERLES-AU-BOIS	11.2.18.		Battalion moved off at 11 AM & arrived at BERLES-AU-BOIS about 4 PM. Day fine	
— " —	12/2/18		Day spent in general cleaning up etc.	
— " —	13/2/18		Day wet. All parades cancelled. Rifle inspection. Preliminary musketry etc carried on in billets.	
— " —	14/2/18		G.O.C. 3rd Division inspected Battalion at 11 A.M. & spoke on reason of the disbandment. Copy of speech attached. Received orders that this Battalion is to amalgamate with 12th West Yorkshire Regt to form 10th Entrenching Battalion. D Coy at Baths	
— " —	15/2/18		Coys on Preliminary musketry, Squad & Platoon Drill. B & C Coys at Baths. [illegible] over [illegible] Rolls etc. All surplus Officers & N.C.Os to report to O.C. II Corps [illegible] on 18th inst.	
— " —	16/2/18		Battalion reorganization into two Companies No 3 & 4 of 10th Entrenching Batt. C.O's parade at 2.30 P.M. for farewell speech. [illegible]	
— " —	17/2/18		No 3 & 4 Coys parade [illegible] No 1 & 2 Coys at 11 A.M. for inspection by Col [illegible] DSO	
— " —	18/2/18		The Battalion ceased to exist as 8th Bn. The East Yorkshire Regt at 12 midnight 17/18th inst.	

(A7092). Wt. W12839/M1293. 750,000. 1/17. D. D & L., Ltd. Forms/C2118/14.

Army Form C. 2118.

WAR DIARY
or
INTELLIGENCE SUMMARY.
(Erase heading not required.)

Instructions regarding War Diaries and Intelligence Summaries are contained in F. S. Regs., Part II. and the Staff Manual respectively. Title pages will be prepared in manuscript.

Place	Date	Hour	Summary of Events and Information	Remarks and references to Appendices
BERLES AU BOIS.	18/2/18.		Surplus Officers & N.C.O's reporting to [illegible] T/Capt. F. L. Ball, T/Capt. [illegible] Cole, T/Lt. C. S. [illegible], Hon. Lt. & Q.M. [illegible] T/2/Lts H. Burkett, P. Shaw, F. [illegible], C. Green, L. [illegible] & [illegible] Award No. 5692 Sgt. Hands R. C. (Bronze [illegible]); No. 13327 C.Q.M.S. Hill G. E. [illegible] No. 220414 Cpl. [illegible] W., 220418 Pte. [illegible] W., 220410 Pte. Greenwood C. J.; 220413 Pte. [illegible] H. F. 220414 Pte. [illegible] T.	

[illegible] Lt.-Col.
8/[illegible]
18/2/18

A7092). Wt. W12839/M1293 750,000. 1/17. D. D & L., Ltd. Forms/C2118/14.

3RD DIVISION
8TH INFY BDE

MACHINE GUN COMPANY

JAN-DEC 1916.

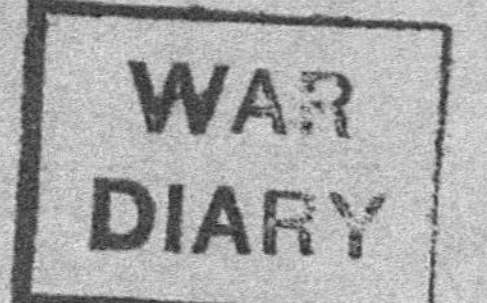

8th Brigade.

3rd Division.

FORMED 22nd January 1916.

8th BRIGADE

MACHINE GUN COMPANY

JANUARY 1 9 1 6

WAR DIARY.

January 1916 — 8th MACHINE GUN COY. B.E.F.

January 22nd RENINGHELST.	Company formed from following units under Command of 2nd Lt (Temp Capt) E.H PETRE 3rd Batt the Suffolk Regt B.M.G.O. 8th Infy Brigade. 2nd Batt the Royal Scots 2nd Lt R.J.O. TALOR. 2nd Lt D.C BROWN & 41. O.R. 2nd Batt the Suffolk Regt 27 O.R. 4th Batt the MIDDLESEX Regt 2nd Lt E.R. SPOTFORTH. 2nd Lt W C. STEELE & 25. O.R. 5th City of London Regt (L.R.B) 2nd Lt W. PULLEN 2nd Lt E.E. POOL & 40. O.R. 1st Batt the Gordon Highlanders. 2nd Lt S.M. ROBERTSON & 1. O.R. The 10th Batt the Welsh Fusiliers 2nd Lt P.T. DALE & 1. O.R 7th Batt K.S.L.I. 1. O.R 2 Batt the Royal Scots 4 Guns limbers horses ammunition Complete 2 " " Suffolk Regt 4 " " " " " 4 " " Middlesex Regt 4 " " " " " 5 City of London Regt 4 " " " " " In Rest Billets at RENINGHELST busy getting Coy in order telling off Sections &c Sgt HILES appointed acting Coy. C.S.M. Sgt TODD 5th City of London Regt acting Coy Q. M. Sgt Sgt ~~McCall~~ McMILLAN acting transport Sgt.
January 23rd	Rest Billets in RENINGHELST.
January 24th	Orders received to relieve 9 M.G.C. in St Eloi Line relieved 9th M.G. C. brought 12 Guns in front line & Supporting positions 4 Guns in reserve at DICKEY BUSCH relief Complete by 12 midnight.
January 25th	Very Quiet day in trenches
January 26th	Quiet day 2 guns under 2nd Lt ROBERTSON moved up to left of line to take over from 76th Bde on extension of 8th Bde line
January 27th	In Trenches very quiet day
January 28th	In Trenches but warned to keep especially alert as it was Kaisers birthday very Quiet day.
January 29	Very Quiet day but Coy stood on Gas alert
January 30th	Very Quiet day
January 31st	Coy relieved at night by 9th M.G. Coy returned Rest Billets RENINGHELST very slow relief 5 am before last man got into Billets

E.H. Petre Capt. Comdg 8th M.G.C

8th Brigade.
3rd Division.

WAR DIARY

8th BRIGADE

MACHINE GUN COMPANY

FEBRUARY 1 9 1 6

WAR DIARY.

8th Machine Gun Coy. B.E.F.

February. 1916

February 1st	in Rest Camp RENINGHELST cleaning up resting after tour in trenches
February 2nd	In rest Camp, busy constructing and improving Camp
February 3rd	Coy. Route march
February 4th	received orders to move to ST OMER rest area packed up etc
February 5th	Coy fell in 9am marched to GODEWAERSVELDE arrived there 1Pm entrained 5Pm. arrived ST OMER 9.Pm marched into rest Billets at EPERLEQUES. 12 midnight very poor billets for men & horses transport lines 1 mile from rest of Coy.
February 6th	in rest Billets at EPERLEQUE very poor billets overcrowded. Cleaning up & church parades
February 7th	Started scheme of training with preliminary drill & inspection by C.O.
February 8th	received orders to take over billets at MENTQUE 2 miles away arrived there 5Pm. very comfortable billets plenty of room for horses & men good training ground
February 9th	Started training working till 3Pm. men played football in Pm
February 10th	Route march with transport brought guns into action etc
February 11th	very wet day spent lecturing mechanism etc
February 12th	Wet drill in am lecture in Pm.
February 13th	Church Parades in am Coy met Cheshire Field Coy in first round of Bde tournament R.E. won by 2 goals good game
February 14th	Continued scheme of training worked section & section in open country
February 15th	received orders to stand to and entrain at ST OMER at 9 hours notice packed up
February 16	Still under orders to move
February 17th	orders to move Cancelled 12 noon but ordered to hold ourself in readiness at moments notice drill in Pm
February 18th	worked scheme with 4 separate sections
February 19th	All day route march
February 20th	Church parades
February 21	drill mechanism etc
February 22nd	Snowing all day no work out of doors lectures etc
February 23rd	Still snowing Phy. Trg. route march
February 24th	Very heavy snow no work out of doors
February 25th	Still Snowing.

War Diary

8th M. G. Coy. B. E. F.

February 1916 (Cont)

February 26th	orders received to pack up and entrain for POPERINGHE on 28th inst
February 27th	orders to move cancelled
February 28th	Mechanism drill &c
February 29th	orders to move as for 28th. packed up

[signature] Captain

Cmnag 8th M. G. Coy.

8th Brigade.

3rd Division.

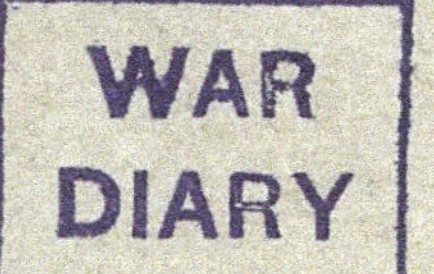

8th BRIGADE

MACHINE GUN COMPANY

MARCH 1 9 1 6

War Diary

8th M.G. Coy B.E.F.

March 1916

March 1st	Left MENTQUE 5 am marched to ST OMER entrained there for POPERINGHE at 9 am left 2 Lts POOL & STEELE behind with 4 Guns no room on train. Detrained at POPERINGHE 2 Pm marched to Camp SCOTTISH LINES with 12 Guns / Pm. partly in huts partly under canvas.
March 2nd	In SCOTTISH LINES but standing 2nd Lts POOL & STEELE rejoined with 4 Guns.
March 3rd	Capt. PETRE. 2nd Lts TAYLOR, PULLEN, & ROBERTSON to 76th Bde Battle H Qrs. BLUFF reconnoitring line CAPT. PETRE stayed there taking over B.M.G.O. for 8th Bde Temporarily other officers returning to SCOTTISH Lines Coy still standing by. Very heavy shelling found trenches in very bad state weather had been bad & terrific bombardment. Saw number German prisoners captured by 2nd Suffolks
March 4th	Capt PETRE still in trenches Coy in SCOTTISH. LINES. 2nd Lt STEELE to hospital sick
March 5th	12 Guns relieved 57th Coy in line 4 Guns in reserve in SCOTTISH LINES
	No 17544 Pte HYSLOP died in F.A. where he had been admitted yesterday fairly heavy shelling but quieter at night
March 6th	2 Guns relieved Guns M.M.G. in BLAUPOORT. FARM 2 more Guns moved up to line making 16 Guns in line in Positions as under
	1 Gun GORDON. TERRACE } under 2nd Lt TAYLOR
	1 " DETACHED POST. }
	2 " GORDON. POST }
	2 " CANAL. POST 3 2nd Lt BROWN
	1 " 36 S } 2nd Lt ROBERTSON
	1 " 37 S. }
	1 " GRAND. FLEET STREET. 3 2nd Lt DALE
	2 " BDE. HQRS. 3 2nd Lt POOL
	2 " R.10. 2nd Lt PULLEN.
	2 " BLAUPOORT. FARM 2nd Lt SPOFFORTH
March 7th	Snowing hard fairly Quiet
March 8	Still Snowing fairly Quiet. but more Shelling

War Diary

8th M.G. Coy. B.E.F.

March 1916

March 9th	Snow thawing a little ground very wet fairly quite
March 10th	Very cold & wet in trenches relieving officers in 36 S. 37 S & Grand Fleet Street every 24 hours it is as much as they can stand. men at H.Q. get good rest
March 11th	Still very cold but fairly quite a little shelling in Pm. No 14575 Pte WOODS. wounded fairly badly
March 12th	fairly quite weather warmer
March 13th	CAPT PETRE sick sent to hospital 2nd Lt TAYLOR assumes command
March 14th	enemy more active shelling BLUFF & support trenches
March 15th	Enemy still shelling hard
March 16	Heavy shelling especially support positions
March 17th	Enemy shelling Batteries & support positions also back area between YPRES & H. Qrs.
March 18th	Bde H. Qrs & Coy H Qrs heavily shelled between 12 noon & 1 Pm & again at 7.30 to 8 Pm. several direct hits on buildings No 17482 Pte Rains & 17525 Pte Bartlett badly wounded
March 19th	Coy relieved by 76th M G Coy their CO came up in Pm. and reconnoitred positions very slow relief left all officers & Sgts & 1 man per team to instruct new Coy. who had just arrived from England 4 Guns on extreme left not relieved
March 20th	4 Guns on left relieved by 150th M. G Coy whole Coy now relieved after 15 day tour very trying weather abominable all time
March 21st	resting & cleaning up in Billets at RENINGHELST
March 22nd	in Billets refitting with clothes Gun stores &c
March 23rd	Drill &c in Billets
March 24th	Drill &c in Billets
March 25th	2nd Lt. SPOFFORTH & 2 guns to St ELOI to support attack by 9th Inf Bde on mound of death these guns were not to be used except in case of a very heavy counter attack
March 26th	orders received to stand by till further orders
March 27th	9th Bde attacked successfully at St ELOI Coy still standing by at RENINGHELST

War Diary

March 1916 — 8th M.G. Coy B.E.F.

March 28th	Coy still standing by in RENINGHELST 2nd Lt TAYLOR visited two guns in line and found them undamaged they had not been called upon
March 29th	Coy relieved 9th M.G. Coy in trenches found trenches in a very bad state after attack however officers & men knew their positions and relief carried through successfully although a good deal of shelling.
March 30th	Very busy in line rebuilding emplacements & C.T.s leading to them very heavy mutual bombardment but men worked splendidly under very trying conditions no casualties very lucky
March 31st	Repetition of previous day shelling not so bad

R. J. O. Taylor 2nd Lieut
Cmmdg 8th M.G. Coy

8th Brigade.

3rd Division.

WAR DIARY

8th BRIGADE.

MACHINE GUN COMPANY

APRIL 1 9 1 6

War Diary

8th M. G. Coy. B. E. F

April 1916

April 1st	Building emplacements & C.Ts very heavy shelling men worked very well under most trying circumstances every gun came in for some shelling only two casualties shelled all night Craters changed hands apparently several times front line Guns in action a lot specially at night. Wounded severely 17988 Pte MILLS " " 17499 Pte ALDRED.
April 2nd	Still heavy shelling but no casualties. Pte Mills died of wounds.
April 3rd	relieved by 3 CANADIANS left Coy Commander very detailed sketch & summary of information as he had not been able to get round positions successful relief although very nervous with enemy shelling back to RENINGHELST. Camp by 12 midnight
April 4th	In camp All ranks very tired & feel effects of strain
April 5th	In Billets 2nd Lt Pool sent to hospital very ill left RENINGHELST for rest Billets at midday 8 miles back near FLETRE very comfortable billets
April 6th	In rest Billets in accordance with Divisional order all ranks having complete rest for 4 days.
April 7th	In rest Billets beautiful weather
April 8th	In Rest Billets
April 9th	Church Parades
April 10th	Started training Gun drill
April 11th	Coy Route Marched
April 12th	Route march in am lecture in pm
April 13th	Sectional route marches & drill Captain PETRE back from hospital & took over command
April 14th	Coy drill in am lecture in pm
April 15th	Route march with transport mounting & dismounting guns & selecting positions
April 16th	Church parades
April 17th	Coy Gun drill and Guns on improvised range 2nd Lt DULLEN to hospital
April 18th	Orders to move. 2nd Lts ROBERTSON & BROWN to LA CLYTTE to reconnoitre trenches Coy busy getting ready to move

War Diary

April 1916 | 8th M.G. Coy. B.E.F.

April 19th — Coy inspected by Maj. Gen. HALDANE G.O.C. DIV. Captain PETRE to LA. CLYTTE reconnoitring trenches

April 20th — Coy left Billets at 9am to Billets near LA. CLYTTE by 1 P.M relieved 151st M.G. Coy in Line relief Complete by 12 midnight 5 Guns in front Line at M.1. N1. N5. O2. O4 8 Guns in support 3 in reserve at H.Qrs. hard to give men in trenches decent relief

April 21st — fairly heavy Shelling no Casualties

April 22nd — trench Mortaring & Shelling front line near M.1 Gun team badly Shaken but no damage done relieved team at night

April 23rd — Heavy Shelling no Casualties

April 24th — Fairly Quiet but enemy trench Mortaring M. trenches heavily no Casualties

April 25th — heavy trench Mortaring front line BOIS. CARRE heavily Shelled no Casualties. 3rd Div took over Command from 50th Div

April 26th — Heavy trench Mortaring & Shelling on front line Gass alarm Stood to heavy bombardment & reported attack on Bde on left

April 27th — Stood to Gass alarm heavy trench Mortar fire & Shelling on trenches and back area no casualties

April 28th — Bois Carre fairly heavily Shelled with 5.9. no Casualties

April 29th — front line heavily Shelled particularly O.S & M.S. 2nd Lt. DALE wounded

April 30th — Gas alarm at 1.5 am Stood to 1. Gun under 2nd Lt TAYLOR sent to R. Bde H.Q VIERSTRAAT Enemy attacked opposite M.1 trench. M1 Gun in action attacked stopped dead a number of dead Germans on wire at daylight fairly quiet day. but certain amount of Shelling

G. W. H. Petre Capt
Comdg. 8th M.G. Coy

8th Brigade.

3rd Division.

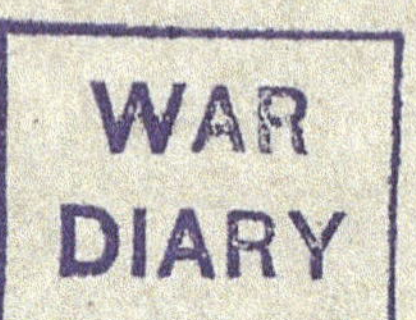

8th BRIGADE.

MACHINE GUN COMPANY

1916

M A Y 1 9 1 6

8 Bde M.G. Coy
Vol 5

Copy of War Diary

Coy M. G. C.

From May 1st to 31st 1916

8th Coy M.G.C

Instructions regarding War Diaries and Intelligence Summaries are contained in F. S. Regs., Part II. and the Staff Manual respectively. Title pages will be prepared in manuscript.

WAR DIARY
or
~~INTELLIGENCE SUMMARY.~~

(*Erase heading not required.*)

Army Form C. 2118.

Place	Date	Hour	Summary of Events and Information	Remarks and references to Appendices
SCHOOL FAM NR LA CLYTTE M.N & O Trenches	May 1st		Fairly Quiet Day. 2nd Lt ROBERTSON. Cpl. REDROND Pte ~~Williams~~ WILLIAMS L Cpl MIERS for 18 day Course. 4 men to Field Ambulance. We have 13 guns in line all ranks getting a rough time. Some of the men with 20 days in line & only 4 out	
Do " "	" 2nd		Fairly quiet day but a lot of trench mortaring in front & support line. 9498 Pte STARTIN transferred to ARTISTS RIFLES on application of Elder Brother. 2 officers & 10 other ranks from Infantry Battalions attached for Course in Lewis Gunnery. The number to be sent each week. Course to start Monday finish on Saturday	
"	3rd		Quite day but front line shelled a little	
"	4		Heavy shelling all day & lot of trench mortaring enemy using a lot of fish tailed bombs although they did not do much damage very unnerving. Pte PITT wounded	
"	5th		Quieter day but enemy still very offensive seems to specialize in various forms trench mortars. 2nd Lt STEELE returned from Field Ambulance	
	6th		Much quieter day, but enemy bombed & trench mortared O Trenches badly had to shift gun in O 2 4 bays to right by trench mortars knocked emplacement completely out lucky to have no Casualties. Gun & most of gun stores alright	

T.134. Wt. W708—776. 500000. 4/15. Sir J. C. & S.

8th Coy. M.G.C.

2

WAR DIARY
or
INTELLIGENCE SUMMARY.
(Erase heading not required.)

Army Form C. 2118.

Instructions regarding War Diaries and Intelligence Summaries are contained in F. S. Regs., Part II. and the Staff Manual respectively. Title pages will be prepared in manuscript.

Place	Date	Hour	Summary of Events and Information	Remarks and references to Appendices
SCHOOL FARM near LA CLYTTE	May 7th		Heavily shelled in front line mostly heavy shrapnel & some heavy trench mortars two men wounded badly but [illegible]. Church parade at H.Qrs. Rev. E. LEE. 1/10 Pte CATTERMOLE & 447 PUTMAN	
M.N.&O. trenches			L.R.B. attached wounded	
"	8th		Much quieter day little shelling in back areas no damage done	
"	9th		Quiet day but men in front line getting very worn [by] perpetual shelling. 39 O.R. reinforcements from base to replace L.R.B who are returning to unit	
	10th		A lot of shelling but little damage done. No 8969 Pte SLEIGH slightly wounded	
	11		Fairly quiet day 2nd Lt BROWN to field ambulance sick	
	12th		Very quiet day certain amount fish tails & T.Ms in front line but no shelling	
	13th		Front line heavily shelled in am also lot of trench mortars & fish tails 2 men badly wounded in front line. CARRE FARM shelled direct hit with 5.9 on emplacement 2 men [illegible] but another [illegible] gun and ammunition buried but undamaged. Wonderful escape for men. W.T.E. [illegible] shelled in P.M. 2 men badly wounded in W. trench, [illegible] heavy H.E. shrapnel & few 5.9s. [illegible] M. CASSIDY behaved very pluckily bandaging Pte BUTLER under fire very trying day. 17498 ~~[illegible]~~ L/Cpl. COE Ptes 17504 FLACK 17520 BUTLER seriously wounded No 9578 L/Cpl ELLIOT slightly wounded	

T.134. Wt. W708-776. 500000. 4/15. Sir J. C. & S.

8th Coy. M.G.C.

3

Instructions regarding War Diaries and Intelligence Summaries are contained in F. S. Regs., Part II. and the Staff Manual respectively. Title pages will be prepared in manuscript.

WAR DIARY
or
INTELLIGENCE SUMMARY.
(Erase heading not required.)

Army Form C. 2118.

Place	Date	Hour	Summary of Events and Information	Remarks and references to Appendices
	May			
SCHOOL FARM near LA CLYTTE	14th		Much quieter day but good deal shelling in front line enemy paying no much attention to N 5 & heavily touched N 4 emplacement but not much damage	
M.N.V.D. Trenches	15		Lot of trench mortaring on large Rum jar pitched on 2nd Lt STEELE dug out penetrated all but one layer of sand bags & then failed to explode very lucky STEELE asleep in dug out at time	
	16		very quiet day 1 Sgt 11 O.R dispatched to join L.R.B.	
	17		Quiet day usual morning & evening issue trench mortars 13 shells no damage	
	18		Support positions shelled with 5.9 & H.E. one 5.9 pitched within 3 yds of FORT MORRO no damage most of them there few were blind shook them badly. Left Battalion H Qrs behind FORT TORONTO heavily shelled with big stuff 1 officer [killed?] & 4 1 O.R wounded very lucky there no casualties in this Coy	
	19		Much quieter day all round not nearly so much shelling also trench mortaring done by shells close to Coy H Qrs no damage done very hot weather	
	20th		Much quieter day. still very hot received preliminary orders for relief Coy to be relieved by 26th Coy going to rest area	
	21st		2 officers of R.E. & party up to O.2 emplacement to try repair. Examined wire in front lot of work to be done very quiet day again	
	22nd		heavy trench mortaring in front line 3 men in M.1 sent to F.A. with shell shock not very serious	

8 Coy M.G.C. 4

Army Form C. 2118.

Instructions regarding War Diaries and Intelligence Summaries are contained in F. S. Regs., Part II. and the Staff Manual respectively. Title pages will be prepared in manuscript.

WAR DIARY
~~or~~
~~INTELLIGENCE SUMMARY.~~
(Erase heading not required.)

Place	Date	Hour	Summary of Events and Information	Remarks and references to Appendices
	May			
SCHOOL FARM near LA CLYTTE	23rd		Quite day very hot weather 2nd Lt PULLEN reported here sick in U.K.	
M. N. trenches	24th		Quite day Sparmodic trench mortaring in front line. Conference of C.Os with Brigadier 8th Bde RIDGEWOOD arranging programme training forthcoming rest. Capt GRIERSON 151 Coy M.G.C came to take over trenches round this way	
	25		Fairly quite during night and am but very heavy bombardment between 2.30-7 pm Brigade on our immediate left had 3 guns had 3 guns Bde Coy put out of action [illegible] VIERSTRAAT and [illegible] forward emplacement to cover our R flank 149 Coy on right got guns into action by 10 pm	
	26th		Relieved to night very hard work getting guns out long carry. 151 Coy under Capt GRIERSON	
	27th		Relief complete reported to Bde by 1 am this morning 8 am left last station arrived in billets long march nearly 12 miles from trenches all ranks rested all day. Better billets for officers men not so bad [illegible] anything but fond of English troops	
	28th		Day spent cleaning up	
	29th		Programme of work training &c commenced [illegible] [illegible] [illegible] [illegible]	
	30th		In rest area training &c	
	31st		In rest area	

[signature]

T.134. Wt. W708-776. 500000. 4/15. Sir J. C. & S.

8th Brigade.

3rd Division.

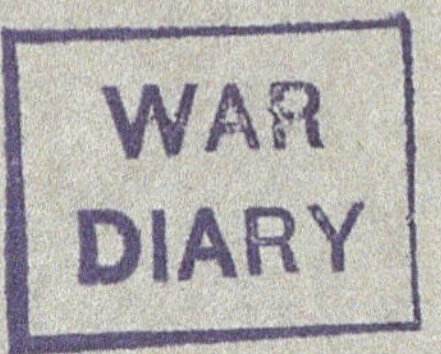

8th BRIGADE.

MACHINE GUN COMPANY

JUNE 1 9 1 6

Instructions regarding War Diaries and Intelligence Summaries are contained in F. S. Regs., Part II. and the Staff Manual respectively. Title pages will be prepared in manuscript.

WAR DIARY
or
INTELLIGENCE SUMMARY.
(Erase heading not required.)

Army Form C. 2118.

8 M G Coy
Vol 6

Place	Date	Hour	Summary of Events and Information — June — 8th Coy M.G.C.	Remarks and references to Appendices
	June 1st		In rest area training &c.	
	" 2nd		Inspected by Brigadier 8th Brigade. carried out defence scheme with 12 Guns	
	" 3rd		Kings Birthday in rest area General Holiday.	
	" 4th		In rest area Church in am. 2nd Lt. Robertson placed under arrest for Drunkeness	
	" 5th		Received orders to be prepared to move at an hours notice, packed limbers & stood by. Heavy bombardment to north.	
	" 6th		In rest area still standing by at hours notice. Preliminary enquiry in charge against 2nd Lt Robertson.	
	" 7th		Still standing by, but continuing training took Coy down and marched them through Gas trench, in Gas school testing tower respirators.	
	" 8th		Time altered to 3½ hrs in which to move carried on training as well as able	
	" 9th		Still standing by to move carried on training.	
	" 10th		Inspected by Brigadier General 8th Brigade carried small tactical scheme received orders to move to Rheninchest left Billets 7.30 PM on ~~[illegible]~~ Rheninchest By 10.30 PM	
	" 11th		In Rheninchest all day Capt Cobre & 2nd Lt Arculus to Inspect line at St Eloi orders received to relieve 9th Coy M.G.C. in Line.	

T.134. Wt. W708—776. 500000. 4/15. Sir J. C. & S.

Instructions regarding War Diaries and Intelligence Summaries are contained in F. S. Regs., Part II. and the Staff Manual respectively. Title pages will be prepared in manuscript.

WAR DIARY
or
INTELLIGENCE SUMMARY.
(Erase heading not required.)

Army Form C. 2118.

Place	Date	Hour	Summary of Events and Information	Remarks and references to Appendices
	June 11th		Night of 12th & 13th 16 Guns to go in	
	June 12th		Coy left billets Rheninghelst 8 P.M. 11 Guns in St Eloi relief complete by 12 Midnight Guns on left spoil bank. Had good deal of trouble getting in Lille road being heavily shelled 9th Coy had lot of trouble getting in Ready Complete at 4 am	
	June 13th		Very quiet day little shelling of Vermozeele in P.M 2 big shells pitched within 10 yds of Coy H.Qrs Vermozeele no Damage 2nd Lt Robertson court Martialed today for drunkeness at Meteren	
	June 14th		Fairly quiet day a little desultory shelling heavy bombardment in Salient nothing very big in this area	
	June 15th		Quiet day Left Sector shelled a good deal sighted position for Guns in Front Line in Left Sector.	
	June 16th		Quiet day sighted position in front line right sector for guns one gun put in in right sector one in left sector very heavy bombardment in South, at night and another extremely heavy bombardment in Salient to North.	
	June 17th		Quiet day a little trench mortaring on right 1 Gun put in front Line on right 1 Gun in front line on left St Eloi shelled again	

T2134. Wt. W708–776. 500000. 4/15. Sir J. C. & S.

Instructions regarding War Diaries and Intelligence Summaries are contained in F. S. Regs., Part II. and the Staff Manual respectively. Title pages will be prepared in manuscript.

WAR DIARY
or
INTELLIGENCE SUMMARY.
(Erase heading not required.)

Army Form C. 2118.

Place	Date	Hour	Summary of Events and Information	Remarks and references to Appendices
	June 18th		Not so quiet more artillery activity right sector had rather bad time trench mortars & shrapnel very heavy St Eloi shelled with 5·9 crumps & shrapnel this afternoon no damage done Sgt Walker wounded Orders issued for relief of on night 19th/20th	
	June 19th		Very quiet day very little shelling a little trench mortaring Coy relieved tonight by 6th Coy Can Bde fairly quick relief.	
	June 20th		Relief completed by 1·30 am Coy marched to Rheninghelst arrived there at 5·0 am Received orders to move across country to Bde Rest area on 21st	
	June 21st		Left Rheninghelst 9-am entrained at Poperinghe (Hopoutre Siding) left at 1·15 pm St Omer at 4 P.M entrained in ½ hr to St Martin au Laerds by 5 P.M & into billets very good billets for all ranks	
	June 22nd		Day spent cleaning up	
	" 23rd		Training started mostly preliminary drill etc	
	" 24th		In training area nr billets	
	" 25th		Church Parade Staff ride in P.M for C.O.	
	" 26th		Brigade Route March	
	" 27th		On Range Ball Firing	

T.134. Wt. W708–776. 500000. 4/15. Sir J. C. & S.

Instructions regarding War Diaries and Intelligence Summaries are contained in F. S. Regs., Part II. and the Staff Manual respectively. Title pages will be prepared in manuscript.

WAR DIARY
or
INTELLIGENCE SUMMARY.
(Erase heading not required.)

Army Form C. 2118.

Place	Date	Hour	Summary of Events and Information	Remarks and references to Appendices
	June 28th		Brigade Route March 12 or 13 miles men marched very well	
	June 29th		Coy in training area did an attack with 8th E Yorks.	
	June 30th		Capt. A. L. Wrenford Worcester Regt took over Command. Capt E. H. Pelve 2nd in Command.	
			[illegible] Capt. 7th M. G. Coy	

T.2134. Wt. W708–776. 500000. 4/15. Sir J. C. & S.

8th Inf.Bde.
3rd Div.

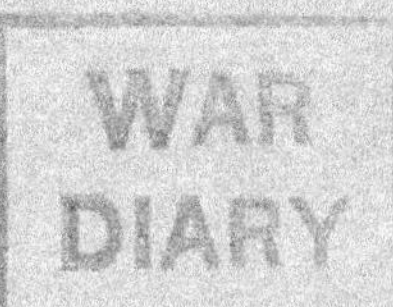

8th MACHINE GUN COMPANY.

J U L Y

1 9 1 6

8 M G Coy
Army Form C. 2118. 3

Vol 7

Instructions regarding War Diaries and Intelligence Summaries are contained in F. S. Regs., Part II. and the Staff Manual respectively. Title Pages will be prepared in manuscript.

WAR DIARY
or
INTELLIGENCE SUMMARY
(Erase heading not required.)

Place	Date	Hour	July — Summary of Events and Information — 8th M.G.C. In the Field	Remarks and references to Appendices
	July 1st		Coy entrained at Wizernes 1 P.M arrived at Candas at 11 P.M proceeded by road to Berneuil	
	July 2nd		Arrived Berneuil 2 am rested all day.	
	" 3rd		By road to Flesselles left 6 P.M to Flesselles at 12 midnight.	
	" 4th		Capt C Shepherd-Cross D.L.O.Y. took over Command of Coy Capt. A.L. Wrenford to 4th R Fusiliers. Capt C.H. Petre 2nd in Command. Left Flesselles 9 P.M by road to Allonville at 2 am	
	" 5th		Arrived Allonville by road at 2 am left 8 P.M for Corbie.	
	" 6th		Arrived Corbie at 2 am left at 8 P.M arrived Bois les Celestin at 11.30 P.M Bivouacked in the	
	" 7th		Left Bois les Celestin at 10.0 am marched to Fontaine Farm halted 2 hrs. and on to Carnoy where Coy Hdqrs are to be relieved 53 Coy in line 8 Guns up in front line & Support line 8 Guns with Limbers & Horses in reserve at Hdqrs getting direct fire on German trenches at 2000 yds.	
	" 8th		Capt. Petre & Cross reconnoitred line very quiet can look over parapet quite safely enemy nearly 2500 yds away	
	" 9th		Capt Cross & all Hdqrs reconnoitred line quiet day nothing much doing either way	

Instructions regarding War Diaries and Intelligence Summaries are contained in F. S. Regs., Part II. and the Staff Manual respectively. Title Pages will be prepared in manuscript.

WAR DIARY
or
INTELLIGENCE SUMMARY

(Erase heading not required.)

Army Form C. 2118.

Place	Date	Hour	Summary of Events and Information	Remarks and references to Appendices
	July	9th	2nd Lt Steele wounded but not badly	
	"	10th	Enemy artillery more active evidently more guns have been brought up preliminary orders	
	"		for attack received we attack in centre between villages of Longueval & Bazentin-le-Grand	
	"	11th	Enemy artillery much more active scheme of attack received 1 Section with supports 1 sec	
			with Bde reserve 2 sec in front line employing overhead fire timed for tomorrow	
	"	12th	Enemy Artillery more active attack put off for 24 hrs.	
	"	13th	Busy working preparations for attack tomorrow at dawn.	
	"	14th	Attacked at 3·25 am 4 guns with support in Sunken road S.16. C. & S.15. D (Longueval 1/10,000)	
			7th K.S.L.I & 8th E. Yorks assaulting troops Guns moved up to Sunken Rd on assault going	
			forward and again after first attack failed directed fire on Enemy's trenches At same	
			time 4 Guns were detailed to act with Brigade Reserve these were dug in at S 22 A	
			& 8 Guns were left in Position in our front line trench between S.N.C & S.22 D to conduct	
			overhead fire on enemy position during attack at 2·15 am orders were received for four	
			of these Guns to be moved forward to act under orders of O.C. Bde R (2nd R Scots) and	
			positions were subsequently taken up by them in S.22 a. At 3·25 4 Guns in front	
			(Montauban-alley) opened fire on enemy position firing for 2 minutes then raising sights	
			& firing 3 minutes Guns remained in position in sunken road until 2 P.M. when enemy	
			position having been taken they moved up to took up position in Enemy support line	
			to assist in consolidating positions, there was no counter attack	

2449 Wt. W14957/M90 750,000 1/16 J.B.C. & A. Forms/C.2118/12.

Army Form C. 2118.

Instructions regarding War Diaries and Intelligence Summaries are contained in F. S. Regs., Part II. and the Staff Manual respectively. Title Pages will be prepared in manuscript.

WAR DIARY
or
INTELLIGENCE SUMMARY
(Erase heading not required.)

Place	Date	Hour	Summary of Events and Information	Remarks and references to Appendices
	July	14th	Disposition of Guns after successful attack. 3 Guns in Enemy support line 1 Gun in Enemy front line supporting sections. 6 Guns from Bde reserve in Enemy support trench 2 Guns from Bde reserve in Sunken road. 4 Guns remaining in Montauban alley. 1 Gun out of action sent back for repairs	sent back for repairs
			The following casualties occurred	
			Killed 17466 Pte Friel E. 12164 Pte Reeves A.J. 9948 Watkins E. - Pte Wood W. G. (R.A.M.C. att)	
			Wounded 2nd Lt D.C. Brown 17452 Sergt Stewart D. 17817 Sgt Vance S. 6538 Pte Baker E.H. 27684 Christopher L 14632 Copley J. 17467 Galbraith P. 17481 Quigley W. 17486 Sommerville J. 5573 Pte West W. 17574 Pte Williams J.	
	"	15th	Coys Hdqrs moved to Quarry at [illegible] firing was applied on various bodys of enemy troops from our front line heavy artillery fire on both sides very little damage done to our trenches 1 Gun damaged by shrapnel Gun damaged on [illegible] returned mended & put in line replacing damaged gun sent for repair.	
	"	16th	Heavily shelled 1 Gun completely smashed by shell no casualties to Gun team	
			Casualties Wounded 17453 Cpl Jones W. 17479 Pte McMillan Attached Pte Houghton KSLI Johnson S.B. 1/ Macquire 2nd R.S. Pte Murphy 1st R.S.F.	
	"	17	Two Guns from support line to S.17 A.34 & S.17 A.6.3. to protect right flank of Brigade	
	"	18	Assisted attack on Delaville wood by 76 Bde by fire on Enemy position from 2 right guns in front line Casualties 17460 Pte Campbell wounded	
	"	19	Moved all Guns in front line & support line relieved by 13th & 85 Coy M.G.C. & with R.S.? took up following dispositions 8 Guns in and around Longueval village. 2 Guns in [illegible]	

2449 Wt. W14957/M90 750,000 1/16 J.B.C. & A. Forms/C.2118/12.

Instructions regarding War Diaries and Intelligence Summaries are contained in F. S. Regs., Part II. and the Staff Manual respectively. Title Pages will be prepared in manuscript.

WAR DIARY
or
INTELLIGENCE SUMMARY
(Erase heading not required.)

Army Form C. 2118.

Place	Date	Hour	Summary of Events and Information	Remarks and references to Appendices
	July	19th	posts in S 23 C. 3 guns being [illegible] left in reserve at Coy Hqrs Heavy shelling during [illegible]	
			& while taking up positions but casualties very light Coy Hdqrs in quarry heavily shelled	
			with heavy shells & Gas shells respirators & Goggles had to be worn everybody suffered	
			from effects of the gas. but no casualties reported everyone alright in [illegible] Casualty	B Henry 16306
	"	20th	Longueval heavily shelled & it was found necessary to put men & Guns under cover [illegible]	
			3 Guns in reserve & 2 Guns from positions taken up previous at S 23 C took up following positions	
			2 Guns in and about the Waterlot Farm 3 guns in East front of Trones Wood from extreme	
			northern Point Shelling again heavy in Longueval Gun Damaged on 15th not returned	
			Supporting 2nd Royal Scots the Bombing attack on trenches S of Waterlot Farm	
			in direction of Guillemont this attack was practically successful but the	
			2nd Royal Scots driven back from their original objective by enfilading M G Fire & took	
			up position half way between original position & objective our M.G. were unable	
			to give them any direct assistance as the fire would have endangered the	Scots R.
			Casualties 12161 Pte Burgess A 14170 Pte Harman H.T. 1832 Sgt Barton 9704 Pte	Parkins
	"	21st	1 gun from Extreme Northern edge of Trones Wood moved to C Y S 18 C 29½ & Tollivers	
			given to 2 Guns at Waterlot Farm & remaining 2 guns in Trones Wood to assist R Scots	
			in night attack on German trenches situated S.E. of Waterlot Farm. Casualty	11300 Pte Body E
	"	22nd	O.C. Royal Scots asked for 2 guns from support line S of Longueval to assist in Waterlot Farm	
			& trenches vicinity these two Guns moved forward in the course of the afternoon and took	
			up position at 10 pm in new trench which had been dug between N.E. Corner of	Trones Wood

2449 Wt. W14957/M90 750,000 1/16 J.B.C. & A. Forms/C.2118/12.

Instructions regarding War Diaries and Intelligence Summaries are contained in F. S. Regs., Part II. and the Staff Manual respectively. Title Pages will be prepared in manuscript.

WAR DIARY
or
INTELLIGENCE SUMMARY

(Erase heading not required.)

Army Form C. 2118.

Place	Date	Hour	Summary of Events and Information	Remarks and references to Appendices
	July	22nd	+ Waterlot Farm were to fire in case of attack in direction of Guillemont at 10 P.m. Verbal orders from Bde ordering an attack by Bde on German trenches to S.E. of Waterlot farm + for 2nd Royal Scots to complete their attack of previous night which had partially failed this attack took place morning 22 + 23 M Gs were not to fire unless in case of enemy attack but were to hold present position while the Brigade attacked this attack took place at 3.35 am 22 + 23rd	
	"	23rd	30th Div attacking village of Guillemont on Divisions Right while the 5th Division were attacking on the Divisions left the Enemy's position from High to Delville Wood. The attack took place at 3.35 am of the 24th + was a failure. Our guns did not come into action but the two Guns in position north + South of Waterlot farm were moved forward to consolidate the German trenche East of Waterlot farm, which had been captured by the 7th K S L I + 8th East Yorks. This trench had to be evacuated later in the day + the guns were brought back to their former positions Lieut Mackie H.Q. of the 106th [illegible]	
		24	Fairly quiet through the day but very heavy shelling in the evening during which [illegible] attacked on our position in Delville wood this attack was repulsed with heavy losses to the enemy but we received heavy casualties by shell fire amongst the Company. One Gun in the position near the railway in Trones Wood was completely buried in spite of digging all night + next day this gun has not been found. No 5 Gun in position in Longueval Alley was moved to take its place. A Draft of 14 men arrived from the base were sent up to the various Guns with ration party at night [illegible] of these were killed wounded or missing on way up	

2449 Wt. W14957/M90 750,000 1/16 J.B.C. & A. Forms/C.2118/12.

Instructions regarding War Diaries and Intelligence Summaries are contained in F. S. Regs., Part II. and the Staff Manual respectively. Title Pages will be prepared in manuscript.

WAR DIARY
or
INTELLIGENCE SUMMARY

(Erase heading not required.)

Army Form C. 2118.

Place	Date	Hour	Summary of Events and Information	Remarks and references to Appendices
	July	24th	Casualties Wounded 17457 Cpl Smith J.F. 17527 Pte Dyer H. 17489 Pte Taylor H. 21216 Pte Kay J. Missing 34177 L/c Childs A.R. 9609 Pte Walker H. 36475 Lee A.E. Missing believed wounded 17472 Pte Kay A. 8470 Pritchard W.	
	"	25th	Heavy shelling continued till about 6 am after which the day was fairly quiet. Four Guns of the 5th M.G. Coy arrived and took up positions in addition to our Guns in the Waterlot Farm Wood sector. At the same time six Guns of the 99th M.G.C. arrived to take up position in Longueval. All the Guns were in addition to those we already had in position. All 8th Brigade Infantry were relieved by a Bde of 2nd Div. & orders were received from 8 Bde for our Guns to remain in position for 24 hrs after infantry relief. Casualties. Wounded 33701 L/c Cooper J. 37133 Alston H. Missing 37138 Pte Johnson	
	"	26th	On receipt of orders from 8th Bde all guns were taken from their positions at 3.30 pm. A rendezvous was made at the quarry whence the Company marched to billets at Méaulte. On arrival relief was reported complete. Capt. Petre E.H. to F.A. suffering from effect of Gas. 2nd Lt E.D.C. Foster M.G.C. from Grantham reported for duty. Lieut A.C. Machie took over duties of second in command during the absence of Capt E.H. Petre sick.	
	"	27th	Commenced training & held kit transport & Gun equipment inspection. The following previously reported missing returned to the Company 17417 Pte Mitcham 36421 Pte Rogers 36470 Pte Stansfield. Notification of death of 12165 Pte G. Burgess & 17526 A.J. Brown at No 1 CCS at Rouen both of wounds received in action. 9719 Pte Lockett C. awarded 14 days F.P. No 1 for not complying with an order	
	"	28th	Training continued 2nd Lt Pullen appointed transport officer 10 reinforcements received.	

2449 Wt. W14957/M90 750,000 1/16 J.B.C. & A. Forms/C.2118/12.

Army Form C. 2118.

Instructions regarding War Diaries and Intelligence Summaries are contained in F. S. Regs., Part II. and the Staff Manual respectively. Title Pages will be prepared in manuscript.

WAR DIARY

or

INTELLIGENCE SUMMARY

(Erase heading not required.)

Place	Date	Hour	Summary of Events and Information	Remarks and references to Appendices
	July	29	Training continued 13 O/Ranks reinforcements arrived.	
	"	30	Inspection of Company & Billets by C.O. Church Parade for C of E & R.C.	
	"	31	Training continued.	

[illegible] Lieut.
O/C 5th M.G. Coy

2449 Wt. W14957/M90 750,000 1/16 J.B.C. & A. Forms/C.2118/12.

8th Brigade.

3rd Division.

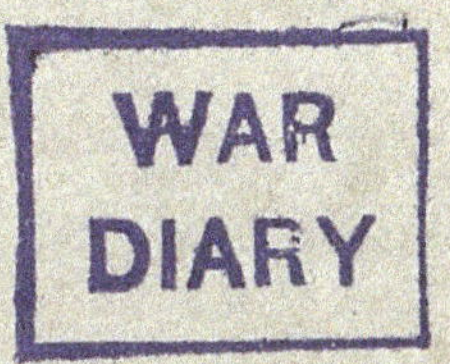

8th BRIGADE

MACHINE GUN COMPANY

AUGUST 1 9 1 6

1st to 31st August 1916

Instructions regarding War Diaries and Intelligence Summaries are contained in F. S. Regs., Part II. and the Staff Manual respectively. Title Pages will be prepared in manuscript.

WAR DIARY
or
~~INTELLIGENCE~~ SUMMARY
(Erase heading not required.)

8th M.G. Coy.

Army Form C. 2118.

Vol 8

Place	Date	Hour	Summary of Events and Information	Remarks and references to Appendices
MÉAULTE	1st		Company in Billets, Training continued, Company Canteen started.	
-do-	2nd		Training continued, No 17516 Pte WRIGHT awarded 7 days F.P. No1 for Absent from Parade. Promotions. 17463 Cpl CASSIDY M. promoted Sergt. vice Walker to U.K. Wounded 18.8.16 17495 " FOREMAN. A -do- -do- do. Vince -do- -do- 14.7.16 17485 " SMALL W appointed Paid L/Sergt. vice Bertram do- 30.7.16. 17497 L/Cpl CABLE. H. promoted Corporal to complete establishment. 6053 " EDWARDS E.C -do- -do- -do- 17540 Pte SPIERS H. appointed unpaid L/Cpl.	
-do-	3rd		Training continued 'B' Section fired on the Range	
-do-	4th	9.30AM	Company inspected by C.O afterwards by G.O.C 3rd Division Divisional Horse show two Coy Limbers competed, but not awarded prizes	

2449 Wt. W14957/M90 750,000 1/16 J.B.C. & A. Forms/C.2118/12.

Army Form C. 2118.

Instructions regarding War Diaries and Intelligence Summaries are contained in F. S. Regs., Part II. and the Staff Manual respectively. Title Pages will be prepared in manuscript.

WAR DIARY
or
~~INTELLIGENCE SUMMARY~~

(Erase heading not required.)

Place	Date	Hour	Summary of Events and Information	Remarks and references to Appendices
MÉAULTE	5th		Training continued C Section fired on the range 2/Lt. SOUTER. C.S.B. to field ambulance sick	
-do-	6th	9.30AM 10AM.	Divine service for C of E & R Cs. Inspection of Billets by C O.	
-do-	7th		Training continued	
-do	8th		Training continued 'A' Section fired on Range Capt. E.H. PETRE. Struck off the Strength having been evacuated to U.K. suffering from gas poisoning Lieut. A.C. MACKIE to field ambulance sick	
		2pm	Brigade Sports	
-do-	9th		'D' Section fired on the range, Remainder of Coy route march.	
-do-	10th		Training continued	
-do-	11th		Training continued, Transport inspected by G.O.C. 5th Brigade	

2449 Wt. W14957/M90 750,000 1/16 J.B.C. & A. Forms/C.2118/12.

Instructions regarding War Diaries and Intelligence Summaries are contained in F. S. Regs., Part II. and the Staff Manual respectively. Title Pages will be prepared in manuscript.

WAR DIARY
or
~~INTELLIGENCE SUMMARY~~
(Erase heading not required.)

Army Form C. 2118.

Place	Date	Hour	Summary of Events and Information	Remarks and references to Appendices
MÉAULTE	12th		Company moved with 5th Brigade to HAPPY VALLEY 2/Lt. SPOFFORTH. E.R. rejoined from M.G. School.	
HAPPY VALLEY	13th		Divine Service for C of E & R.Cs. Inspection of much equipment by section officers C.O. reconnoitred ground between GUILLEMONT & MAUREPAS. Promotion 17477 Pte MITCHELL R. promoted Corporal to complete establishment Reversion 10336 Lcpl MAY G.W. reverts to Private on joining a service Company	
-do-	14th		Company moved with 5th Brigade to camp near BRONFAY FARM. appointments 17463 Pte EDWARDS. A. } 17509 " MARTIN A.J. } appointed unpaid Lance Corporals. 34457 " DROY. A.C. } Strength 35319 Pte BARNARD C. Rauc. attached for duty & taken on the Strength	

2449 Wt. W14957/M90 750,000 1/16 J.B.C. & A. Forms/C.2118/12.

4

Instructions regarding War Diaries and Intelligence Summaries are contained in F. S. Regs., Part II. and the Staff Manual respectively. Title Pages will be prepared in manuscript.

WAR DIARY
or
~~INTELLIGENCE~~ SUMMARY
(Erase heading not required.)

Army Form C. 2118.

Place	Date	Hour	Summary of Events and Information	Remarks and references to Appendices
NEAR BRONFAY FARM.	15th		Training continued	
-do-	16th		Company moved to TALUS BOIS. with 3rd Brigade Transport left at BRONFAY FARM. under 2/Lt PULLEN.	
TALUS BOIS	17th		Training continued	
-do-	18th		"C" Section under 2/Lt BARLEY moved up to support the 9th Brigade at Bombing practice 6053 Cpl EDWARDS E.G. was slightly wounded by the premature explosion of Bomb.	
			Strength	
			17497 Cpl CABLE H. Struck off the strength having been evacuated to the Base sick	
			42571 Sergt HOWIE R. Reported MISSING on the way up to the trenches	
		11.30PM	Lieut BARLEY. Reported that Sergt REDRUP & Pte DEADMAN had been found Drunk	

2449 Wt. W14957/M90 750,000 1/16 J.B.C. & A. Forms/C.2118/12.

5

Army Form C. 2118.

Instructions regarding War Diaries and Intelligence Summaries are contained in F. S. Regs., Part II. and the Staff Manual respectively. Title Pages will be prepared in manuscript.

WAR DIARY
or
INTELLIGENCE SUMMARY

(Erase heading not required.)

Place	Date	Hour	Summary of Events and Information	Remarks and references to Appendices
TALUS. BOIS	18th	11.30pm	At STANLEY DUMP. Sergt. KELLY was sent up to take the place of Sergt. HOWIE. Sergt. HIBBERT was sent up with an escort to bring back Sergt REDRUP & Pte DEADMAN under escort.	
—do—	—do—	12 M.N.	2/Lt. BARLEY moved two guns from STANLEY DUMP to ASSEMBLY TRENCH leaving the other two guns at STANLEY DUMP	
—do—	19th		The two guns left at STANLEY DUMP were moved up to relieve two guns of the 9th M.G.C. in ASSEMBLY TRENCH. No casualties.	
—do—	20th	9 AM.	The company marched from TALUS BOIS to SAND PITS	
SAND PITS	21st		The company moved into Billets at MÉAULTE The Brigade was bombed by German aeroplanes just outside MÉAULTE causing a few casualties to E. YORKS. & A.S.C.	
MÉAULTE	21st		Sergt. REDRUP & Pte DEADMAN Remanded for Court martial by the C.O. Lieut D.J.G DIXON } reported to the company for duty & were taken on Lieut. R ALLAN } the strength Lieut D.J.G DIXON assumed the duties of 2nd in Command Lieut. AC. MACKIE Struck off the Strength Evacuated to U.K. Sick	

2449 Wt. W14957/M90 750,000 1/16 J.B.C. & A. Forms/C.2118/12.

6

Army Form C. 2118.

WAR DIARY
or
INTELLIGENCE SUMMARY

(Erase heading not required.)

Instructions regarding War Diaries and Intelligence Summaries are contained in F. S. Regs., Part II. and the Staff Manual respectively. Title Pages will be prepared in manuscript.

Place	Date	Hour	Summary of Events and Information	Remarks and references to Appendices
MÉAULTE	22nd	10.40AM	The Company Transport went by road to POULAINVILLE under Lieut. PULLEN	
– do –	23rd	9AM.	The Company marched to MERICOURT & entrained there for CANDAS. On de-training the company marched to Billets at PROUVILLE	
			The Transport moved by road from POULAINVILLE to PROUVILLE.	
PROUVILLE.	24th	11.45AM	The Company was paid out.	
		2PM.	Foot inspection by Section Officers	
			Pte LOVE. awarded 7 days F.P.No1:- for using obscene language to a NCO	
			Lieuts NB THOMPSON. } reported for duty were taken on the Strength -do- J.A. ROCH }	
			REINFORCEMENT a Draft of 32 Other Ranks arrived from M.G.C. Base Depôt	
– do –	25th	7AM.	The Company marched into Billets at WAVANS	
WAVANS	26th	8.30AM	The Company marched into Billets at GUINECOURT	
			No17474 Pte MARTIN D } Reported missing on C.Os parade at 8.30 am 17480 " NICOL C }	

2449 Wt. W14957/M90 750,000 1/16 J.B.C. & A. Forms/C.2118/12.

I

Army Form C. 2118.

WAR DIARY
or
INTELLIGENCE SUMMARY
(Erase heading not required.)

Instructions regarding War Diaries and Intelligence Summaries are contained in F. S. Regs., Part II. and the Staff Manual respectively. Title Pages will be prepared in manuscript.

Place	Date	Hour	Summary of Events and Information	Remarks and references to Appendices
GUINECOURT	27th	8 AM	The Company marched to billets at MAREST The Division was inspected by the G.O.C on the march through ST. POL. Ptes MARTIN & NICOL missing from previous day reported about 9 P.M. & were placed under arrest in the Guard Room. Pte MARTIN was Drunk	
-do-	-do-	5.30 PM	Promulgation of Trial at a F.G.C.M. held at MEAULTE on the 22 August 1916 No 17519 Sergt J. REDRUP was found Guilty of Drunkenness Sect 19 A.A. Sentenced to be reduced to the rank of Corporal at the same court. No 13156 Pte. P. DEADMAN. was found guilty of Drunkenness Sect 19 A.A. & sentenced to 56 days F.P. No 1. The above sentences were promulgated on parade & the Reduction of Sergt J REDRUP was carried out before the NCOs of the Company.	
-do-	27th	8.30 AM	The Company marched into Billets at HALLICOURT. 17480 Pte NICOL G was awarded 28 days F.P. No 1 & forfeits 2 days Pay under R.W. for Absence without leave 17488 Pte STEWART A. was awarded 7 days F.P. No 1 for using obscene language to a NCO. 17474 Pte MARTIN escaped from the Guard Room about 5.15 am. Cpl PAGE C who was the NCO Commanding the Guard. was placed under arrest & remanded for C.M. by the C.O	

2449 Wt. W14957/M90 750,000 1/16 J.B.C. & A. Forms/C.2118/12.

8

Army Form C. 2118.

WAR DIARY
or
INTELLIGENCE SUMMARY
(Erase heading not required.)

Instructions regarding War Diaries and Intelligence Summaries are contained in F. S. Regs., Part II. and the Staff Manual respectively. Title Pages will be prepared in manuscript.

Place	Date	Hour	Summary of Events and Information	Remarks and references to Appendices
HAILLICOURT	29th	2 PM.	The Company marched into Billets at NOEUX-LES-MINES Pte MARTIN was found in NOEUX-LES-MINES & again placed under arrest.	
NOEUX-LES-MINES	30th	2 PM.	A & D Sections & 3 guns of B Section relieved 11 guns of The 97th M G Coy in the HULLUCK SECTOR. The Transport Plus C Section & 1 gun of B Section remained at NOEUX-LES-MINES The Company Headquarters moved to Machine gun House PHILOSOPHE Pte MARTIN D remanded for Court martial on charges Being Absent without leave Drunkenness & escaping from the Guard room Very Wet day & relief had a hard time,	
PHILOSOPHE	-do-	10.15 PM	Relief completed at. 10.15 PM. during the night of August 30-31st. Nos 3 & 4 guns fired a 1000 rounds each at 36 C N.W. 3 $\frac{1}{10,000}$ H.19. D.9.6 & H.20. A.2.2 respectively. No retalliation	

2449 Wt. W14957/M90 750,000 1/16 J.B.C. & A. Forms/C.2118/12.

9

Instructions regarding War Diaries and Intelligence Summaries are contained in F. S. Regs., Part II. and the Staff Manual respectively. Title Pages will be prepared in manuscript.

WAR DIARY
or
INTELLIGENCE SUMMARY
(Erase heading not required.)

Army Form C. 2118.

Place	Date	Hour	Summary of Events and Information	Remarks and references to Appendices
PHILOSOPHE	31st	9 AM	The C O visited all the guns in the line	
			Lieut. J A. ROYDS reported for duty.	
			Lieut. ANDERSON. was given orders to return from the Trenches to NOEUX-LES-MINES to conduct a Lewis gun course for NCOs & men of the Brigade the COURSE has to commence on September 1st & last. a week	
			31. August 1916	
			[signature] Capt. Cmdg No 9 Coy M G Corps	

2449 Wt. W14957/M90 750,000 1/16 J.B.C. & A. Forms/C.2118/12.

8th Brigade.

3rd Division.

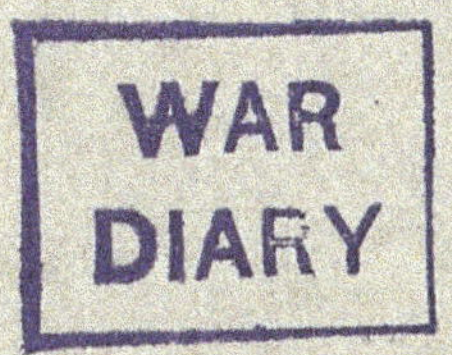

8th BRIGADE.

MACHINE GUN COMPANY

SEPTEMBER 1 9 1 6

Army Form C. 2118.

WAR DIARY
or
~~INTELLIGENCE SUMMARY~~
(Erase heading not required.)

Instructions regarding War Diaries and Intelligence Summaries are contained in F. S. Regs., Part II. and the Staff Manual respectively. Title Pages will be prepared in manuscript.

8th Machine Gun Company.

Vol 9.

Place	Date	Hour	Summary of Events and Information	Remarks and references to Appendices
PHILOSOPHE	1.9.16		The following firing took place on the night 31/1 Sept. 1916 Two guns fired:- 1 gun in Trench R.46 fired 1000 rounds at trench H.13.d.04. 1 gun in Trench R47 fired 1000 rounds at Sentier Rd at H 19 d 56 No Retaliation, Remaining gun teams carried out work on emplacements & trenches. Lieut J A ROYDS assumed duties of 2nd in Command vice Lieut DIXON posted temporarily to D Section. C.O. visited all guns in the line. The guns of B Section & all spare men of A.B.&D Sections moved into Billets at PHILOSOPHE.	
do	2.9.16	9 p.m. – 1 AM	4 guns fired:- one gun in Trench R44 fired 500 rounds at main St BENIFONTAINE H.14b.4.35 one gun in trench R45 fired 500 rounds at Cross Roads, H 20 d 79 one gun in trench R46 fired 1000 rounds at C.T. H19d 49 1250x one gun in trench R47 fired 1000 rounds at Cross Roads H13.695. No retaliation – a quiet day – a considerable amount of work done to loop holes & trench in VILLAGE LINE. G.O.C. 3rd Div. visited line.	

Army Form C. 2118.

Instructions regarding War Diaries and Intelligence Summaries are contained in F. S. Regs., Part II. and the Staff Manual respectively. Title Pages will be prepared in manuscript.

WAR DIARY
or
~~INTELLIGENCE SUMMARY~~

(Erase heading not required.)

Place	Date	Hour	Summary of Events and Information	Remarks and references to Appendices
PHILOSOPHE	3rd Sept		The following firing took place ~~during~~	
			4 guns fired. –	
			one gun in trench R 46 fired 1000 rounds at H26 - B53	
			one gun ~~for~~ in trench R 47 fired 1000 rounds at H20 - a19	
			one gun in trench ~~R~~ No 7 fired 500 rounds at H13 - d 2½ 4½	
			one gun in trench No 8 fired 500 rounds at H13 - d 2½ / 6½, ~~trench~~ Trench Junction	
			Inspected M.G. emplacements.	
			32 men (being 8 men per battn of the Brigade) were attached to the Coy permanently (3rd Div. G. 2423) + were taken on the strength that day.	
			C.O. visited all guns in that line – very quiet day.	
	5th Sept		5 guns fired	
			one gun ~~fired~~ in trench R46 fired 1000 rounds at H 20 c - 6½ 3½ Range 1750x	
			one gun in trench R 47 fired 1000 rounds at H 20 a 18 Range 1500x	
			one gun in trench R 45 fired 500 rounds at H19 D68 Cross Roads Range 1150x	
			one gun in trench No 7 fired 500 rounds at H13 b 88 Range 2400x	
			one gun in trench No 8 fired 500 rounds at do – do 2240x	
			C section Lewis gun class + all remaining ranks except TO. transport + Q.M.S. moved from NOEUX LES MINES to PHILOSOPHE.	

2449 Wt. W14957/M90 750,000 1/16 J.B.C. & A. Forms/C.2118/12.

Instructions regarding War Diaries and Intelligence Summaries are contained in F. S. Regs., Part II. and the Staff Manual respectively. Title Pages will be prepared in manuscript.

WAR DIARY
or
INTELLIGENCE SUMMARY
(Erase heading not required.)

Army Form C. 2118.

Place	Date	Hour	Summary of Events and Information	Remarks and references to Appendices
PHILOSOPHE	4th Sept		Corpl Dyer having rejoined the Coy after being wounded on the SOMME has been posted to "A" Section	
			Lt ROYDS visited all guns in the line, quiet day, no retaliation some rain.	
'do'	5th Sept		Five guns fired	
			One gun in trench R46 fired 1000 rounds at H20 C6½ 3½ (Suspected MG) Range 1450x	
			One gun in trench R47 fired 1000 rounds at H20 A18 (Suspected MG) Range 1500x	
			One gun in trench R45 fired 500 rounds at H19 D.68 (Cross roads & CT) Range 1150x	
			One gun in trench No 7 fired 500 rounds at H13 B88 (Hulluch trench) range 2400x	
			One gun in trench No 8 fired 500 rounds at H13 B68 (Suspected TM) do do range 2240x	
			No 17474 Pte D MARTIN tried by FGCM at HQ 1st RSF —	
			CO took CO 2nd i/c of No 9 Coy MG Coy round all gun positions and arranged method of relief	
			2nd Lt BARLEY instructed attached men.	
			C Section paraded for instruction under Cpl Redrup remainder of men under Sgt Collins continued work on billets in preparation for the winter	

2449 Wt. W14957/M90 750,000 1/16 J.B.C. & A. Forms/C.2118/12.

Army Form C. 2118.

WAR DIARY
or
INTELLIGENCE SUMMARY
(Erase heading not required.)

Instructions regarding War Diaries and Intelligence Summaries are contained in F. S. Regs., Part II. and the Staff Manual respectively. Title Pages will be prepared in manuscript.

Place	Date	Hour	Summary of Events and Information	Remarks and references to Appendices
PHILOSOPHE	6th Sept		Two guns fired	
			One gun in trench R46 fired 1000 rounds at H26 B45·40 Range	2000x
			One gun in trench R47 fired 1000 rounds at H13 D4·9 Range	1200x
do	7th Sept		Coy relieved by No 7 M G Coy, relieving party left PHILOSOPHE at 10am. Relief complete about 5pm.	
			Coy moved into billets at NOEUX-LES-MINES.	
			Men attached to Coy for Lewis Gun class returned to their units	
do	8th Sept		The Coy paraded at 7·50am for baths	
			The Coy paraded at 12 noon for pay. The remainder of the day was spent in cleaning clothing & equipment.	
			Inspection of kit & overhauling of guns & gun equipment.	
do	9th Sept		"A" Section guns were examined by Coy Artificer.	
			Physical Drill 7 am	
			Gun Drill 9·30am	
			Lectures on Map reading 12 noon. Afternoon spent in issuing & refitting clothing. Class for Attached men continued	

2449 Wt. W14957/M90 750,000 1/16 J.B.C. & A. Forms/C.2118/12.

Army Form C. 2118

Instructions regarding War Diaries and Intelligence Summaries are contained in F. S. Regs., Part II. and the Staff Manual respectively. Title Pages will be prepared in manuscript.

WAR DIARY
or
INTELLIGENCE SUMMARY
(Erase heading not required.)

Place	Date	Hour	Summary of Events and Information	Remarks and references to Appendices
NOEUX LES MINES	10th Sept (Sunday)		Church parades:- RC - C of E - & Presbyterians Inspection of billets by C.O.	
do	11th Sept		The CO & 2nd i/c rode PHILOSOPHE to the 9th Brigade HQ & also called at 76th MG Coy HQ MAZINGARBE. Carrying party consisting of 3 officers 120. O.R. paraded 6.45.-pm They were conveyed to the trenches in the Coy limber & 2 G.S. wagons from train. Promulgation of sentence on Pte Martin.	
do	12th Sept		Carrying parties only returned to morning parades. Lt DIXON left the Coy on appointment to 2nd i/c of 123 M.G.C. Pte Mitchell left for BOULOGNE Pte Stamp left for Rest Camp	
		7.30am	2nd Lt J. A. WILSON, reported for duty from CAMIERS 4 guns of "A" section sent to Div'l. Armourer for overhauling.	

2449 Wt. W14957/M90 750,000 1/16 J.B.C. & A. Forms/C.2118/12.

Army Form C. 2118.

Instructions regarding War Diaries and Intelligence Summaries are contained in F. S. Regs., Part II. and the Staff Manual respectively. Title Pages will be prepared in manuscript.

WAR DIARY
or
INTELLIGENCE SUMMARY

(Erase heading not required.)

Place	Date	Hour	Summary of Events and Information	Remarks and references to Appendices
NOEUX LES MINES	13th Sept	11AM	Inspection of Transport by G.O.C.	
			Class for attached men continued	
			Section under S.O. in morning.	
		9.30am	Carrying party 3 officers 120. O.R. paraded. Motor Lorries to trenches	
	14th Sept			
		9.30 AM	2nd Lt BARLEY	
			Corpl HOOD	
			Reported to Divl Gas School at VERDUN	
		about 4 am	Carrying party returned.	
		9.15 am	Carrying party 3 officers – 128. O.R. paraded & were conveyed by buses to trenches.	
	15th Sept	9.30 –12	Gas School at VERDUN	
		10am	FGCM at our H.Q. on Corpl Page (No 8 MG Coy)	

2449 Wt. W14957/M90 750,000 1/16 J.B.C. & A. Forms/C.2118/12.

Army Form C. 2118.

Instructions regarding War Diaries and Intelligence Summaries are contained in F. S. Regs., Part II. and the Staff Manual respectively. Title Pages will be prepared in manuscript.

WAR DIARY
or
INTELLIGENCE SUMMARY
(Erase heading not required.)

Place	Date	Hour	Summary of Events and Information	Remarks and references to Appendices
NOEUX LES MINES	15 Sept		Coy paraded for pay	
		3pm	2nd Lt ARCULUS to 142nd Field Ambulance.	
		9.30 pm	Carrying party 3 officers 120 O.R. paraded	
do	16th Sept		C.O confined to bed with a kick on the knee	
		3.pm	Removed to 142nd Field Ambulance	
			Corpl Smith & Corpl Edwards on strength	
		6pm	Issue of blankets	
			Carrying party cancelled.	
do	17th Sept Sunday	10 AM	Parade:- checking & inspecting guns & equipment on limbers	
		11am	Church parade. C of E	
		9am	R. C.	

2449 Wt. W14957/M90 750,000 1/16 J.B.C. & A. Forms/C.2118/12.

Army Form C. 2118.

Instructions regarding War Diaries and Intelligence Summaries are contained in F. S. Regs., Part II. and the Staff Manual respectively. Title Pages will be prepared in manuscript.

WAR DIARY
or
INTELLIGENCE SUMMARY

(Erase heading not required.)

Place	Date	Hour	Summary of Events and Information	Remarks and references to Appendices
	17th Sept.		Inspection of billets	
NOEUX LES MINES.	12.30. P.M.		Promulgation of sentence on Corp. Page before N.C.O's of Coy	
		2.30 p.m.		
Do	18th Sept.	9.30. A.M.	Coy paraded for ~~taking~~ testing of Box Respirators by Divl. Gas Officer checking gun equipment ready for moving up to trenches	
			Heavy rain most of the day.	
Do			Lt Royds went to Divl H.Q. re M.G. Targets & had an interview with Major Horwick "Q" branch. Also attended C.O's conference 8th Brigade H.Q. 5 p.m. – 7 p.m.	
			Lt Royds also accompanied Bde Major to PHILOSOPHE & arranged with No 9 M.G. Coy re relief.	
Do	19th Sept.		2nd Lt Spofforth + 1 O.R. on leave to U.K.	
		2 P.M.	Coy moved off to PHILOSOPHE.	

Army Form C. 2118

Instructions regarding War Diaries and Intelligence Summaries are contained in F. S. Regs., Part II. and the Staff Manual respectively. Title Pages will be prepared in manuscript.

WAR DIARY
or
INTELLIGENCE SUMMARY
(Erase heading not required.)

Place	Date	Hour	Summary of Events and Information	Remarks and references to Appendices
PHILOSOPHE	19th Sept.	3.15 p.m.	Coy arrived at PHILOSOPHE at M.G.C. H.Q. & received orders there from Bde "Relief cancelled. Remain in billets at NOEUX	
			Coy marched back to NOEUX LES MINES.	
NOEUX LES MINES.		4.30 p.m.	Coy arrived at NOEUX at 4.30 p.m.	
do	20th Sept.	10.30 P.M.	Lt Royds went to Bde "H.Q." 10.30 A.M. Received orders to prepare for moving at any moment. Orders issued for packing everything possible	
	10 P.M.		Movement orders received from Brigade.	
do	21st Sept.	9. A.M.	Coy moved off & marched to AUCHEL. Fine day.	
AUCHEL		2.15 P.M.	Coy arrived at AUCHEL.	
		5. P.M.	Rifle & foot inspection.	
		7. p.m. – 8.30 P.M.	Lt Royds went to "H.Q." at ALLOUAGNE for C.O.s conference. G.O.C. did not arrive. C.O.s returned to billets.	

2449 Wt. W14957/M90 750,000 1/16 J.B.C. & A. Forms/C.2118/12.

Army Form C. 2118.

Instructions regarding War Diaries and Intelligence Summaries are contained in F. S. Regs., Part II. and the Staff Manual respectively. Title Pages will be prepared in manuscript.

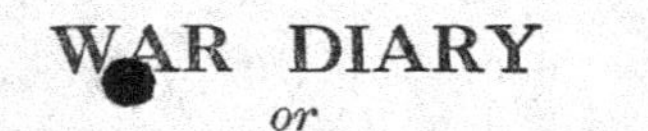

WAR DIARY *or* INTELLIGENCE SUMMARY

(Erase heading not required.)

Place	Date	Hour	Summary of Events and Information	Remarks and references to Appendices
	22nd Sept	9.A.M.	Fine day. Coy moved off from AUCHEL via CAUCHY À LA TOUR FERFAY (10-40) with Bde Column up to X roads at BELLERY & moved independently via AUCHY AU BOIS - LIGNY LEZ AIRE (1-1.20) QUHEM (2.30-3 p.m. watered & fed horses)	
AUDINCTHUN			BOMY (4 p.m.) COYECQUES (5 p.m.) via NOUVEAUVILLE arriving AUDINCTHUN (6.15 p.m. Billets for men good, for officers not too plentiful. No men fell out on the march about 20 miles	
	23rd Sept	9. A.M.	Rifle & foot inspection.	
		10. A.M.	Inspection of billets	
		10.30 -1230.	Sections under S.O.	
		2-4.30.	Lectures & demonstration. Class for attd men resumed.	
			Lt Royds went to reconnoitre the training ground & met Bde Major at COYEQUES visited proposed sights for ranges.	
	24th Sept	9.30 A.M.	Parade for inspection. Spent a quiet day, preparing targets etc for range.	
			Lt Royds & S.O rode over to RECLINGHEM to inspect site for range practice.	

2449 Wt. W14957/M90 750,000 1/16 J.B.C. & A. Forms/C.2118/12.

Army Form C. 2118.

WAR DIARY
or
INTELLIGENCE SUMMARY
(Erase heading not required.)

Instructions regarding War Diaries and Intelligence Summaries are contained in F. S. Regs., Part II. and the Staff Manual respectively. Title Pages will be prepared in manuscript.

Place	Date	Hour	Summary of Events and Information	Remarks and references to Appendices
AUDINCTHUN	24th Sept		(Beautiful day)	
		11.AM.	Transport inspected by ADVS.	
	25 Sept		Sent to Field Cashier at DELETTE for Coy money.	
		5.30. P.M.	Pay parade.	
			"B" Section to range at RECLINGHEM. Instructional practice at short range	
			Remainder of Coy carried on with training in Transport field AUDINCTHUN.	
	26th Sept		1 O.R on leave to U.K.	
		10-30 -1.	Lt Rogds attended C.O. conference under G.O.C. at COYECQUES	
			2nd Lt Thompson returned from M.G. School CAMIERS.	
			Range practice. Bombing instruction + special programme of training continued.	
	27th Sept.		(Showery) Training programme continued.	
		7.30.-8.45. P.M.	Concert in transport lines round Camp fire.	
Do	28th Sept		Dull + misty a.m. Army Commander visited training area.	
			D section range. A,B,+C Route march + visited strong point + trenches near WANDONNE.	
			Sent limber to St Omer for Pte Markham (Bn orderly) in custody there ~~since~~ missing since night of 23 / 24th.	

2449 Wt. W14957/M90 750,000 1/16 J.B.C. & A. Forms/C.2118/12.

Army Form C. 2118.

Instructions regarding War Diaries and Intelligence Summaries are contained in F. S. Regs., Part II. and the Staff Manual respectively. Title Pages will be prepared in manuscript.

WAR DIARY
or
INTELLIGENCE SUMMARY
(Erase heading not required.)

Place	Date	Hour	Summary of Events and Information	Remarks and references to Appendices
AUDINCTHUN	28th Sept		Lecture at COYECQUES on Gymnastics & Bayonet Fighting, also at same place on aerial photos with Lantern	
		7 p.m.		
	29th Sept		Heavy rain in morning, lectures in billets for men. P.M. Arm Drill & exercises. Lt Royds & 2nd Lt Fallen went to reconnoitre trenches on Hill 104 in connection with Divl scheme.	
	30th		Coy out in the open with limbers practicising coming into action & advancing across open. Lt Royds went to meet Bde Major on Hill 104 to discuss the Divl Scheme.	

J H Royds
Lieut Andg
No 8 Coy M.G.C.

2449 Wt. W14957/M90 750,000 1/16 J.B.C. & A. Forms/C.2118/12.

8th Brigade.

3rd Division.

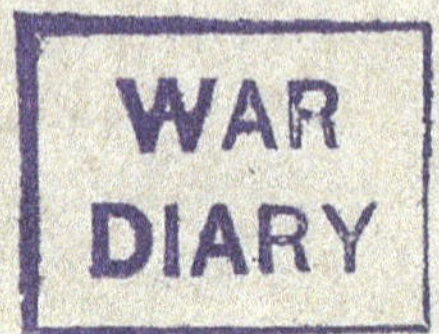

8th BRIGADE.

MCHINE GUN COMPANY

OCTOBER 1 9 1 6

1

Instructions regarding War Diaries and Intelligence Summaries are contained in F. S. Regs., Part II. and the Staff Manual respectively. Title Pages will be prepared in manuscript.

WAR DIARY

or

~~INTELLIGENCE SUMMARY~~

(Erase heading not required.)

Army Form C. 2118.

8th Machine Gun Coy:

Vol 10

Place	Date	Hour	Summary of Events and Information	Remarks and references to Appendices
AUDINCTHUN	1-10-16		2Lieut. SPOFFORTH rejoined from Leave	
		9.30AM	Church parade R.Cs & C. of E. Inspection of billets by C.O.	
		2pm.	Coy bathed under private arrangements	
		3pm.	C.O. attended DIVISIONAL conference on HILL 140 to discuss Divisional scheme, arrived back at 7PM.	
-do-	2.10.16		Very wet morning Coy paid out at 12 noon, Lectures by section officers in billets; Short Route march in the afternoon	
-do-	3.10.16	8 am	Coy moved off to take part in Divisional scheme on HILL 140 very wet morning on Reaching COYECQUE received orders to return to billets operations postponed afternoon spent in Gun Cleaning	
-do-	4.10.16	7.30 am	Coy moved off to take part in Divisional operations another wet morning only 6 GUNS in action, sent forward to hold captured strong points.	
		1.30pm	Trench Mortar Demonstration, arrived back in billets at 3.30 pm. 84 O Ranks returned to M.G Corps Base Depot as Coy was overstrength.	
-do-	5.10.16	10.15AM	Coy moved off marched via RECLINGHEM. Rendezvous VINCLY CHURCH.	
		11.34am	Left Bde Column marched via BEAUMETZ LES. AIRES, LAIRE to PREDEFIN arriving at 3PM. Coy billeted in Chateau	
PREDEFIN	6.10.16	9.30am	Transport moved off under Lieut Pullen marched to PETIT BOURET Drill showery day training continued	

2449 Wt. W14957/M90 750,000 1/16 J.B.C. & A. Forms/C.2118/12.

2/.

Army Form C. 2118.

Instructions regarding War Diaries and Intelligence Summaries are contained in F. S. Regs., Part II. and the Staff Manual respectively. Title Pages will be prepared in manuscript.

WAR DIARY
or
~~INTELLIGENCE SUMMARY~~
(Erase heading not required.)

Place	Date	Hour	Summary of Events and Information	Remarks and references to Appendices
PREDEFIN	7.10.16	9AM	Inspection of fighting kit by Section officers	
		1PM.	moved off Several heavy showers, Reached WAVRANS 4.15pm. halted for tea & rested there until 7.30pm. marched to ST. POL where Coy was due at 9.35 pm. Train very late actually entrained at 1AM.	
ACHEUX	8.10.16	12 NOON	Arrived at ACHEUX railway siding, marched independently to Huts in ACHEUX WOOD under verbal orders of Staff Captain, Camp in very muddy state after heavy rain. Transport arrived at 4pm. having moved from LEALVILLERS where they had billeted the previous night. One O Rank proceeded on leave	
—do	9.10.16		Unpacking limbers & removing surplus stores to QMS Stores Cleaning guns etc	
		2pm	visual training. J D & semaphore. etc.	
—do.	10.10.16		Coy training on ground S.W. of FORCEVILLE — ACHEUX Road advanced drill NCOs in charge of sections, Officers acting as umpires, CO. met Bde major at 7Am & accompanied him round trenches in SERRE Sector, Called at HQ 9th M.G.C. at MAILLY - MAILLET & reported to Bde H.Q at 4pm. discussion on Divisional Scheme of operations returned to camp. 6.30pm.	
—do—	11.10.16		Coy training continued 3 officers & 3 runners went up to the trenches to reconnoitre ground. Coy paid out at 5pm.	
—do	12.10.16		Baths at ACHEUX 9-30 — 11 am Transport moved off at 10 am. to area P 1 near BERTRANCOURT 2 officers & 2 Runners visited trenches to reconnoitre ground	

2449 Wt. W14957/M90 750,000 1/16 J.B.C. & A. Forms/C.2118/12.

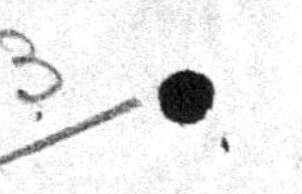

Army Form C. 2118.

Instructions regarding War Diaries and Intelligence Summaries are contained in F. S. Regs., Part II. and the Staff Manual respectively. Title Pages will be prepared in manuscript.

WAR DIARY
or
~~INTELLIGENCE SUMMARY~~

(Erase heading not required.)

Place	Date	Hour	Summary of Events and Information	Remarks and references to Appendices
ACHEUX.	12.10.16		C.O attended conference of O.Cs M.G Coys 2nd DIVISION at LEALVILLERS 2.30 – 3.30 PM. Lieut COURTAULD S.L. reported for duty as C.O Lieut ROYDS J.A. received orders to proceed to Grantham as soon as possible	
– do.	13.10.16		Lt. COURTAULD S.L. assumed command of Coy. Coy training continued	
– do.	14.10.16		Divine Service C of E & R.Cs Inspection of Coy by C.O 100 O Ranks under Lt THOMPSON paraded for fatigue at Railway siding unloading war material Lt. ROYDS J.A. proceeded to U.K.	
– do	15.10.16		2 Lieuts BARLEY, ROCH & 100 O Ranks paraded at 7 PM for fatigue at EUSTON DUMP Cpl MAY & Pte AIRE wounded.	
– do.	16.10.16		Training continued Lieut R.R NEILSON reported for duty & assumed duty as 2nd in Command vice Lt. ROYDS to U.K.	
– do	17.10.16		Bde scheme only 8 guns took part. C & D. Sections.	
– do	18.10.16		Coy marched from ACHEUX to BUS WOOD. A & B. Sections moved off at 2.30 pm under 2 Lieut. PULLEN. H.Q C & D sections moved off under C.O at 5.30 PM.	
BUS WOOD	19.10.16	8 AM.	30 O Ranks under Lieut. WILSON reported to Town major for fatigue Road cleaning	
		2 PM.	Bathing in Divisional Baths very wet day	

2449 Wt. W14957/M90 750,000 1/16 J.B.C. & A. Forms/C.2118/12.

4/

Instructions regarding War Diaries and Intelligence Summaries are contained in F. S. Regs., Part II. and the Staff Manual respectively. Title Pages will be prepared in manuscript.

WAR DIARY
or
~~INTELLIGENCE SUMMARY~~
(Erase heading not required.)

Army Form C. 2118.

Place	Date	Hour	Summary of Events and Information	Remarks and references to Appendices
BUS WOOD	20.10.16		Holy Communion for C of E. Training Continued	
-do-	21.10.16	8AM 7PM.	30 O Ranks on fatigue with town major 3 hostile aeroplanes over our lines 70 O Rank under Lieut ANDERSON. acted as carrying party from EUSTON DUMP to front line	
-do-	22.10.16		Divine service R.Cs + C of E Bde scheme 8 guns took part.	
-do-	23.10.16		Training continued 30 O Ranks on fatigue with town major	
-do-	24.10.16	12 NOON	operation orders received to move to LA SINGAY FARM. move cancelled at 4 PM.	
-do-	25.10.16	8AM	Training continued Lieuts SPOFFORTH THOMPSON & 100 O Ranks marched to COURCELLES for fatigue arrived back at 6 PM.	
-do-	26.10.16	8AM	Training continued 100 O Ranks reported to town major for fatigue Road Cleaning CQMS LANGAN ~~transferred~~ to 76th MGC as CSM. Inspection of billets by C.O.	
-do-	27.10.16		Training continued C.O & Lieut SPOFFORTH visited gun positions in [illegible]	
-do-	28.10.16		Training continued indoors. Very wet day	

2449 Wt. W14957/M90 750,000 1/16 J.B.C. & A. Forms/C.2118/12.

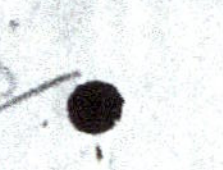

Army Form C. 2118.

Instructions regarding War Diaries and Intelligence Summaries are contained in F. S. Regs., Part II. and the Staff Manual respectively. Title Pages will be prepared in manuscript.

WAR DIARY
or
~~INTELLIGENCE SUMMARY~~

(Erase heading not required.)

Place	Date	Hour	Summary of Events and Information	Remarks and references to Appendices
BUS WOOD	29.10.16		Church parade for RCs & C of E received operation orders to relieve 4 guns 76th & 17th Bde M. G Service in the SERRE Sector.	
– do –	30.10.16		The Coy paraded as under in accordance with OO no 51 [illegible] Bde D. Section 8.30 am C Section 8.45 am B Section 9 am A Section 9.15 am & moved into the line SERRE SECTOR. Coy H.Qrs at COURCELLES relief reported complete at 1.45 pm. very wet day. The following firing took place during the night 30 – 31st Oct. 1916	

No of Gun	No of Rounds fired	Target Engaged	Nature of fire used.	Remarks
1	2000	$K\,29^{d}$ 5 · 3	Short Bursts	No Retaliation
2	1000	$K\,29^{b}$ 1 · 0 to 7 4.	Traversing fire	– do –
3	1500	$K\,30^{c}$ 1 · 5 to 2 7 · 0	– do –	
4	2000	$K\,30^{a}$ 2 0 to 2 5	– do –	– do –
5	2200	$L\,25^{A}$ 3 · 8½	Short bursts	– do –
6	1250	$L\,25^{a}$ 4 · 7	– do –	– do –
7	2000	$K\,30^{d}$ 2½ · 1 ·	– do –	– do –
8	1750	$K\,30^{d}$ 6 6	– do –	– do –
9	2000	N W. Corner of SERRE $K\,30^{d}$ 6 · 0.	Searching Fire	– do –
10	2100	STAR WOOD	– do – & Traversing	Emplacement shelled no damage done
11	2000	SERRE. $K\,30^{b}$ 1 · 1	Short bursts	No Retaliation – do –

2449 Wt. W14957/M90 750,000 1/16 J.B.C. & A. Forms/C.2118/12.

6

Instructions regarding War Diaries and Intelligence Summaries are contained in F. S. Regs., Part II. and the Staff Manual respectively. Title Pages will be prepared in manuscript.

WAR DIARY
or
~~INTELLIGENCE SUMMARY~~
(Erase heading not required.)

Army Form C. 2118.

Place	Date	Hour	Summary of Events and Information			Remarks and references to Appendices
No of Gun	No of Rounds Fired		Target Engaged.	Nature of fire used	Remarks	
No 12 Gun	1750		Enemy wire K29d 4.5 to 5.8	Traversing fire	No Retaliation	
No 13 "	1000		CT & WIRE at S. Corner of SERRE	Searching fire	Sniping over emplacement	No damage
No 14 "	2000		L 35a 90.20 & CT.	Short Bursts	No Retaliation	
No 15 "	1000		CT NE entrance to SERRE	Short Bursts	do	
No 16	1500		do	do	4 Short Bursts from M Gun too high	
Total no fired	26050 Rounds.					
COURCELLES	31/10/16		C O visited all guns in the line, no complaints, trenches in bad condition. The following firing took place during the night 31-1-16			
No of Gun	No of Rounds Fired		Target Engaged.	Nature of fire used	Remarks	
No 1 Gun	2250		K29d 5.8 to 6.6.1	Short bursts	No Retaliation	
No 2 "	2750		K29b 7.0 to 7.4	Traversing fire	do	
" 3 "	2500		K30c 1.5 to 2.0	Short Bursts	do	
" 4 "	2500		K30a 2.0 to 2.5	Searching & traversing	do	
" 5 "	1500		K30a 0.5	Short bursts	do	
" 6	1250		L35a 2.9	do	do	

2449 Wt. W14957/M90 750,000 1/16 J.B.C. & A. Forms/C.2118/12.

Instructions regarding War Diaries and Intelligence Summaries are contained in F. S. Regs., Part II. and the Staff Manual respectively. Title Pages will be prepared in manuscript.

WAR DIARY
or
~~INTELLIGENCE SUMMARY~~
(Erase heading not required.)

Army Form C. 2118.

Place	Date	Hour	Summary of Events and Information			Remarks and references to Appendices
No of Gun	No of Rounds Fired		Target Engaged	Nature of fire used	Remarks.	
No 7 gun	1750		K 35ᵃ 3.7.	Short bursts	No Retaliation	
" 8 "	1500		K 30ᵃ. 6.6	—do.—	—do.—	
" 9 "		Did	not fire Emplacements	& vicinity shelled	with H.E.	
" 10 "	2250		STAR WOOD	Traversing & Searching	No Retaliation	
" 11 "	7000		SERRE K 30ᵇ 2.1	Short Bursts.	—do.—	
" 12 "	3000		3ʳᵈ line wire K29ᵈ 4.5. to 5.5	Traversing fire	—do.—	
" 13 "	Did not		fire building up trench	& Emplacements.		
14 "		——	—do.——			
" 15 "	2000		at wire from L30ᶜ 75.10	Short Bursts	No Retaliation	
16 "	2500		NE entrance to SERRE L30ᶜ 45.50	—do.—	—do.—	
Total No of Rounds fired	25750					

In the field
1-Nov 1916

S. L. Courtauld Lieut Cmdg
No 8 Coy M. G. Corps

2449 Wt. W14957/M90 750,000 1/16 J.B.C. & A. Forms/C.2118/12.

8th Brigade.

3rd Division.

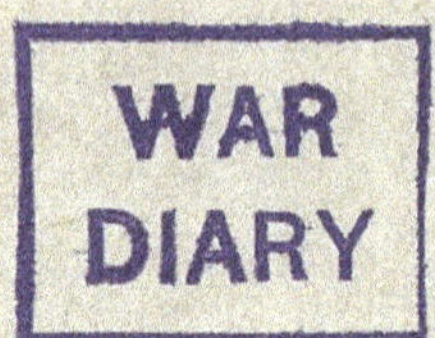

8th BRIGADE

MACHINE GUN COMPANY

NOVEMBER 1 9 1 6

Instructions regarding War Diaries and Intelligence Summaries are contained in F. S. Regs., Part II. and the Staff Manual respectively. Title Pages will be prepared in manuscript.

WAR DIARY
or
~~INTELLIGENCE SUMMARY~~
(Erase heading not required.)

Army Form C. 2118.

4 No 8 Coy M.G.C.

Vol XI

Place	Date	Hour	Summary of Events and Information	Remarks and references to Appendices
In the Field	Nov 1		All 16 guns in the line in SERRE sector as follows:-	
			2 guns of A section under 2/Lt SPOFFORTH in HITTITE trench	
			2 guns of A section under 2/Lt ALLAN in BABYLON "	
			4 guns of B section under 2/Lts BARLEY & THOMPSON in MONK trench	
			C Section under 2/Lts ROCH & WILSON as follows:- 1 gun in PALESTINE	
			1 " " ROLLAND	
			1 " " STAFF COPSE	
			1 " " TOUVENT FARM	
			D Section under 2/Lt ANDERSON as follows:- 2 guns in MONK	
			1 gun " GUNNERS WALK	
			1 " " DUNMOW	
			All guns did overhead fire during the night on enemy 4th, 5th, & 6th line wire & on STARWOOD & selected points in SERRE firing in all 29.500 rounds	
	Nov 2		Night firing continued. Number of rounds fired 33,250	
	Nov 3		Night firing continued. Number of rounds fired 33,500. H.Q. billets were shelled by 5.9's at 7.30 am. No damage or casualties.	
	Nov 4		Night firing continued. Number of rounds fired 32,800, making total number of rounds fired for the tour (6 days) 180,050.	

2449 Wt. W14957/M90 750,000 1/16 J.B.C. & A. Forms/C.2118/12.

Army Form C. 2118.

WAR DIARY
or
~~INTELLIGENCE SUMMARY~~ of No 8 Coy M.G.C.

(Erase heading not required.)

Instructions regarding War Diaries and Intelligence Summaries are contained in F. S. Regs., Part II. and the Staff Manual respectively. Title Pages will be prepared in manuscript.

Place	Date	Hour	Summary of Events and Information	Remarks and references to Appendices
In the Field	Nov 5		Coy was relieved in the trenches by 9th Coy M.G.C. & went back into billets at LOUVENCOURT arriving at 6 pm 2/Lt BARLEY arrived from Course of Instruction CAMIERS	
	Nov 6		The day was devoted to cleaning of clothing, guns & gun equipment etc 2/Lt WILSON & 2 other ranks proceeded to CAMIERS on Course of Instruction 2/Lt PULLEN on leave to U.K.	
	Nov 7		Gun drill & physical training	
	Nov 8		Training continued. 30 other ranks on fatigue cleaning roads etc. Very wet day	
	Nov 9		Training continued. Extract from D.R.O. 17463 Sgt CASSIDY } Military Medal 17474 Pte MARTIN }	
	Nov 10		Training continued. 50 other ranks working party at the Quarries LOUVENCOURT	
	Nov 11		Coy moved into the line. B section relieved 4 guns of 9th Coy in defensive positions in MONK trench. A section & 2 guns of D took up position in HITTITE trench & prepared to do overhead covering fire. C section & 2 guns of D to LA SIGNY farm. H.Q. were established in SACKVILLE street between GREY street & SOUTHERN avenue	

2449 Wt. W14957/M90 750,000 1/16 J.B.C. & A. Forms/C.2118/12.

Army Form C. 2118

WAR DIARY
or
~~INTELLIGENCE SUMMARY~~
(Erase heading not required.)

of No 8 Coy M.G.C.

Instructions regarding War Diaries and Intelligence Summaries are contained in F. S. Regs., Part II. and the Staff Manual respectively. Title Pages will be prepared in manuscript.

Place	Date	Hour	Summary of Events and Information	Remarks and references to Appendices
In the Field	Nov 12		A section & 2 guns of D under 2/Lts SPOFFORTH & ALLAN fired 5000 rnds during night on enemy 4th line & SERRE defences. B section remained MONK trench under 2/Lts BARLEY & THOMPSON. C section under 2/Lt ROCH & 2 guns of D under 2/Lt ANDERSON moved up to assembly positions in SACKVILLE street	
	Nov 13		Division attacked at 5.45 am. The 6 guns in HITTITE trench doing overhead covering fire on enemy 4th line from 5.45 am to 5.55 am & on the enemy 5th line & SERRE defences from 5.55 am till 7.43 am firing in all 20,000 rounds. At 4 pm. C section & 2 guns of D under 2/Lts ANDERSON & ROCH moved forward & took up positions in ROB ROY & MONK trenches. They were heavily shelled while moving up & suffered 6 casualties. Trenches were in very bad condition owing to shellfire	
	Nov 14		A section (4 guns) relieved the 6 guns in ROB ROY & MONK trenches. C section & 2 guns of D moved back to HITTITE trench	
	Nov 15		B section were relieved by 4 guns of 9th COY. A, C, & D sections were withdrawn & Coy moved back into billets at BUS arriving at 12 midnight	

2449 Wt. W14957/M90 750,000 1/16 J.B.C. & A. Forms/C.2118/12.

Army Form C. 2118.

Instructions regarding War Diaries and Intelligence Summaries are contained in F. S. Regs., Part II. and the Staff Manual respectively. Title Pages will be prepared in manuscript.

WAR DIARY
or
~~INTELLIGENCE SUMMARY~~ of No 8 Coy M.G.C.

(Erase heading not required.)

Place	Date	Hour	Summary of Events and Information	Remarks and references to Appendices
In the Field	Nov 16		B section under 2/Lts BARLEY & THOMPSON & D section under 2/Lt ANDERSON returned to the line relieving 8 guns of the 76th Coy. B section to FARGATE & LEGEND trenches & D section to TAUPIN trench. A & C sections & H.Q. moved to billets in COURCELLES.	
	Nov 17		All guns remained in the positions taken up on 16th inst.	
	Nov 18		A section ~~relieved~~ under 2/Lts SPOFFORTH & ALLAN relieved B section in FARGATE & LEGEND trenches. C section under 2/Lt ROCH relieved D section in TAUPIN trench. B & D sections returned to billets in COURCELLES. 7 reinforcements arrived from the base & were posted to C section. 2/Lt ANDERSON admitted to F.A. (sick)	
	Nov 19		All guns remained in positions taken up on 18th inst	
	Nov 20		2/Lt ANDERSON evacuated to C.C.S.	
	Nov 21		B section under 2/Lt BARLEY relieved C section in TAUPIN trench. D section under 2/Lt THOMPSON relieved A section in FARGATE & LEGEND trenches. A & C sections returned to billets in COURCELLES. No 17453 Sgt McMILLAN, C. appointed Acting C.S.M. vice HILES wounded. No 17521 L/Cpl LYON appointed Acting Cpl.	

2449 Wt. W14957/M90 750,000 1/16 J.B.C. & A. Forms/C.2118/12.

Instructions regarding War Diaries and Intelligence Summaries are contained in F. S. Regs., Part II. and the Staff Manual respectively. Title Pages will be prepared in manuscript.

WAR DIARY
or
~~INTELLIGENCE SUMMARY~~

(Erase heading not required.)

Army Form C. 2118.

No 8 Coy M.G.C.

Place	Date	Hour	Summary of Events and Information	Remarks and references to Appendices
In the Field	Nov 22		2 guns to B section moved forward from TAUPIN trench to WOLF trench.	
			2/Lt PULLEN arrived from leave to U.K.	
			Lt NEILSON proceeded on leave to U.K. 2/Lt SPOFFORTH taking over the duties of 2nd i/c.	
	Nov 23		D section were heavily shelled in LEGEND trench but suffered no casualties	
	Nov 24		A section under 2/Lt ALLAN relieved 2 guns of B section in TAUPIN trench & 2 guns D in FARGATE trench. C section under 2/Lt ROCH relieved 2 guns of B in WOLF trench & 2 guns of D in LEGEND trench.	
			B & D sections returned to billets in COURCELLES.	
			Lt COURTAULD promoted to rank of Captain.	
	Nov 25		2 other ranks proceeded to CAMIERS on course of instruction.	
			The following extract of London Gazette 24/11/16:- Undermentioned 2/Lts to be Lt's from 1/11/16 L.H. PULLEN J.A. WILSON E.R. SPOFFORTH H.G. ANDERSON J.A. ROCH	

2449 Wt. W14957/M90 750,000 1/16 J.B.C. & A. Forms/C.2118/12.

Army Form C. 2118.

Instructions regarding War Diaries and Intelligence Summaries are contained in F. S. Regs., Part II. and the Staff Manual respectively. Title Pages will be prepared in manuscript.

WAR DIARY
or
~~INTELLIGENCE SUMMARY~~

(Erase heading not required.)

of No 8 Coy M.G.C.

Place	Date	Hour	Summary of Events and Information	Remarks and references to Appendices
In the Field	Nov 26		Lt. WILSON returned from course of instruction CAMIERS. 2 guns of A section in TAUPIN fired 5000 rounds during the night on enemy 3rd line wire.	
	Nov 27		B section under 2/Lt BARLEY relieved C section in WOLF + LEGEND trenches. D section under 2/Lt THOMPSON relieved A section in TAUPIN + ~~LEGEND~~ FARGATE trenches. A + C sections returned to billets in COURCELLES.	
	Nov 28		A + C sections rifle + clothing inspection in billets. 2 guns of D section in TAUPIN fired 3800 rounds on enemy 4th line wire in the course of the night of 27/28th.	
	Nov 29		A + C sections cleaning guns + gun equipment etc. 2 guns of D section in TAUPIN fired 3100 rounds on enemy 4th line wire. No 19956 Pte SEALY appointed unpaid L/Cpl.	
	Nov 30		A section under 2/Lt ALLAN relieved B section in WOLF + LEGEND trenches. C section under Lts ROCH + WILSON relieved D section in TAUPIN + FARGATE trenches. B + D sections returned to billets in COURCELLES. 2 guns in TAUPIN fired 1200 rounds on enemy 5th line wire being 5 + 7 pm on night of Nov 29/30th.	

2449 Wt. W14957/M90 750,000 1/16 J.B.C. & A. Forms/C.2118/12.

8th Brigade.

3rd Division.

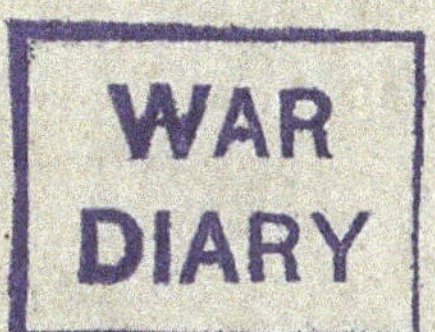

8th BRIGADE.

MACHINE GUN COMPANY

DECEMBER 1 9 1 6

No: 8 Company Army Form C. 2118.
Machine Gun Corps.

Instructions regarding War Diaries and Intelligence Summaries are contained in F. S. Regs., Part II. and the Staff Manual respectively. Title Pages will be prepared in manuscript.

WAR DIARY or ~~INTELLIGENCE SUMMARY~~

(Erase heading not required.)

Vol 12

Place	Date	Hour	Summary of Events and Information	Remarks and references to Appendices
	1/12/16		Rifle + clothing inspection B + D sections. A + C sections in trenches. GOC Division inspected Billets.	
	2/12/16		A + C sections in trenches. B + D sections cleaning guns etc.	
	3/12/16		Divine Service (Voluntary) for B + D sections at 9 am. B section under 2/Lt Barley relieved C section in TAUPIN. D Section under Lt Thompson relieved A section in WOLF and LEGEND. A + C sections returned to billets in COURCELLES	
	4/12/16		B + D sections in trenches. 2 Guns in TAUPIN firing 4200 rounds on enemys 4th + 5th line wire. No 17505 L/Cpl Horrell promoted Cpl from 20-11-16 vide Cpl Parkes evacuated. " 34451 L/Cpl Drey received pay of appointment from 20/11/16 vide L/Cpl Horrell promoted.	
	5/12/16		B + D sections in trenches, the 2 guns in TAUPIN firing 4,600 rounds on enemys 4th + 5th line wire. A + C section cleaning gun equipment + ammunition.	
	6/12/16		A section under 2/Lt Allan relieved 2 guns of B section in TAUPIN + remaining 2 guns took up positions in MONK trench, south of FLAG AVENUE. C section under Lts Roch + Wilson relieved 2 guns of D in WOLF + 1 gun in LEGEND and 1 gun of B section in FARGATE. B + D sections returned to billets in COURCELLES.	
	7/12/16		A + C sections in the line. The 2 guns in TAUPIN fired 4500 rounds on enemys 4th + 5th line wire. B + D sections Rifle + Clothing Inspection.	
	8/12/16		A + C sections in the line. TAUPIN guns fired 3800 rounds on enemys wire.	
	9/12/16		B section under 2/Lt Barley relieved C section in WOLF and FARGATE. D section under Lt Thompson relieved A section in TAUPIN and MONK. Guns in TAUPIN fired 4000 rounds on enemys wire. A + C sections returned to billets in COURCELLES. Lt R.R. Neilson returned from leave to U.K + resumed duty as 2nd I/C. Lt Wilson to F.A.	
	10/12/16		B + D sections in the line. TAUPIN guns firing 4000 rounds on enemy wire. A + C sections Divine Service 10 am. 23021 Pte Nichols reported for duty and taken on the strength.	
	11/12/16		B + D sections in the line. The TAUPIN guns firing 4600 rounds on enemy wire. A + C sections cleaning guns. The following reported for duty from 2nd Bn The Royal Scots. No 11284 Pte McGREGOR J. 43190 " COCHRANE B. 3629 " BLACK J.	

2449 Wt. W14957/M90 750,000 1/16 J.B.C. & A. Forms/C.2118/12.

Army Form C. 2118.

WAR DIARY
or
INTELLIGENCE SUMMARY
(Erase heading not required.)

Instructions regarding War Diaries and Intelligence Summaries are contained in F. S. Regs., Part II. and the Staff Manual respectively. Title Pages will be prepared in manuscript.

Place	Date	Hour	Summary of Events and Information	Remarks and references to Appendices
	12/12/16		A section under Lt Spofforth and 2/Lt Allan relieved B section in WOLF, LEGEND and FARGATE. C section under Lt Roch relieved D section in TAUPIN and MONK. B + D sections returned to billets in COURCELLES. The guns in TAUPIN fired 4250 rounds on enemy wire.	
	13/12/16		A + C sections in the line. The TAUPIN guns firing 4000 rounds on enemy wire. Capt S L Courtauld, Comdg, to U.K. on leave. Lt R.R. Nelson taking over duties of C.O. and Lt Spofforth duties of 2nd I/C. At 8 pm + again at 10 pm shelled in vicinity of billets. No damage or casualties.	
	14/12/16		A + C sections in the line. Guns in TAUPIN fired 5000 rounds on enemy wire. B + D sections cleaning guns	
	15/12/16		B section under 2/Lt Barley relieved C section in TAUPIN, + MONK. D section under Lt Thompson relieved A section in WOLF, LEGEND + FARGATE. A + C sections returned to billets in COURCELLES. Guns in TAUPIN fired 4500 rounds on enemy wire.	
	16/12/16		B + D sections in the line. Guns in TAUPIN fired 4250 rounds on enemy wire. A + C sections rifle and bayonet inspection. Lt Nelson from F A	
	17/12/16		B + D sections in the line. The TAUPIN guns firing 4000 rounds on enemy wire. A + C cleaning guns.	
	18/12/16		A section under 2/Lt Allan relieved B section in TAUPIN + MONK. C section under Lt Roch relieved D section in LEGEND, FARGATE + WOLF. B + D returned to billets in COURCELLES. Guns in TAUPIN fired 5000 rounds on enemy wire.	
	19/12/16		A + C in the line. TAUPIN guns fired 5000 rounds on enemy wire. B + D rifle + bayonet inspection. 2/Lt L. R. Bull reported for duty + taken on strength. 17508 L/Cpl Markham and 10201 Pte Topp returned from course of instruction CAMIERS	
	20/12/16		A + C in the line. TAUPIN guns fired 5000 rounds on enemy wire. B + D cleaning guns. Extract from London Gazette 24/11/16 "2/Lt M B Thompson to be Lt 6/7/16"	
	21/12/16		A + C in the line. TAUPIN guns fired 5000 rounds. A + C relieved at 3.15 pm by D + B respectively.	

2449 Wt. W14957/M90 750,000 1/16 J.B.C. & A. Forms/C.2118/12.

Army Form C. 2118.

Instructions regarding War Diaries and Intelligence Summaries are contained in F. S. Regs., Part II. and the Staff Manual respectively. Title Pages will be prepared in manuscript.

WAR DIARY
or
INTELLIGENCE SUMMARY

(Erase heading not required.)

Place	Date	Hour	Summary of Events and Information	Remarks and references to Appendices
	22/12/16		D & B fired from TAUPIN guns 4,000 rounds. No. 42399 Cpl. Head J.W. and No. 36684 Pte Rashon H.W. proceeded to cadet unit U.K. Undermentioned transferred to M.G.C. with effect from 15/12/16	
			2nd Royal Scots — 43148 Pte Fetter, A. 71867 M.G.C. No:; 30650 " Nimmo, J. 71868; 13755 " Wallace, T. 71871; 43194 " Cunningham, J. 71872; 15898 " Smart, J. 71873; 10339 " Hiles, D. 71874	
			1st R. S. Fus: M.G.C. No — 6793 Pte. McGoff, H. 71875; 12348 " McCormack, R. 71876; 43100 " Kelly, W. 71877; 43105 " Meike, W. 71878; 6749 " Cumming, P. 71879; 43011 " Duff, J. 71880	
			8th East Yorks Regt M.G.C. No — 30945 Pte Baxter, R.H. 71881; 13/875 " Davidson, F. 71882; 3/402 " Hobson, J. 71883; 30953 " Bilton, J. 71884; 15620 " Lennox, W. 71885; 13393 " Cockerill, W. 71886; 10/1422 " Lattimore, W. 71887; 19059 " Vernon, J. 71888	
			7th K.S.L.I. M.G.C. No — 19632 Pte. Symonds, A.G. 71889; 23459 " Burrows, A.G. 71892; 23723 " Martin, S. 71893; 14276 " Morris, J. 71894	
			1st R.O.S.B. — 18094 Pte. Philip, C. 71898	
	23/12/16		B & D in line. TAUPIN guns fired 4,000 rounds. Gun cleaning. No. 36751 Pte. Clunnion and No. 37642 Pte. Liddall evacuated to C.C.S. on 28-21/12/16 respectively and struck off strength of Company	

2449 Wt. W14957/M90 750,000 1/16 J.B.C. & A. Forms/C.2118/12.

Instructions regarding War Diaries and Intelligence Summaries are contained in F. S. Regs., Part II. and the Staff Manual respectively. Title Pages will be prepared in manuscript.

WAR DIARY
or
INTELLIGENCE SUMMARY
(Erase heading not required.)

Army Form C. 2118.

Place	Date	Hour	Summary of Events and Information	Remarks and references to Appendices
	24/12/16		B & D in line. TAUPIN guns fired 3,600 rounds. B & D relieved by A & C at 3-15 p.m. Gun in SERRE Road and gun in LEGEND changed to B & D positions in new part of line taken over by 8th Inf. Brigade. No 8625 Pte Rose evacuated to C.C.S. 19-12-16 and No. 36682 Pte Lowe evacuated to C.C.S. 15/12/16. and struck off strength of Coy.	
	25/12/16		A & C in line. Divine Services (Holy Communion) 8 a.m Billet 38 R.G.A Recreation Hut. 12 noon (H.C.) Billet 38. R.G.A Recreation Hut.	
	26/12/16		A & C in line TAUPIN guns fired 5.000 rounds, gun cleaning and equipment cleaning. Sgt. Gould. H reported for duty as C.Q.M.S and taken on strength as from 24/12/16. VICE Sgt. Whitton returned to D section.	
	27/12/16		A & C. in line. TAUPIN guns fired 4,000 rounds. Feet inspection. A & C relieved by D & B.	
	28/12/16		D & B in line - TAUPIN guns fired 5,000 rounds. Rifle and clothing inspection C.S.M. READE reported for duty and taken on strength. 15193 Pte. Preece A.J evacuated to C.C.S. and struck off strength 26356 Pte. Wood G. discharged to duty and taken on strength 26/12/16 Promotion A/Sgt. Lyon J.W. reverts to A/Cpl.	
	29/12/16		D & B in line. TAUPIN guns firing 4,000 rounds. Cleaning equipment and rifle inspection. 12418 Pte Markham H. to F.A.	
	30/12/16		D & B. in line. TAUPIN guns fired 4.000 rounds. Feet inspection 10-30 a.m. Promotion - Lieut. S.L. COURTAULD to be A/Captain while in command of company Lieut. J.A. WILSON evacuated to C.C.S. 24-12-16. D section was relieved by C section B section by A section.	

2449 Wt. W14957/M90 750,000 1/16 J.B.C. & A. Forms/C.2118/12.

Army Form C.2118.

WAR DIARY
or
INTELLIGENCE SUMMARY
(Erase heading not required.)

Instructions regarding War Diaries and Intelligence Summaries are contained in F. S. Regs., Part II. and the Staff Manual respectively. Title Pages will be prepared in manuscript.

Place	Date	Hour	Summary of Events and Information	Remarks and references to Appendices
	31/12/16		C. & A. sections in line – TAUPIN guns fired 4,000 rounds. Rifle inspection 36533 Pte. Parker H. to Fld. Amb. 35590 Sgt. T. Kelly and 36543 Pte. F. Gibbs from Fld. Ambulance	
			Ralph R. Westmacott for Captain Comdg. No: 8 Coy. M. G. Corps.	

2449 Wt. W14957/M90 750,000 1/16 J.B.C. & A. Forms/C.2118/12.

3rd Division

War Diaries

8/M. G. C.

January To 31st December

1917

Machine Gun Corps. **WAR DIARY** *or* **INTELLIGENCE SUMMARY** *(Erase heading not required.)* No. 8 Coy. Army Form C. 2118.

Instructions regarding War Diaries and Intelligence Summaries are contained in F. S. Regs., Part II. and the Staff Manual respectively. Title Pages will be prepared in manuscript.

Vol 13

Place	Date	Hour	Summary of Events and Information	Remarks and references to Appendices
	1/1/17.		C+A Sections in line. 36543 Pte Gibbs returned from Field Ambulance. 17642 L/Cpl Edwards A. to be full Cpl vice Cpl Hood to Cadet School 22-12-16. 17508 Unpaid L/Cpl Makeham to be paid L/Cpl vice Edwards A. promoted 22-12-16.	
	2/1/17.		Foot inspection + preparation for relief. C Section relieved by B. A Section relieved by D. TAUPIN guns fired 3500 rounds. 36533 Pte Parker H. + 34477 Pte White F.O. from Field Ambulance 1-1-17. Compliments of the Season from the Major General.	
	3/1/17.		Rifle + Clothing inspection. C. Reeves 2/Lieut joined Coy as reinforcement + taken on strength from 2nd Jany, 1917. B+D Sections in line. TAUPIN guns fired 3000 rounds 42887 Pte White F. to Field Ambulance.	
	4/1/17.		B+D Section in line. TAUPIN guns fired 4000 rounds. Parade under CSM for drill etc. J. A. Wilson Lieut. evacuated to England sick 27-12-16. Authy XIII Corps A/600/27 d/31/12/16. 4071 Pte McIntyre J. from Field Ambulance 1-1-17. 57430 Pte Herriott A from Field Ambulance 3-1-17.	
	5/1/17		Foot inspection + preparation for relief. B Section relieved by C. D Section relieved by A. TAUPIN guns fired 4000 rounds. The Military Cross awarded Lt F. H. Pullen 3/1/17.	
	6/1/17		Rifle + Clothing inspection. B+D in line. TAUPIN guns fired 3000 rounds. 37306 Pte Selway J. to Field Ambulance. 9727 Pte France H. evacuated.	
	7/1/17.		Coy relieved by the 14th M.G.Coy. Coy moved back in motor lorries to BEAUVAL.	
	8/1/17.		Coy in BEAUVAL for day of 8th. Preparations for move next day.	
	9/1/17.		Move to St HILAIRE. Billets good. Good standings for horses.	
	10/1/17.		Orderly Officer 2/Lt Reeves. 10am Rifle inspection, cleaning + sorting gun kit. 17509 L/Cpl Martin W. to be full Cpl. 10356 L/C. May Gld. to be paid L/Cpl. 2/Lt Bull F.R. posted to "C" Section " Reeves C " " "B" "	

2449 Wt. W14957/M90 750,000 1/16 J.B.C. & A. Forms/C.2118/12.

Army Form C. 2118.

Instructions regarding War Diaries and Intelligence Summaries are contained in F. S. Regs., Part II. and the Staff Manual respectively. Title Pages will be prepared in manuscript.

WAR DIARY
or
INTELLIGENCE SUMMARY
(Erase heading not required.)

Place	Date	Hour	Summary of Events and Information	Remarks and references to Appendices
In the Field.	11/1/17.		Orderly Officer 2/Lt Rull F.R. 10-11am Physical Training. 11-15 to 12-15 Cleaning guns + equipment 2-30 pm. Inter-Section Football.	
	12/1/17.		Orderly Officer 2/Lt Allan. 10-11am Physical Training, 11.15-12.15 Sorting + cleaning gun kit. 2-30 pm Inter-Section Football. Cpl Smith promoted to Sgt + posted to 'B' Section. Cpl Martin posted from 'D' to 'C'.	
	13/1/17		Orderly Officer Lt. Thompson M.B. 10-11am Physical Training. 11.15-12.15 Gun cleaning. Gun inspection by C.O. at 12 noon.	
	14/1/17		Kit inspection at 12 noon. Orderly Officer Lt Rock J.A. Evacuated to C.C.S:- 46312 Cpl Cooper J.C. 51306 Pte Selway J. 97534 Pte Palmer J. 34477. Pte White J.	
	15/1/17.		Orderly Officer 2/Lt Reeves C. 9-9.45am Physical Training. 10-11am Mechanism. 11-12 noon Gun Drill. 12-1 pm. Judging distance.	
	16/1/17		Orderly Officer 2/Lt Rull F.R. 9-9.45am Physical Training. 10-11am Stoppages. 11-12 noon Fire Orders. 12-1 pm Range Cards. H.Q. Section parade under 'D' Section for Physical Training + under Sgt Small for Signalling. Novices class under Sgt Young at 10 am.	
	17/1/17.		Orderly Officer 2/Lt Allan R. 9-9.45am Physical Training. 10-11am Mechanism. 11-12 noon Gun Drill. 12-1 pm Semaphore. Novices class under Sgt Young at 10 am.	
	18/1/17.		Orderly Officer Lt Spofforth E.R. 9-9.45am Physical Training. 10-11am Stoppages. 11-12 noon Gas Helmet Practice. 12-1 pm. Packing Limbers. Novices class under Sgt Young.	
	19/1/17.		Orderly Officer. 2/Lt Barley F.J. 9-9.45am Physical Training. 10-11am. Mechanism. 11-12 noon Gun Drill 12-1 pm Ident. + Reco. of Targets. Novices class under Sgt Young.	
	20/1/17.		Orderly Officer Lt Rock J.A. 9-9.45am Physical Training. 10-11am Stoppages. 11.12 noon Fire Orders. 12-1 pm Semaphore. Novices class under Sgt Young.	
	21/1/17.		Orderly Officer 2/Lt Rull F.R. Church Parade at 10am for R.C's in Church Domart. C of E Service at 10 am in Barn adjoining D. Sections Billet. Kit inspection at 12-0 noon.	

2449 Wt. W14957/M90 750,000 1/16 J.B.C. & A. Forms/C.2118/12.

Army Form C. 2118.

WAR DIARY
or
INTELLIGENCE SUMMARY

(Erase heading not required.)

Instructions regarding War Diaries and Intelligence Summaries are contained in F. S. Regs., Part II. and the Staff Manual respectively. Title Pages will be prepared in manuscript.

Place	Date	Hour	Summary of Events and Information	Remarks and references to Appendices
In the Field.	22/1/17.		Orderly Officer 2/Lt Allan R. 2 Guns handed in to Ordnance from each Section for overhauling. Coy moved to new billets in Berneuil.	
	23/1/17		Orderly Officer 2/Lt Spofforth C. 9-9.45am Physical Training. 10-11am A+B Section On Range. C+D Sect Mechanism. 11-12 noon A+B On Range. C+D Gun Drill. 12-1pm Revolver Practice A+B. Semaphore C+D	
	24/1/17.		Orderly Officer 2/Lt Barley F.J. 9-9.45am Physical Drill. 10-11am Squad Drill. 11-1pm Coy Drill under CSM.	
	25/1/17.		Orderly Officer 2/Lt Reeves C. 9-9.45am Physical Drill. 10-11am C+D Range. A+B Stoppages. 11-12 noon C+D Range. A+B Parade under C.S.M. 12-1pm C+D Revolver A+B Identn + Recr of target. Following appointed unpaid L/Cpls 36779 Pte Pritchard. H, 71887 Pte Lallimore W, 13156 Pte Deadman R.	
	26/1/17.		Orderly Officer 2/Lt Bull L.R. 10-11.[illegible]am A+B Range C+D Mechanism. 11-12 noon A+B Range. C+D CSM's Parade. 12-1pm. A+B Range C+D Semaphore. 9-9.45am Physical Training. A/Cpl Lyon T. to be A/Sgt vice Sgt McMillan C. evacuated to U.K. with effect from 26th inst.	
	27/1/17.		Orders received to pack ready to move. Day spent in packing	
	28/1/17.		Coy moved with Division to billets at Authieule. Men + Officers in huts.	
	29/1/17.		Coy moved with Division to Bonnieres.	
	30/1/17.		Coy moved with Division to PETIT-HOUVIN.	
	31/1/17.		Coy moved with Division to ROCOURT.	

[signature] Lt & Adjt
8th Coy M.G.C.

No. 8 Coy. Machine Gun Corps

Army Form C. 2118.

Instructions regarding War Diaries and Intelligence Summaries are contained in F. S. Regs., Part II. and the Staff Manual respectively. Title pages will be prepared in manuscript.

WAR DIARY
or
INTELLIGENCE SUMMARY.
(Erase heading not required.)

Vol 14

Place	Date	Hour	Summary of Events and Information	Remarks and references to Appendices
In-the-Field	1/2/17.		Unloading limbers + fixing up billets. Gun cleaning + Kit inspection	
	2/2/17.		10-11 am. Inspection of guns + gun kit. 11-1 pm – Mechanism + Stripping	
	3/2/17.		9-9.45 am. Physical Training. 10-11 am. Gun Drill. 11-1 pm Coy Parade under C.S.M. for drill.	
	4/2/17.		Coy moved to billets in ORLINCOURT	
	5/2/17.		9-9.45 am. Physical Training. 10-11 am. Mechanism etc 12-1 pm. C.S.M. Parade	
	6/2/17.		Route march. Range-finding class under Adjutant.	
	7/2/17.		9-9.45 am. Physical Training. 10-11 am Belt Filling. 11-1 pm Stoppages etc.	
	8/2/17.		Coy moved to LIENCOURT. Coy billets inspected by C.O. at 7.30 am. Coy moved off 7.45 am.	
	9/2/17.		9-9.45 am. Physical Training. 10-11 am. Mechanism. 11-1 pm. C.S.M.'s Parade.	
	10/2/17.		9-9.45 am. Physical Training. 10-11 am. Gun Drill. 11-1 pm. C.S.M.'s Parade.	
	11/2/17.		10 am. Church Parades for C of E in School Room, LIENCOURT. 10.30 am. R.C's in Village Church. 11 am. Nonconformists + Presbyterians.	
	12/2/17.		9-9.45 am. Physical Training. 10-11 am. Mechanism. 11-12 noon Gun Drill. 12-1 pm. C.S.M.'s Parade. Novices class under Sgt Young to be continued.	
	13/2/17.		9-9.45 am. Physical Training. 10-11 am. Gas helmet inspection by Cpl Burnside. 11-12 noon Stoppages. 12-1 pm Fire Orders. 2-3 pm Range cards + judging distance. Practice with Barr + Stroud. Novices class as usual.	
	14/2/17.		9-0 am.-1 pm. A+B Sections Range. 9-9.45 am. C+D Sections Physical Training. 10-11.30 am. C+D – Mechanism. 11.30-1 pm. C+D – Gun Drill. 2-3 pm. All Sections under C.S.M. Novices class as usual.	
	15/2/17.		9-9.45 am. A+B – Physical Training. 10-11.30 am. A+B – Mechanism. 11.30-1 pm. Gun Drill. 9-1 pm. C+D – On Range. Novices class as usual. No 17506 Cpl Makeham C. transferred from B to D Section. No 17496 Sgt Collins F. evacuated. No 34457 L/Cpl Droy A.E. to be Cpl vice No 46312 Cpl Cooper evacuated 5-1-17. No 17506 L/Cpl Makeham E to be Cpl vice No 44445 Cpl Moir reduced to ranks 12/2/17. The following L/Cpls to receive pay of appointment. No 17502 L/Cpl Renton R. vice L/Cpl Lyons appointed A/Sgt 26/1/17. No 19956 L/Cpl Sealy J. vice No 34457 L/Cpl Droy A.E. promoted Cpl 5/1/17; No 36513 L/Cpl Radford H. vice No 17506 L/Cpl Makeham promoted to Cpl 12-2-17.	
	16/2/17.		9-1 pm A+B Section on Range. 9-9.45 C+D – Physical Training. 10-11.30 am. Stoppages. 11.30 to 1 pm. Fire Orders 2-3 pm. All Sections – Indication of targets + judging distance. Novices class under Sgt Young	

A5834 Wt. W4973/M687 750,000 8/16 D. D. & L. Ltd. Forms/C.2118/13.

Army Form C. 2118.

WAR DIARY
or
INTELLIGENCE SUMMARY.
(Erase heading not required.)

Instructions regarding War Diaries and Intelligence Summaries are contained in F. S. Regs., Part II. and the Staff Manual respectively. Title pages will be prepared in manuscript.

Place	Date	Hour	Summary of Events and Information	Remarks and references to Appendices
In-the-Field	17/2/17.		9-1 pm. C+D Sections on Range. 8.45am A+B Sections Unloading limbers. 9am A+B Washing limbers. 2-3 pm All Sections C.S.M's Parade. Novices class under Sgt Young.	
	18/2/17.		10 am. C+D " - Washing limbers. A+B Sections Church Parade for C of E. 11am. A+B Church Parade for R.C. 10 am A+B " Church Parade for Presbyterians + Nonconformists. 3-0 pm C.O's Parade. Dress Fighting Order.	
	19/2/17.		9-9.45am. Inspection by Section Officers. 10 am. Inspection by C.O. 10-30 am. Inspection by G.O.C. 11-12 noon. Cleaning guns + kit. 1.30-4.30 pm. Digging trenches (Practice)	
	20/2/17		9-1 pm. Bathing Parade. 2-3 pm. Gas test Lachrymatory. Novices class under Sgt Young.	
	21/2/17.		9-9.45am. C+D Sections Physical Training. 10-11.30am. C+D Mechanism. 11.30-1pm. C+D Gun Drill 9-1-0 pm A+B on Range. Novices class as usual.	
	22/2/17.		9-9.45am A+B Sections Physical Training. 10-11.30 am A+B Mechanism. 11.30-1.0 pm. A+B Gun Drill 9-1-0 pm. C+D " on Range. 2-3 pm All Sections C.S.M's Parade. Firing on range + Gun Drill practiced wearing Small Box Respirators. Novices Class as usual.	
	23/2/17.		9-1-0 pm. A+B Sections on Range. 9-9.45am ~~A+B~~ Sections C+D - Physical Training. 10-11.30 am C+D Stoppages. 11.30-1-0 pm. C+D Fire Orders. 2-3 pm All Sections - Bombing instruction by Bde Bomb. Off. Novices class taken over by 2/Lt. Vickers R.R.	
	23/2/17		The following reinforcements joined our Coy:-	

No.	Rank	Name	Initials	No.	Rank	Name	Initials	No.	Rank	Name	Initials
14614	Pte	Connelly	J.	81369	Pte	Hargreaves	R.	82319	Pte	Hodkinson	P.
82320	"	Hodgson	J.	81692	L/C.	Mauer	J.	53971	"	Mattison	M.
67724	"	McManus	J.	53970	Pte	Thompson	G.R.	81367	"	Tilley	S.
63276	"	Tripp	J.	81366	"	Wilson	E.	81275	"	Atack	E.
81699	"	Crewse	E.	81706	"	Fearn	G.E.	82382	"	Goodwin	R.
67817	"	Humphrey	T.	81279	"	Hoyle	W.	82388	"	Hill	S.C.
37104	"	Nersey	T.	82374	"	Mould	B.	82379	"	Midway	H.
7986	"	Taylor	G.	81705	"	Williams	J.E.	81500	"	Hoare	H.F.
58939	L/C.	McCrimmon	N.								

A5834 Wt. W4973/M687 750,000 8/16 D. D. & L. Ltd. Forms/C.2118/13.

Instructions regarding War Diaries and Intelligence Summaries are contained in F. S. Regs., Part II. and the Staff Manual respectively. Title pages will be prepared in manuscript.

WAR DIARY
or
INTELLIGENCE SUMMARY.
(Erase heading not required.)

Army Form C. 2118.

Place	Date	Hour	Summary of Events and Information	Remarks and references to Appendices
In the Field	24/2/17		Coy trench digging from 9-0 am to 1-0 pm. C.S.M's Parade from 2-3 pm.	
			The following evacuated + struck off Coy strength.	
			No 17496 Sgt Collins F. No 57873 Pte Rodine G. No 26336 Pte Wood G.	
			" 71876 Pte McCormack R. " 10646 " Florence D.	
			Reinforcements posted as follows:- 'A' Section 6 - 'B' Section 8 - 'C' Section 4 - 'D' Section 7.	
	25/2/17		Church Parades:- C of E 10-0 am. R.C. 10-0 am. – at LIENCOURT. Guns cleaned, belts filled, limbers loaded, ammunition put on fighting limbers ready for move to trenches.	
	26/2/17		9-0 am. Loading limbers. 10-0 am. Blankets to be at Q.M.S.s store rolled in bundles of 10. 11-0 am. Dinner. 12-0 noon. Inspection of billets. 12.15 pm. Coy parades - fighting order - haversacks on back. Coy arrived in ARRAS at 7.15 pm + took over billets from 76th M.G. Coy.	
	27/2/17		B + D Sections paraded for trenches at 11-0 am + relieved 76th M.G. Coy in line.	
	28/2/17		B + D Sections in line, rest of Coy cleaning billets, guns etc.	

Robt McNeilson [signature]. Lieut + Adjt.
No 8 Coy, M.G. Corps

A5834 Wt. W4973/M687 750,000 8/16 D. D. & L. Ltd. Forms/C.2118/13.

Army Form C. 2118.

Instructions regarding War Diaries and Intelligence Summaries are contained in F. S. Regs., Part II. and the Staff Manual respectively. Title pages will be prepared in manuscript.

WAR DIARY
or
~~INTELLIGENCE SUMMARY~~.

(Erase heading not required.)

8 M.G.C. Vol 15

Place	Date	Hour	Summary of Events and Information	Remarks and references to Appendices
In the Field	1/3/17		B+D Sections in line, fired 4000 rounds on selected enemy Communication Trenches. A+C Sections cleaning billets, + Kit inspection. No 58939 L/Cpl McCrimmon ? + No 18692 L/Cpl Massen reverted to ranks at their own request.	
	2/3/17.		B+D Sections in line, fired 4000 rounds. A+C Sections cleaning guns + gun kit.- Mechanism	
	3/3/17.		B+D Sections in line, fired 4000 rounds. A+C Sections paraded at 9.0 am to dig M. Gun emplacements for overhead barrage fire.	
	4/3/17.		B+D Sections in line fired 4000 rounds. A+C Sections digging emplacements	
	5/3/17.		B+D Sections in line fired 4000 rounds. 'A' Section with 2 guns + 'D' Section with 4 guns co-operated with 1st Gordons in carrying out raid on German trenches 16000 rounds were fired in connection with raid which was successful.	
	6/3/17.		B+D Sections in line fired 4000 rounds. A+C Sections paraded for baths at 11.0 am + for digging at 2.0 pm.	
	7/3/17.		A Section relieved D Section at 3.0 pm. C Section relieved B Section at 3.0 pm.	
	8/3/17.		A+C Sections in line fired 4000 rounds. B+D Sections paraded 2.0 pm for cleaning + kit inspection.	
	9/3/17.		A+C Sections in line fired 4000 rounds. B+D Sections paraded at 9am for digging emplacements, making cellars &c.	
	10/3/17.		A+C Sections in line fired 4000 rounds. B+D Sections paraded at 9am for digging &c	
	11/3/17		A+C Sections in line fired 4000 rounds. B+D Sections paraded at 9am for digging etc. 11.0 am. R.C. Service in Hospital St John. 6 pm. Rosary + Benediction at Catholic Church.	
	12/3/17.		A+C. Sections in line fired 4000 rounds. B+D Sections paraded for digging at 9 am.	
	13/3/17.		A+C Sections in line fired 4000 rounds. B+D Sections paraded for digging at 9 am.	
	14/3/17.		A+C Sections in line fired 4000 rounds. B+D Sections paraded for digging at 9 am.	
	15/3/17.		A+C Sections in line fired 4000 rounds. B+D Sections paraded for digging at 9 am.	
	16/3/17.		A+C Sections in line fired 4000 rounds. B+D Sections paraded for digging at 9 am.	

A5834 Wt. W4973/M687 750,000 8/16 D. D. & L. Ltd. Forms/C.2118/13.

Instructions regarding War Diaries and Intelligence Summaries are contained in F. S. Regs., Part II. and the Staff Manual respectively. Title pages will be prepared in manuscript.

WAR DIARY
or
~~INTELLIGENCE SUMMARY.~~
(Erase heading not required.)

Army Form C. 2118.

Place	Date	Hour	Summary of Events and Information	Remarks and references to Appendices
In-the-Field	17/3/17.		16 Guides reported at Orderly Room 10 am from Sections. Coy relieved at 3.0 pm by 9th M.G. Coy. B+D Sections, Orderly Room + Q.M. Stores moved at 8 pm to billets in Hauteville. A+C Sect remained in ARRAS under C.O. to continue digging. Remainder of Coy under 2nd i/cmd at Hauteville for training.	
	18/3/17		A+C Sections in ARRAS. B+D Sections cleaning billets + kit inspection at 2.0 pm. Two guns of B Section under 2/Lt Barley on Anti-Aircraft duty at Wanquetin.	
	19/3/17.		A+C Sections in ARRAS. B+D Sections:- 9-9.45am. Physical Training 10-11am. Gun cleaning 11-1pm. Drill.	
	20/3/17.		A+C Sections in ARRAS. B+D Sections:- 9-9.45am Physical Training. 10-11am Belt Filling N.C.O's Use of compass. 11-1 pm Range taking.	
	21/3/17.		A+C Sections in ARRAS. B+D Sections 9-9.45am Physical Training. 10-11am Mechanism 11-12 noon Use of elevating + traversing dials. 12-1 pm. Advanced gun drill. 2-3 pm N.C.O's Lecture on Map reading. O.Ranks. Cleaning guns.	
	22/3/17.		A+C Sections in ARRAS. Two teams of D Section relieved 2 teams of B Section at Wanquetin. Remainder of B+D Sections 9-9.45am Physical Training. 10-11am Stoppages. 11-1 pm. Map reading. 2-3 pm. Semaphore. Preparations made in case of order to "Stand By" is given. Men to mark their pack, greatcoats +c.	
	23/3/17.		A+C Sections in ARRAS. B+D Sections 9-9.45am Physical Training. 10-11am Lecture Indirect Fire. 11-1 pm. Use of ground + cover in advancing with guns in the open. 2-3 pm Gun Cleaning.	
	24/3/17.		A+C Sections in ARRAS. B+D Section. 9-9.45am Physical Training. 10-11am Lecture on use of night firing box + Auxiliary aiming mark. 11-12 noon Practice with range taker. 2-3 pm. Firing with use of night firing box	

Instructions regarding War Diaries and Intelligence Summaries are contained in F. S. Regs., Part II. and the Staff Manual respectively. Title pages will be prepared in manuscript.

WAR DIARY
or
~~INTELLIGENCE SUMMARY.~~
(Erase heading not required.)

No. 8 MACHINE GUN COMPANY.
No. .... Date........

Army Form C. 2118.

Place	Date	Hour	Summary of Events and Information	Remarks and references to Appendices
In the Field	25/3/17		B + D Sections relieved A + C Sections in ARRAS at 7 pm. Two guns of C Section relieved two guns of B Section at Wanquetin.	
	26/3/17		B + D Sections in ARRAS. A + C Sections Kit inspection + gun cleaning.	
	27/3/17		Coy paraded at 7·30 am, fighting order + proceeded to training area LIENCOURT to practice attack over practice trenches.	
	28/3/17		B + D Sections in ARRAS. A + C Sections:- 9-9·45 am Physical Training. 10-11 am Mechanism 11-1 pm. Use of elevating + traversing dials, and advanced gun drill. 2-3 pm. N.C.O's Lecture on Map reading. O.R. Gun cleaning.	
	29/3/17		B + D Sections in ARRAS. A + C Sections: 9-9·45 am Physical Training. 10-11 am Stoppages. 11-1 pm. Map reading on ground. 2-3 pm. Semaphore. Two teams from A Section relieved two teams of C Section at Wanquetin. No 7799 Pte Rutter A. appointed unpaid L/Cpl. No 13156 L/Cpl Deadman to be paid L/Cpl vice L/Cpl Sealey evacuated 2/3/17.	
	30/3/17		B + D Sections in ARRAS. A + C Sections:- 9-9·45 am Physical Training. 10-11 am Lecture Indirect Fire. 11-1 pm Use of ground + cover in advancing with guns in the open. 2-3 pm Gun Cleaning.	
	31/3/17		B + D Sections in ARRAS. A + C Section parade at 9·30 am for baths at WANQUETIN. 2-3 pm Firing, with use of night firing box + luminous sights.	

[signature] Lt + Adjt.
No 8 Coy. M. G. Corps.

A5834 Wt. W4973/M687 750,000 8/16 D. D. & L. Ltd. Forms/C.2118/13.

Instructions regarding War Diaries and Intelligence Summaries are contained in F. S. Regs., Part II. and the Staff Manual respectively. Title pages will be prepared in manuscript.

WAR DIARY
or
~~INTELLIGENCE SUMMARY~~.
(Erase heading not required.)

Army Form C. 2118.

No. 8 MACHINE GUN COMPANY.
No.
Date

Vol 16

Place	Date	Hour	Summary of Events and Information	Remarks and references to Appendices
In The Field	1-4-17		Coy paraded at 9-0 am to pack limbers and to move billets in HAUTEVILLE	
	2-4-17		Training resumed 9-0 x 9-45 am Physical Training 10-0 x 1-0 PM Washing limbers 2-0 x 3-0 PM cleaning guns and kit	
	3-4-17		9-0 x 9-45 am Physical Training 10-0 x 11-0 am Mechanism 11-0 x 1-0 PM advancing over open and use of cover 2-0 x 3-0 PM gun cleaning N.C.Os map reading	
	4-4-17		Coy paraded limbers packed, men in fighting order ready to move to ARRAS 10-15 am	
	5-4-17		Whole Coy in cellars in ARRAS filling belts and preparing for action D Section continued building overhead firing emplacements	
	6-4-17		Whole Coy moved into RONVILLE. CAVES	
	7-4-17		Coy in CAVES, party of 24 men finishing D Sections emplacements	
	8-4-17		Coy in CAVES, party of 24 men finishing D. Sections emplacements	
	9-4-17		1-40 am Coy moved into assembly positions and all guns into	
	"		emplacements ready to give barrage fire on first	
	"		and second objectives	

A5834 Wt. W4973/M687 750,000 8/16 D. D. & L. Ltd. Forms/C.2118/13.

Instructions regarding War Diaries and Intelligence Summaries are contained in F. S. Regs., Part II. and the Staff Manual respectively. Title pages will be prepared in manuscript.

WAR DIARY
or
~~INTELLIGENCE SUMMARY~~.
(Erase heading not required.)

No. 8 MACHINE GUN COMPANY.
No.
Date

Army Form C. 2118.

Place	Date	Hour	Summary of Events and Information	Remarks and references to Appendices
In the Field	9-4-17		The barrage was formed by 14 guns as follows:-	
			4 guns A. Section	
	"		2 guns B. Section	
			4 guns C. Section	
	"		4 guns D. Section	
			2 guns B. Section in Brigade reserve with Headquarters.	
	"		At ~~5.30~~ Zero 5.30 am the 14 guns opened fire and continued firing on	
	"		first then second objectives till Zero + 2 hours 16 minutes, The	
			Coy then cleaned guns and got ready to move forward,	
	"		2 guns of B. Section then reported to C.O. 2nd Royal Scots and	
	"		2 guns of B. Section to C.O. 7th K.S.L.I. under 2/Lieut F.J. Barley	
			and went forward with them, These guns then reported to	
	"		C.O.s concerned at Zero + 4 hours 40 minutes, and then came	
	"		under orders of C.O.s	
	"		A. Sections 4 guns and D. Sections 4 guns then followed in	
	"		rear of the 8th Inf Brigade, C. Section and H.Q. were in	
	"		Brigade reserve, The first and second objectives were taken	
			and A. C. and D. Sections went forward and took up positions	
	"		for barrage fire behind third objective, The Infantry however	
	"			

A5834 Wt. W4973/M687 750,000 8/16 D. D. & L. Ltd. Forms/C.2118/13.

Instructions regarding War Diaries and Intelligence Summaries are contained in F. S. Regs., Part II. and the Staff Manual respectively. Title pages will be prepared in manuscript.

WAR DIARY
or
~~INTELLIGENCE SUMMARY~~.
(Erase heading not required.)

Army Form C. 2118.

Place	Date	Hour	Summary of Events and Information	Remarks and references to Appendices
In the Field	9-4-17		failed to gain the third objective and our guns remained in their positions during the night 9/10th during the 9th our Casualties were	
			A. Section	
			46134 Cpl Griffiths. D.T. Killed — B. Section	
			36530 Pte Hudson C do — 81279 Pte Hoyle. W Wounded	
			15158 " Hill. J. do	
			81366 " Wilson C. do	
			81867 " Tilley W do	
			37376 " Brakes J Wounded	
	10-4-17		On the 10th our guns of A.C. and D. Sections remained in their overhead firing positions and gave barrage fire when called upon to assist the repeated attacks of our Infantry on the third objective the BROWN. LINE, This objective was finally gained in the afternoon of the 10th	
	11-4-17		On this day Coy H.Q. moved up with Bde H.Q. from position in old German front line to position behind WANCOURT	
			A. and D. Sections took up overhead firing positions behind third objective C. Section remaining in reserve at Coy H.Q.	
	12-4-17		A. and D. Sections gave barrage fire to assist the Infantry in	

A5834 Wt. W4973/M687 750,000 8/16 D. D. & L. Ltd. Forms/C.2118/13.

Instructions regarding War Diaries and Intelligence Summaries are contained in F. S. Regs., Part II. and the Staff Manual respectively. Title pages will be prepared in manuscript.

WAR DIARY
or
INTELLIGENCE SUMMARY.
(Erase heading not required.)

No. 8 MACHINE GUN COMPANY.
No.
Date

Army Form C. 2118.

Place	Date	Hour	Summary of Events and Information	Remarks and references to Appendices
In the Field	12-4-17		their advance on line MONCHY. GUEMAPPE. WANCOURT.	
			C. Section relieved B. Sections	
	13-4-17		Gained a footing in MONCHY but no change on the rest of the front So our guns remained in their positions B. Section at Coy H.Q.	
	14-4-17		at 6 am our guns were relieved by those of the 29th Division and the whole Coy came back to billets in ARRAS	
	15-4-17		Coy paraded at 7 am for Baths and clean clothing, 11-0 am Kit inspection by C.O. 12-0 x 1-0 PM Cleaning guns and Kit	
			Sgt Kelly T. appointed acting C.S.M. vice C.S.M. Reade C. to Field ambulance, Sick	
	16-4-17		Gun cleaning all day, The following O.Rs evacuated.	
			71876 Pte Timms R, 8986 Pte Lawton W.	
	17-4-17		10-0 am Belt filling and overhauling belts and guns,	
			11-30 am inspection of guns and gun Kit by C.O.	
	18-4-17		9-0 x 9-45 am Physical Training, 10-0 x 11-0 am Inspection of Box respirators, Smoke Helmets and gas practice, 11-0 x 12-30 PM Drill under Sectional officers	
	19-4-17		9-30 am Inspection by C.O. Route march after inspection.	
	20-4-17		9-30 x 10-15 am Physical Training 10-30 x 11-30 am Squad drill 11-30 x 12-30 PM Coy drill under C.S.M.	

Instructions regarding War Diaries and Intelligence Summaries are contained in F. S. Regs., Part II. and the Staff Manual respectively. Title pages will be prepared in manuscript.

WAR DIARY
or
INTELLIGENCE SUMMARY.
(Erase heading not required.)

No. 8 MACHINE GUN COMPANY.
No. ......
Date ......

Army Form C. 2118.

Place	Date	Hour	Summary of Events and Information	Remarks and references to Appendices
In the Field	21-4-17		9.30 x 10-15 am Physical Training 10-30 x 12.30 am Squad and arms drill	
	22-4-17		10.0 am Guns and gun kit overhauled, Each section fired one gun fitted with new barrel & muzzle cup, Gun limbers packed during day ready for action.	
	23-4-17		9.0 am Coy standing to in fighting order ready to move, at 1. hours notice, 3.0 p.m. Coy moved up to trenches behind TILLOY and remained there for the night	
	24-4-17		9.0 pm. Coy moved to positions in trenches around and in front of MONCHY	
	25-4-17		Coy in trenches, MONCHY. sector, Casualties, Killed 2. wounded 4.	
			36513. L/Cpl. Radford H. (D) Section. wounded	
			17529 " Holley J " "	
			67817 Pte Humphreys T.W.H " " (Since Died of wounds 12.15 P.M. 4-5-17)	
			5144 " Roberts J.A (C) Section "	
			32771 " Love L.R. (D) " Killed	
			43124 " Ives A.R. (D) " "	
	26-4-17		Still in trenches, Casualties, 71872. Pte Cunningham J. wounded, Died of wounds in Dressing Station,	
	27-4-17		In Same positions, Casualties 8276 Pte Read W. missing believed Killed	
	28-4-17		do do 43886 Sgt Young, J. wounded 10356. L/Cpl May G.W. wounded, 84479 Pte. Winsborrows A.H. wounded, 85861 Pte Wall. L. wounded)	

A5834 Wt. W4973/M687 750,000 8/16 D. D. & L. Ltd. Forms/C.2118/13.

Instructions regarding War Diaries and Intelligence Summaries are contained in F. S. Regs., Part II. and the Staff Manual respectively. Title pages will be prepared in manuscript.

WAR DIARY

~~or~~

~~INTELLIGENCE SUMMARY~~.

(*Erase heading not required.*)

No. 8 MACHINE GUN COMPANY.
No. ....
Date. ....

Army Form C. 2118.

Place	Date	Hour	Summary of Events and Information	Remarks and references to Appendices
In the Field	29-4-17		In same positions Casualties 2/Lieut VICCARS. R.B. leg injury 82380 Pte Goodwin. R. wounded,	
	30-4-17		Same positions, Casualties (nil)	
			8-5-17. [signature] Lieut & adjt No 8 Coy M. G Corps	

A5834 Wt. W4973/M687 750,000 8/16 D. D. & L. Ltd. Forms/C.2118/13.

8th Infantry Brigade

Extract from War Diary of 8th M. G. Coy, from 23/4/17 to 15/5/17

23/4/17 Coy ready to move at 1 hours notice. Coy eventually moved up at 3 pm to trenches behind TILLOY, + remained there for the night.

24/4/17 At 9 pm Coy, less 'C' Section moved to positions in trenches around + in front of MONCHY. 'C' Section in BROWN LINE.

25/4/17 Coy in trenches MONCHY Sector. The following casualties occurred on this day:- 'D' Section – Killed No 32771 Pte Love L.R., 43124 Pte Ives A.R. Wounded – 36513 L/Cpl. Radford H, 17529 L/Cpl Holley J., 67817 Pte Humphreys T. 'C' Section. – 51144 Pte Roberts J.A.

26/4/17 Coy in trenches MONCHY Sector. No 71872 Pte Cunningham J was seriously wounded + died later in the day.

27/4/17 Coy in trenches MONCHY Sector. No 8276 Pte Read W. was reported 'Missing'.

28/4/17 Coy in trenches MONCHY Sector. Following casualties occurred. 'C' Section. 43886 Sgt Young J., wounded, 85681 Pte Wall A, wounded, 'A' Section, 10356 A/Cpl May G.W. wounded, 82380 Pte Goodwin R. wounded, 'D' Section, 84479 Pte Winsborrow A.E.H.,

29/4/17 Coy in trenches MONCHY Sector. 2/Lt Viccars sustained sprained knee

30/4/17 Coy in trenches MONCHY Sector

1/5/17 We had 11 guns in front line + SHRAPNEL TRENCH. On the night 1st/2nd May 'C' Section with 4 guns moved up to SHRAPNEL TRENCH

2/5/17 The following casualty occurred:- Wounded 71875 Pte McGoff H, 66784 Pte Dockerty P.

3/5/17 During the attack on this morning our guns stood by ready to fire if the 'S.O.S' signal was given. We had the following casualties Killed: Lieut M.R. Thompson, 2/Lt L.R. Bell, 17474 Pte Martin D, 17531 Pte Cook C. 12274 Pte Runacres F, 81705 Pte Williams J.S, 71882 Pte Davidson F, 14071 Pte McIntyre P, Wounded. – 10201 Pte Topp W, 36799 Pte Parry C, 84270 Pte Reed W.G. 15175 Pte Lappin T.

4/5/17. Coy in the trenches. The following casualties occurred:- Killed 81275 Pte Atack E, 53971 Pte Matterson M, 53970 Pte Thompson. G.R, 9647 Pte Kemble W,

5/5/17. Coy in the trenches. The following casualties occurred:- Killed.- 36460 Pte Harper T, 26335 Pte Humphreys P, 11211 Pte Hay G, 81692 Pte Masser J.

2./

5/5/17 (Contd) Casualties. Wounded:- 73423 Pte Williams J.H., 65226 Pte Tripp J., 27734 Pte Bollans J., 65093 Pte Gilbert F.C., 17512 Pte Payne D, 34442 Pte Pendreigh W, 17457 Sgt Smith J.T., 9710 Pte Jones E.

6/5/17 Coy in the trenches. Slightly wounded, since rejoined, 11562 Pte Garratt W.

7/5/17 On night of 6/7th Coy was relieved by 9th Coy & moved back to Hengist Trench, with the exception of 'C' Section which remained in MONCHY DEFENCES. Following casualties occurred:- 34457 Cpl Droy A.E., wounded, 57309 Pte Buckley T. J., 6514 Pte Pipkin J., 71892 Pte Burrows C.

8/5/17 Coy in Hengist Trench.

9/5/17 Coy in Hengist Trench. 'B' Section relieved 'C' Sect in MONCHY DEFENCES. Following wounded:- 71878 Pte Meikle W, 82319 Pte Hodgkinson F, 81699 Pte Greaves R. Night of 9/10th Coy took over front line & SHRAPNEL TRENCH positions 1, 2, 3, 4, 5, 6, 7, & 8 from 76th Coy. 'B' + 'A' Sections taking over.

10/5/17. 'B' + 'A' Sections in the line.

11/5/17 'B' + 'A' " " " ". Night of 11/12th 'C' + 'D' Sections relieved 'B' + 'A' Sections.

12/5/17 'C' + 'D' Sections in the line.

13/5/17 'C' + 'D' " " " ". Night of 13/14th 3 guns were relieved by 87th Coy. 17508 Cpl Makeham R + 57723 Pte Mannion C were wounded.

14/5/17 Night of 14/15th remaining guns withdrawn.

15/5/17. Coy moved to DAINVILLE.

[signature] Lieut + Adjt.
No 8 Coy, M. G. Corps.

17/5/17

Instructions regarding War Diaries and Intelligence Summaries are contained in F. S. Regs., Part II. and the Staff Manual respectively. Title pages will be prepared in manuscript.

WAR DIARY
or
~~INTELLIGENCE~~ SUMMARY.
(Erase heading not required.)

Army Form C. 2118. 8/3

Vol 17

Place	Date	Hour	Summary of Events and Information	Remarks and references to Appendices
Field.			On May 1st we had 11 guns in Front Line + Shrapnel Trench	
			On the night 1/2nd May, 'C' Section, with 4 guns moved up to Shrapnel Trench.	
			During the attack on morning of 3rd May, our guns stood-by, ready to fire if the S.O.S signal was given	
	4/5/17		Coy in the trenches	
	5/5/17		ditto	
	6/5/17		ditto	
			Night of 6/7th May Coy was relieved by 9th Coy + moved back to Hengist Trench with the exception of 'C' Section which remained in Monchy Defences	
	8/5/17		Coy in Hengist Trench	
	9/5/17		ditto . 'B' Section relieved 'C' Section in Monchy Defences	
			Night of 9/10th Coy took over Front Line + Shrapnel Trench positions 1, 2, 3, 4, 5, 6, 7, + 8 from 76th Coy. 'B' + 'A' Section taking over	
	10/5/17 11/5/17		'B' + 'A' Sections in the line	
			Night 11/12th 'C' + 'D' Sections relieved 'B' + 'A' Sections.	
	12/5/17 13/5/17		'C' + 'D' Sections in the line.	
			Night of 13th/14th 3 guns were relieved by 87th Coy.	
			Night of 14th/15th remaining guns withdrawn.	
	15/5/17		Coy moved to Dainville.	

A5834 Wt. W4973/M687 750,000 8/16 D. D. & L. Ltd. Forms/C.2118/13.

2.

Instructions regarding War Diaries and Intelligence Summaries are contained in F. S. Regs., Part II. and the Staff Manual respectively. Title pages will be prepared in manuscript.

WAR DIARY or INTELLIGENCE SUMMARY.

(Erase heading not required.)

No. 8 MACHINE GUN COMPANY.
No. ....
Date. ....

Army Form C. 2118.

Place	Date	Hour	Summary of Events and Information	Remarks and references to Appendices
Field	16/5/17		Coy paraded for baths. Inspection of billets by C.O. 4 new Officers joined the Coy. 2nd/Lt McKichnie, 2/Lt Essex, 2/Lt Cashmore.	
	17/5/17		Coy paraded in Drill Order + were marched to Remerville to hear address from G.O.C. 3rd Division. Instructions came thro later that it was postponed. 2·30 pm. Guns cleaning under Section Officers.	
	18/5/17		Coy moved to billets in GOUY-EN-ARTOIS 4 new men posted to Sections as follows:.	

A				B				C				D			
54189	Pte	Pearl	J	82389	Pte	Ward	A	86918	Pte	Sloane	A	8986	Pte	Lawton	W
64193	"	Geddes	J	84284	"	Tickener	R	30695	"	Doveridge	C	71876	"	Nimmo	J
83235	"	Edwards	A.W	59781	"	Railey	R	60048	"	Hill	R	63984	"	McGrath	T
43554	"	Carrick	W	84894	"	Cooper	A	71291	"	Ramsden	G	88477	"	Camp	A
64646	"	Combe	E. J					42777	"	Langston	G	84658	"	Phillips	D
60067	"	Flint	J					59241	"	Camp	C	57909	"	Clive	C
35182	"	Pickering	F					37597	"	Bird	C	54766	"	Lees	F
								68539	"	Tildesley	C	57027	"	Smart	G.S
								83996	"	Emmett	H	84663	"	Cowley	J
								83932	"	Tee	T	82450	"	Martin	C.J
											J.J.	84892	"	Davis	H.F
												67843		Gillett	T
												84091	"	Clarke	L
												12242		Heaydon	A
												17486		Somerville	J
												44187	L/C	Parfitt	G.W

A5834 Wt. W4973/M687 750,000 8/16 D. D. & L. Ltd. Forms/C.2118/13.

3.

Army Form C. 2118.

Instructions regarding War Diaries and Intelligence Summaries are contained in F. S. Regs., Part II. and the Staff Manual respectively. Title pages will be prepared in manuscript.

WAR DIARY
or
~~INTELLIGENCE~~ SUMMARY.

(Erase heading not required.)

Place	Date	Hour	Summary of Events and Information	Remarks and references to Appendices
Field	18/5/17		Appointments.- 13156 L/C Deadman apptd A/Cpl vice 46134 Cpl Griffiths D. killed, with effect from	10/4/17
			36779 " Pritchard H " " " 17477 " Mitchell R wounded, " "	22/4/17
			71887 " Lattimore W " " " 344457 " Droy A.E. wounded " "	7/5/17
	19/5/17		Coy moved to billets in Le HAMEAU.	
	20/5/17		11-0am Inspection of kits + Box Respirators + P.H. Helmets by Section Officers	
	21/5/17		9-1-pm Overhauling + cleaning belts, gun kit etc.	
	22/5/17		9-9.45 am Physical Training, 10-11am. Mechanism, 11.12 noon Gun Drill. 12-1 pm Fire Orders	
			Appointments	
			17476 Cpl Mitchell W to be A/Sgt vice 17457 Sgt Smith J.F. wounded, with effect from 5/5/17	
			12607 Pte Arnall A, 344497 Pte White F, 73421 Pte McGregor J, 71875 Pte Smart J. to be unpaid L/Cpls	
			Transfer Sgt Forman A transferred to 'B' Section + to be Section Sgt.	
	23/5/17		9-9.45am Physical Training, 10-11am Stoppages, 11.0 x 12 noon Squad Drill. 12.1pm Coy Drill	
	24/5/17		7-30 x 8 am. Physical Training, under Orderly Officer, on Transport Fld. 9 x 10 am. Mechanism	
			10-15 x 11-15am Gun Drill. 11.30 x 12 30 pm Range Taking + Indication of Targets	
			Novices Classes as follows. 7.30 x 8.0 am Squad + Arms Drill. 9.8 12 30 pm. Mechanism, Gun Drill &c	
	25/5/17		7.30 x 8am Physical Training, 9 x 10 am. Stoppages, 10.15 x 11-15 am Squad Drill. 11.30 x 12 30. Coy Drill	
			Novices' Classes as usual. No 57723 Pte Manson C posted to 'C' Section	
	26/5/17		7.30 x 8am. Physical Training. 9 x 10 am Mechanism. 10.15 x 11.15am Gun Drill. 11.30 x 12 30 pm. Fire Orders	
			Novices' Classes as usual	
	27/5/17		R.C. Service in Village Church, IZEL-LEZ-HAMEAU. R.Cs paraded at 10.0 am under Sgt Mitchell	
			C of E. Service in Transport Field, under Orderly Officer at 10.45 am	
	28/5/17		7.30 x 8 am - Physical Training, 9 x 12.30 pm A + B Sections On Range. 9-10 am C + D. Gun Drill	
			10-15 x 11-15am - Fire Orders. 11.30 x 12.30 pm. Indn of Targets + Range Cards	

A5834 Wt. W4973/M687 750,000 8/16 D. D. & L. Ltd. Forms/C.2118/13.

4

Instructions regarding War Diaries and Intelligence Summaries are contained in F. S. Regs., Part II. and the Staff Manual respectively. Title pages will be prepared in manuscript.

WAR DIARY
or
~~INTELLIGENCE SUMMARY.~~

(*Erase heading not required.*)

Army Form C. 2118.

Place	Date	Hour	Summary of Events and Information	Remarks and references to Appendices
Field.	28/5/17		2 Special Squads formed, (composed of 16 OR, including each NCO with 1 RE Sapper attached to each Squad) for construction of Model Splinter-proof M. G. Emplacements. To parade each day 9-0 × 12-30 pm Work under supervision of Lieut R R Neilson. Novices' Classes as usual	
	29/5/17		7.30 × 8.0 am. Physical Training. 9.0 × 12 30 pm. C + D Sections on Range. 9.0 × 10 am A + B Sections Gun Drill. 10.15 × 11.15 am. Fire Orders. 11.30 × 12 30 pm. Indn of Targets + Range Cards Construction Squads as usual. Novices Classes as usual. 2 per Section to parade under Lieut Neilson for Range Finding.	
	30/5/17		7.30 × 8 am Physical Training. 9 × 10 am. Mechanism + Stoppages. 10.15 × 11.15 am Squad Drill 11.30 × 12.30 pm. Coy Drill. Construction + Novices' Classes as usual.	
	31/5/17		7.30 × 8 am. Physical Training under Qualified Instructor. 9 - 12.30 pm Cleaning belts, gun kit etc. Packing Limbers.	

[signature] Lieut + Adjt
No 8 Coy. M. G. Corps

"A" Form.

Army Form C.2121 (in pads of 100).

MESSAGES AND SIGNALS.

No. of Message ....

Prefix .... Code .... m.	Words	Charge	*This message is on a/c of:*	Recd. at .... m.
Office of Origin and Service Instructions.	Sent		.... *Service.*	Date ....
	At .... m.			From ....
	To			
	By		(Signature of "Franking Officer.")	By ....

TO { 8th Inf. Bde

Sender's Number.	Day of Month.	In reply to Number.	AAA
* M.G. 303	1		

In accordance with instructions, I
sent an experienced Officer and Sergeant
today to reconnoitre B. de VERT from
our front line AAA
They arrived in HILL Trench just
before our practice barrage started
at 4.0 A.M. AAA The enemy's
retaliation mostly fell just behind
our front line AAA Enemy
snipers were very active all
day and seemed to have
the upper hand; the enemy
showed himself freely and my
sergeant ~~shot~~ shot six AAA
With regard to bringing direct
M.G. fire to bear on
B. de VERT, my Officer Lieut. BULL

From

Place

Time

P.T.O.

The above may be forwarded as now corrected.

(Z)

.... Censor.

Signature of Addressor or person authorised to telegraph in his name.

* This line should be erased if not required.

750,000. W 2186—M509. H. W. & V., Ld. 6/16.

reports that it would be possible to do this from INFANTRY HILL, about O.2.d. Central; but as it would take several minutes to get forward to this point & get into action, ~~the~~ our infantry would then be approaching B. de VERT, and opportunity for firing would be limited. AAA Lieut Bull considers that the best position for the purpose would be DALE Trench; from this trench one can see the whole of the West side of the B. de VERT, which appears to stand on a spur; guns could be got into position here before Zero, open fire immediately, and cover the infantry advance for a considerable distance. The fire would be direct and observed and range 900^x–1050^x. AAA With regard to firing from positions near the Copse at O.8. Central, Lieut Bull reports that the ground here did not seem favourable, as there is a gradual slope up to the B. de VERT. AAA

I would therefore suggest that 4 guns are placed in DALE Trench, to open fire on the B. de VERT at Zero; and then to advance & cover the left flank of the Bde and consolidate positions won; while 2 guns assemble in SADDLE Trench about O.8.a. 4.0, and advance on right flank of Bde. and consolidate.

S.L. Cumberland
Capt
Cmdg: 8th M.G. Coy.

1/5/17

To 8th Inf. Bde

Herewith Report on Operations by 8th M.G. Coy. on 3rd May 1917.

On night 2/3 May, guns assembled in following positions :–

(1.) 3 Guns A Sectn in assembly positions in SADDLE Trench about O.8.a.7.2

(2.) 2 Guns D Sectn + 1 Gun A Sectn in assembly positions in DALE Trench about O.2.c.7.3.

(3.) 4 Guns B Sectn in Barrage positions in trench about O.7.b.3.9.

(4) 4 Guns C Sectn in Barrage positions in PICK Trench about O.7.b.3.3.

At Zero hour (3.45 AM.) on 3rd May, the following action was taken :–

(1.) These guns had orders to advance with the 4th line of Infantry + give direct covering fire on BOIS du VERT. In the event, the guns went forward with no troops immediately in front, as the 2nd Royal Scots diverged to the left, and the Middlesex (56th Div.) to the right. On nearing the Copse at O.8 Central, they were held up by heavy M.G. fire. It was not feasible to give covering fire, as it was dark. Lieut BULL was wounded (he died in the afternoon in ARRAS) and 2 O.R. killed. One gun was temporarily abandoned near the Copse, + the other two dug in, between the Copse + our old front line, about O.8.a.7.1.

A report was received, timed 7.0 AM, from Lieut. Spoffath, who was in command of these guns, giving his position + saying that TOOL Trench was held by the enemy. He was ordered to hold on where he was. At nightfall the 3rd gun was recovered, and mounted

HOSTILE ARTILLERY LIST - 30/4/17.
RIVER SCARPE to CAMBRAI ROAD.

No.	Position	Prob. Cal.	No.	Position	Prob. Cal.
KNOWN EMPLACEMENTS ACTIVE.					
I.B.14	I.18.a.82.03-c.81.88		O.B.7	O.10.d.39.90-44.75	
I.B.1	I.16.d.85.17-94.10		O.B.16	O.17.a.26.63-27.46	
I.B.17	I.17.d.30.15-45.10	105H	O.B.17	O.17.a.27.37-25.21	
I.D.10	I.29.b.72.69-75.51		O.B.21	O.11.d.41.17-47.00	
I.D.8	I.24.c.11.88-19.79	77	O.B.25	O.12.d.33.63-37.48	
I.D.4	I.23.d.79.86-77.50	150	O.B.26	O.12.c.50.23-53.10	
I.D.2	I.23.d.12.49-04.34		O.B.27	O.18.a.20.08-22.03	
I.D.9	I.29.a.98.78-93.65		O.B.28	O.18.a.70.07-c.72.99	
I.D.11	I.29.d.45.80-48.68		O.B.18	O.17.d.39.06-51.16	
I.D.12	I.29.d.36.58-27.40		O.B.19	O.17.d.68.30-77.45	
I.D.13	I.29.d.18.31-18.15	150	O.B.31	O.18.b.20.41-17.26	
I.D.14	I.29.d.93.28	150	O.B.33	O.6.c.05.87 -07.83	
	30.c.07.50		O.B.34	O.6.c.00.69 -03.64	
I.D.16	I.30.d.52.89-62.54		O.B.35	O.6.c.12.45 -14.40	150
I.D.17	I.30.d.41.34-44.13		O.B.36	O.6.c.35.40-55.10	
I.D.18	I.36.b.29.81-23.71	105or	O.B.37	O.6.c.96.34 -d.01.26	
		150	O.B.38	O.6.c.83.06 -	
* I.D.19	I.36.b.55.53-64.36			12.a.83.88	
I.D.22	I.24.b.10.21-15.09		O.B.39	O.6.c.29.11	
I.D.23	I.24.d.22.97-29.87			12.a.40.90	
I.D.25	I.29.b.28.16-d.28.97			O.18.c.70.86-68.55	
I.D.26	I.35.b.39.57-39.38	105		O.18.c.15,65	
I.D.27	I.36.b.62.01-d.68.90			O.18.c.20.30	
	I.36.a.90.65	A-A	O.B.42	O.10.b.87.81-87.67	
	I.24.a.40.73-52.48		O.B.41	O.10.b.78.96-77.83	
J.C.1	J.31.a.69.27-91.00		O.D.31	O.23.a.28.99-28.83	
	J.25.c.85.85-70.90		O.D.13	O.23.a.17.31-16.17	
	J.25.d.05.88		O.D.26	O.23.b.42.70-40.66	
P.A.1	P.1b.20.83 -24.78	A-APits	O.D.32	O.24.b.03.85-08.73	
P.C.5	P.19.c.49.58-56.49		O.D.33	O.23.a.58.68-57.50	
				O.24.d.83.51-91.58	
KNOWN EMPLACEMENTS - ACTIVITY DOUBTFUL.					
I.C.3	I.33.b.52.55-51.48			I.24.c.28.30-41.41	
I.D.3	I.23.d.05.15-03.01		O.B.22	O.4.b.98.53 -	
I.D.6	I.23.d.40.01-			5.a.02.68	
	29.b.48.93		O.B.29	O.11.b.14.11-d.14.99	
I.D.5	I.23.d.63.31-63.21			O.17.b.60.30-50.40	
I.D.7	I.29.b.50.90-55.80		O.D.25	O.23.a.80.71-83.68	
I.D.15	I.29.d.90.19-97.05		J.C.2	J.31.c.85.91-d.10.68	
I.D.24	I.29.b.42.54-37.39				
BATTERIES CONSIDIRED ACTIVE BUT NOT YET CONFIRMED BY PHOTOS.					
	O.24.a.65.08			J.25.b.00.35	
	J.7.a.5.3. (Hvy.Gun)		P.C.9	P.26.c.90.27 (Hvy.Gun)	
NEW ZONE NUMBERS AND CO-ORDINATES.					
J.C.3	J.32.a.94.30-98.20		P.A.7	P.14.d.17.82-20.70	
J.C.4	J.32.c.60.32-53.21		P.A.8	P.14.d.17.52-17.40	
P.A.3	P.14.b.29.17-31,11		P.C.11	P.19.d.23.62-23.42	
P.A.4	P.14.b.35.01-d.40.89		P.C.12	P.20.a.43.41-37.30	
P.A.5	P.14.c.94.20-98.07		P.C.13	P.20.a.60.74-55.58	
P.A.6	P.14.d.02.94-10.87		P.C.14	P.20.a.99.74-96.60	
	Co-ordinates amended. P.C.4 -			P.19.a.30.30-20.09.	

* Batteries active during the past 24 hours.
Batteries not on yesterday's list underlined.

(2) These guns had orders to open covering fire on B. de VERT, & then advance to cover the left flank of the Bde. Covering fire was not feasible, owing to the darkness; the guns advanced with the Infantry, & came under heavy M.G. fire. Lieut Thompson, who was in Command of the guns, and 2.O.R. were killed and 3 O.R. wounded. The guns & teams lay in shell-holes during the day, and at nightfall reported to 2/Lt. Barley, who posted them for defensive purposes in SHRAPNEL Trench, about O.2.c.3.5.

(3.) These guns carried out Barrage fire, according to programme, firing on GREEN WORK from Zero to Zero + 10 min, & then lifting 100x every 2 min. until Zero + 26 min (Cease fire). The Section then advanced and took up positions in SHRAPNEL Trench, about O.2.c.2.1, and guns were laid on "Protective Barrage" lines (target O.4.c.8½.1) Later on, 4000 Rounds were fired on this target, as the Section Commander (2/Lt. Barley) heard that a fresh attack was to be made at 9.0 AM.
One gun had been destroyed by shell fire during the 1st barrage, and 2 O.R. killed and 1 O.R. wounded.
A new gun was sent up to the Section at nightfall, but was not mounted, owing to shortage of personnel.

(4.) These guns carried out Barrage fire according to programme, firing on the BOIS de VERT from Zero to Zero + 10 min, and then lifting 100x every 2 min, until Zero + 26 min. (Cease fire).
The Section then advanced and took up positions in SHRAPNEL Trench about O.8.a.1.5, and guns were laid on "Protective Barrage" lines (target O.10.a.8.2).
The Section Commander 2/Lt Allan, was slightly wounded in the face, but remained at duty; there were no other casualties & no guns were lost.

In the Field
5/5/17.

S. L. Com[...]
Comdg: No 8 C[...]

HOSTILE ARTILLERY LIST - 2/5/17.
RIVER SCARPE TO CAMBRAI ROAD.

No.	Position.	Prob. Cal.	No.	Position.	Prob. Cal.
	KNOWN EMPLACEMENTS ACTIVE.				
I.B.14	I.18.a.82.03-c.81.88		* P.C.4	P.19.a.30.30-20.69	
* I.B.1	I.16.d.85.17-94.10		* P.C.5	P.19.c.49.58-56.49	H.V.gun
I.B.17	I.17.d.30.15-45.10	105H	P.C.2	P.19.a.71.89-77.74	
* I.D.5	I.23.d.63.31-63.21	77	* P.C.11	P.19.d.23.62-23.42	
I.D.10	I.29.b.72.69-75.51		P.C.12	P.20.a.43.41-37.30	
I.D.8	I.24.c.11.88-19.79	77	P.C.13	P.20.a.60.74-55.58	
I.D.4	I.23.d.79.86-77.50	150	P.C.14	P.20.a.99.74-96.60	
I.D.2	I.23.d.12.49-04.34		* O.B.25	O.12.d.33.63-37.48	
* I.D.13	I.29.d.18.31-18.15	150	O.B.26	O.12.c.50.23-53.10	
* I.D.14	I.29.d.92.28-	150	O.B.27	O.18.a.20.08-22.03	
	30.c.07.50		O.B.28	O.18.a.70.07-c.72.99	
* I.D.15	I.29.d.90.19-97.05		O.B.19	O.17.d.68.30-77.45	105
I.D.16	I.30.d.52.89-62.54		O.B.31	O.18.b.20.41-17.26	
I.D.17	I.30.d.41.34-44.13		O.B.33	O.6.c.05.87 -07.83	
I.D.18	I.36.b.29.81-23.71	105-150	O.B.34	O.6.c.00.69 -03.64	
I.D.29	I.30.c.17.68-11.57		O.B.35	O.6.c.12.45 -14.40	150
I.D.12	I.29.d.36.58-27.40		O.B.36	O.6.c.35.40 -55.10	
I.D.25	I.29.b.28.18-d.28.97		O.B.37	O.6.c.96.34 -d.01.26	
I.D.19	I.36.b.55.53-64.36		O.B.38	O.6.c.83.06 -	
I.D.22	I.24.b.10.21-15.09			12.a.83.88	
I.D.23	I.24.d.22.97-39.87		O.B.39	O.6.c.29.11 -	
I.D.26	I.35.b.39.57-39.38	105		12.a.40.90	
* I.D.27	I.36.b.62.01-d.68.90	77	O.B.41	O.10.b.78.96-77.83	
I.D.28	I.18.c.10.03-		O.B.42	O.10.b.87.81-87.67	
	24.a.22.90		O.B.43	O.12.b.46.58-46.43	
	I.36.a.90.65	A-A	O.B.44	O.18.b.47.97-57.86	
*	I.36.d.10.70	A-A		O.18.c.70.56-68.55	
	I.24.a.40.73-52.48			O.18.c.15.65-	
J.C.1	J.31.a.69.27-91.00	210		O.18.c.20.30	
J.C.2	J.31.c.85.91-d.10.68	150	* O.D.13	O.23.a.17.31-16.17	77
*	J.25.c.85.85-70.90		* O.D.29	O.23.b.84.71-91.63	
	J.25.d.05.88-		O.D.31	O.23.a.28.99-28.83	
P.A.1	P.1.b.20.83 -24.78	A-APits	O.D.26	O.23.b.42.70-40.66	
P.A.2	P.13.c.79.10-78.27		* O.D.32	O.24.b.03.85-08.73	
P.A.7	P.14.d.17.82-20.70		* O.D.33	O.23.a.58.68-57.50	
P.A.8	P.14.d.17.52-17.40			O.24.d.83.51-91.58	
P.A.10	P.13.d.64.55-59.35				
P.C.5	P.19.c.49.58-56.49				
* P.C.3	P.19.a.59.53-54.40				
* P.C.6	P.25.a.51.72-66.94				
	KNOWN EMPLACEMENTS - ACTIVITY DOUBTFUL.				
I.D.3	I.23.d.05.15-03.01		O.B.16	O.17.a.26.63-27.46	
I.D.6	I.23.d.40.01-		O.B.17	O.17.a.27.37-25.21	
	29.b.48.93		O.B.21	O.11.d.41.17-47.00	
I.D.7	I.29.b.50.90-55.80		O.B.18	O.17.d.39.06-51.16	
I.D.11	I.29.d.45.80-48.66			O.17.b.60.30-50.40	
I.D.9	I.29.a.98.78-93.65		O.D.25	O.23.a.80.71-83.68	
X.	I.24.c.28.30-41.41				
	BATTERIES CONSIDERED ACTIVE BUT NOT YET CONFIRMED BY PHOTOS.				
	O.18.c.50.40			J.25.b.00.35	
	O.24.a.65.08		P.C.9	P.26.c.90.27 (Hvy.Gun)	
	J.7.a.5.3. (Hvy.Gun)				
	POSITION PROBABLY ABANDONED - O.B.7				

NEW ZONE NUMBERS AND CO-ORDINATES.

I.D.29	I.30.c.17.68-11.57	P.C.15	P.19.c.57.11-62.16
I.D.30	I.24.c.43.40-30.29	P.C.16	P.25.a.36.66-27.50
P.A.9	P.14.c.55.25-56.12	P.C.17	P.14.c.81.07-
P.A.10	P.13.d.64.55-59.35		20.a.65.90

* Batteries active during last 24 hours.
[illegible]tteries not on yesterday's list underlined.

Instructions regarding War Diaries and Intelligence Summaries are contained in F. S. Regs., Part II. and the Staff Manual respectively. Title pages will be prepared in manuscript.

WAR DIARY
or
INTELLIGENCE SUMMARY.
(Erase heading not required.)

No. 3 MACHINE GUN COMPANY. No. .... Date. 78

Army Form C. 2118.

Vol 18

Place	Date	Hour	Summary of Events and Information	Remarks and references to Appendices
In the Field	1/6/17		Coy moved from LE HAMEAU + took over from 29th Division in trenches at MONCHY-LE-PREUX. All guns in the line.	
	2/6/17 to 12/6/17		All guns in trenches at MONCHY.	
	13/6/17		'A', 'B' + 'C' Sections were relieved + moved into billets in ARRAS. 'D' Section remained in trenches.	
	14/6/17		Coy, (less 'D' Section) paraded for Baths.	
			Posting. - Cpl Parker to 'A' Section.	
	15/6/17		Parades. - 10-12·30 pm. Cleaning guns, ammunition etc.	
	16/6/17		Parades. - 9 x 9·45 am. Physical Training, 10 x 11 am. - Squad Drill. 11·15 x 12·30 pm Coy Drill	
	17/6/17		Coy, (less 'D' Section) marched to billets in HABARCQ. 'D' Section were relieved in the line + moved to ARRAS where they embussed + rejoined Coy at HABARCQ.	
	18/6/17		Coy moved from HABARCQ to billets at LIENCOURT.	
	19/6/17		Parades. - Cleaning guns, ammunition etc.	
	20/6/17		Parades 9 x 10 am. Gun Drill. 10·15 x 11·15 am. Stripping + cleaning guns. 11·30 x 12·30 pm Coy Drill. The u/m O.Ranks, transferred from 193rd M.G. Coy, posted to 'A' Section 27783 Pte Guy A.W., 87745 Pte Osborne A, 87740 Pte Odell G.W., 14095 Pte Turner A.	
	21/6/17		Parades. - 7·30 x 8 am. Physical Training, 9·0 x 10·0 am Stoppages, 10·15 x 11·15 am Fire Orders, 11·30 x 12·30 pm Distance judging + range taking.	
	22/6/17		Parades. 7·30 x 8·0 am. Physical Training, 9·0 x 10·0 am Mechanism, 10·15 x 11·15 am Squad Drill 11·30 x 12·30 pm Coy Drill.	

A5834 Wt. W4973/M687 750,000 8/16 D. D. & L. Ltd. Forms/C.2118/13.

Instructions regarding War Diaries and Intelligence Summaries are contained in F. S. Regs., Part II. and the Staff Manual respectively. Title pages will be prepared in manuscript.

WAR DIARY
or
INTELLIGENCE SUMMARY.
(*Erase heading not required.*)

No. 8 MACHINE GUN COMPANY.
No. ....
Date. ....

Army Form C. 2118.

Place	Date	Hour	Summary of Events and Information	Remarks and references to Appendices
In the Field	23/6/17		Parades.- 7.0 × 7.45 am Physical Training. 9.0 × 10.0 am Stoppages. 10.15 × 11.15 am Stripping & care of guns. 11.30 × 12.30 pm. Coy Drill.	
			31977 Sgt Barker transferred from 'C' Section to 'A' Section.	
	24/6/17		Parades.- 10.0 am. R.C's service in Village Church, LIENCOURT. 11.0 am. C. of E service in Fld Amb. hut, LIENCOURT	
			The ufm reinforcements posted to Sections as follows:-	
			'A' Section. 87410 Pte Furnival W. 87338 " Underwood C.F. 60249 " Waddington W.	
			'B' Section. 84392 Pte Robb J.	
			'C' Section. 87536 Pte Prismall D. 87028 " Taylor F.	
	25/6/17.		Parades.- 7.0 × 7.45 am. Physical Training. 9.0 × 10.0 am. Mechanism. 10.15 × 11.15 am. Gun Drill 11.30 × 12.30 pm. Fire Orders. (Including Inwards & Outwards traversing, Vertical Searching & combined sights)	
	26/6/17		Parades. 7.0 × 7.45 am Physical Training. 9.0 × 10.0 am Judging distance. Range Cards, Range taking. 10.15 × 11.15 am Squad Drill. N.C.O's Communication drill under C.S.M 11.30 × 12.30 pm. Coy Drill.	
	27/6/17		Parades.- 7.0 × 7.45 am. Physical Training. 9.0 × 10.0 am Stoppages. 10.15 × 11.15 am Stripping & care of guns. 11.30 × 12.30 pm Packing limbers & fitting Pack Saddlery.	
	28/6/17		Coy moved from LIENCOURT to billets at BOUT DES PRES (less Transport)	
	29/6/17		Coy entrained at DOULLENS and detraining at ACHIET LE GRAND, marched to camp at COMTECOURT. Transport moved to COMTECOURT by road.	

A5834 Wt. W4973/M687 750,000 8/16 D. D. & L. Ltd. Forms/C.2118/13.

Army Form C. 2118.

Instructions regarding War Diaries and Intelligence Summaries are contained in F. S. Regs., Part II. and the Staff Manual respectively. Title pages will be prepared in manuscript.

WAR DIARY
or
INTELLIGENCE SUMMARY.

(Erase heading not required.)

Place	Date	Hour	Summary of Events and Information	Remarks and references to Appendices
In-the-Field	30/6/17		Coy moved into trenches in the LOUVERVAL Sector taking over from the 144th M. G. Coy. B + D Sections + 2 guns of C Section in the Outpost + intermediate lines. 2 guns of 'C' Section in 3rd line. 'A' Section in Reserve line	
			No. 8 MACHINE GUN COMPANY. No. .... Date 3/7/17	
			E R Spofforth Lieut + Adjt. No 8 M. G. Coy.	

A5834 Wt. W4973/M687 750,000 8/16 D. D. & L. Ltd. Forms/C.2118/13.

Instructions regarding War Diaries and Intelligence Summaries are contained in F. S. Regs., Part II. and the Staff Manual respectively. Title pages will be prepared in manuscript.

11

WAR DIARY

or

~~INTELLIGENCE SUMMARY.~~

(Erase heading not required.)

Army Form C. 2118.

Vol 19

Place	Date	Hour	Summary of Events and Information	Remarks and references to Appendices
In the Field	1-7-17 to Night 9/10/7/17		On 1st July Coy relieved 144th M.G. Coy in the line in MORCHIES Sector east of BAPAUME. 'B'+'D' Sections in the line manning 10 guns. 'C' Section at MORCHIES in Company Reserve with 2 guns and 'A' Section in Brigade Reserve in front of BEUGNY. Coy in line then until relieved by 76th M-G. Coy on night 9/10th July. The whole front was very quiet during this period, we had no casualties. Two new emplacements were completed and occupied by 76th Coy when they took over on Night of 9th/10th. On night of 9th/10th	
	10-7-17		'A'+'C' Sections with 4 guns each moved into DIVISIONAL LINE + remained there. Rest of Company to HAPLINCOURT in training.	
	11-7-17		'A'+'C' Section in DIV. LINE.	
			'B'+'D' " . 10-0 am.- Rifles, Anti-gas appliances, clothing inspection. 10-30 x 12-30 pm.- Cleaning guns, ammunition &c.	
	Night of 16th/17		A+C " in DIV. LINE.	
			B+D " . 9-0 x 10-0 am - Gun cleaning. 10.15 x 11.15 am Squad Drill. 11-30 x 12-30 pm Coy Drill under C.S.M.	
	13-7-17		B+D " . 9-0 x 10-0 am - Physical Training, 10-15 x 11-15 am. 'B' Section on German gun 'D' Section Gun Drill 11-30 x 12-30 pm 'B' Section Gun Drill. 'D' Section German Gun. 10-15 x 12-30 pm. Range finders + Signallers on parade under Adjutant.	
	14-7-17		B+D " . 7-30 x 8-0 am. Physical Training. 9-0 x 10-0 am Judging distance. Range Cards. Range taking. 10-15 x 11-15 am. Squad Drill under C.S.M. 11-30 x 12-30 pm - Company Drill.	
	15-7-17		B+D " . 9-30 am. C. of E. Service at Theatre HAPLINCOURT. R.C. " " Kite Balloon H.Q. HAPLINCOURT.	
	16-7-17		B+D " . 7-30 x 8-0 am.- Physical Training. 9-10 am. Mechanism. 10-15 x 11-15 am Gun Drill. 11-30 x 12-30 pm Fire Orders.	
	Night of 16th/17th 7/1917		On the night of 16th/17th B+D Section took over new front from 76th + 9th M.G. Coys with 9 guns in the line. A+C Sections were relieved in DIV. LINE by Sections of 8th, 9th + 76th Companies and on completion of relief went back to HAPLINCOURT for training.	

Instructions regarding War Diaries and Intelligence Summaries are contained in F. S. Regs., Part II. and the Staff Manual respectively. Title pages will be prepared in manuscript.

WAR DIARY

or

~~INTELLIGENCE SUMMARY.~~

(Erase heading not required.)

Army Form C. 2118.

Place	Date	Hour	Summary of Events and Information	Remarks and references to Appendices
In the Field			B + D Sections held line from 16th/17th + were relieved by A + C. Sections on the night of 25th/26th July.	
			A + C. Sections in line from 25th/26th until 31st July.	
			From 17th to 25th A + C Sections were training	
			" 26th to 31st B + D " " "	
			Training consisted of:- Physical Training, Squad + Coy Drill, Mechanism, Stoppages, Stripping + care of gun, Advanced gun drill. Range taking + distance judging, Range - Application, Grouping, Swinging Traverse &c.	

[signature] Lieut + Adjt
No 8 M. G. Coy.

A5092 Wt. W12839/M1293 750,000. 1/17. D. D & L., Ltd. Forms/C2118/14.

Army Form C. 2118.

Instructions regarding War Diaries and Intelligence Summaries are contained in F. S. Regs., Part II. and the Staff Manual respectively. Title pages will be prepared in manuscript.

8th M. G. WAR DIARY ~~or INTELLIGENCE SUMMARY~~. COMPANY.

(Erase heading not required.)

Vol 20

Place	Date	Hour	Summary of Events and Information	Remarks and references to Appendices
In the Field	1/8/17		'A' + 'C' Sections in the Line in LOUVERVAL Section.	
			'B' + 'D' " at Camp, HAPLINCOURT training.	
"	2/8/17		On the night 2/3rd 'A' + 'C' in the Line were relieved by 'B' + 'D' Sections, the former going back to HAPLINCOURT for training &c.	
"	3/8/17 to 9/8/17		'B' + 'D' Sections in the Line.	
			'A' + 'C' " at Camp HAPLINCOURT, training &c.	
"	10/8/17		On the night 10/11th 'B' + 'D' Sections in the Line were relieved by 'A' + 'C' Sections, the former going back to HAPLINCOURT Camp for training &c.	
	11/8/17 to 17/8/17		'A' + 'C' Sections in the Line	
"			'B' + 'D' " at Camp HAPLINCOURT, training etc.	
	18/8/17		On the night 18/19th 'A' + 'C' Sections in the Line were relieved by 'B' + 'D' Sections, the former going back to Camp HAPLINCOURT, for training etc.	
	19/8/17 to 25/8/17		'B' + 'D' Sections in the Line.	
"			'A' + 'C' " at Camp HAPLINCOURT, training etc.	
			On the night 25/26th 'A' Section came into Line + co-operated in raid on number of Shell Holes held by enemy. Four guns 'A' Section were to fire (if called upon) on selected targets on flanks of point raided. However, no rounds were fired and raid was unsuccessful.	
"	26/8/17		On the night 26/27th 'B' + 'D' Sections in the line were relieved by 'A' + 'C' Sections, the former going back to HAPLINCOURT, for training etc.	

A7092 Wt. W12839/M1293. 750,000. 1/17. D. D & L., Ltd. Forms/C2118/14.

Instructions regarding War Diaries and Intelligence Summaries are contained in F. S. Regs., Part II. and the Staff Manual respectively. Title pages will be prepared in manuscript.

WAR DIARY
or
~~INTELLIGENCE SUMMARY.~~
(Erase heading not required.)

Army Form C. 2118.

Place	Date	Hour	Summary of Events and Information	Remarks and references to Appendices
In the Field	27/8/17 to 31/8/17		'A' + 'C' Sections in the line. 'B' + 'D' " at Camp HAPLINCOURT training etc. The work done by Coy when in line consisted mainly of:- Construction of M.G. emplacements, dugouts, shelters for Reserve S.A.A. Connection by wire of Section HQs with Bn H.Q. + with M.G. Coy H.Q. The training done by Coy when in Camp HAPLINCOURT consisted of:- Company Drill. / Squad Drill. / Advanced Gun Drill. Stripping + Care of guns. / Mechanism. Stoppages. / Indirect Fire, Barrages &c. On Range:- Application + Grouping / Vertical Searching + Traversing. The whole Front was very quiet during the month and we had no casualties. [signature] Lieut + Adjt No 8 M.G. Coy. No. 8 MACHINE GUN COMPANY. No. .... Date........	

A7092 Wt. W12839/M1293. 750,000. 1/17. D. D & L., Ltd. Forms/C2118/14.

(1.)

Army Form C. 2118.

Instructions regarding War Diaries and Intelligence Summaries are contained in F. S. Regs., Part II. and the Staff Manual respectively. Title pages will be prepared in manuscript.

WAR DIARY
or
~~INTELLIGENCE SUMMARY.~~
(Erase heading not required.)

No. 8 MACHINE GUN COMPANY.
No. ....
Date. ....

Vol 21

Place	Date	Hour	Summary of Events and Information	Remarks and references to Appendices
In-the-Field.	1-9-17.		'A' + 'C' Sections in the line in LOUVERVAL Section. 'A' Section with 4 guns in Right Sector. 'C' Section with 4 guns in Left Sector. Coy H.Q. in Sunken Road near BEAUMETZ. 'A' Section fired 4000 rounds on selected points. 'B' + 'D' Sections at HAPLINCOURT training. 'C' Section " " " " " ".	
	2-9-17.		'A' Section in line fired 4000 rounds. 'C' Section in line fired 1000 rounds. 'B' + 'D' Sections training.	
	3-9-17.		'A' + 'C' Sections in line. Firing: same as on 2nd. M.G. shelters + emplacements improved during night. 'B' + 'D' Sections training.	
	4-9-17		On the night 4th/5th Company was relieved by 169th M.G. Coy. + moved to camp at YTRES.	
	5-9-17		Erected tents, bivouacs &c.	
	6-9-17 to 8-9-17		Company training.	
	9-9-17		C of E's paraded for Service. R.C's attended Service at ruins YTRES Church.	
	10-9-17 11-9-17 12-9-17		Company training.	
	13-9-17		Company had Box Respirator tested thro' Gas at prepared chamber in ROCQUIGNY. During afternoon Company fired machine guns on Range.	
	14-9-17		Company took part in a practice attack over selected ground.	
	15-9-17		Company training.	
	16-9-17		C. of E's attended a Service of the Brigade held by the Bishop of Khartoum, near YTRES. R.C's attended Service in ruins YTRES Church.	
	17-9-17		Coy marched to BAPAUME where they entrained at 8-0 pm and detrained at PROVEN Station	
	18-9-17		on morning of 18th, and marched to a camp situated in No. 2 WATOU Area.	

A7092 Wt. W1289/M1293. 750,000. 1/17. D. D. & L., Ltd. Forms/C2118/14.

(2)

Instructions regarding War Diaries and Intelligence Summaries are contained in F. S. Regs., Part II. and the Staff Manual respectively. Title pages will be prepared in manuscript.

WAR DIARY

or

~~INTELLIGENCE SUMMARY.~~

(Erase heading not required.)

No. 8
MACHINE GUN
COMPANY.

In.........
Date.........

Army Form C. 2118.

Place	Date	Hour	Summary of Events and Information	Remarks and references to Appendices
In-the-Field	19-9-17		Company training.	
	20-9-17		Company moved to another camp at BRANDHOEK.	
	21-9-17 22-9-17		Company training.	
	23-9-17		Company relieved 28th M.G. Coy in the line on the night 23rd/24th. The Company was then located as follows:- A Section { 2 Guns at BORRY FM. D.25.b.6.8. { 2 " " BECK HOUSE. D.19.d.1.3. B " 4 " " BREMEN Redoubt. D.20.c.9.1 C " { 2 " " LOW FM D.25.a.7.6 { 2 " " D.25.d.0.6 D " 4 " in reserve near MILL COTT, about I.5.b. Coy H.Q at MILL COTT at I.5.a.0.7. Transport at H.16 Central.	Ref Map ZONNEBEKE 1/10000
	24-9-17 and 25-9-17		The two days 24th & 25th were employed in reconnaissance, and preparation for the M.G. Barrage. 12 open emplacements for the Barrage were constructed during the nights 24th/25th and 25th/26th; a reserve of S.A.A in boxes was formed at each of these emplacements. On the night 25th/26th the following moves took place:- A & C Sections moved to their Barrage positions; there were 8 emplacements in a rough line between D.19.d.7.9½ and D.19.d.6.4. forming "G Battery". B Section got into position for Barrage in BREMEN Redoubt, occupying 4 emplacements between D.20.c.9.1 and D.20.c.9.0, and forming "H Battery". D Section moved to their assembly trenches near LOW FM.	
	26/9/17		Zero hour for the attack was 5.50 am. 26/9/17. The M.G. Barrage opened at Zero, the signal being the opening of the 18 pdr barrage. The general idea was to put down a Creeping Barrage in front of the advancing Infantry, and then to lay guns in readiness to open an S.O.S. Barrage in front of the final objective.	

A5092 Wt. W1289/M1293 750,000. 1/17. D. D & L., Ltd. Forms/C2118/14.

(3)

Instructions regarding War Diaries and Intelligence Summaries are contained in F. S. Regs., Part II. and the Staff Manual respectively. Title pages will be prepared in manuscript.

WAR DIARY
or
~~INTELLIGENCE SUMMARY.~~
(Erase heading not required.)

No. 8 MACHINE GUN COMPANY.
No. ....
Date ....

Army Form C. 2118.

Place	Date	Hour	Summary of Events and Information	Remarks and references to Appendices
In the Field	26-9-17		For this purpose, the Brigade front was divided into two portions; G Battery (with 8 guns of 8th M.G. Coy) covering 300x on the Left, and E + F Batteries (with 12 guns of 233rd M.G. Coy) covering 500x on the Right. Each gun had therefore to cover 40x of front; rate of fire was 1 belt per 5 minutes. Guns opened fire at 1650x at Zero, and ceased fire at 2600x at Zero plus 2 hrs 15 min; lifts were generally of 200x. G Battery fired this barrage according to programme, with the exception that a gun of A Section was put out of action by shrapnel after firing about 5 belts, and another gun developed a mechanical defect and was unable to keep pace; (these 2 guns were sent back for repair later in the day.) The remaining 6 guns of the Battery were distributed so as to cover the gap made by the stoppage of these 2 guns. On ceasing fire at Zero + 2 hrs 15 min, the guns were laid on their S.O.S. barrage lines, at a range of 2600x. Later in the day when it was learnt that the final objective had not quite been reached, the S.O.S. barrage was brought back to 2400x. In addition to the Creeping Barrage, H Battery, in a forward position in BREMEN Redoubt, was detailed for searching fire in areas beyond the final objective. The 4 guns (B Section, 8th M.G. Coy) composing this Battery, opened fire at 2000x at Zero + 2 hrs, on an area in D.22.a; they searched upwards, and ceased fire at 2400x, at Zero + 2 hrs 30 min. H Battery fired this barrage according to programme. On ceasing fire, the guns were laid on their S.O.S. barrage lines, at 2200x. (This barrage would come down about THAMES WOOD) Word having come through that the final objective had been taken, the 4 guns of D Section were sent up at 7.30 am to consolidate, 2 guns being detailed to HILL 40 + 2 guns to LEVI Cottages. The Section was much delayed by sniping, and the Section Officer + several men became casualties on the way up. On finally arriving at the front line, there were only sufficient men and ammunition left to serve two guns; the guns were therefore sited in pairs in shell holes, on the ridge between the WINDMILL CABt and the Railway Station. At about 6.30 pm, while the teams were engaged in digging emplacements, the enemy delivered a counter-attack. One gun came into action and fired a few bursts, but the line was forced back a short distance;	

A7092 Wt. W128:9/M1293. 750,000. 1/17. D. D & L., Ltd. Forms/C2118/14.

(14)

Instructions regarding War Diaries and Intelligence Summaries are contained in F. S. Regs., Part II. and the Staff Manual respectively. Title pages will be prepared in manuscript.

WAR DIARY
or
~~INTELLIGENCE SUMMARY~~.
(*Erase heading not required.*)

No. 8 MACHINE GUN COMPANY.
to ....
Date ....

Army Form C. 2118.

Place	Date	Hour	Summary of Events and Information	Remarks and references to Appendices
In the Field	26/9/17		and as the teams were much reduced in numbers, the guns could not be got away and were lost. During the counter attack (5.30 pm on 26th) the S.O.S. signal was sent up and G & H Batteries opened fire on their S.O.S. lines. After an hour, they were ordered to cease fire, as in view of the uncertainty of the situation it was thought best to keep a good reserve of filled belts for direct fire. Later in the evening, the position was reported secure on the Brigade front, but uncertain on the left; 2 guns of A Section (G Battery) were therefore taken off their S.O.S. lines and laid for direct fire on the South slopes of Hill 37, their traverse being between DELVA FM and [illegible] HOUSE.	
	27/9/17		At nightfall of the 27th, the enemy made a general counter-attack; our aeroplanes had seen him massing his troops, and ample warning was given to our S.O.S. M.G. Batteries. All S.O.S. guns opened fire immediately on seeing the S.O.S. rockets, and continued for 1¾ hours, by which time the counter-attack had been defeated.	
	do		In addition to the foregoing fire, H Battery in BREMEN Redoubt carried out harassing fire at intervals during the 26th and following days, on THAMES, THAMES WOOD, [illegible] FM, the Railway, and similar targets.	
	Night 30/9/17 1/10/17		The Division was relieved on the morning of Oct 1st, the 8th M.G. Coy was withdrawn at 3-0 am on that morning. The total number of rounds fired during operations was 83,000. The casualties were as follows	

Officers		Other Ranks				
3 Wounded (including 1 remained at duty)		Killed	Wounded	Gassed	Sick	Missing
1 Sick		1	20	13	1	4

Total 4 Officers. 39 O Ranks

[signature]
Lieut & Adjt
No 8 Machine Gun Coy.

A.5004. Wt. W1228/M1293. 750,000. 1/17. D. D. & L. Ltd. Forms/C2118/14.

Instructions regarding War Diaries and Intelligence Summaries are contained in F. S. Regs., Part II. and the Staff Manual respectively. Title pages will be prepared in manuscript.

WAR DIARY
or
~~INTELLIGENCE SUMMARY.~~
(Erase heading not required.)

Army Form C. 2118.

8 M G Coy
Vol 22

Place	Date	Hour	Summary of Events and Information	Remarks and references to Appendices
In the Field	1-10-17		Coy was relieved in the line, East of YPRES, the guns being withdrawn at 3.30 am. Sections marched down to Camp South of YPRES. Enemy aeroplanes active during night dropping bombs on roads and in vicinity of Camp. Weather conditions ideal for flying. Coy embussed in the afternoon and travelled to WATOU by Lorry from which place the Coy marched to camp situated at WINNIZEELE	
	2nd		Day spent in cleaning clothes, equipment, rifles, gas. Weather bright & warm in day.	
	3rd		8.0 am Reveille, 8.30 am Breakfast, 10 X 10.30 am Inspection of Clothing, equipment, rifles, gas appliances & feet. 10-30 X 12.30 pm Cleaning and overhauling arms kit. Following appointments made. No 17505 Cpl Hewell F appointed A/Sgt 71887 L/C Lattimore " A/Cpl 64193 Pte Geddes " unpaid L/Cpl	
	4th		Reveille 7.0 am Breakfast 8.0 am. Coy paraded 9.50 am and marched with 8th Inf Brigade Group to RENESCURE area. Coy halted for dinner at midday, march being resumed 1.30 pm. Coy arrived in Billets at 5.30 pm. The weather was cool [illegible]	

A7092 Wt. W12839/M1293. 750,000. 1/17. D. D & L., Ltd. Forms/C2118/14.

Instructions regarding War Diaries and Intelligence Summaries are contained in F. S. Regs., Part II. and the Staff Manual respectively. Title pages will be prepared in manuscript.

WAR DIARY
or
INTELLIGENCE SUMMARY.
(Erase heading not required.)

Army Form C. 2118.

Place	Date	Hour	Summary of Events and Information	Remarks and references to Appendices
Field	4-10-17		strong winds & drizzle	
	5th		Coy paraded at 6-0 am & marched from RENESCURE to ST. OMER Entrained at ST. OMER 11-0 am & detrained at BAPAUME Station at about 8-0 pm Coy marched to Camp outside HAPLINCOURT.	
	6th		Coy moved to Camp in BEAULENCOURT area. weather cold & wet	
	7th		Reveille 7-0 am Church parades - R.C's paraded for service at 10-30 am in Cinema BEAULENCOURT.	
	8th		Overhauling & cleaning of guns etc. Following appeared in Coy Orders at 10-0 am, 7/10/17 Army clocks were put back to 12-0 midnight. all clocks and watches will be altered accordingly.	
	9th		Coy Training. Following reinforcement joined from Base depot: 2/LT. Dickinson F.W. The u/m men evacuated and struck off strength of Coy. 68531 Pte Gildersley H. (wounded S.I.) 84240 Pte Carter W.	
	10th		Company Training. 17509 Cpl Martin rejoined the Coy from C.C.S. & posted to "C" Section	
	11th		Coy Training - 71887 A/Cpl Lattimore W.H. promoted Cpl vice 13156 Cpl Goodman P. transferred to U.K. 30-9-17	
	12th		Coy marched at 12-0 noon to FAVREUIL - MORY - BEUGNATRE area and were in Divisional Reserve. weather cold & wet	
	13th		Company Training. Following published in Coy Orders	

A7092. Wt. W128,9/M1293. 750,000. 1/17. D. D & L., Ltd. Forms/C2118/14.

Army Form C. 2118.

WAR DIARY
or
INTELLIGENCE SUMMARY.
(Erase heading not required.)

Instructions regarding War Diaries and Intelligence Summaries are contained in F. S. Regs., Part II. and the Staff Manual respectively. Title pages will be prepared in manuscript.

Place	Date	Hour	Summary of Events and Information	Remarks and references to Appendices
Field	13th		"Steel helmets will be worn by all Ranks when on duty."	
	14th		C of E's parade for Service in Church Army Hut at 10-0 am	
			R.C's parade for Service near Horse lines of 9th East Yorks at 11-0 am	
			17509 Cpl (A/Sgt) Sherratt. F promoted Sgt vice 17626 Sgt Mitchell W transferred to M.K. 2/10/17	
	15th		9-0 X 12-45 pm Coy Training, 3 - 4-30 pm Coy Bathed at FAVREUIL	
	16th		Company Training.	
	17th		" "	
	18th		" " Following published in Coy orders. All Ranks are warned that the Germans have used "Garlic or Mustard Gas on the Corps front. Box Respirators must be put on at once if there is any suspicion that these Shells are being fired in their Vicinity."	
	19th		Coy Training.	
	20th		do do	
	21st		C of E's paraded for Service in Church Army Hut BEUGNATRE at 10-0 am. R.C's paraded for Service in Chapel opposite Church Army Hut at 10-0 am	
	22nd		Company Training. Following published in Coy orders.	

A7092 Wt. W128.59/M1293 750,000. 1/17. D. D & L., Ltd. Forms/C2118/14.

Instructions regarding War Diaries and Intelligence Summaries are contained in F. S. Regs., Part II. and the Staff Manual respectively. Title pages will be prepared in manuscript.

WAR DIARY
or
INTELLIGENCE SUMMARY.
(*Erase heading not required.*)

Army Form C. 2118.

Place	Date	Hour	Summary of Events and Information	Remarks and references to Appendices
Field	22.10.17		"In view of the unsatisfactory behaviour of S A A of I[illegible] manufacture in Machine & Lewis guns, arrangements will be made to confine its use to Rifles only."	
	23rd		Company Training. A R O No 705 dated 15/4/17 re "Cutting of wood" republished in Coy. Orders.	
	24th		Company Training. The following reinforcements joined Coy from Base Depot No 116779 Pte Archibald R. 116224 Pte Armitage H 116245 Pte Ansley S C 116239 Pte Ashcroft J. 116419 Pte Allen W J 116962 Pte Brown W D 51132 Pte Clark S.	
	25th		Company Training.	
	26th		do do	
			F G C M in the case of No 68537 Pte Tildesley H held at these H.Q at 10-30am. Charge:- When on Active Service conduct to the prejudice of good order & military discipline in that he, when at [illegible] discharged a Very pistol, thereby wounding himself. Plea: not Guilty. Finding Guilty. Sentence 28 days F P No 1	
	27th		Company Training	
	28th		C of E's parade 9-40 am for Service in Church Army Hut. RC's parade 9-40 am for Service in Chapel opposite Church Army Hut. Promotion 34677 L/Cpl White F to be Cpl. vice 42597 Cpl Parker A G	

Instructions regarding War Diaries and Intelligence Summaries are contained in F. S. Regs., Part II. and the Staff Manual respectively. Title pages will be prepared in manuscript.

WAR DIARY
or
INTELLIGENCE SUMMARY.
(Erase heading not required.)

Army Form C. 2118.

Place	Date	Hour	Summary of Events and Information	Remarks and references to Appendices
	28/10/17		Transferred to U.K. 11-10-17. Appointment. No 58939 Pte McCrimmon K. to be L/Cpl unpaid Transfer:- No 17508 Cpl Makeham E. Transferred to D Section	
	29th		Sections at disposal of Section officers C & D Sections paraded 4-30pm moved off 4-45pm to Trenches A & B " " 4-45pm " " 5-0pm " " NOREUIL Sector. Following published in Coy orders:- FEET- Before starting for the Trenches, all men will wash their feet, rub them with whale oil, and put on dry socks, this will be carried out in the presence of an officer Relief. The Coy will relieve No 9 M G Coy in the line. 3rd Division Trench Standing orders:- The attention of all Ranks is called to Trench Standing orders, issued to gun teams on 20/10/17.	
	30th		16 Guns in the line. NOREUIL Sector. Following Reinforcement from Base Depot No 103711 L/Cpl Pirrie C A	
	31st		16 Guns in the line, Casualties NIL.	

[illegible signature]
8th Coy M.G.C.

A7092 Wt. W12839/M1293. 750,000. 1/17. D. D & L., Ltd. Forms/C2118/14.

(1.)

Instructions regarding War Diaries and Intelligence Summaries are contained in F. S. Regs., Part II. and the Staff Manual respectively. Title pages will be prepared in manuscript.

WAR DIARY
or
~~INTELLIGENCE SUMMARY.~~
(*Erase heading not required.*)

Army Form C. 2118.

No. 8 MACHINE GUN COMPANY.
No. ......
Date 2-12-17

VM 23

Place	Date	Hour	Summary of Events and Information	Remarks and references to Appendices
Field.	1-11-17		Company in the line in NOREUIL Sector, with 16 guns. 25,000 rounds were fired on selected points in enemy defences, in accordance with Artillery scheme. Dugouts and M.G. nests proceeded with. No 71887 L/Cpl LATTIMORE W.H. awarded Military Medal for Gallantry in the Field.	
"	2-11-17		25,000 rounds fired on selected points. Work on dugouts + M.G. nests proceeded with	
"	3-11-17		25,000 " " " " " " " " "	
			Lieut. R. ALLAN awarded Military Cross.	
"	4-11-17		25,000 rounds fired on selected points. Work on dugouts + M.G. nests proceeded with.	
"	5-11-17		25,000 " " " " " " " " "	
"	6-11-17 / 7-11-17		4 Guns took part in a raid carried out by 13th Kings' L'pool Regt. At 12 midnight 6/7th a M.G. barrage was put down on enemy trenches, the guns firing till 12.30 a.m., by which time the raiding party had reached their own trenches. 5000 rounds were fired in this barrage. 25,000 rounds fired during night on selected points. Work on dugouts + M.G. nests proceeded with.	
"	8-11-17		25,000 rounds fired on enemy defences. Work on dugouts + M.G. nests proceeded with. No 13603 Pte Chapman J, rejoined from Corps Rest Station.	
"	9-11-17		25,000 rounds fired on selected points in enemy defences. Work on M.G. nests proceeded with	
"	10-11-17		25,000 " " " " " " " " " "	
"	11-11-17		25,000 " " " " " " " " " "	
			No 66798 Pte LUMSDEN D. rejoined from Field Ambulance.	
"	12-11-17		25,000 rounds fired on enemy defences. Work on dugouts + M.G. nests proceeded with. No 71880 Pte DUFF J., admitted to Field Ambulance	

A7092. Wt. W12839/M1293. 750,000. 1/17. D. D & L., Ltd. Forms/C2118/14.

(2)

Instructions regarding War Diaries and Intelligence Summaries are contained in F. S. Regs., Part II. and the Staff Manual respectively. Title pages will be prepared in manuscript.

WAR DIARY
or
~~INTELLIGENCE SUMMARY.~~
(Erase heading not required.)

No. 8 MACHINE GUN COMPANY.
No. ....
Date ....

Army Form C. 2118.

Place	Date	Hour	Summary of Events and Information	Remarks and references to Appendices
Field	13-11-17		25,000 rounds fired during night. Work on M.G. nests + dugouts proceeded with.	
"	14-11-17		25,000 " " " " " " " " "	
"	15-11-17		25,000 " " " " " " " " "	
"	16-11-17		25,000 " " " " " " " " "	
			No. 108676 Pte PARRY W. admitted to Field Ambulance. No. 17308 Cpl MAKEHAM E., left Coy for Base Depot, CAMIERS, to attend a Special Course of Instruction at GRANTHAM.	
"	17-11-17		25,000 rounds fired during night on selected points. Work on dugouts + M.G. nests proceeded with.	
"	18-11-17		25,000 " " " " " " " " " " "	
"	19-11-17		A, B + C Sections, forming two Batteries, moved to prepared Battery positions in RAILWAY RESERVE.	
"	20-11-17		At 6-20 am, the 9th Brigade on our left, carried out successful attack on enemy front line. Our Batteries assisted in this attack by (1) Standing barrage on enemy support line. (2) Searching selected localities in back area. Throughout the day 80000 rounds were fired. At 3-45 pm the S.O.S. was signalled - the two batteries firing 24000 rounds on S.O.S. lines.	
	21-11-17		From 5-30 am to 6-0 am our batteries co-operated with the Artillery by firing on possible assembly positions for counter-attack, 24,000 rounds being fired. The expected counter-attack did not develop. Lieut S. FERRY joined Coy from Base Depot. No. 103711 L/Cpl PIRIE C.A. + No. 81388 Pte HOARE H. were wounded.	
	22-11-17		D. Section fired 5000 rounds on selected points in enemy defences.	
	23-11-17		D Section " 4000 " " " " " "	
			Nos. 71880 Pte DUFF J., + 108676 Pte PARRY W. evacuated - sick.	
	24-11-17		11,000 rounds fired on enemy positions. 'A' Section moved back to original defensive position. Captain S.L. Courtauld left Coy to proceed to GRANTHAM. Lt. R.R. Neilson appointed C.O. Lieut S. Ferry appointed 2nd in command.	

A7092 Wt. W1289/M1293 750,000. 1/17. D. D & L., Ltd. Forms/C2118/14.

(3)

Instructions regarding War Diaries and Intelligence Summaries are contained in F. S. Regs., Part II. and the Staff Manual respectively. Title pages will be prepared in manuscript.

WAR DIARY

or

~~INTELLIGENCE SUMMARY.~~

(Erase heading not required.)

No. 8 MACHINE GUN COMPANY.

No. ....

Date ....

Army Form C. 2118.

Place	Date	Hour	Summary of Events and Information	Remarks and references to Appendices
Field	25-11-17		18,000 rounds fired on selected points in enemy defences	
"	26-11-17		9,000 " " " " " " "	
			B + C Sections moved back to original defensive positions.	
"	27-11-17		8,500 rounds fired during night on selected points in enemy defences	
"	28-11-17		15,500 " " " " " " " " " "	
			No 19594 Pt Richards W.C. admitted to Field Ambulance with burnt back (accidental injury).	
"	29-11-17		20,500 rounds fired during night on selected points in enemy defences.	
			Lieut. HOGBIN R.C. evacuated sick.	
"	30-11-17		17,000 rounds fired during night on selected points in enemy defences	

[illegible] Lieut.
Cmdg No 8 M.G. Coy.

A7092 Wt. W12859/M1293 750,000. 1/17. D. D & L., Ltd. Forms/C2118/14.

(1) 8th MG Coy

Instructions regarding War Diaries and Intelligence Summaries are contained in F. S. Regs., Part II. and the Staff Manual respectively. Title pages will be prepared in manuscript.

WAR DIARY
or
INTELLIGENCE SUMMARY.
(*Erase heading not required.*)

Army Form C. 2118.

Vol 24

Place	Date	Hour	Summary of Events and Information	Remarks and references to Appendices
Field.	1-12-17.		Company still in MOREUIL Sector. Guns fired 13000 rounds during night on selected targets in accordance with Artillery Scheme. Captain R.R. NEILSON commenced leave 1st - 15th. Lieut L.H. PULLEN reported back from leave + took over command of Company.	
	2-12-17.		14,000 rounds fired.	
	3-12-17.		20,000 " " .	
	4-12-17.		14,500 " " . Pte LOVERIDGE C. proceeded on leave 4th - 19th December.	
	5-12-17.		17,000 " " .	
	6-12-17.		20,000 " " . Lieut. W. ADAM joined from Base Depot. 2/Lt T.F. ESSEX admitted to Field Ambulance, wound turning septic. Pte McTAVISH J. admitted to Fld Ambulance - sick (eyes). L/Cpl A. BLACK proceeded on leave 6th - 20th Decr.	
	7-12-17.		15000 rounds fired. Enemy aeroplane brought down by L/C. MEADEN T. gun firing 500 Tracer bullets from RAILWAY RESERVE. Plane seen to fall behind enemy front line.	
	8-12-17.		21000 rounds fired.	
	9-12-17.		11,000 " " . Company "stood to arms" one hour before dawn in anticipation of attack, guns were laid on S.O.S. lines; no attack developed. Pte HISLOP P. on leave 9-23 Decr.	
	10-12-17.		9000 rounds fired. Pte KELLY M., " McINTYRE J., " MARTIN S } rejoined from leave. Pte SYMONDS A.G. admitted F. AMB - Sick.	
	11-12-17.		Company "stood to arms" before dawn. Company relieved by 9th M. G. Coy - relief complete by 12.0 midnight. Billets in old camp BEUGNATRE. Sgt ROBERTS R. to Infantry Training Course.	

A5834 Wt. W4973/M687 750,000 8/16 D. D. & L. Ltd. Forms/C.2118/13.

(No. 2)

Instructions regarding War Diaries and Intelligence Summaries are contained in F. S. Regs., Part II. and the Staff Manual respectively. Title pages will be prepared in manuscript.

WAR DIARY
or
~~INTELLIGENCE SUMMARY.~~

(Erase heading not required.)

Army Form C. 2118.

Place	Date	Hour	Summary of Events and Information	Remarks and references to Appendices
Field.	12·12·17.		Company in Divisional Reserve. Stood to arms at 6·30 am, heavy bombardment on front. Orders at 7·30 am to occupy Corps Line. 8 guns in 'A' + 'B' Battery moved off but turned back on receipt of orders. At 1·0 pm 8 guns again ordered up + positions taken up by 'A' + 'B' Battery. Enemy penetrated front line at APEX – counter-attacks unsuccessful.	
	13·12·17.		At 1·0 am 6 guns ordered up to Corps line to relieve 2 guns 76th M.G. Coy, 4 guns 233 M.G. Coy who in turn took up positions under 9th Infantry Brigade in MOREUIL Sector. Pte SYMONDS A.G. evacuated – sick.	
			Company H.Q. established at VRAUCOURT. 2 Guns in reserve at Transport lines. Situation on front – quiet. Cpl COOPER O. from leave.	
	14·12·17.		Emplacements + shelters improved. Counter-attack by 9th Inf. Brigade, with help of 1 Battalion M.G. Coy + T.M. Btty of 8th Brigade proposed + positions reconnoitred. Attack did not take place. Guns withdrawn from Corps line to BEAUGNATRE.	
	15·12·17.		25th Division took over near sector held by 8th Brigade. Transport lines + Camp moved to MORY.	
	16·12·17.		Company moved by busses to BLAIRVILLE AREA, transport by road, + occupied billets at HENDECOURT. Pte OUSBY T. from leave. 2/Lt SHEPHERD E.R. on leave 16–30th Decr.	
	17·12·17.		Overhauling + cleaning guns, kit inspection etc. C.O. rejoined from leave. Weather cold + frosty. Pte HAMPTON G.R. on leave 17/12/17 to 17/1/18.	
	18·12·17.		Company training. Pte LENNOX W. on leave 18·12·17 to 1·1·18.	
	19·12·17.		Company training. 2/Lt ARNOLD F. joined for duty from Base Depot. Court of Inquiry into absence of Pte OSBORNE G. 8th M.G. Coy. Finding:– "Illegally absent + still so absent".	
	20·12·17.		Company training. 2/Lt T. F. ESSEX evacuated. Sgt NEAVE A. joined from Base Depot. C.Q.M.S. IFOULD H. on leave 20·12·17 to 3·1·18.	

A5834 Wt. W4973/M687 750,000 8/16 D. D. & L. Ltd. Forms/C.2118/13.

(No. 3)

Instructions regarding War Diaries and Intelligence Summaries are contained in F. S. Regs., Part II. and the Staff Manual respectively. Title pages will be prepared in manuscript.

WAR DIARY
or
INTELLIGENCE SUMMARY.

(Erase heading not required.)

Army Form C. 2118.

Place	Date	Hour	Summary of Events and Information	Remarks and references to Appendices
Field.	21-12-17.		Company marched to MORY. Transport in advance. L/Cpl LONGWORTH J.H. joined from Base Depot.	
	22-12-17.		Inspection by 6th Corps Commander at 11.0 am including Transport. Address - Inspection of billets, accompanied by Third Divisional General. At 5.0 pm Company paraded + marched to trenches in MORRVIL SECTOR to relieve 13th M.G. Coy. Relief complete by 10.0 pm. 16 guns in line. Pte JOHNSON S. on leave 22-12-17 to 5-1-18.	
	23-12-17.		3000 rounds fired on enemy defences. Weather cold + frosty. ~~turning~~ to ~~rain~~. Lieut. FERRY S. transferred to 192 M.G. Coy. L/Cpl BLACK A. from leave.	
	24-12-17.		6000 rounds fired; weather cold + frosty, turning to rain.	
	25-12-17.		1250 rounds fired. Thaw restrictions adopted from 7-0 am. Heavy fall of snow. Pte BANNISTER F. on leave 25-12-17 to 9-1-18.	
	26-12-17.		1250 rounds fired. Pte HUSBANDS S. + Pte HISLOP P. from leave.	
	27-12-17.		5000 rounds fired. Weather cold + frosty. Pte HUSBAND S. evacuated to C.C.S.	
	28-12-17.		2750 rounds fired. Company relieved in the line by 120th M.G. Coy. Night quiet. Relief complete by 10-0 pm. Sections marched ~~to~~ independently to Camp at MOYENVILLE. Last Section arrived at 3-0 am. 29th. Snowing very heavily.	
	29-12-17.		Cleaning up. Pte CARDEN A.G. on leave 29-12-17 to 12-1-18.	
	30-12-17.		Kit and clothing inspection. Thaw set in. Lieut. BARLEY F.J. on leave 30-12-17 to 13-1-18.	
	31-12-17.		Company training. More snow + hard frost.	

No. 8 MACHINE GUN COMPANY.
No. ....
Date 2-1-17

[signature]
Lieut. + Adjt
No. 8 M.-G. Coy.

A5834 Wt. W4973/M687 750,000 8/16 D. D. & L. Ltd. Forms/C.2118/13.

3RD DIVISION

8TH INFY BDE

8TH MACHINE GUN COMPANY

JAN-FEB.1918

Instructions regarding War Diaries and Intelligence Summaries are contained in F. S. Regs., Part II. and the Staff Manual respectively. Title pages will be prepared in manuscript.

WAR DIARY or INTELLIGENCE SUMMARY.

(Erase heading not required.)

No. 8 M. G. COMPANY. Army Form C. 2118.

Vol 25

Place	Date	Hour	Summary of Events and Information	Remarks and references to Appendices
Field.	1/1/18		Company given holiday. Following men cross-posted to 76th M. G. Coy:- Pte Hislop P, Pte Guy A, Pte Kelly M, Pte Pratt S, Pte Medway H, Pte Williams A, Pte Hill R.C. L/C Cantum + Pte Bishop on leave to U.K.	
"	2/1/18		Company continued training.	
"	3/1/18		Company training. L/C. Renton R + Pte Wilson J. on leave to U.K. 2/Lt Shepherd E.A rejoined from leave.	
"	4/1/18		Company training. Pte Williams C Pte Balaam W. leave to U.K.	
"	5/1/18.		Company training. Lt Pullen L.H. (M.C) to 3rd Division HQ as A/D.M.G.O. C.S.M. Reade C., Pte Page C. leave to U.K. Pte Lennox G. rejoined from leave	
"	6/1/18		Services for C of E's, R.C. + Nonconformists. No 107470 Pte Ballingall A.B. evacuated to C.C.S. + struck off strength of Company. Pte Clive C + Pte Shirra J. leave to U.K. Following N.C.O's proceeded to CAMIERS for M. G. Course:- Sgt Cassidy M, Cpl Marsland M, L/Cpl McGrimmon K, L/Cpl Stewart R. From Part II Orders. (1) Promotions. No 17502 L/Cpl Renton R to be Cpl from 27-11-17 vice No 36570 Cpl Rand J reverted to Private. No 64193 L/Cpl Geddes J. to be Cpl from 29/11/17 vice No 17508 Cpl Mateham to U.K.	
	7/1/18.		Company training. Pte White C. + Pte Stamp W. leave to U.K. Sgt Harrell F on Physical Training Course at St POL. Pte Kelly W. on Signalling Course at 3rd Division.	
	8/1/18.		Company training. Pte McGrath T. leave to U.K. VI Corps Commander visited the Camp at 10-am + saw the Company at training, afterwards inspecting the Company billets + horse lines.	

A5834 Wt. W4973/M687 750,000 8/16 D. D. & L. Ltd. Forms/C.2118/13.

2

Instructions regarding War Diaries and Intelligence Summaries are contained in F. S. Regs., Part II. and the Staff Manual respectively. Title pages will be prepared in manuscript.

WAR DIARY
or
~~INTELLIGENCE SUMMARY.~~

(Erase heading not required.)

Army Form C. 2118.

Place	Date	Hour	Summary of Events and Information	Remarks and references to Appendices
Field	9-1-18		Company training. Pte Gillett T. leave to U.K. CQMS. Gould H + Pte Johnson S. rejoined from leave.	
	10-1-18		Company training. Pte Schorey J. on leave to U.K.	
	11-1-18		Company training. Pte Bannister J. from leave to U.K. Pte Clarke evacuated to C.C.S and struck off strength.	
	12-1-18		Company training. Pte Anderson J. leave to U.K. A lecture was given by Dr C.W. KIMMINS on "Education after the War". 3 Officers and 9 N.C.O's attended.	
	13-1-18		Services for C. of E, R.C. and Presbyterians. Sgt Small W. on leave to U.K. Sgt Roberts rejoined from Infantry Training Course.	
	14-1-18		Company training. Pte Stansfield on leave to U.K. L/Cpl Rutter to Infantry Training Course.	
	15-1-18		Company training. Sgt Roberts leave to U.K. Pte Allen W. evacuated to C.C.S. and struck off strength.	
	16-1-18		Company moved into Camp at ERVILLERS + came into Divisional Reserve to 40th Division. Pte Pain A. leave to U.K. Pte Carden A.G. rejoined from leave	
	17-1-18		Company training. Pte Glen C. leave to U.K.	
	18-1-18		Company training.	
	19-1-18		Company firing on range. Pte Stirman H. leave to U.K. 2/Lt Arnold to LE HAMEAU on Anti-Aircraft Course. From PART II ORDERS. No 59570 Cpl MARSLAND N. promoted Sgt from 13-12-17.	

A5834 Wt. W4973/M687 750,000 8/16 D. D. & L. Ltd. Forms/C.2118/13.

3.

Instructions regarding War Diaries and Intelligence Summaries are contained in F. S. Regs., Part II. and the Staff Manual respectively. Title pages will be prepared in manuscript.

WAR DIARY
or
INTELLIGENCE ~~SUMMARY~~.

(*Erase heading not required.*)

Army Form C. 2118.

Place	Date	Hour	Summary of Events and Information	Remarks and references to Appendices
Field.	20.1.18		Service for Presbyterians. Divisional Band played in the Camp of the Company from 2.0 pm to 4.0 pm.	
			Following rejoined from leave to U.K.:- Ptes Bishop C, Wilson J, Aves E, King C. Cpl Benton R, L/Cpl Canham J.	
	21.1.18		Company firing on range. Pte Hargreaves leave to U.K. Pte Rakaw W. from leave	
	22.1.18		Company on range. Pte Stewart R leave to U.K. C.S.M. Reade C + Pte Williams C rejoined from leave. 2/Lt Arnold F.J rejoined from Course	
			Lieut Pullen L.H. rejoined from Division as A/D.M.G.O.	
	23.1.18		Company continued training. Pte Meadows W. to U.K. on leave.	
	24.1.18		Company training. Pte Hoggan R. to U.K. on leave. Pte Stamp from leave to U.K.	
			From Part II Orders.	
			No. 57723 Pte MANICOM. E.J., promoted A/Cpl from 23.1.18.	
	25.1.18		Company moved into line in the CROISILLES Sector, relieving 101st M.G. Coy. Relief complete by 7.0 pm. Pte Sherrod J. to U.K. on leave. Pte McGrath J. from leave to U.K. Eight reinforcements joined + posted to Sections as follows	
			'A'. 2. – 'B'. 2. – 'C'. 3.	
	26.1.18		Company in line. Pte Wright to U.K. on leave. Pte Schorey from leave to U.K.	
	27.1.18		Company in line. Rounds fired 2,500. Pte White J. to U.K. on leave.	
			Pte White C. from leave to U.K.	
	28.1.18		Company in line. Rounds fired 4000. Pte Anderson from leave to U.K.	
			Pte Taylor G. on leave to U.K.	

4

Instructions regarding War Diaries and Intelligence Summaries are contained in F. S. Regs., Part II. and the Staff Manual respectively. Title pages will be prepared in manuscript.

WAR DIARY
or
~~INTELLIGENCE SUMMARY~~.

(Erase heading not required.)

Army Form C. 2118.

Place	Date	Hour	Summary of Events and Information	Remarks and references to Appendices
Field.	29.1.18		Company in line. Rounds fired 4000. Sgt Small W. + Pte Stansfield from leave to U.K.	
	30.1.18.		Company in line. Rounds fired 4,200. 2/Lt E.W. DICKINSON to U.K. on leave.	
	31.1.18		Company in line. Rounds fired 4,500. Pte Gillett T. from leave to U.K.	

No. 8 MACHINE GUN COMPANY.
No. ....
Date 3.2.18.

E R Spofforth Lieut & A/Adjt
for O/Cmdg No. 8 M. G. Coy.

A5834 Wt. W4973/M687 750,000 8/16 D. D. & L. Ltd. Forms/C.2118/13.

Instructions regarding War Diaries and Intelligence Summaries are contained in F. S. Regs., Part II. and the Staff Manual respectively. Title pages will be prepared in manuscript.

WAR DIARY
or
~~INTELLIGENCE~~ SUMMARY.
(Erase heading not required.)

8th M.G.C.
February 1918.

Army Form C. 2118.

Place	Date	Hour	Summary of Events and Information	Remarks and references to Appendices
In the Field	1-2-18		Company in line in CROISILLES Sector. Situation normal. Work on Emplacements + dugouts continued.	
do	2-2-18		Considerable Artillery activity. Enemy M Guns fairly active during day owing to mist inflicting several casualties on working party. 3000 rounds fired on S.O.S.	
do	3-2-18		A raid suspected. All ranks warned to be on the alert for S.O.S. but raid did not take place.	
do	4-2-18		Company in line. Situation quiet. 4500 rounds fired during night.	
do.	5-2-18		" " " Work on Emplacements + dugouts proceeded with.	
do	6-2-18		S.O.S. went up at 5-30 am. 7250 rounds fired on S.O.S. lines. Situation quiet at 8.30 am + remained so. Work on Emplacements to continued.	
do.	7-2-18		Situation normal. Work continued.	
do	8-2-18		Situation normal. Work continued. Lieut. E.R. SPOTFORTH to U.K. on Tour of duty.	
do.	9-2-18		Situation quiet. Work on Emplacements to proceeded with.	
do.	10-2-18		" " " " " " " "	
do.	11-2-18		" " " " " " " "	
do.	12-2-18		" " " " " " " "	
do	13-2-18 to 21-2-18		" " " " " " " "	
	22-2-18		Considerable Artillery activity between hours of 3 to 4 a.m. Enemy Machine Guns active. Work on Emplacements + dugouts continued.	

D. D. & L., London, E.C.
(A8001) Wt. W1 71/M2031 750,000 5/17 Sch. 52 Forms/C2118/14

Instructions regarding War Diaries and Intelligence Summaries are contained in F. S. Regs., Part II. and the Staff Manual respectively. Title pages will be prepared in manuscript.

WAR DIARY
or
~~INTELLIGENCE~~ SUMMARY.
(*Erase heading not required.*)

Army Form C. 2118.

Place	Date	Hour	Summary of Events and Information	Remarks and references to Appendices
In the Field	23.2.18		Company in line. Nothing of special interest to report. Work on Emplacements &c continued.	
do.	24.2.18		Night passed quietly. Nothing to report. Work continued.	
do	25.2.18		" " " " " " " "	
do.	26.2.18		At 9-20 pm the S.O.S. signal went up, the enemy attempting a raid. Guns opened fire immediately on their S.O.S. lines. The enemy was repulsed, being unable to reach our lines. No of rounds fired = 31,300. Situation afterwards quiet.	
do.	27.2.18		Nothing of interest to report. Situation unchanged. Work on Emplacements continued.	
do.	28.2.18		Situation normal. Work on Emplacements &c proceeding.	

25-2-18

H. N. [illegible] Captain [illegible]
for O.C. "A" Coy [illegible]

D. D. & L., London, E.C.
(A8001) Wt. W1 71/M2031 750,000 5/17 Sch. 52 Forms/C2118/14

3RD DIVISION
8TH INFY BDE

TRENCH MORTAR BATTERY.

MAY - AUG 1916

III

Instructions regarding War Diaries and Intelligence Summaries are contained in F. S. Regs., Part II. and the Staff Manual respectively. Title pages will be prepared in manuscript.

WAR DIARY
or
~~INTELLIGENCE SUMMARY.~~
(Erase heading not required.)

8/1 Trench Mortar Battery

Army Form C. 2118.

Vol 1

Place	Date	Hour	Summary of Events and Information	Remarks and references to Appendices
M.N.O Trenches	8.5.16	2.30pm	Usual enemy activity with trench mortars. We retaliated with 69 rounds & his fire ceased.	
do	9.5.16	7.30am	Enemy's trench mortars again active; afternoon quiet, six rounds fired.	
do	10.5.16	7.30am	Enemy opened with very heavy mortars; afternoon quiet, six rounds fired.	
do	11.5.16	5.30am	Enemy opened fire with light mortars, we retaliated with our 3.7 & gun exploded. Afternoon & evening quiet	
do	12.5.16	12 noon	Trench mortars quiet. Artillery active on both sides. Afternoon & evening quiet.	
do	13.5.16	2.30pm	Enemy very active with trench mortars and very heavy artillery fire later.	
do	14.5.16	2.30pm	Enemy quiet all day. They exploded a mine opposite N4.	
do	15.5.16	8.30am	Enemy sent over a few light mortars during morning. Afternoon & evening quiet	
do	16.5.16	12.2pm	Enemy's artillery fairly active. Trench mortars quiet.	
do	17.5.16	7.am	Trench mortars moderately active. Retaliated with 4 2" bombs. Stokes not fired. Quiet day.	
do	18.5.16	7am	Very misty & quiet. Afternoon some activity & 2" was fired. Heavy shrapnel on left. Quiet night.	
do	19.5.16	9 am	Enemy's trench mortars active. Replied with 2" & 3.7. Moderately quiet afterwards. Afternoon quiet. Evening heavy shrapnel on our right.	

T.134. Wt. W708—776. 500000. 4/15. Sir J. C. & S.

8/1 Trench Mortar Battery

Army Form C. 2118.

Instructions regarding War Diaries and Intelligence Summaries are contained in F. S. Regs., Part II. and the Staff Manual respectively. Title pages will be prepared in manuscript.

WAR DIARY
or
~~INTELLIGENCE SUMMARY.~~
(*Erase heading not required.*)

Place	Date	Hour	Summary of Events and Information	Remarks and references to Appendices
M.N.O Trenches	20.5.16	7am.	Silenced rifle grenades with 3.7. Quiet morning afterwards. Bois Carrè heavily shelled between 5–7 pm.	
do	21.5.16	7am	Enemy's rifle grenades silenced by our mortars. Quiet morning. Some artillery activity on both sides.	
do	22.5.16	4pm	Trench mortars very active between 3 & 4 pm. We replied with 2" gun & Stokes & silenced them.	
do	23.5.16	11am	Enemy's trench mortars fairly active. We retaliated with 2" & Stokes & silenced them.	
do	24.5.16	4pm.	Enemy's trench mortars & artillery active, we retaliated & silenced them. Rest of the day quiet.	
do	25.5.16	8am	Enemy's trench mortars active, we retaliated & silenced them. Enemy's artillery very active on our right during afternoon.	
do	26.5.16	4pm	Enemy quiet all day.	
	27.5.16 – 31.5.16		Battery in training at Noote Boom. Battery taken over by me on 30.5.16.	

C W Sawyer 2Lt
OC 8/1 T.M.B.

T.134. Wt. W708–776. 500000. 4/15. Sir J. C. & S.

Instructions regarding War Diaries and Intelligence Summaries are contained in F. S. Regs., Part II. and the Staff Manual respectively. Title pages will be prepared in manuscript.

WAR DIARY
~~or~~
INTELLIGENCE SUMMARY.

(*Erase heading not required.*)

Army Form C. 2118.

3

8th T M B

Vol 3

Place	Date	Hour	Summary of Events and Information	Remarks and references to Appendices
ST MARTIN AU LAERT	July 1	11 AM	Left ST MARTIN AU LAERT entrained at WIZERNES arrived CANDAS 11.30 pM.	
BERNEUIL	2	2 AM	arrived BERNEUIL	
FLESSELLES	3	8 AM	Left BERNEUIL arrived FLESSELLES 2 PM.	
ALONVILLE	4	8 PM	Left FLESSELLES arrived ALONVILLE 11.30 pM.	
CORBIE	5	8 PM	Left ALONVILLE arrived CORBIE 1.30 pm	
BOIS de CELESTINES	6	8 pM	Left Corbie arrived BOIS de CELESTINES 11.30 pM.	
BRONFAY FARM	7	8 AM	Left CELESTINES arrived BRONFAY FARM 1 PM.	
CARNOY		4 pM	Left BRONFAY FARM for CARNOY relieved 53 T M B	
MONTAUBAN	8		Holding trenches from MONTAUBAN VILLAGE to CATAPILLA LANE. Some shelling during day 3 casualties. Mortars not within range of enemy lines	
	9		Forward dump commenced, some Shrapnel during day & night 2 casualties	
	10		Day & Night quiet continued making forward dumps 1 Wounded	
	11		Enemy Artillery more active MONTAUBAN VILLAGE heavily shelled about 9 PM 1 Killed 2 Wounded	
	12		Detonating & carrying ammunition to forward dumps. Enemy Artillery very active in vicinity of MONTAUBAN VILLAGE no casualties.	

T.134. Wt. W708–776. 500000. 4/15. Sir J. C. & S.

Instructions regarding War Diaries and Intelligence Summaries are contained in F. S. Regs., Part II. and the Staff Manual respectively. Title pages will be prepared in manuscript.

WAR DIARY ~~or~~ INTELLIGENCE SUMMARY.

(*Erase heading not required.*)

Army Form C. 2118.

8th T.M.B

Place	Date	Hour	Summary of Events and Information	Remarks and references to Appendices
	July 13th		Removed guns from MONTAUBAN - CATTERPILLAR LANE trench also guns in reserve to QUARRY NORTH of MONTAUBAN preparatory to joining infantry in attack	
TRENCH	14th	3.20AM	In conjunction with Infantry attacked & captured enemy first & second line between BAZENTIN LE GRAND and LONGUEVAL	
			CASUALTIES OFFICERS 1 Killed - 1 Wounded - OTHER RANKS 11 Wounded ~~missing~~	
	15th		Holding & consolidating captured trenches, Enemy Artillery active but doing little damage - No Casualties	
	16		Making new ammunition dumps and carrying 15 new gun positions Casualties 4 Killed - 4 Wounded.	
	17		Carrying ammunition to gun emplacements. Enemy Artillery active on our front but doing no material damage.	
	18		Enemy Artillery very active our position being heavily shelled.	
		3PM	sent 2 Guns to assist 76th Brigade at LONGUEVAL	
"	19		Enemy Artillery very active DELVILLE WOOD heavily shelled withdrew to MONTAUBAN ALLEY TRENCH.	
"	20		HOLDING MONTAUBAN ALLEY TRENCH, our Artillery very active - Enemy quiet	

T.134. Wt. W708-776. 500000. 4/15. Sir J. C. & S.

Instructions regarding War Diaries and Intelligence Summaries are contained in F. S. Regs., Part II. and the Staff Manual respectively. Title pages will be prepared in manuscript.

WAR DIARY or ~~INTELLIGENCE~~ SUMMARY. 8th T. M. B

(*Erase heading not required.*)

Army Form C. 2118.

Place	Date	Hour	Summary of Events and Information	Remarks and references to Appendices
	JULY			
WATERLOT FARM	21		Sent 4 Guns to WATERLOT FARM. Enemy artillery very active. MONTAUBAN & QUARRY very heavily shelled. 2 Casualties	
	22		Enemy Artillery quiet during early part of day. Started again towards evening 2 Casualties	
	23		Enemy Artillery very active, reserve Trenches heavily shelled. 2 Casualties	
	24		MONTAUBAN QUARRY ROAD heavily shelled 10 PM our Artillery opened out & bombarded for some time 4 Casualties	
	25		Relieved by 5th T M B arrived HAPPY VALLEY 2 AM next morning	
	26	4 PM	Left HAPPY VALLEY arrived MEAULTE 5.30 PM.	
	27		In rest MEAULTE	
	28		Training & reorganising Battery	
	29		Battery Training	
	30		Rest.	
	31		Battery Training	

W J Murcher 2Lt
OC 8th T M B.
31-7-16.

T:134. Wt. W708-776. 500000. 4/15. Sir J. C. & S.

…uctions regarding War Diaries and Intelligence Summaries are contained in F. S. Regs., Part II. and the Staff Manual respectively. Title pages will be prepared in manuscript.

WAR DIARY
~~or~~
~~INTELLIGENCE SUMMARY.~~
(*Erase heading not required.*)

Vol 4

8th Y. M. B.

Army Form C. 2118.

Place	Date	Hour	Summary of Events and Information	Remarks and references to Appendices
Méaulte	Aug: 1		Resting and training new men	
"	" 2		— do —	
"	" 3		— do —	
"	" 4		— do —	
"	" 5		— do —	
"	" 6		— do —	
"	" 7		— do —	
"	" 8		— do —	
"	" 9		— do —	
"	" 10		— do —	
"	" 11		— do —	
"	" 12	2 pm	Left Méaulte, arrived at Happy Valley at 3-30 p.m.	
HAPPY VALLEY	" 13		In training	
"	" 14	3-15 pm	Left HAPPY VALLEY, arrived at camping ground close to BRONFAY FARM at 5 p.m	
BRONFAY FARM	" 15	3 pm	Left camping ground at BRONFAY FARM, arrived CARNOY 4 pm	
	" 15	8 pm	Took over trenches South of GUILLEMONT to assist 9th & 76th Brigades. Carrying ammunition to gun position.	

T.134. Wt. W708–776. 500000. 4/15. Sir J. C. & S.

Army Form C. 2118.

[...]structions regarding War Diaries and Intelligence Summaries are contained in F. S. Regs., Part II. and the Staff Manual respectively. Title Pages will be prepared in manuscript.

WAR DIARY
~~or~~
~~INTELLIGENCE SUMMARY~~
(Erase heading not required.)

8th T.M.B.

Place	Date	Hour	Summary of Events and Information	Remarks and references to Appendices
Trenches South of GUILLEMONT	Aug: 16	5.38 pm.	Fired two minutes rapid previous to infantry making attack.	
	" 17	8 pm.	Started slow bombardment from 8 pm. till 10 pm. when second attack took place. – 9 casualties (all wounded).	
	" 18		Holding trench. Started two minutes bombardment at 2.38 pm previous to 3rd attack at 2.40 p.m. Casualties – 2 killed – 8 wounded.	
	" 19		Holding trench. Firing at intervals. Casualties – 1 killed, 3 wounded.	
	" "	11 pm	Relieved by 35th Division at 11 pm.	
	" 20		Marched to SANDPIT arrived 5 pm.	
SAND PIT	" 21		Left SANDPIT arrived MÉAULTE 9-15 am. Battery resting.	
MÉAULTE	" 22		In training	
"	" 23	5-15 a.m.	Left MÉAULTE entrained at MERICOURT. Detrained CANDAS. Marched to BARLETTE arrived 6-30 pm.	
BARLETTE	" 24		In training	
"	" 25	7.30 am	Left BARLETTE arrived CHATEAU DE BEAUVOIN 11-30 am.	
CHATEAU DE BEAUVOIN	" 26	8.15 am	Left CHATEAU DE BEAUVOIN arrived BLANGEMONT 1 p.m.	
BLANGEMONT	" 27	8 am	Left BLANGEMONT, arrived TANGRY 1-30 pm.	

2449 Wt. W14957/M90 750,000 1/16 J.B.C. & A. Forms/C.2118/12.

uctions regarding War Diaries and Intelligence Summaries are contained in F. S. Regs., Part II. and the Staff Manual respectively. Title Pages will be prepared in manuscript.

WAR DIARY

~~or~~

~~INTELLIGENCE SUMMARY~~

(Erase heading not required.)

8th T.M.B.

Army Form C. 2118.

Place	Date	Hour	Summary of Events and Information	Remarks and references to Appendices
TANGRY	Aug. 28	8 am.	Left TANGRY arrived RUITZ 1 pm.	
RUITZ	" 29	2.30 pm.	Left RUITZ, arrived NOEUX LES MINES 4-30 pm.	
NOEUX LES MINES	" 30	1-30.	Left NOEUX LES MINES arrived PHILOSOPHE 3 pm.	
	" "	"	Relieved 97th T.M.B., and took over trenches HULLUCH sector between boyeau 77 and Posen Alley.	
	" 31		Holding trenches as stated above.	

W. L. Murchie 2 Lt.
OC 8th T M Bty

2449 Wt. W14957/M90 750,000 1/16 J.B.C. & A. Forms/C.2118/12.

www.ingramcontent.com/pod-product-compliance
Lightning Source LLC
Chambersburg PA
CBHW081433300426
44108CB00016BA/2359

* 9 7 8 1 4 7 4 5 0 4 5 9 1 *